COLLISION OF WORLDS

COLLISION OF WORLDS

A DEEP HISTORY OF THE FALL OF AZTEC MEXICO AND THE FORGING OF NEW SPAIN

DAVID M. CARBALLO

OXFORD
UNIVERSITY PRESS

OXFORD
UNIVERSITY PRESS

Oxford University Press is a department of the University of Oxford. It furthers the University's objective of excellence in research, scholarship, and education by publishing worldwide. Oxford is a registered trade mark of Oxford University Press in the UK and certain other countries.

Published in the United States of America by Oxford University Press
198 Madison Avenue, New York, NY 10016, United States of America.

Library of Congress Cataloging-in-Publication Data
Names: Carballo, David M., author.
Title: Collision of worlds : a deep history of the fall of Aztec Mexico and the forging of New Spain / David M. Carballo.
Other titles: Deep history of the fall of Aztec Mexico and the forging of New Spain
Description: First edition. | New York : Oxford University Press, [2020] |
Includes bibliographical references and index.
Identifiers: LCCN 2019041866 (print) | LCCN 2019041867 (ebook) |
ISBN 9780190864354 (hardback) | ISBN 9780190864378 (epub) |
ISBN 9780197503829 (online)
Subjects: LCSH: Mexico—History—Conquest, 1519-1540. |
Aztecs—History. | Indians of Mexico—History—16th century. | New Spain—History.
Classification: LCC F1230.C36 2020 (print) | LCC F1230 (ebook) | DDC 972—dc23
LC record available at https://lccn.loc.gov/2019041866
LC ebook record available at https://lccn.loc.gov/2019041867

1 3 5 7 9 8 6 4 2

Printed by LSC Communications, United States of America

To my mother, Anne

Contents

Preface

This book presents a deep history of the encounter that resulted in the fall of Aztec Mexico and birth of New Spain, with a focus on material things and the co-creative actions of Mesoamericans and Spaniards. It is an archaeological perspective that frames significant moments in human history within the context of centuries or millennia, and one that also considers mute objects and places of the past simultaneously with the written narratives of people who were witness to it, or heard tales from elders who were. In relating the story of the historic encounter in this somewhat unconventional manner, I have relied on the support of friends, students, and colleagues, many of them specialists of particular parts within Mexico and Spain. I am very grateful to Stefan Vranka at Oxford University Press for his encouragement of the project, which then crystallized into a formal proposal when I had the opportunity to write one as a Santander Visiting Scholar at the David Rockefeller Center for Latin American Studies, Harvard University. Funding for trips to Mexico and Spain as part of the research was generously provided by the College of Arts and Sciences at Boston University and by Luis Octavio Ruzo, whom I thank for not only his support, but also his friendship and intellectual curiosity. Support of my archaeological work in Mexico, which I draw on especially in Chapter 2, has been provided by grants from the National Science Foundation, National Geographic Society, University of California Center for US-Mexico Studies, and the Foundation for the Advancement of Mesoamerican Studies.

I am tremendously grateful to Mark Bazer, Jennifer Carballo, Benjamin Juárez, Carolina López-Ruiz, and Amalia Pérez-Juez for reading parts or all of the manuscript and providing very helpful suggestions. Guidance on certain ideas and bodies of literature was graciously provided by Lourdes Budar, Joanna Clapps-Herman, Tom Cummins, Johnathan Edmonson, Susan Evans, Daniela Hernández Sariñana, Ken Hirth, Roberto Junco, Aurelio López Corral, Leonardo López Luján, Stephanie Marciniak, Becky Martin, Deb

Nichols, Alejandro Pastrana, Franco Rossi, Curtis Runnels, Mike Smith, Ariel Texis, John Watanabe, and David Webster. Pedro Cahuantzi Hernández, Guadalupe Espinosa Rodríguez, Lane Fargher, Aurelio López Corral, Nicholas Saunders, and Mari Carmen Serra Puche all kindly assisted with figures, and photos of pre-Hispanic and colonial monuments within Mexico were authorized by the Instituto Nacional de Antropología e Historia. Students in my course AR 365, run through the Boston University Study Abroad Program in Madrid, helped me to gauge what was interesting—and what was not—about certain topics. For inspiration and *amistad* in Mexico and Spain, I thank the Carballo and Eibe families, the Ramírez Lima family, Raúl "Bruce" Martínez Mejía, María Guadalupe Espinoza, Mónica Blanco García-Méndez, Rubén Martínez Galloso, Antonio Luque, Dan Bejar, Café Tacuba, and everyone involved with the Arizona State University Teotihuacan Research Laboratory. Finally, I thank my kids, Tony and Daniel, for asking, "are you done with your book yet?" just the right amount of times. I dedicate it to my mother, Anne, who sparked my interest in studying cultures and their diverse ways of doing and knowing.

Guide to Pronunciation and Spelling

Many terms in this book are in or derived from Nahuatl, the lingua franca of the Aztec Empire. Nahuatl is still spoken by almost two million people today, but its sixteenth-century manifestation differed somewhat and is referred to as "Classical" Nahuatl. The orthography of Classical Nahuatl follows conventions of sixteenth-century Castilian Spanish, which came to the Americas with its own peculiarities. For instance, there was no letter *w*, so that phoneme is often rendered 'hu' as in Teotihuacan (Teo-ti-WA-kan). The letter *x* signaled a 'sh' sound, meaning the word "Mexica" would not have the hard *x* that Anglophones use today for the country name Mexico; the eponymous ethnic group was pronounced Me-SHEE-ka. Nahuatl is an agglutinative language, like German. Terms rendered by two or three words in English might be combined into a single, long word. Most consonants are pronounced as in English, and vowels are pronounced as in Spanish, with certain exceptions:

hu	pronounced 'w' like in way
qua, quo	pronounced 'kw' like in quest
que, qui	pronounced 'k' like in key
tl	pronounced like the bridge between the English words "at least" with the tongue touching the upper palette of the mouth
tz	pronounced 'ts' like in cats
x	pronounced 'sh' like in shell.

The penultimate syllables of words are stressed in Nahuatl and I do not use Spanish accents for Nahuatl terms. Otherwise, I generally use the most common spelling for proper nouns and translate the names of certain dynasts and other historical figures into English, such as the Spanish king Carlos I as Charles. I spell Charles' grandmother's name Isabela, because the double *l* in Spanish designates a 'y' sound and a single *l* is phonetically intelligible in English. During his life, Cortés' first name was rendered Hernando or Fernando, never Hernán—and his surname did not end in *z*, though that is seen in posthumous orthography by Neil Young and others. I have chosen the not wholly satisfactory spelling Moctezuma for the Mexica leader, which is a compromise between the well-known but inaccurate Montezuma and the little-known but accurate Moteuczoma or Motecuhzoma. More rarely, foreign terms come from Mayan, whose different languages are spoken today by over six million people in Mexico and Central America. Mayan makes use of a glottal stop, which is indicated by an apostrophe.

Deep Timeline

Mesoamerica		Iberia
Aztec Empire	1500	Joint kingdoms of Castile and Aragón
Migrations, founding of Mexico-Tenochtitlan		Hybrid ships, reconquest of Al-Andalus
Postclassic Period		Dry compass, first universities
Toltec city of Tula	1000	***Reconquista Era***
		Islamic conquests
Maya florescence		Visigoths and other Germanic groups
Classic Period	500	
Teotihuacan largest city in Americas		***Roman Era***
Cholula Great Pyramid		Roman Hispania
Volcanic eruptions in central Mexico	1 CE/BCE	
Complex math with use of zero		Punic Wars (Rome-Carthage)
		Celtiberians
	500 BCE	Cancho Roano
Urbanization in multiple regions		
		Iron Age
Olmecs	1000 BCE	Phoenician colonies
Formative/Preclassic Period		Trade with northern Atlantic
Early ballcourt at Paso de la Amada	1500 BCE	
		Bronze Age
First farming villages	2000 BCE	***Copper Age***
		Dolmens and other megalithic monuments
Archaic Period	//	
		Neolithic Period
	5000 BCE	First farming villages
Independent cultivation of maize, beans, squash, chiles, and other crops		Importation of wheat, lentils, sheep, pigs, and other crops and animals domesticated in Fertile Crescent
Clovis culture, hunter-gatherers	10,000 BCE	
Paleoindian Period		
	15,000 BCE	
First peoples arrive to Americas from Northeast Asia	20,000 BCE	Cave art in Cantabria and other regions
	25,000 BCE	***Upper Paleolithic Period***

Fifteenth–Sixteenth-Century Timeline

Aztec Core/New Spain		Spain/Spanish Caribbean
	1590	
Díaz del Castillo d. in Guatemala		Muñoz Camargo takes his history to Spain
	1580	
Cocolitzli disease epidemic		
	1570	Phillip II's Ordinances for the Indies
Foiled rebellion of Cortés' sons		Colonization of Philippines
	1560	Capital moved to Madrid
Sahagún and Nahua scribes begin to draft history of New Spain		Phillip II succeeds Spanish throne
	1550	Cortés d. near Seville, Valladolid debates
Cocolitzli disease epidemic		
Invasion of Yucatan by Montejos	1540	Passage of New Laws regulating Indies
Mendoza first Viceroy, Colegio de Santa Cruz		
Invasion of Guatemala by Alvarados	1530	Cortés returns to Spain with Tlaxcalteca
Fall of Tenochtitlan, arrival of Franciscans		Marriage of Charles I and Isabela of Portugal
Expeditions led by Grijalva, Cordoba, and, finally, Cortés	1520	Revolt of the Comuneros
		Laws of Burgos, Charles I succeeds throne
	1510	Dominicans arrive, Montesinos' sermon
Malinche b. in Olutla		d. of Isabela and Ferdinand
Moctezuma II *tlatoani* of Tenochtitlan	1500	De la Cosa *mappa mundi* depicts Americas
		Treaty of Tordesillas
Ahuitzotl *tlatoani* of Tenochtitlan	1490	Conquest of Granada, Columbus
Triple Alliance conquest of Soconusco		Cortés b. in Medellín
	1480	Establishment of Tribunal of the Inquisition
Triple Alliance wars with Tarascans		Castile and Portugal war over Canary Islands
Nezahualpilli *tlatoani* of Texcoco	1470	Marriage of Isabela of Castile and Ferdinand of Aragón
Triple Alliance launch "flower wars" vs. Tlaxcalteca and other rivals		Habsburgs elevated as Holy Roman Emperors

Aztec Core/New Spain		Spain/Spanish Caribbean
Tenochtitlan floods/dike construction	1460	Accurate maps depicting eastern Atlantic coast
Moctezuma I *tlatoani* of Tenochtitlan	1450	and islands
Nezahualcoyotl of Texcoco and Itzcoatl of Tenochtitlan ally vs. Tepanecs	1440	Emirate of Granada is a vassal state to Castile
Chimalpopoca *tlatoani* of Tenochtitlan	1430	
Mexica fight for Tepanecs vs. Acolhua	1420	
Ixtlilxochitl *tlatoani* of Texcoco	1410	Fernando I ("de Antequera") jointly regent of Castile and king of Aragón
Early stages of Tenochtitlan's Great Temple	1400	Initial colonization of Canary Islands

I

Mexico, Spain, and Their Deep Histories of Place

> [T]he two worlds, old and new, European and American, fuse in the heat of the flame, in the rush of the sea, and in the solitude of high mountain air. The elements become human. They are also universally linked in communication, meeting and embracing. [F]ew cultures in the world possess such continuity as those of Indo-Afro-Ibero America.
>
> —Carlos Fuentes (1992)[1]

The quincentennial of what has traditionally been known as the conquest of Mexico—but is better termed the Spanish invasion of Mesoamerica or the Spanish-Mexica war of 1519–1521—provides an opportunity to reflect on this momentous encounter and its consequences for shaping the world of today. When Spaniards, primarily from the kingdom of Castile, came into contact with the Aztec, Maya, and other indigenous Mesoamerican civilizations, they marveled at the size of their temples, marketplaces, and orderly plans of their urban centers, especially the Mexica-Aztec capital of Tenochtitlan. Spaniards and Mesoamericans were each struck by how the others standing before them were in some ways similar and in other ways vastly different from themselves. It was the meeting of two worlds that had developed along their own trajectories, separated by the vast ocean between what Mediterranean legends knew as the Pillars of Hercules (the Strait of Gibraltar) and the Aztecs knew as "the land by the waters" (Anahuac). Their collision was violent, but it also intertwined the richly layered history of both places to create something distinctive, serving to forge a New Spain that became a template for similar colonial endeavors in the rest of Latin America. By connecting trans-Atlantic and trans-Pacific colonial exchange networks, it was a key event in creating the globalized world we inhabit.

As a point of entry for this encounter, we can consider Cholula, Mexico, and Medellín, Spain—two towns where deeply layered human history is palpable. The same is the case for many places across the globe, but for these towns history is also inextricably linked through events of five centuries ago when Medellín's most famous son, the conquistador Hernando Cortés, led a brutal massacre in Cholula's main plaza. The years bracketing this massacre were witness to the dismantling of the powerful Aztec Empire by a few hundred Spaniards, enabled by a force of tens of thousands of indigenous Mesoamericans looking to upend the existing political order in hopes that the foreigners would grant them greater authority than the Aztecs had. Although the culmination of these events has been recounted often in the five centuries since, the cultural and societal developments over centuries or millennia on both sides of the Atlantic have been less frequently examined in tandem. Doing so allows us to more fully understand this mutually transformative encounter through its deep histories of place and its manifestation in the material world.

Cholula is a charmed town. It sits in a fertile valley with a dramatic backdrop provided by some of the most impressive volcanoes in the world. Colonial period buildings painted in bright pastels gleam against a blue sky. It is a sacred place, with church spires and cupolas visible in every direction—though not, as legend has it, one for every day of the year. It is also a university town, with a youthful energy spilling from its cafes and nightclubs. Although it, too, sits in a fertile valley, Medellín is austere by comparison, with whitewashed houses and church façades of exposed stone. The town is dominated by a long fortress perched on a hill that provides a strategic vantage point for surveying a natural transportation corridor along the Guadiana River. Novelist James A. Michener's categorization of Medellín as "one of the most mournful places in Europe"[2] overstates the solemnity, but it lacks the vibrancy of Cholula, or of other Spanish towns like Salamanca or Seville, to which Cortés and other conquistadors escaped during their formative years.

A closer look at the landscapes of Medellín and Cholula, including the prominent hills that anchor the towns, reveals their fascinating layers of history—encapsulations of Spain and Mexico. Human occupation along the Guadiana River near Medellín began in the Paleolithic period, hundreds of thousands of years ago. The population was sparse through the Bronze Age, but by the eighth to sixth centuries BCE, Iron Age inhabitants had the wherewithal to acquire at least an occasional pottery vessel from as far away as Greece or carved ivory from North Africa. Conisturgis was the most important settlement in the Guadiana region, and archaeological discoveries from the necropolis on the fortified hill show connections to the Phoenicians—the great Mediterranean seafarers of the time. The Romans made Medellín a proper town (*Metellinum*) and constructed large retaining walls on the hill to form an acropolis of public buildings, including a theater that could seat over 3,000 spectators and was adorned with elegant statuary. Medellín next passed briefly to the Germanic Visigoths before being conquered by Muslim Arabs and Berbers, who built ingenious cisterns for storing water (*aljibes*). The fortress was eventually reconquered and expanded in the thirteenth century under Christian forces led by Ferdinand III of the kingdom of Castile-León and was completely rebuilt in the fourteenth century. Following the Christian *Reconquista* of the region, the inhabitants of Medellín built their sacred structures on the side of the hill. These included the church of San Martín, which was erected directly on top of the remains of a Roman temple formerly dedicated to Pluto, and where in 1485 the future conquistador was baptized (Figure 1.1).[3]

Mesoamerica denotes the land and cultures comprising much of modern Mexico and northern Central America, which largely became the viceroyalty of New Spain during the colonial period. Initial settlement of the Americas was later than in Europe, so Cholula does not have any artifacts as ancient as the Paleolithic period. Once settled, however, Cholula's urban trajectory kept pace with Medellín's. Early inhabitants of the first millennium BCE took advantage of dependable water provided by local springs and traded with other parts of Mesoamerica. The feature of the landscape that dominates Cholula today looks to be a large hill with a bright yellow church dedicated to the Virgin of the Remedies on its summit (Figure 1.2). But it is not a natural hill. The sixteenth-century Choluteca called it the Tlachihualtepetl ("man-made mountain") in deference to the efforts of those who a millennium earlier had built the largest structure ever constructed in the Precolumbian Americas. By some estimates, Cholula's Great Pyramid is the largest by volume in the world. With a maximum basal length of some 1,300 feet (400 m) and height of 217 feet (66 m), the total volume is nearly twice that of the Great Pyramid on the Giza plateau in Egypt.[4] It was once taller than it is today, but the Spanish truncated Cholula's sacred mountain in the sixteenth century to build the first of a series of churches.

Figure 1.1. Medellín, Spain, with fortress in background, statue of Cortés in plaza, and church of San Martín to left.
Photo by the author.

The origins of Cholula's Great Pyramid were in more modest structures that the Choluteca began erecting during the first century CE and that are encased inside the final construction phase, which has only been partly reconstructed by archaeologists along some of its lower courses. It is difficult to be certain what culture built these early versions, but they exhibit cultural continuity with central Mexican traditions seen centuries earlier. The city was a natural crossroads between the mountainous Basin of Mexico—home to successive urban civilizations, the Teotihuacanos, Toltecs, and Aztecs—and the tropical lowlands around the Gulf of Mexico. Sixteenth-century accounts such as the *Historia Tolteca-Chichimeca* name the Olmeca-Xicalanca, peoples with apparent ties to the coastal Gulf of Mexico, as settlers of Cholula during the eighth century. In the twelfth century, the city was conquered by the Tolteca-Chichimeca, whose roots the Choluteca whom Cortés massacred identified with directly. By the time the Tolteca-Chichimeca arrived, the Great Pyramid had been abandoned and left to be reclaimed by nature, its formidable mass eventually covered with grass and shrubs. The center of conquest-era Cholula was a temple honoring the god Quetzalcoatl, the

Figure 1.2. Cholula, Mexico, with Great Pyramid looming in background and colonial buildings in foreground.

Photo by the author. Reproduction authorized by the Instituto Nacional de Antropología e Historia, Mexico.

Feathered Serpent, whose devotees made the city one of the most important pilgrimage spots of pre-Hispanic Mesoamerica.[5] The Spanish destroyed it to erect the monastery of San Gabriel, around which they developed the grid of colonial-era Cholula.

In Cholula and Medellín we have some of the important episodes in how early Mesoamerica became Mexico and how early Iberia became Spain, as well as the cultural and historical entanglement of the two countries. Archaeologists consider their layers of occupation as deep history that spans millennia of cultural, technological, political, and religious development. We borrow from other disciplines such as anthropology, geography, and the history of art and architecture to create a historical understanding that grounds the richly detailed textual sources in the material world and tangible stuff of life—those physical places and things that archaeologists call "sites" and "artifacts." It is the lens through which the encounter between Spain and Mexico of five centuries ago is viewed in this book, as part of historical processes with antecedents and consequences registered in the material record, rather than being a discrete event described primarily through text—though we will also consider the texts. They are processes that continued after the fall of the Aztec Empire and served as a template for the forging of much of today's Latin America.

Facts on the Ground

How do experts of this encounter and the cultural developments that preceded it know what we say we know? What evidence do certain claims rest on? Many different ways of knowing are at our disposal in investigating the human past. Our understanding of more recent history relies heavily on written texts, which have proliferated exponentially over the past few hundred years. Scholars of more recent historical periods tend to be in disciplines within the humanities or certain social sciences. More distant history, such as the origins of our species and our colonization of different corners of the planet, lacks written texts. As a result, researchers tend to follow natural science approaches, as are used in paleontology or genetics. Yet the boundaries between disciplines and methods are not clear-cut. Some researchers might consider the aesthetics of Paleolithic cave art or the social organization of the people who created it—representing more humanistic or social science concerns—whereas we can understand more recent history through genetics, the history of disease, and other more natural-science approaches.

In terming this a "deep history" of European colonization of the Americas, I am thinking like an archaeologist in that the deeper one excavates in the ground, the further back in time the layers of cultural occupation date to. An approach with this temporal depth crosses fields of study since it engages early periods that lack written documents (often termed "prehistoric"), other periods that have minimal textual sources typically written by more literate neighboring cultures or by slightly later cultures in the same area (often termed "proto-historic"), up to the pivotal period of encounter, invasion, and early colonialism—all during the early decades of the printing press and widespread dissemination of the written word. What types of information should we prioritize? When presented with accounts of, for instance, between 3,000 to 6,000 Choluteca massacred by Cortés and his forces, out of a total population of 40,000 households, how can we evaluate the accuracy of such information?[6] Or in considering the historical geography of Medellín and its broader region of Extremadura, the so-called cradle of the conquistadors, how can we discern what influences from earlier cultures and historical periods were most critical to forging a culture of trans-Atlantic conquest and imperialism? Creating a more accurate understanding of the complex and conflicting history of this encounter, invasion, and the colonial experience it produced requires mixing lines of evidence and the methods for studying them.

As a starting point, we have the axiom of historical scholarship that all texts possess biases of their authors. It probably does not come as a surprise that the letters that Cortés wrote to the king of Spain (Charles I, also known as Charles V of the Holy Roman Empire) to justify his illegal military actions are considered to have been authored with considerable bias. The actions were a breach of the chain of command because Cortés' immediate superior, Diego Velázquez de Cuellar, the governor of Cuba, had authorized exploration but not invasion, which forced Cortés to justify his actions as legitimate and virtuous.[7] These letters are, nevertheless, the earliest written eyewitness accounts we have. They caused a sensation in Europe when they were first published by giving a wide audience the sense that they were witness to historic events on par with Rome's imperial expansion, but from previously unknown lands and in "real time."[8] Accordingly, although we should not rely on Cortés' letters blindly in fashioning great-man narratives of earlier historians,[9] we would also be foolish to ignore them. Likewise, the more detailed surviving accounts of indigenous Mesoamerican societies during the early decades of New Spain accumulated by Spanish friars include rich information on pre-Hispanic life and Native perspectives on the conquest. Yet these clearly need to be read with a critical eye, particularly with regard to religion, since these men of the cloth were keenly interested in converting Mesoamerican populations away from what they deemed pagan beliefs and rituals. Further complicating matters, later accounts were often compiled by authors who were not themselves eyewitnesses to invasion and colonization. In some cases they may have drawn from oral or written accounts of eyewitnesses, the most famous example being the hypothesized existence of "Crónica X," a lost chronicle or series of texts that appears to have provided source material to other sixteenth-century authors, including key histories written by the Dominican friar Diego Durán and by Hernando Alvarado Tezozomoc, a great-grandson of Moctezuma.[10]

Forms of bias in sources authored by Native peoples or peoples of mixed Mesoamerican-European ancestry (called *mestizo*) can be less obvious to non-specialists. Recent conquest scholarship has shown how all parties involved in these transformative events acted strategically within the complex webs of power, politics, and societal transformation in which they found themselves. An important fact of pre-conquest and early colonial Mesoamerican societies was their micro-patriotism.[11] There was no unified Mesoamerican, Aztec, or Maya perspective on the Spanish invasion because the large groups of people we refer to by those terms were diverse and identified primarily as city-states and secondarily as a number of ethnic groups. For example, the dominant culture group within the political formation broadly known as the Aztec Empire is better termed by their ethnic designation Mexica, or as Tenochca, based on their capital city of Tenochtitlan. This empire was in actuality ruled as a confederation between three city-states, the Triple Alliance, with the second most powerful being the Acolhua ethnic group centered on their capital city Texcoco, and the third the Tepanec ethnic group with a capital at Tlacopan (later corrupted to Tacuba in Spanish). Texcocans eventually joined the Spanish and other Native allies to topple the island city of Tenochtitlan, and their descendants wrote histories that celebrated the contributions of their family members as conquistadors in their own right.[12] The Mexica were not even unified on their home island, since the Tenochca shared it with their ethnic brethren the Tlatelolca. The city of Tlatelolco possessed a superior canoe port and a larger marketplace than Tenochtitlan, and the Tenochca had annexed it decades before the Spanish arrived. When the Franciscan friar Bernardino de Sahagún, the prolific compiler of Mesoamerican lifeways, recorded perspectives on pre-Hispanic political history and the events leading up to the conquest, we can sense the bias toward the denizens of their imperialistic sister-city on the part of several scribes from Tlatelolco and other city-states who worked with him.[13]

Whether a text is written in Spanish, an indigenous language such as Nahuatl (the lingua franca of the Aztec Empire) combined with Spanish, or in non-alphabetic or hieroglyphic text in one of the few pre-Hispanic books that survived the massive Spanish campaigns to burn them all during the early colonial period, we can identify and mitigate biases by probing authorship and possible agendas. We must also look to non-textual material remains—such as art, architecture, and artifacts—to provide additional lines of information that may complement or contradict what chroniclers recorded in their manuscripts. For much of this book, these will be the most important lines of evidence, particularly when exploring pre- and protohistoric periods, but also in framing the transformation of Mesoamerica into New Spain in terms of physical spaces and material things.

Archaeologists study humanity's past through the material remains people have left behind. This could include books or other texts, but more typically includes ruined buildings, discarded tools, or the bones of the past people themselves. When applicable, it may include art and imagery also studied by art historians, or may draw on the work of social and cultural anthropologists who study living people from the same geographic area. At its best, archaeology is cross-cutting and can incorporate information from other specialties in order to look at the broad scale of change in human societies over millennia, while also being able to zoom into the cultural minutiae of a particular moment in time when an individual person made or used something—a hearth, a clay figure, an article of clothing. This broad, multi-scalar lens on the places and things fashioned by past peoples can provide a tangible authenticity to human history sometimes lacking in written texts. For example, returning to the earlier issue of how many people lived in Cholula or other Aztec-period cities when the Spanish and their Mesoamerican allies invaded, we can make informed estimates based on the physical urban footprint and occupational density of settlement. We take into consideration the more macro-scale of the distribution of buildings, pottery sherds, or other types of material culture that archaeologists have documented through systematically surveying individual sites or entire regions. In this particular domain, Cholula poses problems, because it was never dis-occupied following the conquest, meaning that the colonial and contemporary occupation overlie much of the pre-Hispanic occupation and render it impossible for systematic archaeological survey. In other pre-Hispanic or conquest-period cases, settlements were abandoned and archaeologists have been able to record their size or distribution in a region, to more accurately estimate population geography and demographic trends. Alternatively, we could focus on micro-scale analyses and examine in detail the bone remains of particular individuals or the floorplans of their houses in order to build up site or regional estimates of population or the impact of discrete events, such as a specific battle or massacre.

Another key issue in considering this particular instance of European colonization revolves around identification of the cultural developments that were most critical to Iberians, especially from the western half of the peninsula, having developed the technology and predilection to cross the Atlantic to conquer and colonize. This is also a topic whose illumination requires a long look back, to consider various episodes of history and the cumulative yet capricious nature of technological and cultural change through time. It is a perspective that is applicable not only to setting up the relatively short interval of the pivotal Spanish-Mexica war of 1519–1521, but also to the longer endeavor of colonialism in Iberia and its legacies to later Mexico and Latin America more broadly.[14] Recent investigations by scholars of the "New Conquest History" highlight the decisive roles played by diseases that Europeans introduced to the Americas, the political decentralization and micro-patriotism of Native peoples, and the greater use of metal weapons and naval technologies in European warfare.[15] These last factors are ripe for archaeological evaluations: bioarchaeologists study the history and demographic impacts of disease, while field archaeologists combine the material record with textual sources to advance understanding of the organization of pre-Hispanic political formations and technologies.

Trans-Atlantic perspectives that emphasize material culture are rare, but one notable exception is the work of the social anthropologist George Foster, who over half a century ago took stock of the tangible legacies of the conquest and colonial period in his book *Culture and Conquest: America's Spanish Heritage.*[16] Foster's work is valuable in the linkages it makes between types of material culture found in Spain and Mexico. It is fascinating for those interested in minute cultural details, such as variability in the construction and use of fishnets or ox plows. Archaeologists love these sorts of inventories, though non-specialists may be forgiven if their eyes glaze over. Another trans-Atlantic perspective, but one focused on history and aesthetics and rendered in more imaginative prose, was provided by the great Mexican author Carlos Fuentes for the 1992 quincentennial in *The Buried Mirror: Reflections on Spain and the New World*—the source for this chapter's epigraph. Fuentes considered the fraught history of Hispanic heritage in the Americas and how to best reflect on and project from this mixed inheritance five centuries later, metaphorically employing the mirror, both of the kinds fashioned from obsidian by the Aztecs and the one bringing the viewer into Diego Velázquez's masterpiece of Spanish golden-age painting, Las Meninas.[17] This cultural mixing, or *mestizaje*, defines the creation of Latin America but has deep roots in earlier exchange networks, migrations, political alliances, and colonialism on the part of Mesoamerican and Iberian peoples, on both sides of the Atlantic.

Reflection and Explanation

Five centuries removed from the key events of the fall of Aztec Mexico and multicultural creation of New Spain, we continue to grapple with understanding these events and to contextualize them in the present. It is a task scholars pursue at varied scales of analysis. The one followed here is somewhat intermediate between global histories seeking ultimate causes for how our species has arrived at where we are today and those that focus more intently on a particular chapter of the human story. Macro-histories of human societies typically do not concentrate on particular parts of the globe, such as Mesoamerica and Iberia. Many ignore the Americas altogether, and few emphasize material culture as an interconnected system of things and practices entangled over deep time—underscoring instead certain disparities in technology or ways of harnessing energy. Long-term histories of this sort, sometimes falling under the rubric of "big history," are valuable in their breadth of coverage and in isolating a few key variables in major social transformations, such as the roles played by geography, diseases, energy capture, military and transportation technologies, or the creation of capitalist world systems.[18] They are often less satisfactory in illuminating the particular cultural and historical contours of specific regions of the globe or, when they do, lack information on non-elites derived from more recent archaeological research of settlement patterns and households—prioritizing instead texts and monuments that bias toward elite perspectives.[19] Regional histories, in turn, can be highly focused regarding a specific area or historical moment, and in the case of conquest history there exists a robust and mature corpus of scholarship examining the Spanish-Mexica war in great detail.[20] Yet it is only through zooming out to draw comparisons that we can understand what is interesting or unique about any particular part of the world at a moment in history, or what parallel institutions societies developed due to similarities in social processes.[21]

In the pages to follow, we explore the comparative cultural developments of early Mesoamerica and Iberia and the material manifestations of their entanglement in the focal period of encounter, conquest, colonialism, and Native resilience. We begin millennia before the sixteenth century in both pre-Hispanic Mesoamerica and prehistoric Iberia. Our focus is intermediate, however, in considering only these two parts of the globe so as to balance regional details with broader mechanisms of societal change over long periods of time. We will consider long-term historical trajectories as involving a certain amount of path dependence, meaning that earlier developments served to increase the likelihood of later ones by reinforcing and institutionalizing particular patterns of behavior.[22] This self-reinforcement may be an unconscious process to later people, as with the introduction or invention of key technologies that later became taken for granted, or may be very consciously embraced as part of the historical narratives that were celebrated to define group identity. As examples, we will see how the legacy of specific facets of Teotihuacan and the Toltecs in central Mexico contributed to shaping Aztec urbanism, religion, and imperialism, and how the same was the case for the legacy of the Phoenicians, Romans, *Reconquista* kingdoms, and other cultures in conquest-era Spain. We will follow a materially grounded inquiry into these historical trajectories on both sides of the Atlantic and then their tumultuous collision and enduring consequences through a primary focus on the tangible stuff of life—specifically, deep histories of places, styles, and things.

We will also consider the ways in which various Mesoamerican peoples were active agents in wars of conquest and the creation of the viceroyalty of New Spain. Although the pivotal roles of indigenous Mesoamericans as allies, translators, and conquistadors in their own right have been prioritized only by recent scholarship, their voices were recorded in the early decades of the viceroyalty, collected by chroniclers such as Sahagún.[23] By charting the deep history of Mesoamerica we can better appreciate the political evolution of pre-Aztec kingdoms and city-states, and how it was that some peoples of the Aztec period became confederated or antagonistic, and more or less willing to ally with Spanish forces. We can also see how the interconnectivity of Mesoamerica as a culture area fostered populations that permitted multicultural and multilingual negotiations essential to the encounter. Mesoamericans possessed intimate knowledge of the transportation routes that moved pre-Hispanic merchants and armies across the landscape and became the routes of conquests that were generally directed by the Spanish but would have been impossible without such guides and warriors. Finally, we can understand deep patterns in cultural norms of diet, labor, technology, architecture, warfare, politics, religion, and other domains that were crucial to how military conquest, spiritual conversion, and quotidian lifeways unfolded.

The Path Ahead

Mesoamerica is the stage for most of the events in this book, so we begin with its deep history in Chapter 2. We trace how the transition from nomadic foragers to settled farmers of maize and other crops resulted in the first villages, unifying art styles, and later cities, states, and empires. Cultures such as the Olmecs, Mayas, Teotihuacanos, and Toltecs preceded the Aztecs, who incorporated elements of all of them, particularly the last two from the same region of central Mexico. We then cross the Atlantic in Chapter 3 to examine the waves of conquest and cultural developments on the Iberian peninsula. Farming began at a similar time to Mesoamerica, but in Iberia it was imported from the Fertile Crescent region of Southwest Asia and was joined by animal husbandry and the use of pack animals. Autonomous cultural developments of native Iberians were stimulated by maritime powers that sailed west along the Mediterranean: the Phoenicians, Greeks, Carthaginians, and Romans, each growing in their imperial reach and providing a base for later political and economic developments. Iberians also took advantage of their geographical setting on a peninsular hinge between the Mediterranean and Atlantic worlds, which connected two major maritime spheres of interaction and saw the development of hybrid ships increasingly suited to open ocean crossing. Following the collapse of imperial Rome, Iberia fluctuated between Christian and Islamic rule, with the former emerging victorious after a centuries-long program of national unification known as the *Reconquista*, or "reconquest." Crops introduced by Muslims and administrative strategies implemented by Christian kingdoms in frontier regions were direct predecessors of the plantation-like economies eventually imposed on the Americas. The two trans-Atlantic sequences are then interlaced for thematic comparison in Chapter 4, which focuses on the fifteenth and early sixteenth centuries in Mexico and Spain, with an emphasis on their most consequential kingdoms: the Aztec Triple Alliance and the Crown of Castile-León. Major themes of comparison include ethnic affiliation and national mythos, patterns of urbanism and political and economic organization, military and transportation technologies, and worldview framed through religion and philosophy.

Initial colonial encounters and Cortés' invasion make up Chapter 5. We consider the development of institutions and strategies for Spain's colonization of the Indies, as Columbus, thinking he had landed in India, erroneously branded the Western Hemisphere. There were major disagreements over issues of slavery, land and labor, and continued conquests, with opinion often split along the lines of the Spanish conquistadors and the clergy. Initial expeditions to Mesoamerica encountered Maya cities that were unlike those that Spaniards knew from colonizing the Caribbean. These urban centers were more similar in their large populations and architectural elaboration to what the Spaniards were familiar with from the contemporaneous Islamic world and from Mediterranean antiquity, prompting the Spaniards to draw frequent comparisons with these civilizations. After seeing the potential riches of Mesoamerica, Cortés and others in his expedition opted for invasion rather than the exploration and trading they were authorized to do. It would have been wholly impossible at the time were it not for the support of various Mesoamerican groups who constituted the majority of the fighting force. Critical among these were the tens of thousands of Tlaxcalteca who joined the expedition and a single woman, La Malinche, who became Cortés' translator and concubine. Following the pivotal Spanish-Tlaxcalteca alliance, the first military campaign ended in the tragic massacre at Cholula, both covered in Chapter 6.

The decisive Spanish-Mexica war is the subject of Chapter 7. The war lasted for close to two years but alternated between periods of uneasy diplomacy and violent battles. More Native allies joined the war as it progressed, including, most importantly, the second most powerful Aztec city-state of Texcoco. It was from here that Cortés launched small ships onto the lake surrounding the imperial capital and brought naval and siege battle tactics, borne of millennia of bloodshed in the Old World, to the New World.

Histories of the conquest often end with the fall of Tenochtitlan, but the forging of New Spain required decades of continued military invasions in which central Mexicans, in particular, played leading roles. On the basis of this assistance, the Tlaxcalteca and other Native allies petitioned the Spanish Crown for certain rights and privileges, as a form of negotiation within a system of domination and oppression, even sailing across the Atlantic to Spain multiple times to do so in person. Imperial rule and religious conversion could occasionally be challenged or proactively shaped by Mesoamericans, generating hybrid forms of religious belief, public spectacles, art, architecture, diet, and personal adornment, all inscribed on Mexico's natural and cultural landscape. Such exchanges also crossed the Atlantic to affect European and world history. A specialist of colonial Latin America has remarked, "As a concept, the 'New World' is more a matter of time than place; it is a time in which two ancient world cultures collided through the aggressive act of invasion, to begin a process of continuing dialectical permutations where native participation was neither as passive, reactive, or silent as is so often believed."[24] Chapter 8 closes the volume by considering the conflictive cultural fusion of sixteenth-century New Spain and its legacy to developing what we know today as Latin America, as well as to our globalized and cosmopolitan world order.

On their own, neither Cholula nor Medellín could convey the deep layers of this linked history underlying Mexico and Spain, but together—and with other related sites, buildings, artifacts, and textual testimonies covered in the pages to follow—they tether us to this fascinating episode in the human story.

2

Mesoamerica

A Deep History

The great volcanoes rise above the landscape, clad in a mantle of snow as if they had relinquished their dark powers and fallen into eternal sleep. But the crust of the land is still unstable. It trembles even when asleep, and overnight a fiery monster may burst forth.

—Eric Wolf (1959)[1]

The Aztecs, Maya, and other Mesoamerican peoples believed that our habitable world began as a crocodilian earth monster or a turtle emerging from a primordial sea to carry the earth on its back. Sacred texts dating to the sixteenth century, and the art and calendars of pre-Hispanic periods, tell of this particular act of creation. Although it is tempting to speculate that highlanders like the Aztecs more often recognized the spines of a crocodile in the mountain ridges within their environment while lowlanders like the Maya of the Yucatan saw the shell of a turtle in the flatter terrain around them, similar conceptualizations extend throughout the Americas and do not group neatly with local topography. Indeed, the fact that various peoples of Eurasia, particularly eastern Asia, also conceive of these cosmogenic metaphors suggests a deeply shared understanding dating from the Paleolithic period that was carried in the minds and stories of the first humans to enter the Western Hemisphere. The nineteenth-century anthropologist E. B. Tylor proposed that the "world turtle" was evidence of a mutual cosmogony among humankind. Tylor's book *Anahuac: or, Mexico and the Mexicans, Ancient and Modern* also introduced the indigenous peoples of Mexico to a wide, Anglophone audience.[2] The Nahuatl term of the book's title translates as "close to water" and was used in Aztec times to designate either the island of Tenochtitlan-Tlatelolco, the highland lake basin of the Aztec core (the Basin of Mexico), or a larger territory of the empire between the Gulf of Mexico and Pacific Ocean. Another representation of Mesoamerica is attributed to Hernando Cortés himself, when he returned to Spain in 1528 to tell Emperor Charles V in person about the lands he had conquered. He purportedly crumpled a ball of paper before the sovereign as a visual illustration of New Spain's rugged topography.[3]

These metaphors for the land of Mesoamerica capture some of its dramatic mountain ranges and immense environmental diversity, which is matched by its cultural diversity (Figure 2.1). Mesoamerica's topographic relief and tropical latitudes create an array of ecozones and microclimates, and make it one of the richest areas of the world in terms of species of plants and animals. Native peoples exploited and exchanged these diverse resources, first more symbiotically through trade and later also involving tax and tribute demanded by kingdoms and imperialistic states.[4] Such exchanges kept highlanders and lowlanders in contact from the time of the first settled villages of four millennia ago to the Aztec Empire on the eve of Spanish arrival. They fostered shared traits that became the basis for defining Mesoamerica as a culture area: intensive maize agriculture, a dual-calendar system combining the solar year with a 260-day ritual year, the world's

Figure 2.1. Map of Mesoamerica listing modern countries, major landforms, and select cultural subregions.

first team sport using rubber balls, and urban societies that built temple-pyramids and used hieroglyphic writing.[5] Nevertheless, Mesoamerican peoples did not perceive themselves as culturally united on the eve of the Spanish invasion, and in certain cases their sense of regionalism or micro-patriotism turned groups against one another in the conquest and creation of the colonial political order of New Spain.[6] Mesoamerica's diverse peoples also exchanged goods and ideas with more distant groups—such as ancestral Puebloans from the present-day Southwestern United States and cultures of southern Central America and northern South America, from whom metalworking technologies spread.[7] The boundaries of what scholars designate as Mesoamerica were therefore porous and shifted over its history of occupation; yet we can perceive a strong unity in thought that is considered the "hard nucleus" of Mesoamerican religion and orientation toward the world,[8] and which brings conceptual coherence to the culture area.

Sons and Daughters of the Shaking Earth

Since it is defined by its cultural attributes, Mesoamerica has no discrete natural boundaries. The culture area's landmass is demarcated somewhat to the north by the deserts of northern Mexico and to the south by the narrowing of the Central American isthmus around Nicaragua. Within these latitudes are an array of landforms, climates, and peoples. From the north, two major mountain ranges—the eastern Sierra Madre Oriental and western Sierra Madre Occidental—converge to the south at the Isthmus of Tehuantepec, the narrower strip of land where Mexico is pinched before opening up again at the Yucatan peninsula. Saddled between these long ranges are high plains referred to by their Spanish terms, *altiplano* or *meseta*. These plains are cut east-west through the highlands of western and central Mexico by the Trans-Mexican Neovolcanic Axis, which features a number of active volcanoes with some peaks that reach over 18,000 feet (5,500 m) and are snow-capped throughout the year (Figure 2.2). Highland lakes formed in areas where mountains block the drainage of water, and these became attractive places for human settlement because of their abundant resources. This is best exemplified by the Basin of Mexico, which became the core of the Aztec Empire, the center of New Spain, and today's Mexico City metropolitan zone. In the United States we refer to Denver as the "mile-high" city; Mexico City

Figure 2.2. Eastern Basin of Mexico with Popocatepetl and Itzaccihuatl volcanoes in background.
Photo by the author.

and the former urban core of the Aztec civilization are about a mile and a half high.

Mesoamerica generally gets more humid beginning at the Isthmus of Tehuantepec and adjacent coastal areas extending southeast into southern Mexico, Guatemala, Belize, and western Honduras, much of which is designated as the Maya lowlands for its major culture group. The northern Maya lowlands is the drier half of the Yucatan peninsula between the Gulf of Mexico and Caribbean Sea, which receives a little over three feet (1 m) of rain per year and has no rivers because the porous limestone bedrock absorbs the water. In contrast, the southern Maya lowlands, centered in the Peten district of Guatemala and adjacent areas, is home to dense rainforest with six to seven feet (2–2.5 m) of annual precipitation feeding rivers and low swampy areas called *bajos*. The Pacific side of Mesoamerica, from the Mexico-Guatemala border through El Salvador and southward, transitions from coast to dynamic highlands periodically rattled by earthquakes and volcanic eruptions. It includes the Maya highlands around today's Guatemala City, which was a second major area of Spanish invasion and colonization. Natural disasters from these active tectonic features and from hurricanes raging inland from the coasts posed challenges to ancient Mesoamericans, as they still do today. Not surprisingly, indigenous peoples viewed this landscape as vigorously animate and in need of appeasement.

Similar to the environmental setting, Mesoamerican languages also exhibit tremendous diversity. This linguistic diversity and need for bilingual translators would impact the way the conquest and creation of New Spain unfolded. The Spaniards first landed on the Mayan-speaking Yucatan peninsula and then moved westward to encounter the Aztec Empire, whose lingua franca was Nahuatl. In between were bilingual populations of trading emporia linking the two major culture spheres, and peoples of surrounding regions possessed their own rich mosaics of languages, some of which are tonal, others agglutinative, and all of which tell us something about the patterns of migration, cultural contact, and political formation.

Linguists designate the three largest Mesoamerican language families Uto-Aztecan, Mayan, and Otomanguean.[9] Uto-Aztecan represents the indigenous language family with the widest dispersal in the Americas, captured by its name combining Ute of Utah and the northern Rocky Mountains to the southernmost speakers of the Aztecan group—the Pipil of El Salvador. Debates concerning the origins and spread of Uto-Aztecan, particularly whether it spread with farmers of central Mexico or nomadic foragers from the north, relate directly to questions surrounding the origins of the Aztecs. Mayan languages are more concentrated geographically in the northern lowlands of the Yucatan, southern lowlands of northern Guatemala and Belize, and highlands of southern Mexico and Guatemala. The Huastecs of the Sierra Madre Oriental are an isolated Mayan language group who inhabit the Huasteca, adjacent to central Mexico and once incorporated into the Aztec Empire. Mayan languages are about as closely related to one another as are the Romance languages, such as Spanish to Italian. Their current distribution provides a textbook illustration for linguists of how the natural landscape can foster homogeneity or heterogeneity in language, since the relatively flat and contiguous Yucatan peninsula is dominated by a single language, Yucatec Mayan, whereas the fragmented terrain of the Maya highlands is home to dozens of languages. Between the Uto-Aztecan and Mayan language families are speakers of Otomanguean languages, who are found largely in central and southern Mexico and include Otomi, Mixtec, and Zapotec. The Otomi were generally within the Aztec imperial core, whereas the Mixtecs and Zapotecs, centered in today's Mexican state of Oaxaca, included some kingdoms that were conquered and others than remained independent. Speakers of a fourth language family, Mixe-Zoquean, are found today primarily in the Isthmus of Tehuantepec, where the contemporary Mexican states of Oaxaca, Chiapas, Tabasco, and Veracruz meet.

In 1519 central Mexico was linguistically diverse, with resident speakers of Nahuatl, Otomi, and Totonac representing different language families, not just languages. Speakers of all three remain in the region to this day, and even though the region is and has been linguistically diverse, there are strongly shared cultural symbols and a common worldview.[10] As the Aztec imperial language, Nahuatl was the language of administration and commerce. Moving backward in time to periods without texts or with sparse pictographic texts that lack clear phonetic markers to provide clues of the language they correspond to, archaeologists can still see that highland central Mexico was a cultural crossroads of early Mesoamerica, based on the diversity of artifacts and architectural styles.[11] Recent bioarchaeological studies involving bone-isotope analyses and other methods of skeletal and genetic analysis have demonstrated how common migration was throughout Mesoamerican history and that no population remained isolated or static.[12] In the case of central Mexico, its placement within the landmass of Mesoamerica, its rugged topography characterized by corridors that serve to channel movement, and the differentiation of landforms including semi-arid plains and more lush lake basins converged to create natural transit points and make some places more advantageous than others for human settlement. Multiple cultural ties to the northwest, east, and south are seen in the styles of artifacts and buildings unearthed in central Mexico dating to the first millennium BCE, when the region's inhabitants began constructing its first urban centers. These continued in subsequent periods up to the Aztec Empire on the eve of Spanish arrival. Pre-Hispanic central Mexico was a multiethnic mosaic, which intensified through urbanization in its capital cities and by the expansionistic states and empires some of them controlled.

Archaeologists have parsed major periods of Mesoamerican cultural development based on how humans interacted with their environment and created major spheres of stylistic, economic, and political interaction. This differs from chronologies used in Africa, Europe, and Asia based largely on tool technology—an Old Stone Age (Paleolithic) followed by a New Stone Age (Neolithic) and then by Bronze and Iron Ages. It also differs from how Mesoamerican peoples themselves divided cycles of time, though both archaeologists and Mesoamericans view the adoption of maize agriculture as a critical development. In one Aztec creation narrative known as the *Legend of the Suns*, previous "suns"—or cycles of world creation and destruction—lasted for either 676, 364, or 312 years, corresponding respectively to 13, 7, and 6 intervals of 52 years, the sacred measurement of time marking when the solar and ritual calendars realigned to the same day. Only in the present, Fifth Sun did the sentient beings that became "real" humans receive maize from the gods, as well as other key crops such as beans, amaranth, and chia.[13] In archaeological sequences, this transition characterizes what is termed the Archaic period, analogous to the Neolithic period and its associated shift to farming in the Old World.

The Mexican archaeologist Manuel Gamio was one of the first scholars of the ancient Americas to excavate sites so as to understand their sequence of superimposed artifact layers and then use this stratigraphy to stitch together a regional chronology of long-term cultural change. He and his colleagues uncovered Mexico's deep history of place by noting that Aztec layers were preceded by ones connected with the great ruined city of Teotihuacan that were in turn preceded by earlier layers of pre-urban settlement.[14] Later discoveries showed the still deeper history of central Mexico and Mesoamerica as a whole, with the shift from foragers or hunter-gatherers to farmers occurring over millennia, from the Paleoindian to Archaic and Formative (or Preclassic) periods. The Paleoindian period denotes the earliest arrivals of people to the Americas from northeast Asia, a date that has been repeatedly pushed back by new research and now appears to have been at least 18,000 years ago.[15] This initial occupation of Mesoamerica therefore falls in the Pleistocene geological epoch, better known as Earth's last ice age. Around 11,700 years ago, global climate began to warm and become less variable from year to year, marking the transition to the Holocene epoch. All across the planet, humans adapted their subsistence strategies to this global climate change, but evolutionary pathways branched in different directions and unfolded at different rates. Mesoamericans started experimenting with the cultivation of maize and other crops approximately 10,000 years ago (or 8000 BCE), marking the onset of the Archaic period. Change in these plant species was relatively slow, and people did not fully commit to life as settled farmers until approximately 2000 BCE, beginning the Formative period. The pace of cultural change then quickened dramatically as Mesoamericans started building their first towns in the late second millennium BCE and their first cities by the late first millennium BCE. Large urban centers of approximately two thousand years ago attracted migrants who arrived from more rural areas in the same regions or sometimes from other regions hundreds of miles away. From this point onward, Mesoamerica was witness to sequential urban and state-level societies of the first millennia CE Classic period and the subsequent Postclassic period of the first half of the second millennia—the setting for Aztec civilization.[16]

People of the Corn

Many of the earliest archaeological investigations into the origins of agriculture focused on the Fertile Crescent region of Southwest Asia, where the dry climate nicely preserved plant remains and provided archaeologists with some of the earliest evidence of farming. This region subsequently loomed large in models postulating how humans developed or adopted agriculture elsewhere in the globe. Change was thought to have been fast (or "revolutionary") and stimulated by an intellectual breakthrough where people "discovered" planting. Scholars assumed, implicitly or explicitly, that planting was first undertaken by men and that farming preceded settled village life everywhere across the globe. More recent research outside and within Southwest Asia challenges all of these notions. In some places the tempo of first cultivating and then domesticating plants and animals was much more gradual. There was also no intellectual breakthrough involved, as ethnographic studies of forager communities show that they intimately understand the relationship between seeds and crops, and know more about the entire life cycles of more plants and animals than neighboring farming communities do. Moreover, this knowledge, of plants in particular, is usually the domain of women, suggesting their greater agency in cases of past domestication. Finally, in multiple parts of the world, archaeological remains show that foragers lived in sedentary (permanently settled) or semi-sedentary villages prior to this major change in subsistence.[17]

Much of the debunking of early archaeological reconstructions of the transition to farming has come from research in Mesoamerica, and the culture area has seen a great deal of research because it presents an independent case of plant domestication, especially of one of the world's major crops—corn, or maize (scientific name *Zea mays*). First was the debunking of the idea that planting and harvesting was any sort of intellectual breakthrough for foragers. Here, most tellingly, is the fact that one of the initial crops Mesoamericans cultivated were inedible gourds, such as the bottle gourd (*Lagenaria siceraria*) that forager populations planted seasonally for use as containers. They did this for thousands of generations before deciding to commit to farming as a way of life.[18] These foragers clearly understood the relationship between seed and plant, but did not undertake a rapid revolution in their subsistence strategies.

The temporal lag between when foragers first planted gourds as containers and when Mesoamericans committed to becoming dedicated farmers of maize and other crops also illustrates how gradual the transition to agriculture in was Mesoamerica. Remains of cultivated maize plants in the form of phytoliths—microscopic silica structures from plant tissue—have been recovered from the Balsas River region of southwest Mexico dating to approximately 10,000–9,000 years ago (8000–7000 BCE), during the initial Archaic period.[19] Current genetic evidence suggests that key transformations of domesticated maize were present by 4,400 years ago, or 2400 BCE, and a sequence of well-preserved cobs from dry caves and rock-shelters as distantly separated as central Mexico to Honduras indicate that the intervening five millennia or more of maize cultivation had resulted in a much more productive staple crop.[20] The telling signs of more settled lifeways appear archaeologically in the centuries following the evolution of productive maize—traits such as pottery production and the preserved foundations of houses. In this way, inland Mesoamerica conforms better to older models derived from the Fertile Crescent of farmers transitioning to villagers than do parts of the globe where a high biomass of wild plants and animals was regularly available, such as in certain coastal and riverine regions. One example of complex settled life prior to agriculture is the Pacific coast of Peru, where an abundance of marine life delivered to the region's shores by the Humboldt Current was harvested by the builders of impressive urban centers who did not farm edible crops but did plant cotton to make nets for fishing.[21] This contrast between higher and lower biomass areas also accounts for some of the variability in the origins and spread of farming in Mesoamerica. Residents of more marginal zones located in semi-arid inland regions appear to have changed their subsistence strategies based on economic calculations of crop yield as maize became more productive, whereas residents of lusher areas along the coasts appear to have incorporated maize and other domesticated crops for the more social reasons of throwing feasts and serving celebratory foods, potentially including the fermentation of grains into alcohol.[22]

Maize, beans, and squash are together known as the "Mesoamerican trinity" or "three sisters" of agriculture because the plants grow symbiotically and when eaten together provide most of the nutrients needed for basic human subsistence. The three are planted together in traditional Mesoamerican farming in field plots called *milpa*, using the Nahuatl term. Maize is planted first on low, mounded ridges of soil; when it begins to sprout, beans and squash are added to the mix. Maize and beans are natural field companions because maize stalks provide something for the vines of bean plants to wind around during their growth and, in turn, the beans replenish nitrogen extracted by the maize back into the soil. Squashes add to this botanical collaboration by extending their low, broad leaves to provide shade for young maize sprouts and inhibit the growth of weeds, whereas farmers encourage other species of field greens, usually in the chenopod family and lumped in classification as *quelites*, on field edges and fields in fallow. These greens and other domesticated crops—such as chili peppers, tomatoes, amaranth, chia, and various fruits and tubers—round out a vitamin-rich, plant-based diet.[23] Some variability between the highlands and lowlands include the heavy use of arid-adapted (xerophytic) plants such as agave and prickly-pear cactus in the highlands, and more humid-adapted fruits and vegetables, such as papaya and avocado, in the lowlands. The division of labor in Mesoamerican subsistence shifted over time and varied through space, but it is clear that among the Aztec, Maya, and other Mesoamerican groups both women and men participated in key parts of the agricultural cycle.[24] Agricultural activities also provided the basis for supra-household cooperation, and in many systems of Mesoamerican land tenure, fields were held in trust collectively with use rights allocated to individual families.

While early farmers of Eurasia's Fertile Crescent relied on domesticated sheep, goats, and cattle alongside growing grains like wheat and barley, Mesoamerica differed significantly in not possessing any local large animals conducive to domestication. In the realm of subsistence, this absence impacted the Mesoamerican diet by making it more plant focused; sustaining the importance of hunting animals such as deer, rabbits and hares, quail, ducks, and peccary (in the lowlands), as well as fishing on coasts or lakes; the domestication or household raising for food of smaller animals such as turkeys, rabbits, and plump, hairless dogs; and the acquisition of a broader spectrum of protein, including harvesting insects and nutritious lake products.[25] In the realms of agriculture and transportation, this absence also meant that there were no available plow- or pack-animals and that all field tilling and overland movement was on foot. Even though Mesoamericans knew of the wheel and used it for children's pull-toys with two axles, they lacked the incentive of animal traction and did not apply the wheel to transportation. Overland transport included ingenious systems of human porters (*tlamemes*, in Nahuatl) who moved goods far and wide using tumplines, connecting Mesoamerica through the exchange of objects and ideas in the process.

Early Towns and Spheres of Interaction

The Aztecs mythologized the hot and humid tropical lowlands to the east and southeast of them as a land of continual regeneration mimicking the area's natural fertility—where just about anything will grow easily and abundantly (Figure 2.3).[26] Lowland species include the rubber tree (*Castilla elastica*) used for making the balls used in Mesoamerican ballgames, one of the world's earliest varieties of team ball sports, and for utilitarian applications such as connecting stone knives to wooden handles and making durable soles of sandals. Mesoamericans devised a range of ball sports including a type of field hockey, where the ball was hit with sticks, and a type of handball, where it was slapped with padded hands. But the most widely played game, and the one that was most commemorated through depictions in art and in the constructed courts featuring parallel structures bounding a playing alley, was the hip-ballgame, which the Aztecs called *ullamalitzli*. Ballgames may have been played as early as the Archaic period, though definitive archaeological evidence, such as ballcourts and clay figurines depicting ballplayers, currently dates to the initial Formative period. The inhabitants of Paso de la Amada, living on the Pacific coast of the Mexican state of Chiapas, built the earliest known formal, parallel-mounded court during the mid-second millennium BCE. They had also developed social inequality within their community at

Figure 2.3. Map of Mesoamerica with sites mentioned in the text dating to different chronological periods.

this time, evident in the disparity in house sizes and the fact that some of these were renovated and expanded over generations, exceeding the lifespan of any single individual.[27] In Aztec times, this coastal region, called the Soconusco, was the most far-flung province of the empire and was prized for another local tree species, *Theobroma cacao*, which produces the precious beans of our Nahuatl-derived word chocolate.

Cacao beans and rubber balls spread throughout Mesoamerica, including to the similarly hot and humid Gulf of Mexico region of the neighboring Mexican states of Tabasco and Veracruz. For rubber to be of much use as an industrial product, raw latex from the rubber tree (*olli* or *ulli*, in Nahuatl) was cleverly mixed with the sap of a species of morning glory to produce a chemical reaction analogous to vulcanization, only discovered in the West millennia later during the nineteenth century, and create a bouncy and elastic product.[28] The Aztecs called people from this place of rubber *olmecatl*, from which archaeologists derived the ethnonym (ethnic group name) Olmec for the first large-scale society of Mesoamerica. The Formative period Olmec (ca. 1200–600 BCE) flourished in the southern Gulf region beginning three millennia before the Aztecs and the historical people they called *olmecatl*. These later people are attributed as a founding group for Cholula.

Although the Gulf lowlands are abundant in water and vegetation, both of these can pose problems for sedentary life due to torrential floods during the rainy season and acidic soils generated through dense plant decomposition. The occupants of the first large urban center in Mesoamerica, San Lorenzo (ca. 1200–900 BCE), invested significant labor in creating artificially raised living surfaces to keep floodwaters at bay.[29] In a region where stone was in short supply, the Gulf Olmecs constructed ceremonial platforms and at least one palatial residence for their rulers using clay bases and perishable super-structures, elaborated with large columns and drains cut from basalt that were imported to San Lorenzo from a distance of 50 miles (80 km) or more, likely involving some river transport using rafts.[30] Yet the Olmecs are more well-known for their virtuosic transformation of stone in sculpting colossal heads that depict their rulers in an individualized and highly naturalistic manner (Figure 2.4). There are currently 17 known colossal heads from San Lorenzo and other Olmec sites, with many weighing 20 tons and the heaviest approaching 50 tons. No two are identical, lending support to the idea that they represent individuals, but their heads are adorned with similar forms of jaguar imagery and other symbols of power. The Olmec also sculpted monumental thrones that at their bases depict full-bodied rulers seated in the niche of the cave-mouth of a zoomorphic Earth and were sometimes sculpted to hold a rope tied to bound captives.

Since the term "Olmec" comes from a much later period and was applied as an archaeological designation, material culture and stylistic attributes in Mesoamerica dating from the late second and early first millennium BCE are better seen as a multiethnic sphere of interaction. The Olmec interaction sphere was not a unified culture or hegemonic relations initiated by people of the Gulf region; rather it involved diverse networks of exchange in goods, styles, and religious ideas that spread across Mesoamerica and linked lowland and highland regions.[31] The urban centers of the Gulf, with San Lorenzo having been succeeded by La Venta (ca. 900–600 BCE), were the largest and most precocious in terms of their art and architecture. Within the Soconusco and similar lowland environments of southern Mesoamerica, Gulf Olmec influence appears to have been more direct than in the southern and central highlands, where trade and cultural interaction fostered shared premises that were used variably in different social contexts. An example of such variability comes from the central Mexican site of Chalcatzingo, a contemporary of La Venta, where sculptors carved stone with Olmec-style motifs, including

Figure 2.4. Colossal head from Olmec site of San Lorenzo, located in the Museo de Antropología de Xalapa.

Photo by the author. Reproduction authorized by the Instituto Nacional de Antropología e Historia, Mexico.

making thrones, but these did not depict rulers, nor did their relief carvings, which instead convey mythic narratives associated with rain, maize agriculture, and diffuse supernatural powers.[32] At this early date, we already see a pronounced difference between the Mesoamerican highlands and lowlands in which rulership tended to be depicted more symbolically in the highlands and in a more individualized manner in the lowlands, an enduring pattern with exceptions that we will return to.

The broad exchange networks that linked Mesoamerica during the Formative period were focused on precious goods and symbols. Foremost among an array of prestige goods was jade, the dense and lustrous greenstone prized throughout pre-Hispanic Mesoamerica and originating only in the Motagua River Valley of Guatemala—though less dense or less lustrous greenstones were available elsewhere. Jade became associated in Mesoamerica with fertility, preciousness, and high status, and was more valued than gold or silver by the Aztecs. The Olmec prestige-goods economy greatly elaborated the crafting and distribution of jade artifacts. Other preciosities included iron-ore, which was polished but not smelted, and shell—in the case of people located at distances from coasts. These goods do not decompose easily, meaning they have high archaeological visibility. What is missing in the archaeological record are precious materials that decompose easily, such as the colorful feathers of tropical birds and the cotton textiles we know were important lowland products during later periods.

In addition to these items with patchy natural distributions, Formative exchange included pottery decorated within a canon of Olmec imagery and symbols that conveyed ideas about the cosmic order, cycles of time and agriculture, and rulership. It also included more mundane, utilitarian goods, such as obsidian mined from volcanic deposits in the highlands and bitumen derived from tar deposits along the Gulf Coast. Bitumen was important as an adhesive and for waterproofing baskets and the canoes that the Olmec used in moving goods. Based on preserved examples from the Gulf region, Olmec canoes may have measured 16–23 feet (5–7 meters) long and served to navigate this wetland and riverine environment.[33] The more widely distributed utilitarian good was obsidian, a volcanic glass that provides the sharpest edge available in nature and, in the absence of metals, formed the key cutting tools for most of pre-Hispanic Mesoamerica. Exchange of obsidian and other utilitarian goods expanded rapidly following the decline of the Olmec sphere and coinciding with the creation of cities in core Mesoamerican areas such as central Mexico, Oaxaca, and the Maya lowlands—suggesting that this change in economic relations and widespread urbanization were causally linked.[34]

Cities, States, and the Development of Classic Period Mesoamerica

Mesoamericans began urbanizing at an accelerated pace during the last half of the first millennium BCE, resulting in the creation of cities with population estimates numbering in the tens of thousands. Some of these cities became the capitals of state polities, and the subsequent Classic period, comprising much of the first millennium CE, was largely defined by the florescence of urban centers such as Teotihuacan and Cholula in central Mexico, Monte Albán in Oaxaca, and a constellation of city-states in the Maya lowlands. Periodization of the later Formative, Classic, and Late Classic or Epiclassic varies by region, and I purposely blur these boundaries because they are of little value for understanding major societal transformations. We will consider Teotihuacan separately in the section to follow due to the outsized role the city had for the Aztecs, who venerated its ruined monuments, identified it as a center of creation, and modeled much of their sacred urban planning on it.

Prior to Teotihuacan but following the Olmec horizon center of Chalcatzingo were a number of central Mexican settlements that could be classified as ceremonial centers, towns, or cities. The largest of these was Cuicuilco, in the southern Basin of Mexico and within Mexico City's contemporary metropolitan zone. Our knowledge of this important early city is impoverished because it was covered first by a lava field, with hard volcanic rock encasing many of its buildings, and later by the sprawl of the modern city, including the construction of facilities for the 1968 Mexico City Olympics. Survey-based estimates suggest that during its height in the last centuries BCE and first centuries CE, Cuicuilco was home to some 20,000 residents.[35] The city was situated in an ecologically rich area that was well watered by seasonal rains and perennial springs, and had close access to the freshwater lakes of the southern basin. In the Aztec period, this productive area was home to the agriculturally rich city-states of the Chalca and Xochimilca, to the south of Tenochtitlan. Cuicuilco's inhabitants dug canals and reservoirs to manage water and built large, circular platforms to serve as temples. As was the case elsewhere in central Mexico during the Formative period, religious rituals at Cuicuilco prioritized the dualism of water and fire.[36] Fire was personified at Cuicuilco by effigy vessels depicting the Old God, whom the Aztecs knew later as Huehueteotl (Figure 2.5). Water was personified by the Storm God,

Figure 2.5. Effigies depicting Old God of Fire, known as Huehueteotl-Xiuhtecutli to the Aztecs, spanning 1,500 years from (left) Cuicuilco, (center) Teotihuacan, and (right) Tenochtitlan.
Illustrations by Jennifer Salazar.

whom the Aztecs knew as Tlaloc; they would encode this fire-water dualism into the Great Temple at Tenochtitlan and use it as a metaphor for war.

The southern Puebla-Tlaxcala Valley was a second resource-rich area to develop early urban centers, which preceded Aztec period city-states in the region such as Cholula, Huexotzingo, and Tlaxcala. The region possessed smaller lakes and wetlands than the Basin of Mexico. They have mostly dried up today, but two rivers (the Atoyac and Zahuapan) continue to feed productive agriculture. During the Formative period, rituals relating to water—likely linked to agricultural fertility—were performed using megalithic stone basins in the center of the ceremonial precincts of a few towns, usually associated with the primary temple.[37] Well-preserved examples can be found at Xochitecatl, where two large basins were incorporated sequentially into the central axis of its main temple-pyramid. This pyramidal platform is rectangular and was built to monumental proportions of approximately 540 x 400 feet at the base and 120 feet tall (165 m x 120 m x 37 m) (Figure 2.6). The occupants of Xochitecatl also constructed a circular structure, like Cuicuilco's in form but with a spiral ramp ascending to its upper tier. Xochitecatl's ceremonial precinct was built on a promontory that affords spectacular views of the surrounding landscape. Buildings were aligned to incorporate surrounding volcanoes into sightlines, and it is possible that the spiral structure was an effigy of Popocatepetl, the "Smoking Mountain" that looms behind it when viewed from Xochitecatl's plaza, separates the

Figure 2.6. Southern Puebla-Tlaxcala Valley with Formative period hilltop center of Xochitecatl at center and protective roof covering Epiclassic murals of Cacaxtla to left.

Photo by Mari Carmen Serra Puche; used with permission. Reproduction authorized by the Instituto Nacional de Antropología e Historia, Mexico.

Puebla-Tlaxcala Valley from the Basin of Mexico, and remains an animate being to people living in its shadow today, since it is still very much active.[38]

Eruptions of Popocatepetl and another volcano active at the time, called Xitle, had profound consequences for urban societies in central Mexico. On Popocatepetl's northeastern slope, archaeologists unearthed the key site of Tetimpa, a large village that was covered by over three feet (1 m) of ash from a mid-first century CE eruption of the volcano, providing excellent preservation for understanding life at this time and the devastation caused by this event.[39] Tetimpa shows that people in the village lived in clusters of three to four elevated platforms with façades that featured a mix of angled and vertical walls, called *talud-tablero*, organized around a patio with a central altar. This style of façade and the patio arrangement became commonplace later at Teotihuacan. Popocatepetl's catastrophic first-century eruption is classified by volcanologists as a VEI6 event, which for comparison was also true of the late nineteenth-century eruption of the Indonesian volcano Krakatoa—an event that produced the loudest sound in recorded history, being registered 3,000 miles away in central Australia. Popocatepetl's eruption drove populations from the southern Basin of Mexico and southern Puebla-Tlaxcala to resettle in Teotihuacan and Cholula. Occupants of the southern basin were also affected by the smaller scale-eruption of Xitle, which provided the lava flow that covered Cuicuilco. This event occurred in the third century, but deposits at the site indicate its inhabitants lived through earlier eruptions of Xitle and Popocatepetl, and the layers covering the site make it difficult to ascertain how much of the city's population remained when it was finally and fatefully covered.[40]

Urbanization was simultaneously underway elsewhere in Mesoamerica, including to the south in the Valley of Oaxaca and the Maya lowlands. These social transformations were linked through demographic movements and exchanges between peoples of various regions, which fostered the shared attributes that characterized religion and urban planning in Mesoamerica, but each with its own particular flavor. The Zapotecs founded the hilltop city of Monte Albán in the center of the Valley of Oaxaca in the mid-first millennium BCE and a few centuries later had succeeded in incorporating smaller polities into what could be characterized as Mesoamerica's first state, defined by sustained bureaucratic institutions of governance.[41] During the first millennium CE the Zapotecs traded with and migrated to central Mexico and also received emissaries from Teotihuacan. After the fall of Monte Albán, Oaxaca was divided into a number of small Zapotec and Mixtec kingdoms. The Mixtecs in particular were famed for exquisite gold and turquoise working, and later became a prime target for Aztec imperial expansion.

The Maya of the Late Preclassic and Classic periods underwent two major pulses of urbanization. The first, generally contemporaneous with Cuicuilco and Monte Albán in the highlands, saw the rise of the massive city of El Mirador, in northern Guatemala. The colossal platform and acropolis-like arrangement of temples known as the Danta complex at El Mirador was the largest structure erected by the pre-Hispanic Maya and rivals Cholula's Great Pyramid in construction volume. Art and architecture at El Mirador and other urban centers of this period emphasized deities and mythological themes, but transitioned to highlight the role of sacred kinship headed by "holy-blood lords" (*k'ul ajaw*) who were increasingly rendered as individualized authority in mural paintings and sculpture, being named in hieroglyphic texts.[42] The Classic period writing system of the Maya lowlands was further elaborated through the courtly activities that took place in mid- to late first millennium CE city-states. It was the most elaborate writing system in the pre-Hispanic world and, used in conjunction with the most figurative art of the Americas, brings Maya society during this period into a historical light not possible for other Mesoamerican groups with writing systems whose signs were more pictographic and used more sparsely. Yet the Maya, Zapotecs, Teotihuacanos, and other Mesoamericans of the Classic period shared a vigesimal (base-twenty) system of numeration with positional notation that included the concept of zero before it was used in Europe. It permitted large calculations for charting and predicting astronomical events, demarcating time, and situating human actors within sacred cycles of earthly and cosmic renewal.[43]

Classic period Maya texts, mural art, and archaeological remains show that certain youths, likely drawn primarily from the nobility, learned how to write, as well as the workings of the intricate calendrical system, as part of formal schools attached to palaces. A recently excavated example comes from the ancient city of Xultún, Guatemala, where archaeologists, epigraphers, art historians, and cultural astronomers have collaborated to demonstrate a fascinating case of early Mesoamerican pedagogy.[44] Murals in one complex at Xultún depict members of a scribal order who used variants of the title *Taaj*, depending on their rank, interacting with students and the local lord (Plate 1). On another wall are over 40 distinct sets of complex numerical and astronomical calculations, demonstrating the sophisticated mathematical knowledge of Classic period Maya society. We will return to this issue in Chapter 4 in comparing the Aztec and Spanish educational systems.

Although they were never united into a single empire—something the popular media often misrepresents—Classic period Maya city-states were connected with one another and with other culture areas of Mesoamerica through various exchanges. Sometimes they were literally connected on land by roads covered in gleaming white stucco known as a *sacbe* ("white road"). Other times they were connected by water routes along the coasts and penetrating inland through rivers. Maya artisans have left us depictions of log canoes in different media, and archaeologists have discovered a Classic period wooden canoe paddle and port sites from the Gulf of Honduras, along the Caribbean coast of the Yucatan peninsula, and westward into the Gulf of Mexico. These ports span the Late Preclassic through Postclassic periods and were the locations of salt production and other forms of marine-based commerce.[45] Centuries earlier, Maya ports on the coast articulated via river systems with the rain-forest interior that was the core of Classic period cities. Following the ninth-century CE political collapse of Classic period city-states and ensuing demographic decline of the southern Maya lowlands, the Caribbean and Gulf of Mexico coastal economy became more important and new cities developed on the northern and eastern Yucatecan coast, a shift also registered in patterns of obsidian exchange.[46] Christopher Columbus noted this canoe trade in his journal, and a few of these Maya cities were the initial points of Spanish encounter and invasion. Archaeologists working in Veracruz have also recently documented an elaborate port at La Perla del Golfo, which features modified access points cut through the coral reef, the stone foundations of probable docks, and a network of weigh-stations with circular storage facilities containing chemical residues consistent with having stored organic products.[47] The site dates to the mid- to late first millennium CE, meaning it would have mediated waterborne commerce between the Mexican highlands and Gulf and Maya lowlands during the height of Classic period urbanism. This likely included the later phases of the pre-Aztec imperial center of Teotihuacan, a city that integrated vast swaths of Mesoamerica through a multidirectional and multicultural exchange of goods and ideas.

City of the Gods

Urbanism of the Mesoamerican Classic period reached its zenith at Teotihuacan, the ancient ruined city 30 miles (48 km) northeast of Mexico City. We have inherited the names for Teotihuacan (roughly "city of the gods"), its iconic Pyramids of the Sun and Moon, and its central artery, the Street of the Dead, from the Aztecs, who a millennium after the collapse of the city venerated it as a place where the Fifth Sun of creation was set in motion (Plate 2a). The city was a contemporary of imperial Rome, and the urban footprints of the two cities are quite similar, though Rome had more inhabitants. Teotihuacan started urbanizing as a rival to Cuicuilco in the Basin of Mexico during the first century BCE. Although the northern Basin of Mexico receives almost half the annual precipitation of the lusher southern basin surrounding Cuicuilco, making it riskier for rain-fed maize agriculture, the Teotihuacan Valley offered an attractive place to settle because of a system of springs in the southwest valley that allow for permanent irrigation. Teotihuacan underwent a population boom during the first century CE, when migrants fleeing the eruptions of Popocatepetl and Xitle moved to the city, and it served as the capital of the most influential state in Mesoamerica until its unraveling during the sixth century.[48] The urban planning and architectural styles of the city present a mix of synthesis and deviation from earlier central Mexican patterns.

Teotihuacan is anomalous among pre-Hispanic Mesoamerican cities in the construction of multifamily apartment compounds for housing most of its urban inhabitants and in lacking both a ceremonial core organized around a large central plaza and a formal ballcourt, typical in most urban centers, at least during later phases of occupation. It was like only a few other Mesoamerican urban centers, including Tenochtitlan, in its citywide orthogonal (grid-like) layout and level of dense nucleation of the population. Teotihuacanos nevertheless drew from the Formative period canon in a few important ways: they organized their sacred space so that major temples faced west; they emphasized sacred dualisms such as between fire and water in a suite of deities venerated at these temples and in statuary and portable effigies; and they incorporated architectural styles involving arrangements of three structures around a patio and the *talud-tablero* style of façade seen earlier at Tetimpa and elsewhere in southern Puebla-Tlaxala.[49] In addition to the earlier deities the Storm God and Old God of Fire, Teotihuacanos also centralized the cult of the Feathered Serpent (Quetzalcoatl, to the Aztecs) in the city's third-largest pyramid complex, which they covered in sculptures of the deity and consecrated with some 200 human sacrifices, mostly males with skeletal profiles and bodily adornments consistent with the warrior class (Figure 2.7). The Teotihuacanos also erected massive feminine statues by the Moon Pyramid that may depict a goddess analogous to the one the Aztecs associated with terrestrial waters (Chalchiuhtlicue, "she of the jade skirt").

During its apogee, Teotihuacan covered approximately 15.5 square miles (25 square km) and was occupied by between 80,000–150,000 inhabitants, making it larger than any city on the Iberian peninsula at the time.[50] Nearly all of these people lived in a form of multifamily residential architecture that appears to be unique not only for Mesoamerica but also novel or exceedingly rare for a city of Teotihuacan's size anywhere in the premodern world. These apartment compounds housed dozens of individuals who shared craft trades and bonds of kinship or affinity within the walls of this shared residential space (Figure 2.8). Unlike the apartments (the *insulae*) of its larger contemporary Rome, which were multistory residences that housed approximately a quarter of the city's population, primarily lower-status renters, those of Teotihuacan were the predominant housing type of the city, they

Figure 2.7. Front façade of the Feathered Serpent Pyramid at Teotihuacan, which was defaced at its sides and back but covered over in the front, preserving the sculptures.

Photo by the author. Reproduction authorized by the Instituto Nacional de Antropología e Historia, Mexico.

were inhabited by low- and high-status residents alike, and they typically were a single story—Rome's multistory buildings being one reason more people fit in a similar area. Teotihuacan's apartment compounds were clustered into neighborhoods that were nested into larger groups designated wards or districts for their presumed administrative functions. These larger groupings could be as large as a square kilometer, the size of some smaller ancient cities, with their own temples, plazas, and administrative buildings. Archaeological remains in these spaces indicate they were used for rituals and craft production. There is also evidence to suggest spaces for playing ballgames, marketplaces, and district schools similar to those present in later Aztec cities.

A sustained flow of migrants moved to Teotihuacan over its six centuries of prominence. In some cases, they married into compounds whose majority population was local, while in others they established ethnic enclaves on the periphery of the city, exhibiting differing degrees of cultural assimilation. In one case designated the Merchant's Barrio, occupants appear to

Figure 2.8. Plan of the Tlamimilolpa apartment compound at Teotihuacan, which had over 2,000 multifamily compounds.
Illustration based on Linné (1942: Plate 1).

have lived in circular houses, rather than rectangular apartment compounds, and had sustained relations with the Gulf of Mexico and Maya region. Bone chemistry analyses of skeletal remains indicates that the merchants were men who moved goods by foot between Teotihuacan and these areas, while local women from Teotihuacan maintained matrilocal residences—a clear example of pre-Hispanic multiculturalism and ethnic mixing that is now being refined through the analysis of ancient DNA.[51] On the other side of the city, a neighborhood of people from Oaxaca settled and adopted some elements of Teotihuacan material culture while retaining their homeland's system of hieroglyphic writing, conceptualizations of particular deities, and mortuary treatment of the deceased. The initial arrivals, and perhaps later generations and groups of migrants, would have spoken Zapotec. Along with Mayan speakers present in the city, other migrants from the Gulf region and west Mexico, and a debated lingua franca that could have been a proto-Nahua or proto-Otomian language, there would have been at least five languages spoken at Teotihuacan. The city's more pictographic writing system, compared to the one used by the contemporaneous Maya, may have therefore been designed in part to serve its polyglot population. Like other Mesoamericans, the Teotihuacanos portrayed themselves in terracotta figurines. These were molded by hand earlier in the city's history, continuing Formative period techniques, but as more migrants arrived and the population boomed, Teotihuacano artisans started creating molds to mass-produce these small human effigies—imposing some uniformity on the types of identities and social roles they depicted.

Archaeologists estimate that Teotihuacan controlled a territory in the range of 15,000–30,000 square miles (25,000–50,000 square kilometers).[52] It had relations with much more distant polities that could be termed hegemonic or imperialistic, such as certain Maya city-states of central Guatemala and the rich cacao-growing region of Escuintla on Guatemala's Pacific coast, just south of the Soconusco. The city exerted its influence over certain distant areas, including exchange relations and local adoptions of Teotihuacan styles, but does not appear to have ever politically administered them. Like other pre-Hispanic Mesoamerican states, the capital city was densely urbanized but its domain was territorially restricted, though Teotihuacan was both denser and territorially more influential than any of its contemporaries of the Classic period. These attributes of Mesoamerican urbanism and political structure were due largely to the limitations on transportation in the absence of pack animals and complex seafaring vessels.

Mesoamericans of the Classic period warfare also waged war without metal weapons. Teotihuacanos exploited the abundant obsidian mines around their city for making utilitarian tools, weapons, and ceremonial objects, including effigies of humans, serpents, and other entities. Obsidian therefore bridged the physical/technological and the symbolic/ideational worlds.[53] Teotihuacanos created obsidian discs to inset into the eyes, chest, and bodily adornments of sculptures and relief carvings, including the eyes of the Feathered Serpent heads gazing out from the pyramid to that deity (see Figure 2.7). The most valued source of obsidian, both for its homogenous texture (suitable for removing ready-made razor blades) and its green-golden hue (colors associated with vegetation and the sun), was the Sierra de las Navajas mine, northeast of Teotihuacan and near the modern city of Pachuca. The mine was used for millennia during the pre-Hispanic period and continued into colonial New Spain. During the Classic period, miners and crafts producers associated with Teotihuacan lived seasonally at the source. They fabricated tools and ceremonial items for the city and for export through its exchange networks, production activities that were also conducted in the city itself.[54]

Teotihuacan's soldiers were armed with obsidian-tipped darts, short spears thrown with an *atlatl* or spear-thrower, obsidian knives, and wooden clubs. Within the city, some obsidian workshops were located at apartment compounds where primarily utilitarian tools were fabricated, whereas at least one workshop was located next to the Moon Pyramid and specialized in the production of weapons (dart points and knives) as well as ceremonial items of the type that were deposited as consecratory offerings and exported as far away as certain Maya cities. Domestic workshops appear to have been organized as independent commerce undertaken by extended families, but the workshop at the Moon Pyramid precinct would have been overseen by state functionaries, and the finished weapons may have been stored in state armories analogous to the *tlacochcalco* ("house of darts") used later at Tenochtitlan.[55] There were no great technological breakthroughs in the destructive capacities of Classic period Mesoamerica to match the vicious arms race that characterized early Eurasian states. In the case of Teotihuacan, its armies seem to have been successful because of their strength in numbers, their better organization, and perhaps the incentive of social mobility to capture more of the enemy. These advantages were also enjoyed by the Mexica centuries later.[56] Like many people around the world, Teotihuacanos drew on the symbolism of apex predators in their environment as metaphors for military might. This included the raising of animals such as pumas and jaguars, wolves and coyotes, and eagles and other raptors to be sacrificed in dedicatory offerings that consecrated the major pyramid complexes of the city, along with humans whose skeletal remains generally fit the demographic profile of a warrior (males between 15–40 years of age at death, but with exceptions) and were adorned with weapons and war trophies.[57] It also included depictions in the art of the city of warrior animals and warriors outfitted in bird headdresses, animal skins, or other animal regalia. These are consistent with the operation of military orders or sodalities analogous to the eagle and jaguar warriors of the Mexica and other Aztec city-states.

We will return to the topic of human sacrifice in Chapter 4, but it is worth mentioning here that the practice at Teotihuacan was intimately linked to warfare. Nevertheless, not all human sacrifice at Teotihuacan or elsewhere in Classic period Mesoamerica was related to captive taking in battles, as is clear by the lower instances of sacrifices involving women and children. Sacrifice was expanded among Mesoamerica's hegemonic powers as martial state theater, but people also believed in its efficacy in the context of religious offering, with examples extending as far back to the Archaic period, well before any cities or states.

One of the great enigmas of pre-Hispanic Mesoamerica is the political organization of Teotihuacan and the state it controlled. The topic remains debated among specialists, with some consensus that rulership was framed with a more collective face at Teotihuacan. Yet strong individual rulers may have existed at different points in the city's history, and between the third to sixth centuries CE certain relations between Teotihuacan and other parts of Mesoamerica appear imperialistic or at least hegemonic.[58] The proposition of more pluralistic rule, or individual rulers strongly bound to a council, is supported by the fact that there are no compelling depictions of individual rulers in the art of Teotihuacan to match those made by the Gulf Olmec during the Formative period, the Maya or Zapotec during the Classic period, and the Mexica during the Postclassic period, nor have any obvious royal tombs been discovered at Teotihuacan. The imperialism proposition does not mean that Teotihuacan had a far-flung empire to match the Aztec Triple Alliance and, indeed, one of the significant contrasts between these two most influential Mesoamerican states is that Teotihuacan appears to have been held in high esteem and emulated through large portions of Mesoamerica, which would not be the case later for the Mexica.[59] Although Teotihuacan clearly exerted military power abroad, its commercial activities and probable attraction as a site of religious pilgrimage may have served as a less imperialistic base than the Triple Alliance for connecting large parts of Mesoamerica. Nevertheless, events such as the iconoclastic destruction and concealment of the sculptural facades of the Feathered Serpent Pyramid around 300 CE suggest certain social tensions at Teotihuacan.[60] The city and state survived, and indeed thrived, following this event, but it speaks to strong political cleavages.

The demise of Teotihuacan began slowly and involved some mix of a contraction in the control of routes connecting the city with other parts of Mesoamerica by upstart city-states, an increase in the power of intermediate elites who forged patron-client relations in the outer districts of the city that undermined the collective ideology of the state, and a possible period of sustained drought. It then finished in dramatic fashion with the fateful burning of the city center. The pattern of burning is not at all random and speaks directly to the processes behind Teotihuacan's collapse. Evidence of burning visible in surface remains were systematically recorded in nearly all of the temple and palace compounds in the city center, in approximately half of the neighborhood administrative complexes featuring local temples and elite residences, and in as little as 5 percent of other contexts. There was a "Carthaginian quality" to the purposeful termination of the city,[61] though it is important to note that there is currently no evidence that the city's demise was related to conquest by an external adversary, as was the case with Carthage. The pattern of burning observed from surface remains also holds in contexts I have excavated with colleagues, including carbonized roof beams collapsed on floors next to the Moon Pyramid and at temples in the Plaza of the Columns administrative complex, but nothing to match in the Tlajinga district on the southern periphery of the city.[62] Had Teotihuacan been invaded from the outside, we would expect to see evidence of burning on the periphery and at this main entry point along the southern Street of the Dead. Teotihuacan was sacked and burned by people who knew it intimately—some segment of the city's population itself—and who decisively rejected the politico-religious order of the state. This political collapse was not matched by the massive demographic decline seen in the centuries following the collapse of cities in the southern Maya lowlands.[63] Tens of thousands of people continued to occupy the Teotihuacan Valley during the subsequent Toltec and Aztec periods, founding new settlements away from the ruins that became colonial period towns still occupied today. Aztec rulers made regular pilgrimages to Teotihuacan to venerate it as a place of the origin of time, and even excavated in its ruins for art and artifacts that they then offered in consecration of their own sacred buildings. Yet the former urban center was left as a ruin and, like Cholula's Great Pyramid, was reclaimed by the earth.

Reconfiguration and the Rise of the Toltecs

In the power vacuum that followed the collapse of Teotihuacan, central Mexico underwent renewed urbanization in valley systems adjacent to the Basin of Mexico at upstart centers such as Cacaxtla, Xochicalco, Tula, and Cantona.[64] This period (ca. 600–900 CE) is called Epiclassic in central Mexico, and it is contemporaneous with the height of lowland Maya civilization designated in that area as Late Classic. Urban populations in central Mexico were in the lower tens of thousands at this time, whereas a few lowland Maya centers expanded to 60,000 or more.[65] Art and architecture at Cacaxtla and Xochicalco illustrate the strong cultural hybridity of the time, when exchange routes and power relations were being contested and reconfigured by these competing city-states. The civic-ceremonial core erected at Cacaxtla departs from earlier central Mexican site planning in its acropolis-like fortifications, with a configuration more akin to architectural styles from southeastern Mesoamerica, as in its expert use of lime stucco. Cacaxtla's justifiably famous murals, painted during the mid-seventh to early ninth century, also exhibit strong elements of the southeastern aesthetic traditions of the Maya and Gulf Coast peoples.[66] The artists who painted the murals depicted individuals using more naturalistic southeastern figurative styles but associated with central Mexican hieroglyphs, the trappings of jaguar and eagle military orders, and the central Mexican Storm God and Feathered Serpent deities (Plate 2b). Evidence of trade connections to southeastern Mesoamerica are seen in a mural that either depicts an elite merchant or the patron god of merchants (Yacatecuhtli to the Aztecs or God L of the Maya) and are attested to by artifacts from the Gulf region found at Cacaxtla's civic-ceremonial center and elite residences. Sixteenth-century accounts, including one by the mestizo chronicler Diego Muñoz Camargo, link the builders of Cacaxtla to the Olmeca-Xicalanca, as they do for Cholula. Competition between local peoples and new arrivals, and perhaps renewed volcanic activity on the part of Popocatepetl, appears to have resulted in the growth of Cacaxtla at the expense of Cholula, whose Great Pyramid fell into disuse before the city rebounded in the tenth century.[67]

The residents of the hilltop city of Xochicalco projected their political and military ideologies through hybrid art that prioritized sculpture, both in relief and in the round, rather than through murals. Most exuberantly decorated is the Feathered Serpent temple, which is smaller than Teotihuacan's but ornate and rich in imagery that pivots between Teotihuacan and later Toltec and Aztec art. Militarism and conquest are central themes, including the depiction of armed warriors, tribute received from other polities named in hieroglyphs, eagle and coyote imagery that may represent prevailing military orders, and the association of the Feathered Serpent with themes of fertility and rulership.[68] All of these elements of Xochicalco's Feathered Serpent temple are firmly within a central Mexican tradition, as is the continuity from Teotihuacan in images identifying a "house of darts," or *tlacochcalco* armory, which was likely located off Xochicalco's central plaza.[69] Hybrid elements connecting to the lowlands are apparent in certain styles, such as the body posture of male figures carved next to the Feathered Serpent, and in other architectural elements at the site, including the use of carved stelae depicting personages and hieroglyphs, and the presence of ring and macaw-head "goals" at ballcourts. Stelae were present earlier in central Mexico at Cuicuilco and Teotihuacan, but they were carved much more stylistically or were left plain, with some examples retaining evidence of having been painted. Following their decline during the Classic period, the building of ballcourts picked up in central Mexico during the Epiclassic to match contemporaneous urban centers in Oaxaca, the Gulf Coast, and the Maya region.

During the Classic period, porters from the Tula region in the northern Basin of Mexico moved quicklime (calcium oxide) to Teotihuacan in great quantities.[70] These exchange relations kept inhabitants of the region in close ties with the city and may have included a resident Teotihuacano population who lived at the site of Chingú. Following the collapse of Teotihuacan, the layout of Tula reclaimed earlier principles of central Mexican urban planning, including a main plaza with temples to the east and north and a ballcourt to the west—a layout that would be continued by Aztec urban planners. Tula grew to become the largest and most consequential Early Postclassic city in central Mexico, and is estimated to have housed 60,000 people in the city and another 30,000 to 50,000 in its hinterland during its apogee (ca. 900–1150 CE).[71] Its builders, known as Toltecs, realized the basic contours of this urban plan twice, in parts of the site now designated as Tula Chico and Tula Grande. The Aztecs, who viewed themselves as direct heirs of the Toltecs, incorporated many elements of Tula's urban layout and public art into their own urban centers. They also called other large-scale societies that preceded them *toltecatl*, including Teotihuacan and Cholula, but archaeologists have reserved the designation Toltec for Early Postclassic societies and particularly the inhabitants of Tula. The root term *Tollan*, meaning "place of abundant reeds," was the designation for archetypal earlier urban societies and has the dual meaning of a location near water and urban population density—with people clustered as densely as a stand of reeds.[72]

The reasons the Toltecs moved Tula's urban epicenter between the Epiclassic and Early Postclassic periods remain mysterious, because the organization of buildings and their associated decorative motifs in the two plaza groups show continuity. One possibility takes us into the realm of mythistory and sixteenth-century accounts of a great king of Tollan named Ce Acatl Topiltzin Quetzalcoatl ("One Reed [a calendrical designation] Prince Feathered Serpent").[73] This personage—maybe an actual ruler who was memorialized as an *hombre-dios* or "man-god" in oral narratives[74]—is said to have left Tollan in disgrace for lands to the east, to one day return and reclaim his kingdom. He is also said to have promoted the sacrifice of birds and butterflies, symbols of the souls of warriors killed in battle, rather than humans. Could the shift from Tula Chico to Tula Grande represent some dispute among ruling or priestly factions connected to this narrative? Alternatively, may it relate to earlier Teotihuacan and the desecration and covering over of the temple dedicated to the Feathered Serpent? These questions may never be resolved, but they serve as reminders that Mesoamerican polities were not static and monolithic entities, and that, even in the absence of detailed texts from the period, archaeological indicators and later narratives allow us to sense societal tensions and transformations. We will also return to this mythistorical narrative later in the context of the nature of divinity in Aztec religion and the much debated issue of whether or not Moctezuma perceived Cortés to be a returning Quetzalcoatl.

Toltec art and architecture at Tula emphasized sculpture in the round and in relief, more akin to Xochicalco than to Cacaxtla. Some themes, such as the Feathered Serpent and images of jaguars devouring hearts, were present earlier in the sculpture and mural art of Teotihuacan. Others were innovations of the Early Postclassic period that either spread with Toltec political expansion or through more mutual exchanges of goods and ideas. Two types of statues are saddled with misnomers given by early explorers: the chacmool depicts a reclined individual, likely representing a fallen warrior, with a receptacle for offerings on his chest, and was named using an invented Mayan term; and the atlantean statues depict armed, living warriors that may have served as columns to support a roof, like the Atlas of Greek myth (Figure 2.9). A third art style in the civic-ceremonial center of Tula features benches with processions of deities and warriors on their lower talus panel. The Aztecs continued to use all three styles, sometimes in purposeful archaism in a neo-Toltec style analogous to neoclassical styles in Europe and the United States.[75] For the Mexica, the chacmool played a central role as the primary offering to the half of the Great Temple dedicated to Tlaloc, where the statue received sacrificial offerings like blood-soaked paper and human hearts. Neo-Toltec reliefs decorated benches on the House of the Eagle Warriors attached to the temple.

Figure 2.9. Atlantean statues depicting warriors from Toltec city of Tula.
Photo by the author. Reproduction authorized by the Instituto Nacional de Antropología e Historia, Mexico.

Although Tula was the largest city in central Mexico in its day and the Mexica held it in great esteem, it is unlikely that the city controlled a polity as large as Teotihuacan's. It does not seem to have held dominion over the southern Basin of Mexico, which may have been more influenced by Cholula.[76] Based on material remains, it less convincingly meets the standard of an empire than does Teotihuacan or the Aztec Triple Alliance.[77] Tula was nonetheless one of the key pre-Aztec centers, and stylistic similarities with the great Maya city of Chichen Itza have been interpreted along a spectrum of hypothesized interaction ranging from Toltec invasion to peer polities emulating one another. There is no question that the Feathered Serpent cult moved from central Mexico to the Maya region, as did certain styles such as the chacmool, but we have already seen that highland-lowland exchanges were reciprocal from Olmec times, through Teotihuacan, and apparent in the hybrid and syncretic styles of Cacaxtla, Cholula, and Xochicalco. These linkages would continue through the Aztec Empire and other parts of the Postclassic Mesoamerican world, and would prove crucial during the conquest period.

Mesoamerica on the Eve of the Aztecs

Over the course of millennia of cultural development and exchanges, Mesoamerica became an area with a deeply shared nucleus in domains of religion, diet, technology, iconography, time reckoning, and world outlook. It comprised diverse cultures that varied geographically and temporally but were in continued contact in exchanging goods and ideas, hybridizing styles, and forming multiethnic families and neighborhoods. Taking stock of some of the major societal transformations helps to situate Aztec Mexico on the eve of encounter and draw comparisons with similar transformations in Iberia, reviewed in the next chapter. The Archaic to Formative periods in Mesoamerica witnessed an independent development and spread of farming and settled village life. Local large animals—such as deer, peccary, or tapir—were not amenable to domestication, as were smaller species like turkey and dogs, or the penning of rabbits. As a result, the Mesoamerican diet emphasized plants, but was supplemented with these smaller animals, hunted game, fish, and insects. Even the most basic subsistence of maize, beans, and squash is balanced and nutrient rich—especially when the maize is nixtamalized (soaked in water with lime or ash). The lack of large livestock meant that there were no beasts of burden to move goods, people, or plows. Mesoamerican peoples, like others in the Americas, also did not suffer the same sort of epidemic diseases transferred from domestic animals to people in Europe, Asia, and Africa, and as a result did not develop natural defenses to such diseases.

The lack of draft animals also had ramifications in the domains of technological spread and warfare. Since most Mesoamerican transportation was on foot except for canoe transport on waterways, goods moved more slowly and in lower volume than was possible on horseback in Eurasia or by llama caravan in the Andes. Metallurgy arrived relatively late to Mesoamerica and was used more ornamentally than for utilitarian tools. Arsenic bronze developed in West Mexico during the Epiclassic period (ca. 600–800 CE) but did not spread eastward for centuries, until the Aztec period, and was then also joined by bronze alloying copper with tin. The cultural value system of Mesoamerica favored the aesthetics of metals, such as the color of ornaments and the sounds of metal bells.[78] Most Mesoamerican weaponry was therefore made of stone and wood, and battles were not fought using cavalry, chariots, or ships. As a result, in an absence of an arms race and a reduced scale of battlefield casualties compared to ancient Eurasian states, Mesoamerican war was heavily ritualized and was not aimed at large-scale territorial control and cultural or religious conversion. Mesoamericans waged war and undertook raids primarily with the goals of taking captives and trophies in battle and these, in turn, served as material symbols of hierarchical relationships of tax and tribute.[79]

Mesoamericans adapted to and elaborated on their ecological base in innovative ways. In the absence of animals to plow fields for extensive agriculture, Mesoamericans developed ingenious systems to intensify agriculture, including large-scale water management in wetland environments and the construction of stone terraces in mountainous environments. They discovered symbiotic relationships between plants for sustainable *milpa* fields, and in urban centers they collected latrine waste for fertilizer. Labor and long-distance trade was largely on foot, so Mesoamericans devised highly organized systems of reciprocal work obligations (called *tequitl* in Nahuatl), cooperative groups of craft producers and traders somewhat analogous to guilds, and networks of markets to connect vendors and consumers.[80] Some cities, such as Teotihuacan, grew larger than any of their contemporaries on the Iberian peninsula; others, like Cholula, leveraged their role as market and pilgrimage centers to endure as centers of long-standing importance. Although Mesoamerican cities were primarily located inland, and major maritime technologies did not flourish, water-borne commerce moved briskly on the lakes of highland Mexico and along the coasts of the Caribbean, Gulf of Mexico, and Pacific, especially during the Postclassic period. These Native solutions resulted in the highly urbanized mosaic of farmers, merchants, priests, scribes, warriors, and kings, who encountered Europeans for the first time in the sixteenth century.

3

Iberia

A Deep History

Spain, which was to play so great a part in the discovery and colonization of the New World, was once discovered and colonized itself.

—Trend (1967)[1]

The shores of southern Iberia are where the Mediterranean meets the Atlantic: the exit from an inland sea that divides continents to a vast ocean that divides hemispheres. This may be easiest appreciated from the vantage of Cádiz, a spit of land jutting out into these waters that has a claim on representing the oldest continuously occupied city in western Europe. Ancient Cádiz (Phoenician *Gadir*, Roman *Gades*) is said by some Classical period authors to have been founded by the Phoenicians as early as 1104 BCE, though the earliest archaeological remains discovered thus far date to three centuries later. Greek writers situated it and a larger, indigenous Iberian kingdom named Tartessos to the extreme west of their known world, past the Pillars of Heracles. Writing in the late-seventh to mid-sixth century BCE, the lyrical poet Stesichoros recorded a mythistorical reference to this landscape involving the tenth of Heracles' 12 labors—to steal cattle from the three-headed giant Geryon.[2] It is often presumed that the legendary pillars refer to natural features of the landscape, most notably the rock of Gibraltar and its counterpart across the strait in Ceuta (likely Jebel Musa), where Europe comes closest to Africa. Yet they may also designate architectural features of the temple the Phoenicians built at Gadir to honor their patron deity Melqart, whom the Greeks equated with Heracles, or to a pair of temples situated on the Iberian and African sides of the strait.[3] The ancient peoples of the settlements underlying contemporary Cádiz, Seville, Huelva, and their broader region just west of the Strait of Gibraltar connected seafarers of the Mediterranean with those of the Atlantic. In the late fifteenth century, the region became the Spanish port to the Americas, launching the explorations and invasions led by Columbus, Magellan, Cortés, Pizarro, and others.

Western Iberia, especially the division between its north and southwest, served as the key pivot or hinge between the Mediterranean and Atlantic worlds for three millennia.[4] Peoples of the east and southeast were historically more tied to the Mediterranean, from Archaic period Greek colonists to Renaissance period Aragonese merchants. It was also the Greeks who termed peoples living south of the Ebro (*Iber*) River, which empties into the Mediterranean in the northeast of the peninsula, "Iberian." The term later became Latinized to *Hiberi*, and the Romans also used the designation *Hispani*. The centuries of cultural developments from Iberia to Hispania therefore encompass the protohistoric accounts of peninsular cultures recorded by other Mediterranean peoples up to the time of their Romanization as one of the most fully integrated provinces of that empire.[5] The peninsula's four other major rivers—the Duero, Tagus (Tajo), Guadiana, and Guadalquivir—all empty west-southwest to the Atlantic. Northwestern Iberia has always been Atlantic focused, with strong connections to continental Europe, whereas the southwestern regions of Extremadura and western Andalucía mediated between both maritime worlds.

As it was the eventual homeland to many of the conquistadors and the ports to the Americas, we will examine the deep history and pivotal role of southwest Spain most closely in this chapter, while also contextualizing its cultural developments within their broader peninsular and pan-Mediterranean settings. As was true of pre-Hispanic central Mexico, southwest Spain was a cultural crossroads, transformed by the exchanges, migrations, and conquests of various cultures, including the Phoenicians, Tartessians, Celtiberians, Carthaginians, Romans, Visigoths, and Arabs. It was a land rich in metals, which drew many Mediterranean groups westward and connected that early commercial superhighway to the eastern Atlantic in the process. Waves of conquests, cultural mixing, and imperial integration and dissolution are part of the deep legacy of what eventually became Spanish conquistador culture and much of the infrastructural underpinnings of colonialism in New Spain and elsewhere in Latin America. Although the concepts of "discovery" and a "New World" are outdated, the sentiment voiced by J. B. Trend in the epigraph to this chapter holds true today.

Iberia and Its Peoples

Like Mesoamerica, the Iberian peninsula contains a range of environments differentiated by elevation, precipitation patterns, and other climatological factors (Figure 3.1). Within Europe, Spain is relatively diverse ecologically and high in elevation—the highest country in average elevation of those not located primarily in the Alps or Pyrenees. It does not possess the altitudinal extremes of Mesoamerica, however, or have the biotic diversity associated with Mesoamerica's strong vertical dimension and tropical setting. Iberia can be roughly parsed into a cooler and wetter north and a hotter and drier south. The north features a rugged terrain of small valleys; much of the center is dominated by an expansive elevated plateau called the Meseta; and the southwest is traversed by the large valleys cut by the Tagus, Guadiana, and Guadalquivir Rivers, the lower courses of which feed fertile farmland. The lower Guadalquivir Valley is especially well watered and attractive to early farmers. Its Arabic name (Wadi-al-kabir) translates as Great River and shares its riverine prefix with the Guadiana, Guadalete, and other rivers renamed in Arabic during the centuries of Islamic rule. In Roman times, the river was called the Baetis, the source of the name for the affluent province of Baetica.

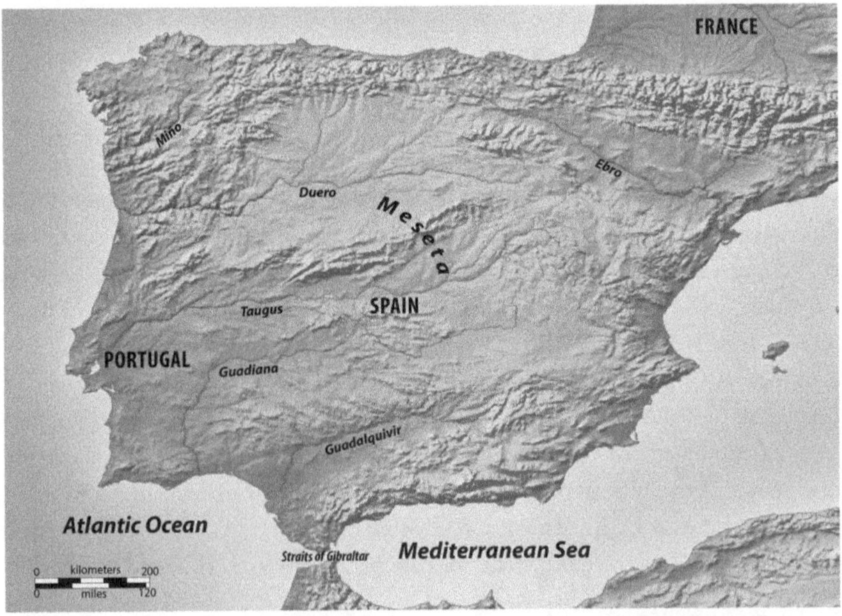

Figure 3.1. Map of Iberia depicting major rivers and natural landforms.

Large parts of the peninsula are less agriculturally productive. The northern Meseta of Old Castile in particular can be a hostile landscape—at an average of 2,000–2,600 feet (600–800 m), it is windswept with thin soils, insufficient water, and extremes of heat and cold.[6] The mountains of the east-west-running Central Sierras divide the northern Meseta of Old Castile from the New Castile's southern Meseta, to the east, and lower valleys of Extremadura, to the west (Figure 3.2). In the latter, the Guadiana River meanders westward through the "Cradle of the Conquistadors" surrounding Cortés' hometown of Medellín and Alvarado's hometown of Badajoz before turning south to empty in the Gulf of Cádiz. The region is lower and greener than the Meseta but not as lush as the lower Guadalquivir. Together, these three regions provided most of the conquistadors, chroniclers, and other sixteenth-century emigrants to the Americas.

The history of human interactions with these environments has shaped Iberia's mosaic of cultures. In addition to the Mediterranean versus Atlantic orientation of coastal peoples, significant differences for inland subsistence include the larger tracts of land in the south, contrasted with the fragmented

Figure 3.2. Landscape in Extremadura.
Photo by the author.

landscape of the north. Whereas the open plains and large valleys of the south could be connected into sizable agricultural estates of the Roman-derived *latifundios* or the *Reconquista*-era *encomiendas*, the pocket valleys of the north were more difficult to patch together into sizable estates and instead fostered cultures of smallholder farmers (*minifundios*) who could often retain greater autonomy from landed gentry or other social elites.[7] Differing cultural practices also affected these differences in landholding. In the medieval period, areas with larger estates tended toward an inheritance system based on primogeniture, in which the oldest son inherited all of the family property, while in the north partitioning could be more equitable among siblings. Many river valleys of the south were productively irrigated to compensate for low annual precipitation, especially with systems feeding Mediterranean crops brought by the Phoenicians and Romans, and Asian and North African crops introduced and productively farmed under Islamic rule.[8] Crops of Islamic Spain such as sugar, rice, and cotton eventually became central to the plantation or *encomienda* economy of lowland regions of the Americas. In contrast, Iberia's high and dry Meseta encouraged the transhumance of grazing animals, particularly sheep and goats, and formed a boundary for the cultivation of warmer adapted vegetation such as olive trees.

Iberians exploited various metal resources on the peninsula, which eventually attracted colonizing Mediterranean populations such as the Phoenicians, Greeks, Carthaginians, and Romans. The Iberian Pyrite Belt crosses the country in an arc from northwest, where gold and tin deposits predominate, through the southwest and southeast, where abundant copper deposits transition to silver deposits from west to east. The southwestern Río Tinto Valley, near Huelva, is so abundant in iron, silver, and copper that salt from ore colors the water red, giving the river its name. Metal deposits are also concentrated in the Sierra Morena region, north of Córdoba, but the northwest of the peninsula has the most expansive deposits, including what would become Rome's most productive gold mine at Las Medulas, in León. The northwest also contains plentiful tin deposits as well, which became important for alloying with copper during the Bronze Age. The Bronze Age and other major chronological designations follow the general Eurasian chronological scheme based on tool technologies. Archaeologists divide the Stone Age into the earlier Paleolithic of nomadic foragers, some of whom produced the wondrous cave art of the peninsula, and the later Neolithic of early agriculturalists—with a transitional Mesolithic between the two. The Iberian Iron Age began when the Phoenicians introduced high-temperature smelting to the southern peninsula in the early first millennium BCE, but was soon followed by an early northern or "Celtic" ironworking tradition introduced via central and Atlantic Europe. Between stone and iron tools was a period of initial experimentation with local copper, giving rise to a Copper Age (also called the Chalcolithic), before it was combined with tin to create bronze. Bronze technology was important for connecting western Iberia in pairing northwestern tin deposits with southwestern copper deposits. More broadly, it fostered connections between the Atlantic and Mediterranean, as more distant tin sources located in the British Isles and more distant copper sources located in Cyprus were also mediated through southwestern Iberia during different phases of occupation. In addition to metals, Mediterranean peoples were also drawn to Iberia for its timber, salt, and fish, as well as for its land and labor resources.

The approximate millennium between early Mediterranean colonists and the conquest of Roman Hispania is termed prehistoric or protohistoric, because textual accounts are few and mostly from the perspective of cultures to the east. During the Second Punic War (218–202 BCE), the peninsula served as a battleground between the newly colonizing Carthaginians and the eventual Roman takeover. After a couple of centuries of peninsular conquests and massive mineral extraction, Roman Hispania became one of the most assimilated provinces and the birthplace of three of Rome's greatest emperors. The early fifth century CE demise of the Western Roman Empire brought waves of Germanic conquerors to Hispania, especially the Visigoths, who were followed by Muslim armies of the early eighth century.

From Ice Age Artists to Scratch-Plow Farmers

The Iberian peninsula contains several key sites for understanding the evolution of our species, initial colonization of Europe, and early expressions of art, rendered in visually arresting cave paintings. The close proximity between Europe and Africa at the Strait of Gibraltar provided an alternative route for early human migrations to the overland one through Southwest Asia. It would have required traversing the Mediterranean-Atlantic interface, but this is a relatively narrow crossing with land in sight, and evidence is mounting of Paleolithic seafaring in southern Iberia and elsewhere in the Mediterranean.[9] Some of the most abundant and best preserved fossilized remains of human ancestors (hominins) demonstrate continuous occupation of the peninsula beginning 1.3 million years ago and including early ancestors in our genus such as *Homo antecessor, Homo heidelbergensis,* and *Homo neanderthalensis* (the Neanderthals). These earliest Europeans are better represented in the site of Atapuerca, located east of Burgos, than anywhere else on the continent. Yet the most famous Paleolithic sites date more recently to the Upper Paleolithic period, when between approximately 34,000–11,000 years ago ice-age artists painted vibrant depictions of the animals they hunted, their own handprints, and other symbolic creations on the walls of Altamira Cave and elsewhere in northern Spain.

The end of the ice age (or Pleistocene) and beginning of our present geological epoch (the Holocene) saw the warming of global climate. Ice-age agriculture would have been possible in the warmer latitudes of the Mediterranean, but climatic fluctuations appear to have prohibited the commitment to farming lifeways that the more stable Holocene climate enabled.[10] These developed first in the Fertile Crescent region of Southwest Asia, and the suite of domesticated plants, animals, and tools and practices for tending them were introduced by colonists from this area across the Mediterranean.[11] The rapid appearance of a package of foods including wheat and other cereals, lentils and other pulses, and domesticated sheep and goat around 7,700–7,600 years ago (5600 BCE) on the coasts of eastern and southern Iberia, followed by their appearance around 7,400–7,300 years ago (5300 BCE) on the Atlantic seaboard, are consistent with maritime colonists introducing farming from the east.

Unlike in Mesoamerica, early agriculture in Iberia and other parts of Eurasia included a significant component of animal husbandry, which had important ramifications for differences in social organization. Iberians have lived for millennia with livestock. Cattle appear to have arrived somewhat later than sheep and goats, with origins from North Africa, and pigs may have been independently domesticated in Europe, or crossbred between native and foreign animals. Farming then spread inland through a combination of independent adoption by native foraging populations and the mixing of these and the coastal colonists. Another difference from Mesoamerica is that, although domestication began at roughly similar times, in Iberia agriculture came as a relatively complete suite of plants and animals that had undergone the transition from wild to domesticated elsewhere. Change to agricultural lifeways was therefore faster than in Mesoamerica, where the local process of domestication took several millennia to unfold before people committed to becoming settled farmers. In Iberia, a second wave of Mediterranean crops came with later seagoing colonists, including the spread with the Phoenicians and Greeks of vine monocultivation and wine consumption in the early first millennium BCE, and olive cultivation with Roman colonization during the end of the millennium.

Like in other parts of the globe, the transition to farming had profound social consequences in Iberia. Plow agriculture using cattle for traction permitted the extensification of farmed fields that were unequally distributed and created greater wealth disparities than were possible in early farming communities in Mesoamerica.[12] There is archaeological evidence of increased social inequality in Iberia at megalithic sites clustered around the Tagus estuary of central Portugal and the Almería region of southeast Spain by the third millennia BCE, during the Copper Age.[13] In the Almería region, the site of Los Millares grew to cover 12 acres (5 ha) and may have been inhabited by 1,000 people, making it larger than anything in Mesoamerica at the time. A series of large, concentric defensive walls represent a degree of architectural elaboration as impressive as anything in the contemporary Mediterranean.[14] Interspersed among the round houses of Los Millares are some 80 elaborate masonry tombs with a subterranean burial chamber used for depositing multiple individuals. Their conical shape is the basis for their characterization as beehive tombs.

Megalithic builders of the Antequera region in eastern Andalucía, just east of the Strait of Gibraltar, erected impressive monumental complexes.[15] Three ruins together now comprise a UNESCO World Heritage Site: the Tholos of El Romeral and the Dolmens of Menga and Viera. The first, a large beehive tomb, is chronologically the latest, dating to the late third or early second millennium. Yet the older dolmens have recently been radiocarbon dated to the fourth millennium. The Dolmen of Menga is the earliest and is classified as a gallery-style dolmen by virtue of not having an interior structure differentiated from its entrance. Like its famous British counterpart at Stonehenge, the Dolmen of Menga may have an astronomical orientation toward the summer solstice sunrise. However, the largest stones in the interior of the dolmen weigh up to 180 tons, making them over four times the weight of the largest monoliths of Stonehenge. Megalithic sites also dot the northwest of the peninsula, where Atlantic seafaring initially made use of log- or hide-boats. More seaworthy plank-boats were fashioned by the second millennium BCE, and Phoenicians introduced sails by the early first millennium, intensifying connections between the Mediterranean and Atlantic worlds.[16]

Light from the East, Legends of the West

The westward exploration and colonization initiated by the Phoenicians and the Carthaginians during the early and mid-first millennium BCE represent one of the most remarkable periods of maritime navigation in human history. It was undertaken primarily by peoples with distant roots in the city-state of Tyre, situated on a small peninsula jutting out from the coast of present-day Lebanon. By crossing the entirety of the Mediterranean and striking out north and south into the eastern Atlantic, these sailors connected two networks of maritime interaction and, with other seafarers such as the Greeks and Etruscans, set the stage for later Mediterranean empires of the Romans, Byzantines, and Islamic caliphate. The millennia or so of circa 1100–250 BCE has traditionally been referred to in Iberian archaeology as the "orientalizing" period, signifying strong influences from the eastern Mediterranean, but recent investigations have illustrated the more nuanced and bidirectional exchanges that occurred between peninsular peoples and others from the east.[17]

Native peninsular peoples of the first millennium BCE are generally grouped into two broad cultural and linguistic categories: Iberian (including Tartessian) and Celtic.[18] People grouped as Iberian resided in the south and east. They had closer contacts with Mediterranean peoples than did Celtic groups living in the central interior and northwest. The Greeks named the Iberians with reference to the northeastern Ebro River, but the most elaborate Iberian art and architecture comes from southeastern Spain in the last half of the first millennium. Iberians spoke languages that were not in the Indo-European family, which they wrote in several undeciphered or only partially deciphered scripts. The languages went extinct with the spread of Latin following Roman colonization, and today only the Basque language (Euskara) remains as a non-Indo-European language within Spain. Basque speakers reside in the north, which lies well outside the Iberian cultural sphere of the first millennium BCE.

Celtic languages are in the Indo-European family and appear to have spread west from central Europe, but the timing and the amount of human migration in this process is much debated. They were also driven to extinction from the Iberian peninsula with Roman colonization, but endure on the British Isles, Ireland, and Brittany. Close connections between peoples of northwestern Iberia and these northern Atlantic cultures can be traced archaeologically over millennia and, irrespective of language, are usefully grouped as Atlantic Celtic based on broadly shared material culture.[19] Accordingly, although the northwestern Spanish region of Galicia likely was home to a mix of Iron Age peoples who spoke Celtic and pre-Celtic languages, shared cultural traits with other Atlantic peoples are apparent millennia before any supposed Celtic migrations. Some continue today, such as the bagpipe, wooden clogs, and a diet heavy in potatoes—the last, following Latin American colonization.

Tartessian designates another non-Indo-European language that can be differentiated from others in the Iberian sphere geographically and by virtue of its distinctive script. The terms "Tartessos" as an area of southwestern Iberia and "Tartessian" as an ethnonym come from sources written by authors from the Greco-Roman world, but these were the earliest occupants of the peninsula to use their own script, which they adapted from the Phoenician alphabet—as was done by the Hebrews, Greeks, Etruscans, Romans, and onward. Phoenician colonization and the Tartessian interaction sphere were critical to this early chapter in Iberian history because of their role as a hinge between the Mediterranean and Atlantic spheres and in moving the material culture and beliefs of the former into the Iberian interior. Both contributed to the region's later role as the so-called cradle of the conquistadors and port to the Americas.

Although Phoenicians and other eastern Mediterranean peoples are better documented than the Iberians and Celts in mid- to late-first-millennium texts, the ethnonyms for them can be confusing. The term "Phoenician" comes from the Greek *Phoinikes*, which is associated with the red-purple dye these people specialized in extracting from murex sea snails in their coastal homeland of what is today Lebanon. Groups of Phoenicians followed this and other trade resources westward and established a Murex dye production facility on the Iles Purpuraires, or "Purple Islands," off the coast of Morocco. Ancient Israelites may have called them *Ponim*, but also by the biblical term that probably reflects a broader self-identification: *Canaans* (from Semetic *Kn'nm*, and perhaps deriving from the Hebrew word for "merchant"), though the strongest ethnic self-identification was by city-state.[20] Phoenicians from Tyre arose as the most powerful city-state in the mid-tenth century BCE and had the most profound impact on the colonization of the western Mediterranean, including not only Gadir and the Spanish coast around Malaga (Phoenician Malaka), but also Rome's great early rival of Carthage, on the coast of Tunisia. The Latinized *Punici* gives us the term "Punic" for the same people who later founded a new Carthage (Cartogo

Novo, today's Cartagena) in southeast Spain. In my focus on the role of these people in Iberia, I will use "Phoenician" for the early founders of cities and trading entrepôts along the southern coast, and then "Carthaginian" when that particular city-state began exerting its influence over western Mediterranean trade in the late sixth century BCE and three centuries later extended the political reach of its empire onto the peninsula.

The Phoenicians of Tyre, Sidon, Byblos, and other cities of the coastal Levant were said by some early authors to have originated from the Red Sea, which may be the etymology of the Greek name for the island of *Erytheia*, Red Island, on which urban Gadir was built.[21] Greater Gadir also included the larger islands of *Kotinoussa* and *Antipolis*—now connected into the peninsula of Cádiz—and references to the polity perhaps also included the larger Gulf of Cádiz around the mouth of the Guadalete River. This coastal archipelago closely matched the geography of Tyre, and was likely chosen by the Tyrian-Phoenicians for its potential as an ocean port, access to inland resources through the Guadalete and Guadalquivir Rivers, and because of the presence of freshwater springs and a low water table that could be easily tapped.[22] Before silting up, the mouths of the Guadalquivir and other rivers on the southwestern coast extended much more inland than at present, allowing ships to navigate as far upriver as Córdoba and effectively making Seville a coastal port through the time of its central role in the colonization of the Americas (Figure 3.3). In the Roman period, the large lagoon at the mouth of the river was known as *Lacus Ligustinus*; once silted to marshland, the port to the Americas moved from Seville to Cádiz.

At the southern tip of Kotinoussa, some 11 miles (18 km) from Gadir's urban core, the Phoenicians erected the famed Temple to Melqart, the patron god of Tyre and whom the Tyrians possibly conflated as an avatar of their supreme god Baal.[23] The Greek association of Melqart with Heracles (Hercules to the Romans) maintained the temple's prominence in mythical and historical narratives of Gadir/Gades. In the mid-fifth century BCE, Herodotus situated Gadir (or Gadira) "outside the Pillars of Heracles, and on the shore of [the Atlantic] Ocean."[24] This "father of Western history" connected greater Gadir with myths of Heracles and expressed skepticism concerning the reported ocean. He mentions other mid-first millennium inhabitants of Iberia as Celts, Tartessians, Iberians, and Kynetes. Some five centuries later, during the early Roman Empire, Strabo records the Temple of Melqart (the *Heraklion*) as housing two bronze stelae with inscriptions to the divine hero. These stelae, or the entire temple complex and two more

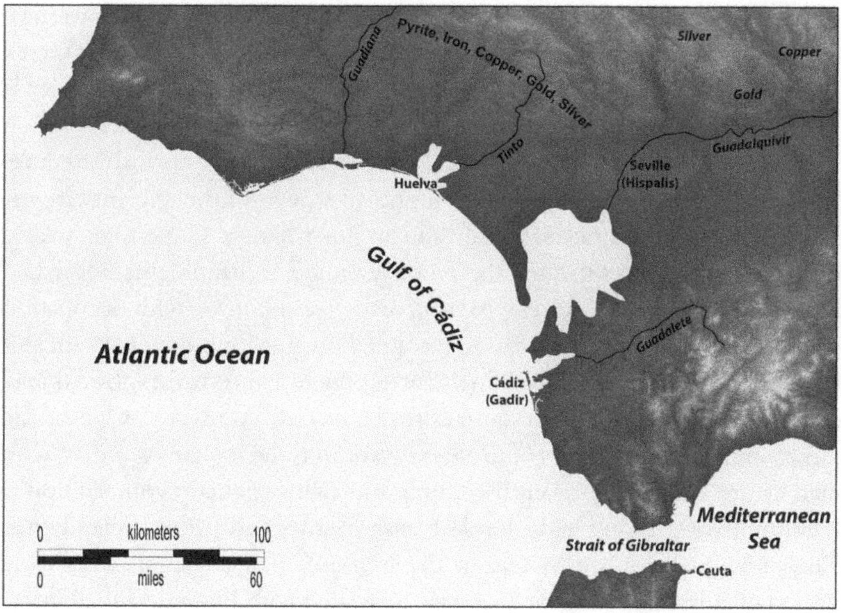

Figure 3.3. Map of the Gulf of Cádiz region with prominent sites and resource zones.

at the sites of Tingus and Lixus, in Morocco, may collectively represent the Pillars of Hercules of lore, if they were in fact built features rather than the natural rock protrusions around the Strait of Gibraltar.[25]

Archaeological investigations have been revealing the material manifestations behind these protohistoric narratives associated with the Gulf of Cádiz region. Although the remains of the Phoenician Temple of Melqart and Roman Heraklion lie below an Islamic period fortress at Sancti Petri, remains of sculpture and architecture associated with that ancient sacred precinct have been discovered. More recent investigations have uncovered traces of other temples and sanctuaries near the urban core of Phoenician-period Gadir, the settlement of its epicenter, and two outlying necropolises. Excavations under the early eighteenth-century San Sebastián Castle revealed the remains of a large architectural complex that matches historical accounts of a Phoenician temple to Baal Hammon—the major incarnation of the deity the Greeks equated with Cronos (giving the precinct the name *Kronion* in Greek sources).[26] The earliest Phoenician materials date to the seventh century BCE and include fragments of amphorae that would have carried trade commodities such as olive oil, wine, or fish sauce.

Another important Phoenician sanctuary, located nearby on the western tip of Erytheia, was dedicated to the goddess Astarte, linked to the Greek Aphrodite and Roman Venus.

The urban epicenter of Gadir has now been definitively established on Erytheia, where recent investigations under layers of historical buildings have revealed more functional and quotidian aspects of the ancient city, including Phoenician houses, burials, and an inner harbor. Close to 30 feet (9 m) below a historical theater, the Teatro Cómico, archaeologists unearthed Phoenician streets and densely packed, orthogonal houses, with occupation beginning in the late ninth century BCE.[27] This small window into ancient Gadir comes complete with vessels for producing and storing food, bread ovens, and the footprints of animals that traversed clay floors. One of the most significant discoveries of these excavations is the remains of a man who died at the end of the seventh century and whose genetic composition is consistent with having had a local, Iberian mother and a Phoenician father. This individual, dubbed Mattan by the archaeologists, encapsulates an early period of cultural mixing, or *mestizaje*, associated with Phoenician colonization of southern Iberia. Other examples of Phoenician-Iberian mixing will surely follow, as genetic studies are maturing and many burials have been excavated in the nearby necropolis at the Casa de Obispo site and another farther south on Koutinoussa.

The broader historical significance of this cultural mixing and hybrid styles present in the interaction sphere of southwestern Iberia is a fertile field of study, encapsulated by the problem of Tartessos. Spanish archaeologists characterize Phoenician traits as "oriental" and the hybrid Tartessian sphere as the result of contact between the indigenous population and various pulses of Phoenician colonization, along with a lesser degree of influences from other Mediterranean cultures.[28] As an ethnonym, Tartessos comes from Greek sources, and the same cultural sphere may be the Tarshish of the Hebrew Bible, both characterizing it as a place rich in silver. The characterization has now been confirmed through isotopic analysis of silver from the Phoenician homeland that originated in Iberia.[29] For years, archaeologists imagined a kingdom with a single, opulent urban center awaiting discovery, but recent perspectives consider early Tartessos to designate a broader region within the triangle between Cádiz, Seville, and Huelva, comprising several urban cores of shifting influence. Greater Huelva may have been important early because of its close proximity to the Río Tinto mines. Greater Seville would have been the most agriculturally productive and has early archaeological documentation of opulent jewelry and substantial settlements such as at Carambolo; additionally, the term "Tartessos" may be a Hellenized version of Tertis, designating the Guadalquivir River.[30] Greater Cádiz would have included sites other than Gadir along the bay and mouth of the Guadalete, such as Castillo de Doña Blanca. Defining a particular site as Phoenician versus Tartessian becomes a thorny issue—and one not totally unlike the problem of the Olmec period in Mesoamerica—but one that is viewed more productively as the gradated horizon of cultural admixture and stylistic emulation.[31]

No matter how it is defined, the Phoenician-Tartessian sphere was the early pivot connecting Atlantic and Mediterranean exchange and had important reverberations into the interior of southern and western Iberia. The Greeks acquired tin from the Atlantic by the sixth century BCE, and most or all of it came from the largest source region in Galicia, having been shipped along the Atlantic coast to Gadir and adjacent port cities and continuing into the Mediterranean.[32] The distance between Gadir and the Galician coast is some 750 miles (1,200 km), which would take approximately 40 days to traverse overland but only a week to sail.[33] This maritime trade is documented archaeologically through the Phoenician or orientalizing material culture found along the coast of Galicia and Portugal and pushing inland along the Tagus River. It includes the depiction of an eastern Mediterranean style galley on a rock carving from Santa Maria de Oia, in southern Galicia (Figure 3.4).[34] These Phoenician ships, with keeled hulls caulked with pitch, represented a major advance in seafaring technology. The upriver Tagus area also has metal deposits, but Phoenician economic incentives appear to have been broader, involving salt production, agricultural land, and slaves.[35] The mouth of the Tagus near Lisbon, the eventual Portuguese port to the Americas, was also a key stopover on Atlantic-Mediterranean navigation, complementing Gadir on the other side of southwest Iberia.

Phoenician colonies and their networks in Iberia were part of a yet larger, pan-Mediterranean network linked to the mother-city of Tyre, situated approximately 2,500 miles (4,000 km) to the east of Gadir. This interregional economy thrived through improved ships, but for centuries did not incorporate coinage, as Phoenician commerce functioned with somewhat standardized metal ingots and equivalencies in goods. Historical accounts indicate that the Carthaginians paid tribute in goods to Tyre until at least the fifth century, but changes in settlement patterns and other archaeological indices suggest that the daughter-city of Carthage began exerting greater authority over western Mediterranean trade in the mid-first millennium BCE,

(a)

(b)

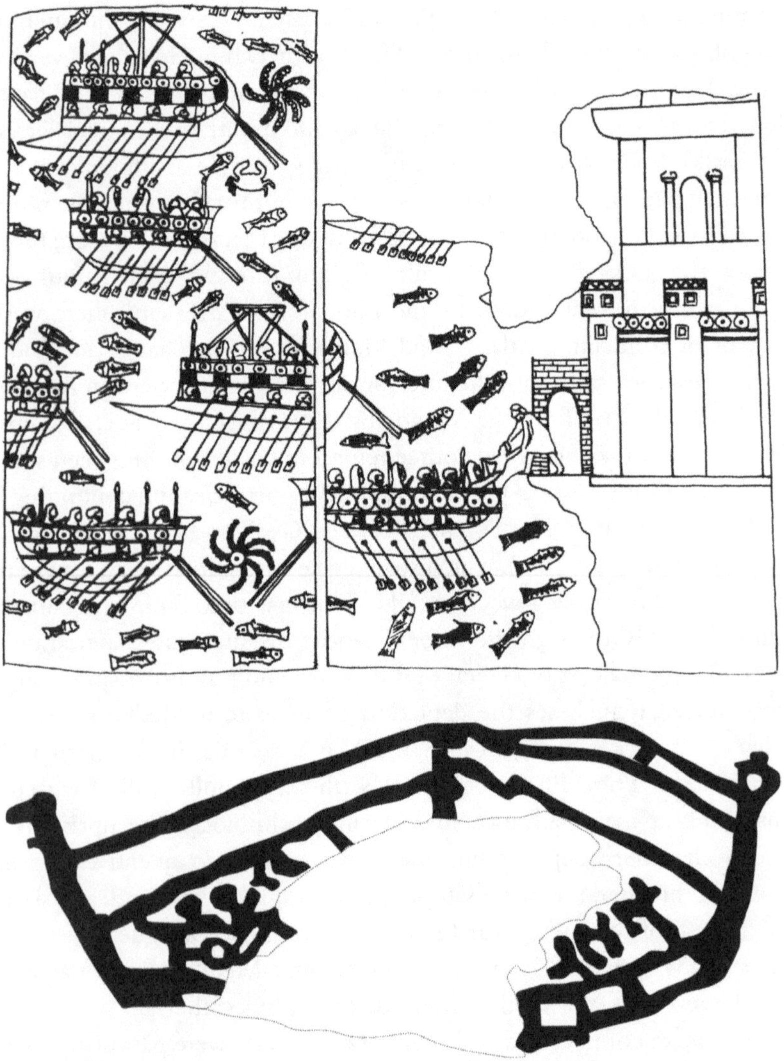

Figure 3.4. Depiction of Phoenician ships in eastern Mediterranean and Atlantic: (top) depiction of harbor of Tyre from Assyrian relief at Nineveh, Iraq, with temple of Melqart to right (redrawn by Pedro Cahuantzi Hernández from Cunliffe 2017: 265); (bottom) detail of eastern Mediterranean galley (note circular shield motif at left) from Laxe dos Cervos rock carving, Galicia, Spain (redrawn by author from Ruiz-Gálvez 2015: Fig. 11.3).

correlating with a decline in Gadir and other coastal centers and a florescence of an inland Tartessian network.[36] Causality is difficult to discern in this case, but the success of Gadir and other Phoenician colonies on the peninsula may have relied on amicable relations with native elites of the Tartessian sphere, which were challenged by upstart inland centers. Furthermore, at a pan-Mediterranean scale, the colonies were increasingly isolated from the motherland of Tyre, which fell under the dominion of the late Assyrian Empire, and by the rise of an independent Carthaginian maritime power.

Greek and Roman authors recorded the impressive navigational feats of the Carthaginians, with two of the most ambitious expeditions captained by Hanno and Himilco.[37] Hanno's was first, in the late fifth century, and may have been assisted by locals from Gadir. He was a political leader of some sort in Carthage—perhaps a *sufete*, a dual-leader of the aristocratic council analogous to the consuls of Republican Rome—and is recorded to have set sail with 30,000 men and women on long galley ships (*penteconters*) to found colonies beyond the Pillars of Heracles. The voyages of these Carthaginians took them into the Atlantic and down the west coast of Africa, where they traded with local peoples and coined the term "gorilla" for strange animals they encountered. Just how far south they explored along the African coast is debated. Himilco's journey or journeys in the first half of the fifth century took him northward into the Atlantic along the Iberian coast to the *Cassiterides*, "Tin Islands," which could have been as far north as the Cornwall region in the British Isles, but more likely represents the tin sources along the Galician coast, where the portages of fjord-like *rias* could have been perceived as islands. It is during this period that stronger Mediterranean (Carthaginian or Punic) influence is seen in northwestern Iberia, including hybridity in typically Celtic jewelry decorated with Mediterranean motifs and Mediterranean sculptural forms decorated with Celtic motifs.[38]

Peoples living in the inland regions of what are today Extremadura and western Andalucía received Mediterranean products through down-the-line trade and adopted their styles in local craft traditions. These contacts accelerated with the decline of the coastal centers in the mid-first millennium. Precolonial exchange of the early first millennium saw an emphasis on Mediterranean prestige goods, which circulated among Iberian elites as a means of social differentiation and exclusion. Metal goods—especially swords, shields, and bodily adornments—were carved as prominent motifs on early stelae, which later became more ornately carved with a thematic focus on full-bodied figures of warriors.[39] Later stelae that postdate Phoenician colonization are stylistically linked to the Phoenician homeland: Tartessian warriors in horned helmets that resemble the bull-headed figures of the god Baal. The thematic focus of these stelae and the deposits of actual weapons and jewelry in the burials of social elites suggest an organization of competing chiefdoms.

The Guadiana River assumed a role as an important conduit between the Meseta and the southwestern port cities, and a necropolis at Cortés' eventual hometown of Medellín provides an important window into this exchange, though the actual settlement is obscured by Roman and later layers on the Cerro del Castillo hill. Tombs of the Tartessian period from the mid-seventh to late fifth centuries contain inscriptions in Tartessian script and furnishings such as ivory combs and gold adornments. In addition to Phoenician-Punic products and styles, including ones derived ultimately from Egypt, Greek products and styles were also in fashion for inland peoples of the Tartessian sphere. They would occasionally include imports like Medellín's fine *kylix* vessel, used for drinking wine and labeled in Greek as a product of the workshop of the artisan Eucheiros, but were more commonly produced locally in Extremadura with the same form but lacking external decoration.[40] Goods circulated in this inland Tartessian network as part of a ritual economy that included shrines and sanctuaries for orientalizing religion. The most well preserved and best understood of these is the site of Cancho Roano, located south of the Guadiana on one of its tributaries.

The sanctuary at Cancho Roano is an impressive structure that illustrates the connections between inland populations and the Mediterranean world exceptionally well, as the manner in which it was abandoned was favorable for preservation of its buried remains.[41] Prior to excavations, it had the form of a large grass-covered mound or tumuli, but the square walls of the complex were discovered by a farmer plowing his field. The multi-occupation sanctuary was ritually burned and filled in with the ash from extensive fires as part of its termination and abandonment. In the final phase of construction, walls were built using a mix of stone and adobe, measuring approximately 80 feet (24 m) on a side (Figure 3.5). Since other contemporaneous sites in the region were principally constructed of adobe and were abandoned gradually, they were much more poorly preserved than Cancho Roano and do not offer direct parallels. Its more elaborate construction also included a slate floor in one room with materials that came from 50 miles (80 km) away. Initial construction was underway in the late seventh or early sixth century, and the sanctuary was abandoned in the beginning of the fourth century.

Figure 3.5. The Tartessian sanctuary of Cancho Roano.
Photo by the author.

In the little over two centuries that it was occupied, Cancho Roano underwent some interesting changes, particularly in the motif of a central altar used for religious offerings. The earliest version, designated as part of Cancho Roano C, features a circular and triangular motif reminiscent of Egyptian iconography that was adopted by the Carthaginians and may relate to the goddess Tanit (Phoenician Astarte, Egyptian Ishtar). Two later superimposed altars, from construction phases designated Cancho Roano A and B, take the shape of an extended bull's hide, seen in other sanctuaries on the Guadiana, such as at Casas de Turuñuelo, as well as at El Carambolo and other Tartessian sphere sites along the Guadalquivir. These bull- or ox-hide altars link to the animal associated with Baal, including to the founding narrative of Carthage, when the first Phoenician settlers were given as much land by the Libyans "as an ox-hide could cover."[42] In addition to these clear links to Phoenician religion, Cancho Roano also possessed the coupling of elemental symbolism relating to water and fire: a nearby spring fed a moat surrounding the sanctuary and two wells within it, and rituals included making burnt offerings and terminating the sanctuary in a conflagration. A conscious effort to link to symbolism of the past can also be seen in the reuse of an earlier warrior stela as a slab in the entrance to Cancho Roano A. Evidence of textile production and other crafting, storage amphorae, the large-scale sacrifice and consumption of animals, and deposits containing fine bronze and gold objects together suggest that Cancho Roano served as an important ritual and economic node within a broader inland Tartessian interaction sphere that linked the Atlantic and Mediterranean worlds.

Elsewhere on the peninsula prior to Carthaginian and then Roman colonization were the Iberians of the southeast, Atlantic Celts or Castro Culture of the northwest, and Celtiberians in between the two on the Meseta. Sculpture of the mid- to late-first millennium became more naturalistic, influenced by Classical Mediterranean styles and exemplified by the female mortuary statues of the southeast and male warrior statues of the northwest. The southeastern or Iberian-sphere statues were given a broader societal context through the 1971 discovery of the Dama de Baza, a seated, authoritative feminine figure found as part of an intact deposit, which helped to illuminate the context of similar female sculptures without sound archaeological context, such as the Dama de Elche (Figure 3.6). The Dama de Baza was part of a tomb deposit with weapons placed before her and ashes of a cremation inside of the statue, which may represent the goddess Tanit or a prominent priestess.[43] The northwestern warrior statues of what is designated regionally as the Second Iron Age (beginning ca. 400 BCE) retain imagery of the earlier warrior stelae, with an emphasis on weaponry and adornment such as gold torques, but sculpted in the round (Figure 3.7). They may have once been positioned as standing sentry at the entrances to the defensible hillforts called *castros* or *oppida* that define the later northwestern cultural sphere, serving to announce their political autonomy.[44] A pattern of smallholding *minifundios* involved the designation of cooperative groups and their collectively managed territories using statuary and specific symbolic motifs as corporate emblems. The Celtiberians are often viewed as having benefited from the "civilizing" influences of the Iberian and Mediterranean spheres, in their adoption of attributes such as the potter's wheel and rectangular house forms. They developed larger and more centralized hillforts than the northwestern castros, including the heavily fortified town of Numantia, which grew to cover 55 acres (22 ha) on the high central Meseta near Soria. Northwestern peoples were organized less hierarchically, based on corporate houses with more flexible kinship and higher social status for women—commented on by Classical authors for its foreignness to them.[45]

Figure 3.6. Iberian funerary sculpture La Dama de Baza, possibly representing the goddess Tanit or a prominent Iberian woman. Museo Arqueológico Nacional, Madrid.

Photo by the author.

The first intent to unify the Iberian peninsula came as part of the Carthaginian invasion and successful colonization of the east and south in the mid- to late third century BCE.[46] This period is often referred to as Barcid because of the Barca family who led Carthage's imperial expansion. The 237–229 campaigns of Hamilcar Barca used Gadir as a base to first extend dominion over southern Iberia, especially the lower and middle Guadalquivir. Hamilcar founded another coastal base in the heartland of Iberian culture near Alicante at Akra Leuké in 231, and colonization continued under his son-in-law Hasdrubal, who in 227 founded a new Carthage (*Qart Hadasht* or Roman Carthago Novo, today's Cartagena) as a port close to key mines of the southeast. Carthaginian colonization of southern Spain thereby included new settlements and investment in existing cities. At Gadir, urban renewal included the erection of a large, tower-style mausoleum with a crowning depiction of Melqart at Sancti Petri next to the earlier Phoenician Temple

Figure 3.7. Celtic warrior statue from Lezenho, Portugal, with circular shield, dagger in right hand, and gold torque around neck. Museu Nacional de Arqueologia, Lisbon.
Photo by the author.

of Melqart.[47] References to the ruined remains of this structure appear in several Islamic period texts, and the original may have once towered 200 feet (60 m) high, making it a conspicuous landmark of greater Gadir/Gades for sailors in the Gulf of Cádiz. Hamilcar's son Hannibal extended these conquests as far north as the Duero River in the west, including the Celtic settlement of Salmantica (today's Salamanca). The Carthaginians did not hold the northern and central Meseta, but consolidated and administered conquests northeast to the Ebro River from Carthago Novo. Hannibal's armies included war elephants, which were famously used later to cross the Pyrenees and Alps into Rome.

The outcome of the fateful Second Punic War (218–201 BCE) resulted in Rome gaining its first continental territories outside Italy and left Carthage weakened, both from the military defeat and from losing the revenue of Iberian mines and tax payments. From this foothold, the rest of the peninsula became a target of further expansion, and the western Mediterranean and adjacent lands of North Africa and western Europe fell under Rome's imperium. The Roman conquest of Hispania involved two centuries of brutal war and the transformation of the mosaic of Iberian cultures that had connected the Mediterranean and Atlantic worlds through economic and religious networks, cultural *mestizaje*, and stylistic hybridization among the smaller political formations, colonies, and incipient empires of the pre-Roman first millennium.

Hispania and All Roads to Rome

In the hills of the northwestern province of León is a magnificent gash in the earth with red cliffs and hillocks reminiscent of a landscape from the American Southwest (Plate 3a). Yet this landscape is completely anthropogenic—the product of massive gold-mining operations in Hispania under the Roman Empire. Las Médulas is a vivid testament to the hydraulically assisted demolition of over eight trillion cubic feet (228 million cubic meters) of mountainside, a process with the evocative Latin term *ruina montium*. It was the largest metal-mining operation in the ancient world, not equaled until the last couple of centuries, and Roman mining operations in northwestern Hispania as a whole reached nearly three times this figure.[48] The conquest of this corner of the peninsula was a protracted affair, begun in the mid-first century BCE under the Roman Republic and completed under the early Roman Empire. Within Spain, the two centuries of Carthaginian and then Roman expansion are generally known as the Baja Epoca (Low Epoch) due to its bitter battles, enslavement, large-scale extraction of peninsular resources, and efforts to impose cultural assimilation. Nevertheless, following imperial consolidation under Augustus and his general and close confidante Marcus Agrippa, the peninsula became a fully integrated Roman territory (Figure

3.8). The emperor Trajan, responsible for expanding Rome to its territorial limits, was born in Italica near the provincial capital of Hispalis (Seville), and the great author and Stoic philosopher Seneca was born farther up the Baetis (Guadalquivir) River in Corduba (Córdoba). Trajan's successors Hadrian and Marcus Aurelius—together three of the five whom Machiavelli elevated as Rome's "good" emperors—had Hispanic roots. The dynamics of conquest, colonialism, and imperial integration of Roman Hispania had profoundly enduring implications for later peninsular history and, in contrast to the earlier Phoenician or Greek enterprises of the first millennium BCE, served as Spanish models in Latin America.[49] Much of the laws, language, religion, urban planning, and other societal and cultural conventions of early colonial Latin America have direct roots in the fierce conquest and more benign rule of Roman Hispania.

Following the Second Punic War, the Romans built from their base of former Carthaginian territories to undertake incremental conquests of Hispania, which was eventually divided into two provinces: *Hispania Citerior*, comprising the eastern, Mediterranean-oriented peninsula and the recent conquests northward made decades earlier by Hannibal and

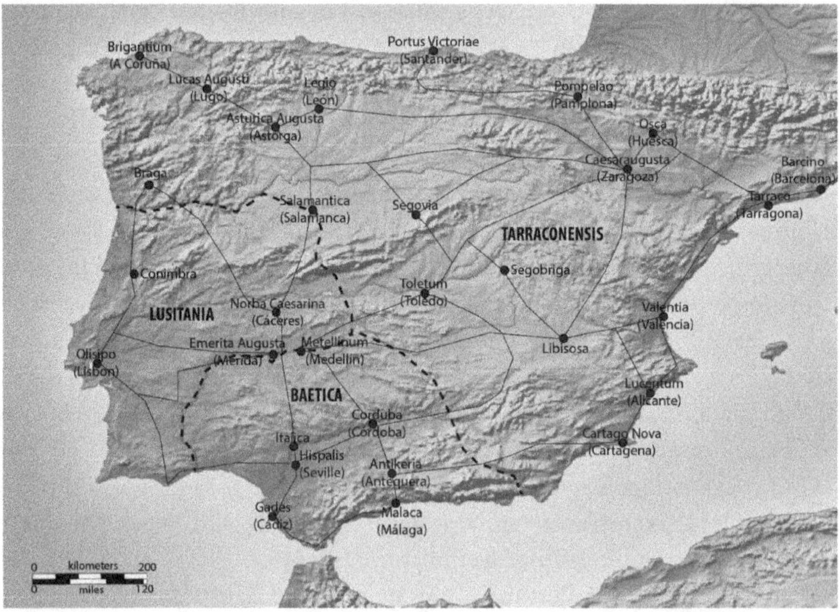

Figure 3.8. Map of Roman Hispania with provinces, cities, and major roads.

the Carthaginians, and *Hispania Ulterior*, comprising the southern, former Phoenician coast westward past the Strait of Gibraltar into the Gulf of Cádiz and southern Portugal. Recent chemical analyses of silver coins from the period illustrate a dramatic change coinciding with the Second Punic War. Coins that were minted mid-conflict (ca. 209 BCE) and afterward contain isotopic ratios of lead and other elements consistent with origins in Iberian silver mines, such as from the Sierra Morena and near Carthago Novo, rather than the eastern Mediterranean sources used previously.[50] The coins are a physical testament to Rome's defeat of Carthage and gain of its provinces. Early coins possibly made it into Roman coffers through war booty or repatriations paid by the Carthaginians, while later ones reflect a period of transition to Roman state control of silver mines in the southern peninsula, which potentially whet the appetite for further conquest.

The conquest of Hispania generally progressed from southeast to northwest, but the process was uneven, the result of indigenous resistance and Rome's own internal political battles.[51] Under the Republic, consuls, magistrates, and generals enjoyed a level of autonomy that fostered conflicting strategies and a near continual state of war in outlying provinces such as Hispania. These wars involved tremendous casualties, sexual violence, and enslavement; they also involved the hybridization of Hispanic and Roman culture and the *mestizaje* of population (a term derived from the Latin *mixtus*), with children of mixed descent recognized legally as *latini* as early as the early second century BCE. Hispania would eventually have the highest percentage of Roman citizens outside of the Italian peninsula. The expansion of Hispania Citerior followed the mid-second century conquests of the Celtiberians in the central and northern Meseta, particularly the siege of Numantia.[52] This conflict lasted two decades and culminated in the Numantians burning their own town and committing mass suicide rather than being enslaved by the Romans. It was idealized in later Spanish memory as an epitome of national sovereignty and resistance, including in a play of the sixteenth century by Cervantes, who later wrote *Don Quixote*.

The expansion of Hispania Ulterior followed the conquests of the Celtic Lusitani, largely in what is today Extremadura and central to southern Portugal. It was during these campaigns, in 80 BCE, that the consul Quintus Caecilius Metellus Pius founded a base of operations in the Guadiana Valley at Metellinum, where centuries later would emerge the town of Medellín, birthplace of Cortes.[53] The transplanting of Roman defensive architecture to Metellinum began the terraced and fortified Cerro del Castillo that would serve for millennia as strategic lookout over the Guadiana, but the development of the town was stunted by the growth of its larger neighbor Augusta Emerita (Mérida), located 18 miles (30 km) to the west. Emerita's rise as one of the great Roman provincial cities began with the campaigns against the final holdouts to Roman dominion in the northwest of the peninsula—Atlantic Celtic peoples such as the Astures, Cantabri, and Gallaeci—and the eventual connecting of the mines of the region, including Las Médulas, to Emerita through the Via de la Plata. In 26 BCE the emperor Augustus himself took the battlefield in the Cantabrian war, concluded a few years later by Marcus Agrippa. Emerita was founded as a sort of retirement community for the veteran soldiers (*emeriti*) of this war—named for them and their patron emperor—in a more agreeable climate for Mediterranean vets than the rainy zone of conflict.

During and following the Cantabrian war, the Romans established a number of fortified towns of enduring quality in the northwest as well, such as Lucus Asturum (Lugo), Bracar Augusta (Braga), and Asturica Augusta (Astorga). Once the region was securely in the imperial fold, the Legio VII Gemina legion was headquartered proximate to the productive mines at Castra Legionis (León). Lucis Asturum, in Galicia, retains the formidable imprint of a heavily fortified Roman town, as impressive walls built primarily in the third century still encircle Lugo today.[54] The settlement was situated strategically near springs as a local water source, where it began as a camp during the Cantabrian wars. It then housed a unit of soldiers from the legion and was connected by the road built between Asturica Augusta and the mining region, where another unit of legionnaires was stationed, and the Galician port town of Brigantium (A Coruña). Excavations outside Lugo's walls provide information on life and death in the town, as they revealed ceramic kilns from large-scale brick and tile manufacture as well as the town's necropolis. At A Coruña, the Tower of Hercules lighthouse was originally erected in the late first or early second century CE when Brigantium became an important port in the Roman Atlantic passage, and its inner core is still preserved within a later structure. Sailors in the eastern Atlantic during the Roman period would make portage at Brigantium before entering the Mediterranean via Olisippo (Lisbon) and Gades. Recent underwater archaeology in the mouth of the Guadiana River illustrates this exchange through the large quantity of excavated amphorae that moved goods between the Mediterranean, Atlantic, and inland river valleys.[55]

Under Augustus, Hispania's two expanded provinces were split into three: Baetica, in the south, centered along the Guadalquivir Valley and former Tartessian heartland, whose descendants were called Turdetani by the Romans; Lusitania, taking the name of the Lusitani, covering much of Extremadura and central and southern Portugal; and Tarraconensis, the largest of the three, stretching from the Mediterranean and key port city of Tarraco (Tarragona) to the Atlantic northwest. Concerted mining activities in the northwest began in the first century CE under Augustus and escalated under his Flavian successors before subsiding in the third century. The Romans required local labor as tax or tribute in realizing an expansive network of 13–16 canals in the hills of Las Médulas, representing approximately 800 miles (1,100–1,400 km) of tunneling.[56] The gold deposits are densest within the first 16 feet (5 m) above bedrock, but are present up to 650 feet (200 m). Pliny the Elder was a financial administrator (*procurator*) in the province during the later first century and visited mines of the region, likely including Las Médulas. He writes that some of the deeper gold nuggets that were extracted weighed up to 10 pounds. Recent paleoenvironmental research near La Molina, Asturias, registers the intensity of mining-related activities on the landscape. Traces of metal pollution found in peat deposits and soils reached levels under the early Roman Empire not seen again for over a millennium during the late modern period, and remains of vegetation show the intensive farming, animal grazing, and deforestation associated with dense population in the region.[57]

With all of these gold riches, and more mundane tin deposits, the name Via de la Plata (Silver Way) seems a misnomer for the major Roman road joining Asturica Augusta to Emerita and then continuing through Hispalis to the port at Gades. However, this long-standing north-south artery connecting Old Castile, Extremadura, and Andalucía is a corruption of either a Latin or an Arabic term for "road" and has nothing to do with silver, which was mined more in the south. Roman development of the urban nodes linking the Via de la Plata created winners and losers. Augustus favored Emerita for urban development, rather than the older settlements of Metellinum and Norba Caesarina (Cáceres), and the city became elaborated with the trappings of Roman urbanity, including a grid plan oriented to a long bridge over the Anas River, three aqueducts, a spacious amphitheater, and an ornate theater (Figure 3.9). Emerita and Metellinum followed divergent yet interconnected trajectories, exemplified by the differences in total size (80 ha/

Figure 3.9. Theater at Mérida, Extremadura, formerly Agusta Emerita.
Photo by the author.

198 acres versus 25 ha/62 acres, respectively), the dimensions of their theaters (80 m/262 feet versus 30 m/98 feet), and disparities in the materials used in elaborating urban art and architecture to promote Emerita as a "Rome in Spain."[58] Prestigious older centers were also respected and elaborated, especially in Baetica and including the still central port of Gades. Roman Gades grew much larger than Phoenician Gadir, and its urban architecture included construction of one of the largest theaters and one of the longest aqueducts in the empire. Excavations at the western San Sebastian precinct show a major enlargement of the *Kronion*, likely serving as a Roman temple to Saturn.[59] The temple to Hercules-Melqart also continued to be important, and the cult honoring this god-hero was elevated to imperial status with Roman coinage depicting his likeness.

The ascendance of the Hispanic emperors led to further infrastructural investment on the peninsula. For all of its brutality in conquest and extraction of resources, Rome was a remarkably inclusive and multicultural empire, exemplified by its flexibility in norms of succession to noble title, including to the highest offices.[60] In the later terminology of New Spain, Trajan would be considered a *criollo*—a provincial, but of the dominant ethnicity and class—and perhaps a *mestizo*, based on some Iberian heritage (Figure 3.10). Neither criollos nor mestizos ever assumed the Hapsburg or Bourbon throne in Spain, something roughly equivalent to Trajan's reign as Caesar (98–117 CE) following Nerva. Trajan was born in the town of Italica, whose ruins are

Figure 3.10. Statue of the emperor Trajan from the town of Baelo Claudia, located on the coast at the Strait of Gibraltar. The marble for the statue was imported from Italy. Museum of Cádiz.
Photo by the author.

in Santiponce, less than four miles from Seville, across the Guadalquivir. His family, the Ulpii, counted among them one of the veterans of the Second Punic War for whom the town was founded, in 206 BCE.[61] In the pivotal battle near Italica, Roman forces reportedly killed 44,000 Carthaginians. Once settled, the Ulpii family prospered in the olive oil trade, for which the province of Baetica was especially famed. Rome's Monte Testaccio, or "Hill of Sherds," along the Tiber River is an anthropogenic feature testament to the empire's commercial networks, with many amphorae coming from Baetica. Trajan made his mark in the military and ascended in rank to assume command of the Legio VII Gemina and protect the exportation of gold from Las Médulas and other mines of the region. His candidacy for emperor came with the backing of the Praetorian Guard and the legions under his direct command in campaigns on the northern frontier of Germany.

Trajan was the last Roman emperor to expand the borders of the empire significantly, primarily through the conquest of Dacia, which brought new silver mines. He was also a major sponsor of infrastructural projects that facilitated transportation and connected the vast territory. These improvements in the circulation of goods and armies involved the construction and renewal of roads, bridges (including over the Taugus River in Lusitania), the harbors at both sides of the Italian peninsula at Ostia and Ancora, and the large marketplace at Rome itself. Approximately three-quarters of the 60 construction projects that can be securely attributed to Trajan were primarily utilitarian in nature, with other examples including hydraulic works such as aqueducts and canals.[62] The date for Segovia's iconic aqueduct in the heartland of Old Castile is debated, but it may have been completed in the early second century under Trajan's reign (Figure 3.11). Trajan was less interested in the founding or embellishment of cities than was his adopted successor, Hadrian. Hadrian was born in Rome, but to a father from Italica who served as a senator in the capital, and a mother from Gades, possibly of Carthaginian descent, which would have made Hadrian a mestizo as well. When Hadrian's father died at age 40, Trajan and another man from Italica

Figure 3.11. The aqueduct at Segovia, possibly built under Trajan.
Photo by the author.

became his guardians. Hadrian visited his ancestral town of Italica once and perhaps twice, but never as emperor.

Hadrian's rule (117–138 CE) was only two years longer than Trajan's, but he oversaw three and a half times the documented construction projects of his predecessor.[63] Hadrian is remembered for setting fortified boundaries on the empire, particularly his eponymous wall through Britain; an emphasis in the construction of religious architecture, including rebuilding the Pantheon; and his love of all things Greek, elevating and embellishing Athens as a cultural capital. Hadrian garnered a high level of co-sponsorship for these projects from the urban elites of 130 cities across the empire. This included Italica, where a construction boom gave the town the third largest Roman amphitheater (even though it was not even a provincial capital), a new center following Greek conventions of orthogonality, a large bath complex, and a monumental cult center to Trajan—part of a broader Hadrianic program to promote the imperial cult, which promoted the divine sanctioning of imperial power. Construction in Italica was of higher quality than is typical for provincial architecture, including the use of superior cement and fine marble brought from Mons Marmorius via a newly constructed road. Italica's amphitheater covers 525 x 450 feet (160 x 137 m) and could hold an estimated 34,000 spectators (Figure 3.12)—the Coliseum, for comparison, measures 617 feet at its largest axis and could hold an estimated 55,000.[64] Hispania and Lusitania had fewer amphitheaters than other Roman provinces in western Europe, but the peninsula has some of the few surviving examples dating

Figure 3.12. The amphitheater at Italica, built under Hadrian.
Photo by the author.

from the Republic, and imperial constructions tend to cluster in Baetica and coastal cities. The presence or size of Roman amphitheaters does not correlate nicely with urban scale, however, and Italica presents a case in point for their association with provincial expression of loyalty to an emperor. Embracing the architectural canons and ritualized slaughter of gladiatorial spectacles in the arena affirmed a community's close ties with the empire.

Italica expanded to cover 75 acres (30 ha) under Hadrian, making it smaller than only provincial capitals such as Emerita and Tarraco, or commercial centers such as Córdoba, which was succeeded by Hispalis as capital of Baetica. Nearby Hispalis undermined Italica's prominence, and by the late second century the ancestral city of Trajan and Hadrian was in decline. Córdoba's long-standing prominence began as a pre-Roman hillfort (*oppida)*, initially founded as a colony during the Republic, and then was refounded as the provincial capital of Colonia Patricia under Augustus, with associated urban renewal.[65] Following the shift in the Baetic capital downriver, Córdoba continued to prosper as an economic hub that attracted migrants to its fertile valley. This presaged the city's rise as the most consequential Islamic city of Spain and one of the largest cities in the world in its heyday in the late first millennium. The family of Marcus Aurelius (emperor 161–180 CE) was also from Baetica, which was by far the most urbanized province of Roman Hispania. The peninsula as a whole had an estimated population of between seven and nine million people in the later second century.[66] Although no Hispano-Roman city ever matched Teotihuacan's estimated population of over 100,000 inhabitants at a roughly contemporaneous time, we lack comparable cumulative population estimates for Mesoamerica during the Early Classic period to match the census-assisted accounts from Hispania. A value in the millions is probable, but whether it was as populated as Iberia at the time or approximately half as much requires more study.[67]

Baetica thrived as a province of Roman Hispania through the system of large agricultural estates known as *latifundia*. These were private landholdings with high yields directed at an exported economy in grains, wine, or olive oil—the last representing the Ulpii family's rise to prominence and the sequence of Hispanic emperors. They presage the encomiendas of the *Reconquista* era that were later exported to colonial Latin America. Something else that would be exported was malaria, which was already a disease associated with the *latifundia* of Baetica, an example of how human land use patterns can encourage a harmful pathogen.[68] Malaria and diseases associated with the long history of Eurasians living with domesticated animals would have tragic consequences when they crossed the Atlantic and encountered populations who had not evolved genetic defenses to them.

It would be difficult to overstate the legacy of Roman Hispania to later peninsular history, especially in the domains of urban networks and infrastructure, language, law, and cultural institutions such as the calendar (Figure 3.13), literature and philosophy, or the *latifundia* estates. Roman cities generally transitioned to become medieval cities of the Visigothic, Islamic, and northern Spanish kingdoms. Christianity spread through the peninsula and became institutionalized and monumentalized through church construction beginning in the late second century. By the year 220 CE there were episcopal sees at Asturica Augusta (Astorga), Emerita (Mérida), and Ceasaragusta (Zaragoza).[69] The introduction of Christian mortuary practices can be seen in necropolises such as at Lucus Asturum (Lugo) beginning in the mid-third century, with a shift away from cremations to extended inhumations in ceramic-tile coffins. Administrative reforms of the late Roman Empire under Diocletian and Constantine included the division of northern Hispania into

Figure 3.13. Mosaic from Italica with the seven astronomical designations for the Roman and then Spanish days of the week (counterclockwise from top: Selene/Moon, Mars, Mercury, Jupiter, Saturn, Helios/Sun, with Venus in center).
Photo by the author.

the provinces of Tarraconensis, Carthaginiensis, and Gallaecia, with Lusitania and Baetica remaining the same.[70] These were renamed *dioceseis* and were restructured with more elaborate bureaucracies and higher but more equitable taxation of the populace. Late Roman imperial reforms also first granted legal status to Christianity (313 CE) and then made it the official faith of the empire (391 CE). This established the major axis of cultural identification and conflict leading up to the *Reconquista* era: religion.

Moros y Cristianos

The era of peninsular unification under Roman Hispania was followed by a medieval era that saw the re-emergence of the Iberian hinge, between a south and southeast of Mediterranean-oriented cultures and colonists, and a north and northwest of continental European- and Atlantic-oriented ones. Following the collapse of Rome, the Germanic Alans, Vandals, Suevi, and Visigoths invaded the peninsula from the north and southeast. The Suevi were concentrated in the northwest but began expanding southward in 439, eventually conquering Lusitania and Baetica. By the end of the sixth century, the Visigoths briefly reunified much of the peninsula with a centrally located capital at Toledo (the former Roman city of Tollentum).[71] Later Christian kingdoms of the former Celtic and Roman mining regions of the northwest drew on this period of Visigothic unification as inspiration in their military campaigns directed against Islamic rule in the south, known as the *Reconquista* or reconquest.[72]

Gothic Hispania of the fifth to early eighth centuries retained much of the Roman urban and road network. During the late Roman period, changes in the built environment of the western peninsula included the construction of larger and more elaborate walls around already established urban centers and the creation of new hilltop settlements, both indicating the need for surveillance and defense.[73] Two major transformations in urban layout relating to Christianity can be seen in cities such as Mérida: Christians changed the practice of burying their dead in necropolises outside urban centers in favor of graves within city walls, and churches and other new forms of sacred architecture were more distributed within cities than was the earlier Roman pattern of nucleated temples and civic spaces. Mediterranean agriculture remained important economically south of the Duero, especially in the production of olive oil as food and fuel, whereas animal raising and colder-adapted crops were important in the north. Taxes appear to have been paid in kind and in coin, with the latter method increasing over time. Material culture simplified in many ways during Visigothic rule compared with the Roman period, yet personal adornment became more ornate in inlayed metalwork such as brooches and belt buckles (Figure 3.14).[74] In Visigothic Hispania of the late sixth century, Christianity became not only a generally shared worldview, but also a means of expressing prestige, which included the founding of more architecturally substantial churches and monasteries by elites as a means of asserting their social distinction.[75] This included the more established zones of former Lusitania (Extremadura and much of Portugal) and Gallaecia (Galicia and northern Portugal), as well as the more lightly urbanized northern Meseta, which had become a contested frontier between the Suevi, Visigoths, and different local populations of Basques and Cantabrians.

Figure 3.14. Visigothic belt buckles, sixth century. Museo de Cáceres.
Photo by the author.

Although Christianity eventually played a unifying role for the northern kingdoms of the *Reconquista*, during the centuries between Roman and Islamic rule its three main denominations on the peninsula were at odds. At first the eastern orthodoxy represented by Byzantium was more closely linked to Rome (even though following the Justinian conquest in 552 its promoters in southeastern Spain spoke Greek) since it was preferable to the heretical Arianism of the Goths, which did not recognize the Holy Trinity. When the Visigoths converted to Catholicism, it linked them more closely to Rome and the Latin legacy, leading to the decline of Arianism and its eventual prohibition by the Third Council of Toledo in 589. The Gothic realignment motivated many Hispano-Romans to migrate from the Byzantine southeast, including the family of the future Saint Isidore, who moved from Spanish Carthage to Seville.[76]

Isidore succeeded his brother as bishop as Seville, and one of his intellectual legacies was in channeling Classical sources such as Aristotle and Pliny the Elder through Augustine and other early Christian scholars.[77] The correspondence and Isidore's *Etymologiae* illustrate an early seventh century scholastic brand of Christianity that looked to the Classical past. Isidore oversaw the Fourth Council of Toledo (in 633), which decreed that all bishops establish seminaries with training in Greek, Hebrew, and liberal arts, similar to his own in Seville. His initiative would be rekindled and expanded half a millennium later under the Dominicans and their early universities. Among Isidore's less enlightened beliefs were his strong anti-Jewish views, also elaborated from Augustine, which he recorded in his writings and enacted as part of the same Fourth Council of Toledo.

Another of Isidore's contributions was in cartography. The encyclopedic *Etymologiae* and earlier *De Natura Rerum* ("On the Nature of Things") present his vision of global geography and the earliest preserved map in what is known as the T-O style, for its schematic rendition of the continents of Europe, Africa, and Asia encircled by the Ocean (Figure 3.15). Isidore's map drew on predecessors of the Classical and early Christian world and influenced later cartographic traditions, which became less schematic in depicting towns, coastlines, and smaller rivers.[78] In Isidore's simplified rendition, the East (Orient) is appropriately at top and the Pillars of Hercules are at the bottom. The T form is created by the waters of the Mediterranean for the body and the Nile and Dom Rivers as the arms—the latter possibly also with the Black Sea. It is debated whether Isidore's depiction and textual references to the Earth as round means that he understood it as spherical or

Figure 3.15. Isidore of Seville's T-O map with circular Ocean and three continents known to Europeans of the seventh century.
Illustration by Pedro Cahuantzi Hernández.

a flat disc, but Aristotle and other Classical authors whom Isidore drew from recognized it was not flat, and this generally was educated consensus in late Antiquity and the early Medieval period. Approximately a century and a half after Isidore's map, in 776, a monk from northern Spain named Beatus illustrated a more cartographically accurate rendition that became the source of a number of medieval maps. Beatus appears to have drawn from both the writings of Isidore and an earlier Spaniard named Orosius, who was a friend and early fifth-century contemporary of Augustine, and like Augustine also lived in Hippo (North Africa).[79] Together, these maps and texts represent the cumulative geographic knowledge and cosmovision of early Christian Spain.

Visigothic Spain of the seventh to early eighth centuries could be considered the strongest in western Europe of the day, but it was conquered relatively quickly beginning in 711 by Islamic armies comprising primarily Berber soldiers led by Arabs. Muslims would rule much of the peninsula for the next half millennium, with later waves arriving from northwest Africa in the eleventh and twelfth centuries.[80] The Arabs originated from the east and their eponymous peninsula, home to the prophet Muhammad, whereas the Berbers were diverse tribes of northwest Africa who mostly lived inland from the former Carthaginian core and Roman provinces of Mauretania and Numidia. The ethnonyms Berber and Moor come, respectively, from Greek designations for "barbarians" and for inhabitants of Mauretania. Berbers were always the ethnic majority of the conquering Islamic forces in Iberia, but the Arabs were the administrative leaders and Arabic the prestige language of state. Much of the Islamic conquest was completed by the year 720. In the course of a little over a decade, forces led by Tarik crossed the Strait of Gibraltar as an exploratory raid (bestowing his name to the rock, *jebel Tarik*), and then were joined by Musa, governor of the Maghreb (also called the Barbary states, derivative of Berbers), for three years of military campaigns before both were recalled to Damascus by the Umayyad caliph.[81]

In the mid-eighth century, the Umayyad dynasty was succeeded by the Abbasids and one of its members, 'Abd al-Rahman, crossed to Spain in 756 with new conquests that created a state lasting two and a half centuries as an independent polity from Damascus. The conquests involved large-scale conversions of native Hispano-Gothic populations to Islam, with an estimated 8 percent designated as Muslim in 800 growing to 25 percent in 900 and 75 percent by 1000, at the height of the caliphate of Al-Andalus (origins of Andalucía) and the most cosmopolitan city in Europe of the day, Córdoba. The strongest state of Al-Andalus was in the tenth century under the rule of 'Abd al-Rahman III, who took the title of caliph al-Nasir in 929, and of his immediate successors, al-Hakam II and al-Mansur, known in Spanish as Almanzor. These caliphs relied heavily on slave and ex-slave soldiers, initially Slavs (cognate of the term), and later balanced by Berbers to strike at the northern Christian kingdoms, including the sack of the holy site of Santiago.[82] Following the decline of Abbasid power in the eleventh century, the Berber Almoravids and Almohads launched invasions from Morocco.

In the northwest, Christian reconquests began shortly after Tarik's invasion, but took centuries elsewhere. Islamic power was also periodically contested by sea and from beyond the peninsula, but none was a serious threat. In the 840s, when a Norse fleet of over 100 ships sailed up the Guadalquivir with the purpose of raiding Seville (Plate 3b), the expedition met an unhappy end: Islamic forces beheaded over two hundred Vikings and hung the bodies of others from the city's palm trees.[83] Muslims in Iberia took to the seas as well but were primarily focused on the Mediterranean rather than in the Atlantic. The chief medieval Atlantic port was the Christian controlled

A Coruña, which was joined by Porto and Lisbon after the twelfth-century reconquest of northern Portugal. Muslim indifference to the northern Atlantic created an entry for merchants from Italian city-states, particularly sailing from Genoa and Venice. Both traded up the Atlantic shore, but the Genoese were more active, after negotiating friendly terms with the Muslims and then the Castilians, while the Venetians were more involved in the Aragonese Mediterranean world.[84]

The legacies of these waves of Muslim conquests and the kingdom of Al-Andalus to later Iberia were profound and enduring. It saw the introduction of a number of new crops that had been domesticated in Asia and Africa. These included grains such as rice and durum (hard) wheat, sugarcane, citrus fruits, other fruits like banana and melon, and Old World cotton—which was also domesticated independently in the Americas.[85] Rice, sugar, cotton, and bananas would all go on to play important roles in the plantation economies of Iberian colonies, first in Madeira and the Canary Islands and later transferred to well-watered regions of the Americas. Although the Romans has constructed hydraulic works that impressed the Muslims, these were generally oriented toward supplying cities with drinking water or mining operations like at Las Médulas. The Arabs in particular instigated a "green revolution" in Al-Andalus by introducing irrigation systems and technological advances such as the water wheel (*noria*) that could grow monsoon-adapted crops in arid environments.[86] A mix of south Asian crops, Roman and Persian hydraulic techniques, and a legal code of water distribution drawing from Arab and Berber tribal norms as well as Roman and Islamic legal precedents created the highly productive farming of Al-Andalus.

Islamic period introductions are reflected in Castilian Spanish through Arabic loanwords.[87] Many are easy to identify by the definitive article al- as a prefix, and some of these reflect the bureaucracy of Al-Andalus, such as *alcalde* (mayor), *almirante* (admiral), *aldea* (village), *alquiler* (rent). Others reflect introduced goods such as *algodón* (cotton), *azúcar* (sugar), *azulejo* (ceramic tile), *café* (coffee), *cero* (zero), *guitarra* (guitar), *limón* (lemon), and *naranja* (orange). These were transferred to Spanish America when Castilian became the language of empire. A different historical trajectory of Islamic conquest and contacts is reflected in two other languages of the peninsula, Galician and Portuguese, which share a common ancestry from the vulgar Latin once spoken in the northwest. Since the northwest became independent from Islamic rule only decades after the conquest of the peninsula, Galician has less than half as many Arabic loanwords as does Portugal, which branched from the shared Galician-Portuguese Romance language base as the Reconquista pushed south.[88] The loans came from Mozarab populations (Christians who lived under Islamic rule) who were more numerous in southern Portugal than those who migrated north, and later entered Galician lexicon from Portuguese and Castilian. The dozen or so Arabisms found in Galician but not Castilian illustrates the complexities of migration and culture contacts that shaped the hybrid Iberian culture known as Mozarabic and Mudéjar—the latter being Muslims and converts who stayed in Iberia after territories were conquered by Christians.

The Iberian *Reconquista* began in the northwest and was framed in religious terms; Spain's patron saint, Santiago (Saint James), emerged as its rallying spirit. On the Galician Atlantic coast, Iria Flavia in today's Padrón was site of the late Roman to early Suevi bishopric known from the fifth or early sixth century and said to have been Santiago's entry point to the peninsula as one of Jesus' first century apostles. Medieval-period documents assert that Santiago was martyred in Jerusalem and his remains returned to Padrón and then moved inland to Compostela. The exact timing of these events is debated, with a traditional narrative of a moving of the remains in the early ninth century and elaboration of a church later that century under King Alfonso III of León, Asturias, and Galicia. Maps of the mid-tenth century depict Compostela as an important church center, though there is no evidence of it having been so in the eighth century.[89] In 997 CE it was attacked by an Islamic army led by al-Mansur, who burned the church and took its bells to Córdoba. The pilgrimage route cutting across northern Spain from the Pyrenees was established by the mid-eleventh century, and construction of a monumental Romanesque cathedral began later that century. Evidence from coins deposited in Santiago's crypt suggests that it was modified from an original form as a mausoleum to a subterranean tomb under the cathedral by 1105 CE.[90]

The late twelfth to early thirteenth centuries represent the heyday of the pilgrimage route to Compostela along the road called the *Via Lactea* (Milky Way), a communication network that stimulated development of urban centers in northern Castile such as Burgos, Vallodolid, and Palencia. It also oriented Castillian trade toward markets of northern Europe, with imports of goods including textiles from Flanders and exports of iron and animal products to England, Flanders, and France.[91] Pilgrims arrived to Compostela by land and by sea—many of the latter disembarking at A Coruña, where there was another church to Santiago (Figure 3.16). Along with those to

Figure 3.16. Santiago the Moorslayer on tympanum of entrance to late twelfth-century church in A Coruña, where pilgrims arriving from sea would disembark before walking to Compostela.
Photo by the author.

Jerusalem and Rome, the journey to Santiago was one of the great medieval pilgrimages, and the ritual-economic network it created served as a conduit for northern European ideas and social structures to reach northern Spain. As its fame grew, the cult of Santiago also became increasingly militaristic and associated with the saint's avatar as Moorslayer (Matamoros). This included the twelfth-century decree by King Alfonso VII recognizing Santiago as the nemesis of infidels as well as the creation of the Order of Santiago, with both military and hospitality charges in protecting pilgrims on the route, whose knights wore the insignia of a red cross whose central element evokes a sword. Texts of the eleventh and twelfth centuries present a mythistory suggesting that Santiago always assumed a military role. These later narratives memorialized a "first" *Reconquista* victory led by the Visigothic nobleman Pelayo (Pelagius) in the hills of Austurias at Covadonga, in 722, with Santiago as an inspiration. The conquering saint was conceived as leading Christian forces to victory in the battle of Clavijo, thought to be entirely mythical, and appearing to Charlemagne in a dream to free Iberia from the yoke of Islam.[92] The Charlemagne narrative illustrates a key point of the centuries traditionally termed the *Reconquista*: at the time it was viewed as a crusade through the Iberian peninsula. Iberian Christians did not journey to the Holy Land to join those crusades because, in their view, they had one at home.

Of the crusading heroes of Spain's Reconquista, none looms larger in popular imagination than Rodrigo Díaz de Vivar, better known as El Cid from the Arabic *sayyid*, meaning "lord" or "master."[93] The title was never used in Rodrigo Díaz's life (d. 1099) but was part of his memorialization in the epic poem *El Poema de mio Cid* written in the early thirteenth century. The poem also designated him El Campeador, for his prowess on the field of battle. El Cid as the archetypal Castilian knight of the Reconquista was particularly memorialized in the early twentieth century, when Spain's national ego was bruised from the loss of its last overseas colonies and in need of a hero. In actuality, Rodrigo Díaz's life was complex. Though he did conquer on behalf of Castilian monarchs, he also fought for Muslim rulers of Zaragoza, essentially as a mercenary. His greatest victory when he sieged and took control of Valencia was accomplished with a mixed army of Christians and Muslims, and he ruled it as a semi-autonomous polity for the last five years of his life, when it then returned to Islamic control.

During the centuries of the *Reconquista* the unsettled frontier between established Christian and Islamic kingdoms moved progressively from Castile to Extremadura to Andalucía. The Castile of El Cid was a buffer zone between the northwestern Christian kingdoms of Asturias-León and Islamic Spain south of the Duero River. As frontiersmen, Castilians were granted relative autonomy through the chartered legal rights granted through the system of *fueros*. With the Camino of Santiago and the gradual movement of the frontier southward, Old Castile north of the Duero became a developed core. In the thirteenth century Extremadura and rural Andalucía became the new frontier. The first retained the culture of a more sparsely settled frontier throughout the *Reconquista* as part of New Castile, whereas the fertile and historically established core of the Guadalquivir Valley simply passed from being a Muslim core to a Christian one. When Seville was taken in 1248 its estimated 45,000 residents made it the most populous city in the kingdom of Castile.[94] The new frontiers won during the Reconquista gave rise to the system of *repartimientos*—allocations of former Muslim lands to Christian landowners. It became a precursor to the *encomienda* system of estates that were entrusted with local, serf-like labor used in nationalizing Spain and its colonial enterprises of the late fifteenth century (Figure 3.17).

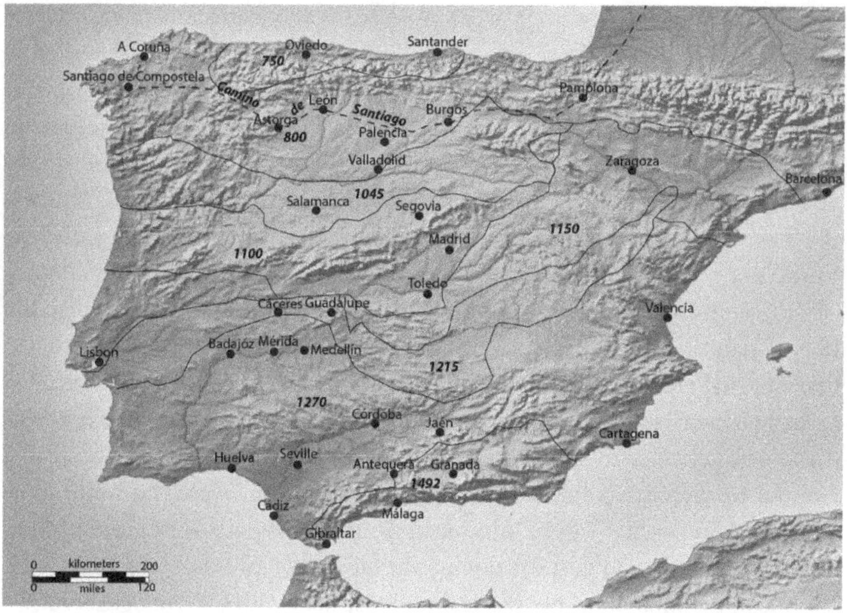

Figure 3.17. Map of Medieval Iberia with Camino de Santiago and rough dates of the Reconquista.

After the pilgrimage to Santiago helped to fortify Castilian trading centers such as Burgos and Valladolid, the kingdom further developed the institutions of a core through centers of learning. In the eleventh century, church councils in Galicia and Castile decreed that cathedral chapters establish schools in parishes throughout the land.[95] The first was established in 1208 or 1212 at Palencia and followed the model of the University of Bologna, with study of the *trivium* (grammar, rhetoric, and logic) and seven liberal arts. Other universities were founded in Castile and elsewhere, including at Salamanca, Valladolid, Toledo, Murcia, and Seville—the last with heavy emphasis on Arabic. Dominic de Guzmán was educated and then taught at Palencia. He founded the *Ordo fratrum predicatorum* ("Fraternal Order of Preachers" or Dominican Order) in 1216, seven years after Francis of Assisi had founded his own. Like Rodrigo Díaz, Dominic was born near Burgos of a minor noble class. Unlike the conquering knight, however, he exemplified a different early instance of what would become an important role in colonizing the Americas: a Christian missionary.

Dominic began his career as an Augustinian, but created the Order of Preachers with the goal of proselytizing. This meant rejecting the Benedictine model of cloistered monks for one that preached the gospel to laypeople, as was also being done by the Franciscans. The Dominicans and Franciscans were therefore similar in their missionizing and their vows of humility and poverty as "mendicants," but they differed in their approaches. Whereas the Franciscans sought to connect sentimentally, by proselytizing directly to the people on the streets, the Dominicans made their appeal intellectually, through universities. Dominic moved from Palencia with other faculty to Salamanca, where they founded a Dominican college and San Esteban convent in 1229. Salamanca would become one of medieval Europe's great universities and would later serve as the training grounds for many of the missionaries who sailed to convert Native peoples of the Americas.[96] Central to the curriculum of the "Salamanca school" were the writings of Thomas Aquinas, the early Dominican from Italy who was later elevated to doctor and sainthood status and whose philosophy would be essential to the European reconciliation of Classical philosophers with Christian theology.

Spain on the Eve of the Catholic Monarchs

Over its millennia of societal development, Iberia witnessed waves of conquerors to the peninsula, including Phoenicians, Carthaginians, Romans, Goths, and joint Arab-Berber forces. These all left their stamp in technology, styles of material culture, social norms and laws, beliefs, and language. Yet they differed in orientation—whether commercial, extractive, or imperialistic—and in how extensively they transformed societal organization. Iberian agriculture came in waves as mostly complete packages or suites of foods: first from the Neolithic Fertile Crescent, next in Mediterranean goods brought by the Phoenicians and others, and finally with south Asian and north African crops and techniques brought by Muslims. Unlike in Mesoamerica, Iberians lived with large domesticated animals that passed diseases to them, and they harnessed these animals for extensive plow agriculture, trade, and battle.

As a hinge between the Mediterranean and Atlantic worlds, Iberians received and contributed goods and ideas to a much more territorially extensive sphere of interaction than existed in pre-Hispanic Mesoamerica. Seafaring technology and navigation expertise improved markedly with Phoenician colonization of the first millennium BCE and later saw the fusion of hybrid boat forms drawing on Mediterranean and Atlantic traditions. The Phoenicians and Celts also introduced iron smelting, which never developed in the Americas. Roman Hispania produced the first political unification of the peninsula and introduced urban and road infrastructure, linguistic homogenization through Latin, and cultural and legal institutions that endure in Iberia and Latin America today. It also introduced the Christian faith, continued by the Visigoths, which later provided a unifying cause in the *Reconquista*, or peninsular crusade against Islamic rule. During this period the conquering patron saint Santiago, the knights who drew inspiration from him, and the mendicant friars who looked to spread the gospel emerged as key figures in the unification of the Christian kingdoms of Spain, with a center of gravity in Castile.

At the extreme southern end of Cádiz, two remarkable bronze statuettes were unearthed at Sancti Petri (Figure 3.18). The first is a Phoenician

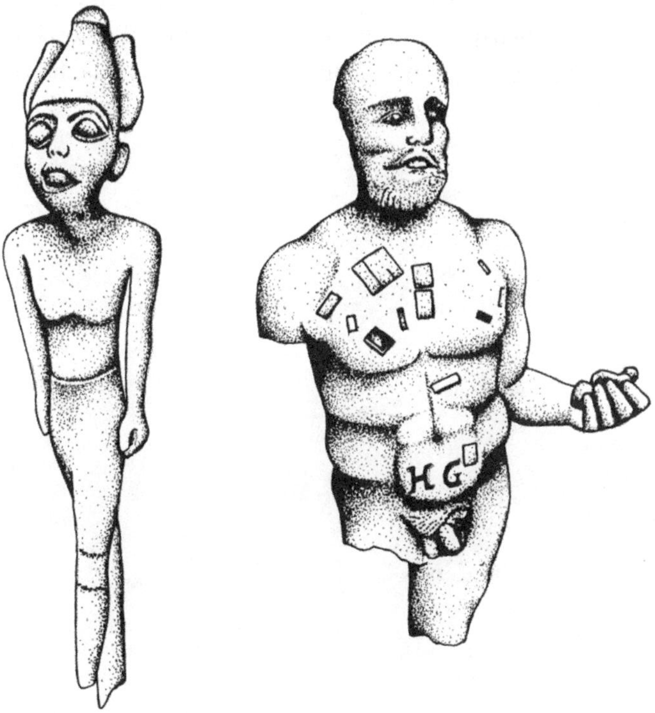

Figure 3.18. Bronzes of (left) Phonecian god Melqart and (right) Roman hero Hercules from Sancti Petri, currently in Museum of Cádiz.
Illustration by Pedro Cahuantzi Hernández.

depiction of Melqart dating to the seventh century BCE. Eastern aesthetics of that period include the Egyptian-style conical headdress and rigid posture with arms at the side and one leg before the other. The second is a Roman depiction of Hercules-Gaditani, the Hercules "of Gadir," labeled with initials etched on his stomach and dating to the second century CE. Western aesthetics of that period include the naturalism of the figure's features and posture. The rectangular elements on the torso are from patches made in antiquity at places where an air bubble introduced during the casting process had created a hole, and Hercules's eyes contain a stone inlay for the pupils, perhaps of obsidian.[97] Although centuries separate the two pieces, their connection thematically as divine heroes, materially as bronzes, and in the Roman initials ultimately derived from script invented by the Phoenicians is clear. So too is the continuity in the demarcation of this part of southwestern Iberia as a sacred spot on the landscape that Mediterranean peoples saw as a threshold to a mysterious ocean. Sailing further beyond the Pillars of Hercules was a goal deeply engrained in the collective consciousness of navigators. From their positioning at this geographical pivot and with the bellicose and expansionistic momentum of the *Reconquista*, Iberians would sail beyond them.

4

Mexico and Spain on the Eve of Encounter

In comparative history, the challenge is to identify significant factors and the ways in which they are related to observed outcomes. A willingness to draw on historical data from both sides of the Atlantic Ocean will be essential in meeting this challenge.

—Walter Scheidel (2016)[1]

During the decade before Spain's 1492 dynastic merger and launching of trans-Atlantic expeditions, both the Aztec Triple Alliance and the joint kingdoms of Castile and Aragón were expanding their domains through conquest. During the 1480s, the Aztec Empire gained its farthest flung province in the Soconusco region, located over 500 miles (800 km) from the Basin of Mexico near the current border between Mexico and Guatemala. It was brought into the imperial domain of the Triple Alliance by the Great Speaker Ahuitzotl, who ruled from Tenochtitlan, and his younger ally and son-in-law Nezahualpilli, of Texcoco. At the same time in Spain, the allied Catholic Monarchs Isabela of Castile and Ferdinand of Aragón were busy with military campaigns against the southern emirate of Granada, situated nearly the same distance from the Castilian heartland as was the Soconusco from the Aztec heartland. The unification of the kingdoms ruled by Isabela and Ferdinand was in some sense akin to the reunification of Hispania Ulterior and Hispania Citerior of the early Roman period.[2] The conquest states of Aztec period Mexico and early modern Spain were the product of myriad, layered cultural and historical processes and exchanges. Both were, of course, ignorant of one another, but the preceding millennia of societal developments in Mesoamerica and Iberia set the stage for their momentous encounter of the sixteenth century.

There were some striking parallels between Aztec Mexico and the merged kingdoms of Spain in how ethnogenesis and imperial prerogative were framed, the centrality of urban centers with noble and priestly classes, and the inspiration derived from conquering religious figures. But there was also major variability in national and ethnic affiliations, the financing and administration of political institutions, religious tolerance and proselytizing, military and transportation technologies, and other aspects of culture and society. Differential technologies explain how the Spanish crossed the Atlantic to Mexico instead of the Aztecs doing the same in the other direction, but provide only part of the story for how invasions led to ultimately successful conquests and the new cultural and political order of colonial New Spain. For that, we need to look at cultural, societal, and historical variables. In both Spain and Mexico, people drew on historical memory of earlier cultures to frame their contemporary identity. Affiliation was most often to kingdoms, but in Spain religious zeal turned to intolerance. Castilian expansion and language homogenization undergirded nation building, whereas in Mesoamerica religious divisions did not define society, and the indirect governance of the Aztec Empire fostered micro-patriotism and primary allegiance to ethnic city-states. Major rivals to the Aztec Triple Alliance included the collectively organized state of Tlaxcala, to the east, and the hierarchically organized empire of the Tarascans, to the west. Cleavages existed within the Triple Alliance itself, where Tenochtitlan had assumed greater power than its previously equal partner, Texcoco. We will look at these and other dimensions of Aztec Mexico and Spain of the Catholic Monarchs as a type of intensive comparison, between two cases and along multiple variables,[3] to understand how they impacted the wars of Mesoamerican conquest and the forging of a new colonial order.

Aztecs and Spaniards: Ethnic and National Identities

It is a puzzling fact of Aztec-period Mexico that so many people saw it as deeply meaningful to claim ancestry from someplace else, particularly from somewhere to the northwest named Aztlan—the source of the ethnonym.[4] Narratives dealing with ethnic origins recorded in sixteenth-century Mexico are full of people on the move. Elements of these narratives are also evident in pre-Hispanic art, indicating that they were not simply a post-contact fabrication. These statements of migrant ancestry are an interesting phenomenon because they are, in some sense, counterintuitive. An obvious way to make claims to a certain territory is to assert that your people have always been there or, as many groups do, that the first of their "real" people emerged or were created in the area. What did Aztec peoples gain by claiming they were relative newcomers?

Outsized attention has gone to the Aztec (here meaning Nahuatl speaking) migrations, particularly the Mexica narrative, whose omen of an eagle perched on a cactus is emblazoned on the Mexican flag and on national currency today. It is important to emphasize that other groups of the period, such as the Otomi and speakers of Otomanguean or Otopamean languages, who linguists would note had deep ancestry in central Mexico, also chronicle their migrations from elsewhere. The Codex Huamantla shows Otomis from that particular *altepetl* (city-state) passing the ruined pyramids of Teotihuacan on their migration eastward (Figure 4.1).[5] New methods of bioarchaeological analysis, including the study of bone isotopes and ancient DNA, are revealing just how mobile groups were in the past, but much of the archaeological record exhibits great continuity between periods. Archaeological excavations at the Otomi city-state of Xaltocan show continual occupation through the early Aztec period of proto-historic migration narratives, indicating that immigrants settled among an existing

Figure 4.1. First folio of Codex Huamantla, depicting the migration of Otomis from Chiapan, in today's state of Mexico, past Teotihuacan (depicted at center by two stepped pyramids with the Fifth Sun above them) and on to Cuauhmantla (Huamantla, Tlaxcala). Biblioteca Nacional de México (http://www.codices.inah.gob.mx/pc/index.php).

population.[6] Accordingly, a critical read of these narratives suggests that migrations did indeed occur, but their historical memory was exaggerated because of the cultural salience that narratives of journeys, divine omens, and some conquering kings had to sixteenth-century Mexicans.

Some of the names given to migrating groups by later peoples who claimed ancestry from them capture the tensions inherent in the projection of an ethnic identity that was simultaneously new or foreign and ancient or local.[7] A prominent example is the dual affiliation of Tolteca-Chichimeca referenced by various Aztec peoples from the Basin of Mexico and Valley of Puebla-Tlaxcala. The term "Tolteca" captures the glorious, civilized past of the agriculturally based, urban artisans who built places such as Teotihuacan, Tula, and Classic-period Cholula's Great Pyramid. This part of the identity is ancient, settled, and noble. However, when balanced by Chichimeca, the identification presents a dichotomous couplet that in Aztec thought was fused and dualistic, as the Chichimeca were the barbaric nomads from the northwestern deserts. This part of the identity is recent, unsettled, and humble. A similar term is for the Teochichimeca, named as a founding community in Tlaxcala. Here the Chichimeca identity is balanced by *teotl*, meaning "sacred." Another proto-historic group of migrants we have already encountered are the Olmeca-Xicalanca, with likely ties to the Gulf of Mexico trading communities at the interface of Aztec and Maya culture. They are said to have already been settled in Puebla-Tlaxcala, at places such as Cholula and Cacaxtla, when the Teochichimeca arrived in the area and took over.

Regardless of the historical accuracy of these migration narratives, the framing of apparently disparate origins projected both the trappings of civilized people and the conquering spirit of barbarians. Framing ethnic identity as Toltec and Chichimec could simultaneously appeal to a sense of legitimate authority grounded in the past and a sense of restless energy of hardscrabble newcomers. It is a rags-to-riches story and would be effective for projecting political authority based on both ancient grandeur and a people not to be messed with. Similar origin narratives are familiar to us from states and empires of the West. The Roman version combined the heroic Trojan War of the *Aeneid* with the half-wild Remus and Romulus suckling from the she-wolf; the version in the United States combines Greco-Roman ideals of governance, rendered in neoclassical styles on the National Mall in Washington, with the humble origins of the Pilgrims and western Pioneers. We will examine Spanish national mythos later in this section.

In addition to these more general appeals to the Tolteca-Chichimeca are origin narratives connecting specific tribes of people to Chicomoztoc, meaning the place of seven caves, each of which birthed a tribe. These narratives have a general order to them with non-Nahuatl speaking groups like the Michoaque emphasized as Chichimec and migrating first, Nahuatl-speaking groups from Aztlan migrating next, and, among these, the Mexica being the last.[8] Textual accounts and figurative depictions equate Chichimec identity with simpler dress and the use of the bow and arrow, whereas Toltec identity was associated with more elaborate attire and use of the more ancient *atlatl* spear-thrower. The introduction of the bow and arrow into the Americas is a much debated topic, with some consensus that it did not arrive to Mesoamerica until the late first millennium CE and may have not been pervasive until the early second millennium.[9] A major component of this debate revolves around the size of projectile points and whether they are consistent with having been attached to larger spears, intermediate darts (spears thrown by atlatl), or smaller arrows. Yet another line of evidence comes from pre-Hispanic art and imagery, and here it is noteworthy that few if any depictions of bow and arrow use exist until only a few centuries before Spanish arrival, when they are depicted in accounts of Mixtec conquests recorded as part of screenfold codices such as the Codex Zouche-Nuttall and the Codex Colombino. Warriors at Teotihuacan and the great Atlantean statues at Tula were depicted armed with atlatls and darts, making this the epitome of Toltec weaponry and the bow a less dignified, Chichimec introduction. The bow and arrow does figure in Aztec ethnic origin narratives, however, and had a foundational role in the demarcation of new cities. A ritual of establishing a new altepetl involved shooting arrows to the four cardinal directions from what was designated as the symbolic navel of a new urban center.

Colonial documents name a number of leaders of the Aztec migrations, but their historicity is often opaque, and the individuals range on a spectrum from patron deities to human rulers. Confusing matters is that individual rulers were often given the name of a deity, such as the case of the revered Toltec king Topiltzin Quetzalcoatl, who is said to have ruled Tollan in the ninth century and to have banned the practice of human sacrifice before being driven out by the divine sorcerer Tetzcatlipoca or the priestly faction associated with that deity.[10] Since the succession of Aztec rulers, referred to as speakers (*tlatoani*) but often glossed in English as king, did not follow rules of primogeniture, histories of ethnic origin stressed collective identity, rather than royal genealogies.[11] One exception to this pattern is the early Chichimec conqueror Xolotl, named after a deity (the twin of Quetzalcoatl) but treated as a human ruler and claimed by later rulers of Texcoco as a founding ancestor of their lineage. Other ethnic origin narratives mix themes of migrating people with the epic journeys of gods, such as the Mexica being led by Huitzilopochtli and the Tlaxcalteca being led by Camaxtli, both patron deities for these groups. These related but disparate narratives of ethnic origins and founding figures formed part of the micro-patriotism that Mesoamericans exhibited during the wars of conquest waged by Spanish and Native coalitions against other groups of Mesoamericans.

Pre-Hispanic art and architecture corroborate the early colonial texts about Mexica migration into the Basin of Mexico and their founding of the future imperial capital of Tenochtitlan. Tenochtitlan's Great Temple (named the *Huey Teocalli* or "Great God's House") was architecturally encoded as a sacred mountain with dualistic symbolism relating to agricultural subsistence and their migration narrative: the water-mountain of the storm god Tlaloc and the snake-mountain (Coatepec), where the Mexica patron deity Huitzilopochtli, associated with the sun and war, emerged from his mother (Earth) as an immaculate conception garbed in full battle gear in order to avenge her by defeating his sister (Coyolxauqui, representing the Moon) and many brothers (the stars).[12] The Mexica symbolized Coatepec as a stop on the route of migration, Mexica ethnogenesis, and broader cosmogenesis through the snake sculptures ringing the base of Tenochtitlan's Great Temple and by the large, circular sculpture of the disarticulated body of Coyolxauqui at the foot of the stairs (Figure 4.2). Dual temples were not present at Teotihuacan or Tula, but both cities featured two temples that stood out in scale, and conjoined temples with two staircases leading to independent shrines predated the Mexica at Aztec cities associated with earlier migration narratives, such as the founding of Tenayuca by Xolotl and his followers (Figure 4.3). A second important stopover in the Mexica migration narrative was at Toltec city Colhuacan, the source of the ethnonym Culhua, which the Mexica sometimes used to emphasize their partial Toltec ancestry.

Another image relating to the founding of Tenochtitlan is the eagle perched on a nopal cactus, carved in the back of a temple-shaped throne known as the Teocalli of Sacred War. The monument encapsulates the politico-religious ideology under the emperor Moctezuma II and commemorates

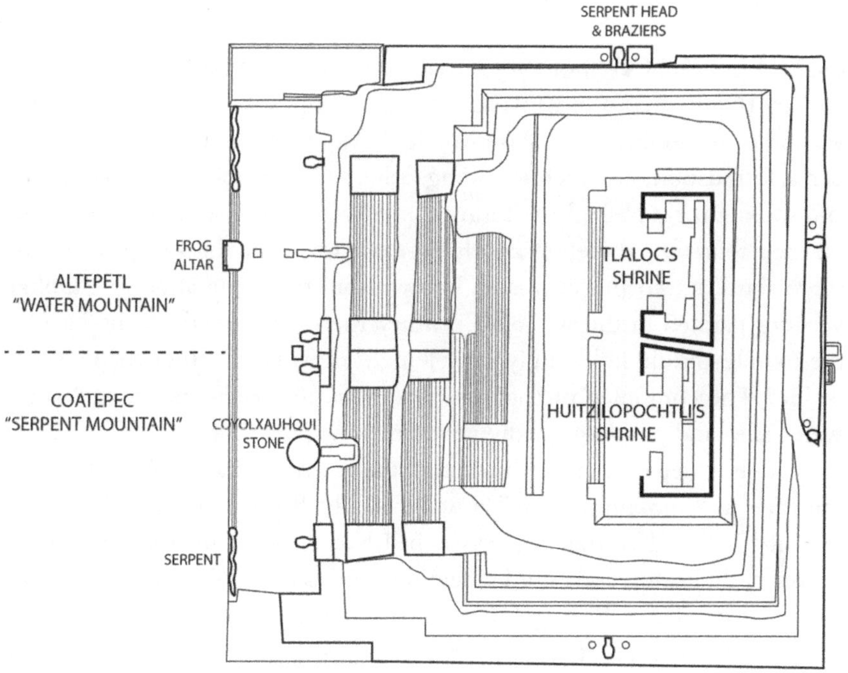

Figure 4.2. Plan of the Great Temple (Templo Mayor) at Tenochtitlan, showing dual symbolism associated with Tlaloc and Huitzilopochtli.
Based on López Luján (2006) and Matos (1988).

Figure 4.3. Dual temple at Tenayuca.
Photo by the author. Reproduction authorized by the Instituto Nacional de Antropología e Historia, Mexico.

the last New Fire Ceremony prior to the arrival of the Spaniards, undertaken in 1507 (Figure 4.4). On its back, a Mexica sculptor carved a pre-Hispanic version of the emblem today on Mexico's flag. This canonical omen of imperial foundation, in which founding fathers and possible co-rulers Tenoch and Mexitzin established the future capital where they witnessed the eagle on the cactus, was therefore clearly part of Mexica mythistory prior to the more abundant corpus of images known from the colonial period. Unlike versions painted in the sixteenth century, the relief carved on the back of the temple-throne holds a glyphic element in its beak, rather than a snake or bird. The conjoined pictographs read *teoatl-tlachinolli*—meaning "sacred water-fire" and standing for divinely sanctioned war.[13] Tetzcatlipoca is one of the deities depicted along the sides of the Teocalli of Sacred War. His name translates as "smoking mirror," an icon of which was often substituted for one of his feet. Through his crystal-ball-like obsidian mirror, he had the power of divination and could reflect the true essence of individuals—what led to Quetzalcoatl fleeing Tollan. Tetzcatlipoca was an important patron deity to the Acolhua of Texcoco and other Aztec groups that predated the ascent of the Mexica of Tenochtitlan. They appear to have also acknowledged the smoking mirror as a paramount deity earlier, but then supplanted him with Huitzilopochtli to mark their distinctiveness and greater authority within the Triple Alliance.[14] This elevation was clear by the time the sculpture was carved, since Moctezuma II commissioned the sculptor to depict Huitzilopochtli and himself flanking the Fifth Sun of creation front and center on the monument.

The Tenochca-Mexica memorialized Tenochtitlan's founding as having occurred in the year 2 House of the Aztec calendar, corresponding to 1325, but archaeological remains attest to the earlier occupation of the island on which the eventual metropolis grew. The political power in the Basin of Mexico at the time of the city's founding were the Tepanecs, who place their migration narratives earlier in time than the Mexica but after the arrival of Xolotl, and who also spoke Nahuatl as well as other languages. The city-states of Tenochtitlan (ethnically Mexica), Texcoco (ethnically Acolhua), and Tlacopan (ethnically Tepanec) formed the Triple Alliance (*Excan Tlahtoloyan*) to resist and then overthrow Tepanec rule, which was centered on the capital city of Azcapotzalco. As was the case in many historical instances of state formation, including Spanish efforts to conquer Mesoamerica, this process involved convincing "some of [Azcapotzalco's] allies that only the lord had changed, not that they had obtained independence."[15]

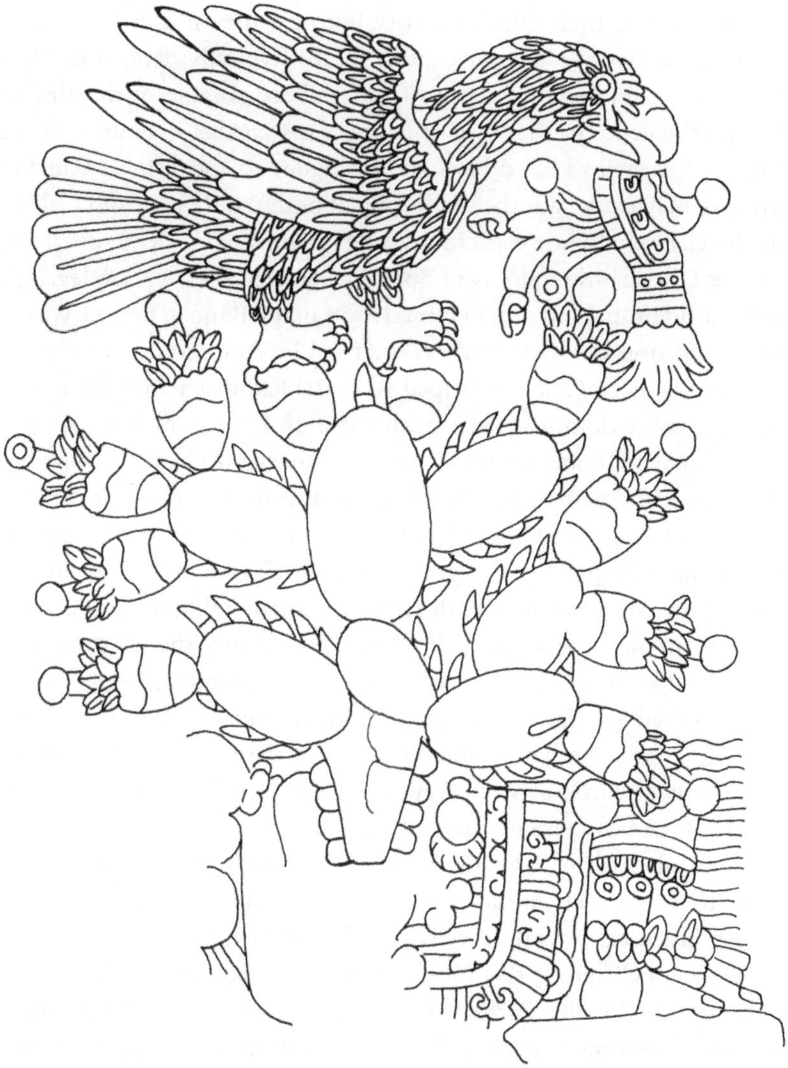

Figure 4.4. Eagle on cactus motif on back of the sculpted effigy temple and possible throne, the Teocalli of Sacred War.

Illustration by Pedro Cahuantzi Hernández.

Spaniards also looked to the deep past and to more recent migration southward in framing their ethnic identity, but here they invoked the centuries of conflict between Christians and Muslims (typically designated "Moors" at the time) and the slow creep of the military crusade of the *Reconquista* through the central and southern peninsula. A parallel in embracing a coupling of the civilized and barbaric, analogous to the Tolteca-Chichimeca narrative in Mexico, was the embracing of both the Roman and Celtiberian past. Reclaiming Rome was a motivating force for much of medieval Europe, and the Christian kingdoms of Spain recognized their urban, legal, philosophical, linguistic, and other cultural roots in the Roman period. We can see this connection clearly in authors such as Elio Antonio de Nebrija, whose 1492 grammar of Castilian helped to crystallize that particular peninsular language as the dominant one for the Spanish Empire. Nebrija drew inspiration from the Roman ruins of Augusta Emerita (Mérida) and the bridges and roads of Hispania constructed under Trajan. He called for reclamation of the Roman past, asking: "What is not transformed by the long passage of time and changed by old age? In human affairs what can survive? Here, where now Mérida stands with its name corrupted, once stood Augustus Caesar's famous city: Emerita."[16] Rome was clearly the ideal for political aspirants of early modern Spain and other former provinces. Nevertheless, newly unified Spaniards, and Castilians in particular, also sought distinction in framing how the hardscrabble peoples of the Meseta had resisted these same Romans, particularly by drawing on the narrative of the siege and mass suicide of the Celtiberian citadel of Numantia.[17] Entwining elements of the Roman and Celtic past, Castilians thereby conceived themselves not only as linked to the great civilization of yore, but also as indomitable, and possessing a fierce, historically documented drive for independence.

We saw in Chapter 3 that Old Castile was the heavily fortified land of the Cid and other knights in the tenth and eleventh centuries. Only later did it become a respectable core with an infrastructure of cathedral towns, monastic orders, and centers of learning like at Salamanca. As the unsettled frontier between established Christian and Islamic kingdoms moved southward from Castile to Extremadura and then to Andalucía—the three regions that contributed the most early conquistadors and colonists to the Americas—frontier culture became essential to framing the conquistadors' worldview. Conquests of Islamic Al-Andalus included continual use of small cavalry forces (*cabalgadas*) and territorial management of frontier zones gave rise to a new administrative post in the thirteenth-century Castilian bureaucracy under the reigns of Ferdinand III and Alfonso X: the *adelantado de la frontera.* This "advance-man" of the frontier was a military official charged with defending border zones, but *adelantados* were able to exploit their semi-autonomy in these under-administered frontier settings, as they would later in the Americas.[18] A variant on this post was the *adelantado del mar* intended by Alfonso X for maritime expeditions associated with the Crusades.

Conquistadors from Extremadura such as Francisco Pizarro and Pedro de Alvarado were granted the designation *adelantado* before and during their invasions of Peru and Guatemala, respectively, while the campaign led by Cortés was legally dubious on the grounds that Diego Velásquez, not he, possessed the title for Mexico. Extremadura retained the strong sense of frontier even as Spain emerged as a unified kingdom. Families of means sent their children to study in the established Castilian core at Salamanca, including the Cortés family, whose paternal roots were in the university town. Tensions between the colonial visions of *adelantados* and conquistadors from the frontier and theologians from the Castilian core would manifest themselves in fierce debates about Spain's American colonies during the early and mid-sixteenth century.

As in Mexico, narratives of Spain's unification also featured mythistorical leaders and patron saints. Pelayo of Austurias was invoked as the king who had begun the reconquest in 722 with the battle against the Muslims near Covadonga. Santiago was transformed from the benign apostle figure of earlier pilgrimages to a conquering icon as Moorslayer. He was said to have appeared on horseback and in battle gear to rally an outnumbered army of Christians versus their Muslim enemies in the ninth-century Battle of Clavijo, which historians doubt was an actual battle but nevertheless became part of fifteenth-century Spanish mythos.[19] In an act fraught with symbolism, Fernando III of Castile-León, upon conquering Islamic Córdoba in 1236, first raised the cross and his royal banners on top of the Great Mosque and next recovered the bells from the Cathedral of Santiago that had been taken by al-Mansur in 997.[20] Recovery of Santiago's bells had been a rallying point for the Christian armies of the *Reconquista*; by returning them to Compostela and taking the former Islamic capital, Fernando had closed one of its most significant chapters. Spaniards also had the model of chivalry personified in the *Amadís de Gaula*, which originated in the fourteenth century but became a best-seller following its mass dissemination with the printing press, in the late fifteenth and early sixteenth centuries. The legends of *Amadís*—involving chivalric romance, exotic travel, battles with monsters, and sorcery, all later parodied by Cervantes in *Don Quixote*—became part of the filter through which conquistadors such as Bernal Díaz del Castillo framed the invasion of Mexico.[21]

The allied campaign of Isabela and Ferdinand against Granada and its final Islamic kingdom on the peninsula united the two most consequential Christian kingdoms of the Spains, Castile and Aragón, under the banner of religion. In their triumphant entry into Granada, the Catholic Monarchs processed with actual banners bearing not only the crests of their kingdoms but also the cross and Santiago, while a herald shouted that a divine triad of God, Santiago, and the Virgin Mary had directed their victory.[22] The *Reconquista* was not initially framed in racial or ethnic terms, and the earlier period of coexistence between Christians, Jews, and Muslims extended into the fifteenth century, nearly two centuries after Jews had been expelled from England and a century after they had in France. The Jewish Sephardim experienced oscillating waves of tolerance and intolerance within the Christian and Muslim kingdoms of the late medieval period, and significant numbers of Muslims in Spain at the end of the fifteenth century were of Hispanic descent. The turn to ethno-nationalism culminated in the 1478 establishment in Seville of the Tribunal of the Inquisition and with the conflation of religious intolerance with the Castilian claim to purity of blood in being "old Christians."[23] In what were clearly kingdoms with hybrid cultural influences, exemplified in styles such as *mudéjar* architecture rendered in Islamic canons at Christian centers, this ethno-nationalism represented a call to put Castilian identity first.

In Mesoamerica, the Postclassic period of circa 1100–1450 was likewise a hybrid system with influences from different cultural regions. We can glean from colonial period documents that the ethnic Nahua (or Nahuatl-speaking) Aztecs viewed other ethnic groups of the empire and neighboring kingdoms in ethnocentric or pejorative terms. Yet there is no indication that purity of blood mattered in ethnic terms within the Aztec imperial system, only in qualification as nobility. Further, although religion was the major framing principle for Aztec warfare and imperial expansion, this was not with the intent of imposing a singular religious tradition on subject peoples. We will return to this intersection of ethnicity, politics, and religion later in this chapter, after first considering key social institutions.

Comparative Social Organization: Cities, Trade, and Politics

Cities were at the heart of political and economic organization of Aztec Mexico and early modern Spain, but they were part of different systems of imperial administration—the first classifiable as hegemonic or indirect control and the second classifiable as territorial or direct control. Cities of the fifteenth century were generally older in Spain than in Mexico, since in most cases their establishment dated to the Roman period and retained their physical linkages following the road network of Hispania.[24] Mesoamericans, on the other hand, had followed the tradition of terminating political-religious capitals such as in the planned burning of Teotihuacan. Only certain market and pilgrimage centers in Mesoamerica, Cholula among them, had more continual urban occupation. Nevertheless, institutions of governance during the fifteenth century and first half of the sixteenth century were much more peripatetic in Spain than they were in Mexico, moving through time with the *Reconquista* frontier, the unification of Christian kingdoms, and imperial strategies of administering territories in Europe and the Americas. Phillip II chose Madrid as the capital of the Spanish Empire some four decades after the fall of the Aztec Empire, in 1561, largely because of its central position within the peninsula. Prior to Madrid's elevation in status, the courts and royal palaces of Castile and then of the unified monarchies alternated between Burgos, Valladolid, Toledo, and Seville. Important administrative functions relating to the Americas, such as the Council of the Indies, moved between Valladolid and Seville, later transferring to Cádiz.

Aztec city-state capitals were more fixed on the landscape and did not shift with strategies of territorial administration. Among both cultures, however, cities were material manifestations of the political power of their rulers. Economic functions of domestic production and marketplace exchange followed, and were manipulated by rulers as part of the institutional economy—the financial underpinnings of political and religious institutions.[25] In all Aztec city-states, the institutional economy comprised bureaucratic positions such as tax collectors who mobilized resources produced by farmers and artisans as part of the domestic economy, but these varied based on the relative power of palaces and temples as part of the state institutions of any given city. In a few cases, such as the great market center of Tlatelolco and the market and pilgrimage center of Cholula, commercial development was structured through more mercantile means and an economy of ritual festivals. It was not as tightly tied to rulers as in Triple Alliance capitals such as Tenochtitlan and Texcoco. These expansionistic capital cities, together with Tlacopan as the junior partner of the Triple Alliance, received tax and tribute from provinces, manipulated and taxed marketplaces, and mobilized urban labor pools for public works and craft production centered at palaces and temples—a practice called *coatequitl*, or "snake/reciprocal work."

The Aztecs had two forms of collective landholding, the first associated with the estates of local lords (the *tecalli*) and the second with urban neighborhoods or corporate-kin groups in rural settings (the *calpolli* or *tlaxilacalli*). Aztec non-elites or commoners could also gain access to land through direct service to individual, lesser lords. A contrast between such dependents in Aztec society and medieval European serfs is that commoners in the Aztec system were not bound to the land and were free to leave their local lord for another deemed by them as a more desirable ruler.[26] The organization of corporate social groups such as the *calpolli* may have originated centuries earlier in the apartment compounds and neighborhoods of Teotihuacan, since the city's multifamily residences also featured communal spaces with central temples or shrines, shared occupational specializations, and internal stratification whereby commoners and elites belonged to the same corporate group.[27]

Some population estimates for Aztec cities can be gleaned by the writings of Cortés and other conquistadors, but these are often problematic when compared to estimates derived from systematic archaeological survey. Conquistador-derived estimates generally seem exaggerated, as they were not taking formal censuses and wanted to aggrandize their exploits, but in a few cases the archaeological estimate is higher.[28] Larger Aztec city-state capitals had inhabitants numbering in the 25,000–50,000 range, with the joint Mexica capital of Tenochtitlan-Tlatelolco being an exception at three to four times this figure. Population estimates for Tenochtitlan vary from a low of 60,000 to a high of one million inhabitants, which is better taken as the population of the entire Basin of Mexico in the Late Postclassic period. The Aztec-period Basin of Mexico underwent a population boom due in large part to the spread of the highly productive plots of drained agricultural field along the lakes, known as *chinampas*. A conservative estimate of 150,000 occupants for imperial Tenochtitlan would have made it over three times as large as Seville or Granada, which were then the largest in Spain. Tenochtitlan may have had as many as 200,000–250,000 residents, comparable to Paris or Constantinople in the lived experience of the conquistadors. The claim by Cortés that Tlaxcala was larger in population than Granada may have been accurate or only a slight exaggeration, as its high estimate is 48,000. Smaller tier Aztec city-state capitals had populations in the low tens of thousands, and provincial urban centers had populations more typically in the thousands.

Population estimates for Aztec and Castilian cities during the early sixteenth century are compiled in Table 4.1. It excludes other cities of the era in Mesoamerica and Iberia to focus on the core kingdoms, which were equally urbanized, but with Tenochtitlan representing a larger outlier. Since most Aztec cities were destroyed during the conquest and then reborn as colonial centers whose architecture covers pre-Hispanic buildings, it can be difficult to appreciate the early sixteenth-century built environment from the archaeological remains in Mexico today. Yet we know from excavations and architectural mapping at Aztec cities that were not covered with colonial

Table 4.1 Population Estimates of Castilian and Aztec Cities of the Late Fifteenth to Early Sixteenth Centuries

Castilian		**Aztec**	
City	Population	City	Population
Seville	45,000	Tenochtitlan-Tlatelolco	212,500
Granada	45,000	Cholula	40,000
Toledo	30,000	Tlaxcala	35,250
Córdoba	30,000	Texcoco	24,000
Valladolid	25,000	Huexotla	17,000
Jaén	20,000	Yautepec	15,000
Málaga	13,500	Calixtlahuaca	13,000
Burgos	12,500	Chalco	12,500
Salamanca	12,500	Otumba	11,000
Segovia	12,500	Cempoala	10,500
Average others	5,000	Average others	4,500

Note: Table does not include Aragónese cities such as Barcelona and Valencia or cities of comparable sizes in west Mexico (such as the Tarascan capital of Tzintzuntzan), the Maya region, or Oaxaca. A midpoint is given when authors provide low and high estimates and in instances when population is separated between urban core and adjacent sustaining area.

Sources: Coleman 2013: 15; Fargher et al. 2011b; Ladero Quesada 2018: 34–35; Plunket and Uruñuela 2018: 225; Smith 2005: Table 4, 2008: Table 6.1, 2017b: Table 14.1; Ossa et al. 2017: Table 1.

buildings, and even some that were, such as Tenochtitlan and Tlatelolco, that a typical urban plan featured a sacred precinct with buildings arranged around a plaza and the main temple on the eastern side. In central Mexico, the only place that can convey the former grandeur of Tenochtitlan is Teotihuacan, where a lack of colonial occupation over the largest monuments and the city's partial reconstruction by archaeologists allows the visitor to appreciate its scale and grid-like organization. In a few Aztec sites, such as Calixtlahuaca and Otumba, the population was relocated to a new colonial center, which had the result of preserving the pre-Hispanic remains and allowing archaeologists to understand a more typically sized city.[29] Others are largely covered over but retain some vestiges of monumental architecture.

Many Spanish cities of the period continued to evolve and grow in later periods, also making it difficult to envision their conquest-era cityscapes. The Spanish cities of Burgos, Segovia, and Toledo were continually occupied but eventually lost their administrative functions to Madrid, with the effect that their historical cores more strongly reflect urbanism of the era (Figure 4.5). Burgos is most closely associated with the Castilian monarchs and was at the vanguard of peninsular culture and commerce when its

Figure 4.5. Toledo, an important urban center in Roman, Visigothic, Islamic, and Christian times.
Photo by the author.

majestic Gothic cathedral was constructed during the thirteenth to fifteenth centuries.[30] Yet Toledo stands out as a religious and political center of the time of the Catholic Monarchs for a few reasons. Toledo's layered urban history—from Roman city to Visigothic capital to important Islamic center to a Christian center—made it a pastiche of cultures that alternated between periods of generally amicable coexistence among the three monotheistic faiths and periods of violence and forced conversions. Toledo was strongly fortified from its perch on the Taugus River, and the Catholic Monarchs designated the city's cathedral—long sacred ground as the location of a former Roman Christian temple, Visigothic church, and mosque—as the highest-ranking or Primate Cathedral within Spain. Many of the monarchs of the House of Trastámara of Castile-León, from which Isabela was descended, are buried in the cathedral. The queen had a special relationship with Gonzalo de Cisneros, who took the name Francisco after joining that order and rose to the top of the Spanish ecclesiastical hierarchy by becoming Archbishop of Toledo and personal confessor to the queen, followed by his promotion to Cardinal and Grand Inquisitor.[31] Cisneros was one of the most influential figures of the period and twice served as Regent of Castile. The first occasion followed the deaths of Isabela, in 1504, and Philip I, in 1506, who was Isabela and Ferdinand's son-in-law and had assumed power of the kingdom. The second occasion was during the transition between Ferdinand, who assumed the titles of regent of Castile and "lord of the Indes," and his grandson, the emperor Charles I. Cisneros financed the Spanish conquest of the Algerian city of Oran, which gave the empire a strategic foothold in the southern Mediterranean. He also founded the university at Alcalá de Henares—the origins of today's Complutense University in Madrid—and oversaw significant reforms to the Spanish Church and its role in the Americas.

An interconnected network of cities was essential to the commercialized Aztec and Castilian economies. Both relied on regular urban markets and periodic rural markets for the circulation of goods. A major difference between the two systems is that all goods in the Aztec economy were transported by human porters in the absence of domesticated pack animals. Trading canoes were used on the lakes of the Basin of Mexico and other highland basins, on the slower moving rivers of the lowlands, and along the coasts. Yet overland goods all moved on the backs of human porters (*tlamemes*), usually on tumplines and framed packs. The technologies of transport were dramatically different from those found in the Mediterranean world; transport by land and sea was cheaper and higher volume.[32]

The Aztec economy was monetized but did not use coinage, as had also been the case in the Phoenician trading colonies of southern Iberia—both examples of how commercial economies do not require the circulation of metal coins. In the Aztec case, a standardized system of equivalencies in commodities such as cacao beans and fine cotton cloth blankets, or "mantas" (*quachtli*), served as the monetary basis of commercial exchange. The medieval Spanish economy included coinage, with King Alfonso VII establishing a mint at Toledo in the late twelfth century, but also involved barter with equivalencies in products such as sheep and wheat—the last still using the Roman unit of measurement.[33] Examples of Aztec equivalencies recorded for a tribute role and two markets in the early colonial period are depicted in Table 4.2. The tabulations emphasize that although the Aztecs valued ornamental metals such as gold, they held colorful stones such as jade and turquoise, and colorful feathers from tropical birds in similar or greater regard.[34] The prioritization of metal wealth, developed through Mediterranean coinage-based economies, did not apply to the Aztecs or other Mesoamerican societies.

Trade was one of the means, along with the military and priesthood, by which individuals in Aztec and Castilian society could rise in social rank, though not in hereditary status. This included highly skilled craft producers and groups of long-distance merchants such as the *pochteca*, who had a symbiotic relationship with the empire. Since they traveled widely, these merchants provided valuable information on the provinces as well as enemy territories, through which they could typically move peacefully since trade superseded political boundaries. Along with imperial scouts and relay runners, long-distance merchants were the eyes and ears of the empire, whose armies provided them with protection. These seasoned merchants and porters established the network of communication routes that kept the imperial and market-based, interregional economies going. They also became critically important for the sequential conquests by the Spanish. The pochteca continued and elaborated upon linkages between the different resource zones of the highlands and lowlands established by earlier cultures such as the Olmecs, Teotihuacanos, and Toltecs. Trade entrepôts played a mediating role in this interregional economy at places such as the southern coast of the Gulf of Mexico, where Nahuatl speakers traded with those speaking Mayan or Mixe-Zoquean languages, and many residents were bilingual—such as Cortés' eventual translator and concubine, Malinche. The Aztec imperial economy of tax and tribute involved processes of negotiation between

Table 4.2 Examples of Monetary Equivalencies in Goods from Aztec Tribute and Market Systems

Tlaxcala Market
1 cacao bean = 5 chiles
1 large tomato = 1 cacao bean
1 prickly pear fruit = 1 cacao bean
1 tamale = 1 cacao bean
1 avocado = 3 cacao beans
1 turkey egg = 3 cacao beans
1 fish wrapped in maize husks = 3 cacao beans
1 small rabbit = 30 cacao beans
1 Castilian hen = 40 cacao beans
1 hare = 100 cacao beans
1 turkey hen = 100 cacao beans
1 turkey cock = 200 cacao beans
Tlatelolco Market
1 quachtli blanket = 100 cacao beans, 1 canoe full of potable water
30–40 quachtli blankets = 1 slave
Tlapa tribute roll
1 quachtli blanket = 10 gourd containers (tecomates)
1 quachtli blanket = 20 cakes of rubber
1 gold tablet = 45 quachtli blankets
1 warrior costume = 112.5 quachtli blankets
1 gourd of gold dust = 232 quachtli blankets

Sources for equivalencies: Tlaxcala market (Anderson et al. 1976: 209–213); Tlatelolco market (Sahagún Book 9, Ch. 10 [Anderson and Dibble 1959: 45–49]); Tlapa tribute roll (Gutiérrez 2013: Table 6.3).

central authorities, provincial tax collectors (*calpixque*), and local inhabitants, with the possibility of significant profiteering from the bureaucratic posts of provincial administration and tax collection.[35]

The fundamental unit of political organization in Aztec Mexico was the *altepetl* or city-state, a polity that hinged on the establishment of hegemony of a noble lord and noble council over free and enslaved commoners. Nobles (*pilli*) and commoners (*macehualli*) were distinguished by birth, but between these hereditary titles was a spectrum of variability in power and wealth, including what may be deemed a "middle class" of fine-craft artisans, long-distance merchants, and officials with governmental, military, or ritual charges.[36] The head of each noble lineage was a lord (*teuctli*), and the ruler or "speaker" (*tlatoani*) was the head of the most powerful lineage or the one elected by a noble council. Aztec nobles were not exempt from paying taxes, but could adorn themselves with certain sumptuary goods prohibited to commoners and noble men could practice polygyny, a practice forbidden to non-elites.[37] Within the system of Aztec polygyny, the practice of noble men taking non-elite wives (hypergamy) presented a means of social mobility: unlike most kinship systems in medieval Europe, such offspring were considered of noble rank and could assume positions of rulership. Other than these practices, the class structures of Aztec Mexico and medieval Europe were not so divergent, and the concordance allowed for successful mixed marriages between Spaniards and Aztecs or other Mesoamericans during the colonial period, once polygamy was abolished. Political organization was quite different, however, in the nationalizing and territorial character of late fifteenth to early sixteenth-century Spain, which contrasted significantly with the micro-patriotism and hegemonic character of Mesoamerican polities.

Like most state societies, protection was one of the benefits that Aztec rulers could claim as a public good to members of the political community, including its long-distance merchants within the empire or beyond its dominion. In cities of the Basin of Mexico, benefits also included urban infrastructure. Tenochtitlan had two aqueducts that brought fresh water into the city—one from the west, originating at Chapultepec, and another to the south from Coyoacan—as well as a system of eastern dikes to keep floodwaters at bay. Urban marketplaces were staffed with officials who oversaw fair trade, and cities and towns had a system of compulsory education with two tiers based on status, reviewed later this chapter. Finally, priests of the Aztec state presented religion as a public good in repaying debts to the gods and ensuring that time itself kept going. The entanglement of public good and state religion is acutely and tragically registered by events of the extreme drought that the inhabitants of the Basin of Mexico faced in the year 1454 (1 Rabbit in the Aztec calendar), an event that caused massive famine. The Great Speaker of Tenochtitlan, Moctezuma Ilhuicamina (or Moctezuma I), opened the city's storehouses to distribute food to his people but also oversaw the sacrifice of children at the Great Temple, as they were seen as the most appropriate offering in a dire time to Tlaloc, the god of rain.[38]

For a trans-Atlantic comparison of the Aztec Empire, we can look to certain structural similarities between it and Republican Rome, when the latter was expanding onto the Iberian peninsula and elsewhere.[39] In both cases, imperial expansion was preceded by a network of highly commercialized city-states and strong interregional interaction spheres that saw the brisk exchange of goods and styles—called the Mixteca-Puebla or international style in Mesoamerica and the Hellenistic era in the Mediterranean. The tempo of Roman expansion was slower than for the Aztec Triple Alliance, which was not even a century old by the time of the Spanish invasion, and this may have resulted in the stronger territorial integration of provinces under Rome, whereas the still developing Aztec system involved more indirect mechanisms of control. Another difference is in the stronger notion of citizenship and republican governance in early Rome compared to the Aztec Empire, though a more participatory system characterized the Triple Alliance rivals of Tlaxcala.

The unifying spirit of early modern Spain followed the historical trajectory of the *Reconquista* and the consolidation of its largest kingdoms. Castile-León was by far the largest and most active state actor in this process. Its estimated population of 4.5 million during the fourteenth to fifteenth centuries constituted approximately two-thirds to three-quarters of the entire peninsula and was five times larger than Aragón's.[40] Yet the Crown of Aragón's mercantile activities in the Mediterranean brought it great wealth. Since the large majority of the early colonists to the Americas came from three regions of Spain—Old Castile, Andalucía, and Extremadura—but a disproportionate number of early conquistadors came from the last, it is often assumed that life in Extremadura was harsher and pushed these men to belligerence. This explanation has merit when framed in terms of historical development and cultural institutions, but not in terms of environment and agricultural productivity. Extremadura, like many other parts of Spain, can have severe summer droughts; yet it receives more annual precipitation than the plains of the Meseta and is intermediate between Old Castile and the Guadalquivir region of Andalucía. With roughly 16–22 inches (400–550 mm) of rainfall, all three areas receive significantly less than central Mexico or most any part of Mesoamerica, but they all had productive farming and livestock that supported millennia of urbanism. The landscape of Guadiana Valley between Cortés' hometown of Medellín and Mérida supported dense populations throughout the Iron Age and Roman period,[41] and we saw in Chapter 3 that Emerita Augusta was a significant urban center during the Roman period that transitioned into the Visigothic period. Through the centuries of Islamic rule and the *Reconquista*, however, it became more of a frontier between the Christian core in Castile and Muslim core in Andalucía. Medieval urban development in these areas therefore outpaced Extremadura's.

Spanish political centralization and the evolution from territorial "reconquest" and administration on the Iberian peninsula to trans-Atlantic conquest lasted centuries, culminating in the fifteenth century. Decades before the Catholic Monarchs, the kingdoms of Castile and Aragón had already become more entwined when Fernando I—known as "de Antequera" for his role in the conquest of that city, which guarded the border to Granada—served as regent of Castile and was elected king in 1412 by the joint parliaments of Aragón, Valencia, and Catalonia (called the Corts and equivalent to the Castilian Cortes).[42] An interesting structural distinction exists between the two kingdoms and finds a parallel in Mesoamerica: the Aragonese Corts had considerably more of a check on dynastic control than was the case in Castile, but in this more pluralistic system of governance women were barred from rulership. Women could rule in more dynastically oriented Castile, even though succession was male-preference primogeniture. This pattern of political organization also characterized Mesoamerican kingdoms. Those that were more focused on dynastic bloodlines, such as the Classic period Maya or Postclassic period Mixtecs, had women rulers, whereas those with noble councils who elected rulers, such as the Mexica, elected only men.[43] Succession to the high office of Great Speaker typically passed among brothers or following the patriline. For instance, following the death of Moctezuma Ilhiacamina (also known as Moctezuma I or "the elder") in 1469 the noble council of Tenochtitlan elected as Great Speaker his three sons in succession—Axayacatl (1469–1481), Tizoc (1481–1486), and Ahuitzotl (1486–1502)—before turning to the son of Axayacatl, Moctezuma Xocoyotzin ("the younger"), who wore the turquoise diadem as paramount ruler when the Spanish arrived. The Tenochca also had a second in command whose title was gendered female, the Cihuacoatl ("Snake Woman"), but was filled by men from the noble lines connected to Tenochtitlan and Texcoco.

A dynastic push for more centralized control in Castile, and then by the linked kingdoms of the Catholic Monarchs, included the installation of *corregidores* who co-opted power from town councils and parliaments that previously had greater autonomy. This administrative office would later be extended to colonial governance of the Americas. Other *Reconquista* era and early modern institutions that would become important to colonial administration were the frontier military governor *adelantado* and the land and labor grants known as the *repartamiento* and *encomienda*. During the *Reconquista*, repartamientos granted Christian settlers land and property that were formerly owned by Muslims. Property could include industrial buildings such as mills, which are heavily represented in documentary sources because royal surveyors took note of them for purposes of taxation.[44] The terms later became differentiated, so that the repartamiento indicated grants of only labor, whereas the encomienda granted land plus labor. These political-economic institutions were grounded in the spoils of war and the incentives of gaining booty, and as a result required further conquests for growth. Once Castilian forces reached the natural sea boundaries of the peninsula, further conquests and the implementation of these *Reconquista* institutions and offices were transferred for administering its initial Atlantic colonies in the Canary Islands, and were then exported across the ocean to the Caribbean.

Initial Spanish conquests into the Atlantic began in the early fifteenth century with the Canary Islands, located west of Morocco. Carthaginian, Roman, Arab, and Genoese expeditions had visited the archipelago in the millennia prior, but the indigenous population, who possess distant links to mainland Berbers and are grouped by the ethnonym Guanches, had never been colonized. The process of colonization first began with mid- to late fourteenth-century missionaries from the island of Majorca under the Crown of Aragón. Norman and French nobles and navigators, sailing from Seville, Cádiz, and other southern Andalusian ports, followed by establishing footholds on the smaller islands of the archipelago in the early fifteenth century, and were primarily interested in acquiring slaves and gold from the coast of west Africa.[45] Profits from these privately financed ventures piqued the interest of, and invited conflict with, both the Castilian and Portuguese Crowns, culminating in a war between the two kingdoms in the 1470s. A treaty would give Castile control over future colonization of the larger islands of the archipelago as a separate kingdom subordinate to the Crown, while the Portuguese held sovereignty over the Azores, Madeira, and Cape Verde Islands. These island conquests represent a prolongation of the *Reconquista* beyond the peninsula and the first Atlantic stepping-stones in Spanish and Portuguese colonization of the Americas.[46] Sugarcane production, introduced to southern Spain by the Arabs, became the major plantation economy of the Canaries until the mid-sixteenth century, when the higher yields from the plantation system that was transposed to the Caribbean made the Canary industry unprofitable.

Forms of forced servitude had deep histories on both sides of the Atlantic, and during the fifteenth and sixteenth centuries European notions of slavery varied by nation and over time.[47] Prior to this period, enslavement was generally a temporary status, brought about by warfare and the taking of prisoners or wealth inequality and debt relations. In the Postclassic Mesoamerican world, slaves were often prisoners of war or the children of impoverished families who sold them into servitude. Men and boys typically served as burden bearers for merchants or nobles, and women and girls served as domestic servants and/or concubines. The latter was the case of Malinche, the translator and concubine of Cortés, whom we will meet in the chapter to follow.[48] The historical tragedy that was the trans-Atlantic slave trade involved new maritime technologies that allowed European colonial powers to take slaves thousands of miles from their homelands and, separated by an ocean, lock them into a permanently lower status. The trans-Atlantic system also increased the racialization of slavery, which became the means by which Europeans increasingly justified lifelong enslavement, particularly of Africans.

Technologies of Imperialism

A range of technologies provided the physical means of the military conquests and territorial expansion of Iberian colonial enterprises. It is worth taking a brief detour here to review them in relation to those that were employed in Mesoamerica at the same time. We often think of Europe's medieval period as a time of regression or stasis. Some inventions of the Classical Mediterranean were indeed forgotten, but medieval Europeans made significant advances in harnessing the energy of animals, wind, and water, which made for improved transportation and production that was not initially as reliant on slave labor as had been the case in the Classical Mediterranean world.[49]

European navigation improved greatly with the invention of the more mobile and precise stern-rudder in the twelfth century. Under Islamic rule, the Strait of Gibraltar region had been more oriented to the Mediterranean and coastal Atlantic fringe, as it relied on galleys not suited for distant ocean voyages on the Atlantic. Iberians of the fourteenth and fifteenth centuries developed hybrid ships that took advantage of the peninsular hinge between maritime worlds to combine traditions from the Mediterranean and northwest Atlantic.[50] This included the caravel (*carabela* in Spanish), which combined Mediterranean-style triangular or "lateen" rigging with Atlantic-style square rigging and became the primary ship of Portuguese and then Spanish navigation on the Atlantic. Other new ships were the larger carrack (*carraca*) and *nao*, whose more spacious hulls were suited for transporting greater cargo, and the smaller brigantine, which had one or two masts as well as oars, making it suited for shallow water. All these hybrid vessels featured large and strong hulls built frame first, a substantial keel running through its center, and the combination of square-rigged sails for speed with the maneuverability of lateen sails. Shipbuilders constructed increasingly larger vessels as the sixteenth century progressed, and it was only later in the century that the Spanish galleon became the primary cargo ship. European sailors made use of the dry compass by the twelfth century, but early modern Spain and Portugal were the initial beneficiaries from refinements to the astrolabe introduced centuries earlier to the peninsula by the Arabs—a legacy that allowed for more precise navigation by charting the declination of the sun or other celestial bodies at the meridian.[51]

By the mid-fifteenth century, cartographers depicted the eastern Atlantic coastlines and island archipelagos such as the Canaries and Azores with increasing accuracy. Even though the ancient Greeks and many educated Europeans of Isidore of Seville's day had known the world was a globe, it had now become widely accepted and debates centered more on how large it was at its circumference and whether or not another continent, the Antipodes, existed in the Ocean between Europe and Asia.[52] Christopher Columbus, after appealing for his plan to lead an expedition westward to the courts of Portugal, England, and France, found willing sponsors with Spain's Catholic Monarchs, who drew up a contract designating Columbus an Admiral of the Indies and Viceroy of Castile with rights to one-tenth of the profits of his expedition. Spain's pivotal year of 1492 continued with Columbus' first journey: departing on August 3 from Palos de la Frontera to the Canaries, and then onward to reach first the Bahamas (an island called Guanahaní by its Taíno inhabitants, rechristened San Salvador by Columbus), continuing to Cuba, and disembarking at Santo Domingo on Hispaniola (today's Dominican Republic and Haiti) on December 6.

Juan de la Cosa accompanied Columbus on his first voyages and suffered the ignominy of running the Santa Maria, a ship de la Cosa owned, aground and abandoning it during the first voyage. He nevertheless redeemed himself in the annals of history by producing the first European map to depict the Americas (Plate 4a). De la Cosa completed his *mappa mundi* in 1500 based on his own knowledge of the Caribbean and northern coast of South America, combined with the accounts of other navigators, such as John Cabot for eastern North America. He likely created his map for Juan Rodríguez de Fonseca, who was sequentially bishop of the diocese of Badajoz, Cordoba, Palencia, and Burgos. Fonseca was a close advisor of Queen Isabela, who entrusted him with administering early expeditions to the Indies, whereas Fonseca and Cisneros alternated in their influence over the Indies under the reign of King Ferdinand.[53] De la Cosa likely had in mind a broader intended audience for his map of not only Fonseca, but also the Catholic Monarchs themselves. His map is detailed in areas where he possessed accurate information (including depicting Cuba as an island, not the mainland that Columbus believed) and imaginatively Eden-like in areas of the Americas where he did not. The map also has a very telling dual orientation. Whereas medieval maps in the T-O tradition following Isidore of Seville oriented East as up, navigational maps after the advent of the compass had reoriented to our familiar perspective with North on top. De la Cosa illustrated much of the detail on the map oriented northward but designed it to be hung with West up, as if to draw the gaze of his intended audience of superiors westward. Text marking the Atlantic Ocean, a depiction of the Virgin and Child within a compass rosette, and an image at the top depicting St. Christopher—possibly an allusion to Columbus, or more generally representing the saint of travelers—are all oriented to West, as if making an appeal to his superiors to Christianize the newly discovered world across the ocean.

Another interesting feature of the map is that de la Cosa set the central meridian to what we would today designate 46°30′ W of the meridian set to Greenwich, England. De la Cosa's meridian represents the line of demarcation negotiated by Spain and Portugal in the Treaty of Tordesillas, made in 1494 in that town of Castile. The treaty modified the line of demarcation established a year earlier by Pope Alexander VI, whom the Portuguese contended had established the line favorably to his native Spain, to be 370 leagues (1,185 miles) rather than 100 leagues west of Cape Verde. The Treaty of Tordesillas was therefore a momentous event in world geopolitics, as it had the effect of establishing the future American colonial dominions of the Iberian kingdoms and revising the papal bull to grant land to Portugal that would become Brazil.

Boat technologies of the Precolumbian Americas did not include ships capable of open-ocean crossings. Some of the more sophisticated vessels were made of bundled reeds on the Pacific coast of South America, plank boats on the coast of California, and the ingenious kayak of the Arctic.[54]

Mesoamerican vessels were exclusively logboats and log canoes that were confined to coastal or riverine travel, but Columbus noted some off the coasts of Yucatan and Honduras, likely paddled by Mayas or Zoques, which he judged as longer than any he knew from the Old World. Later, the conquistador Bernal Díaz del Castillo judged canoes off the coast of Yucatan as capable of holding 40–50 people. In the Aztec core, the lakes of the Basin of Mexico were full of dugout canoes. The Nahuatl term for these is *acalli* ("water-house"), and they were maneuvered closer to land through a gridded system of major canals and smaller passages through fields.[55] Inhabitants of the Basin of Mexico used smaller canoes among the canals, so that a single individual could maneuver them by pushing off the shallow lake bottom, as is still done today in the relic waterways of Lake Xochimilco. Larger examples could reach 50 feet in length and be propelled by 20 oarsmen to carry heavier goods such as lumber, stone, or many passengers. The Aztecs also used canoes for naval battles along the lakes.[56]

As for military technologies, key advances in Europe involving cavalry and artillery bracket the *Reconquista* era. During its inception in the eighth century, the stirrup gave northern European armies a mounted shock force with the estimated equivalence of 10 foot soldiers to every rider in battle, a calculus that spread southward to the Spanish kingdoms. Cavalry were essential to the sustained incursions of Christian armies on the Emirate of Granada, where immediate payoffs to horsemen came in the form of captured herds of cattle, and later by negotiating labor and land allocations through the encomienda.[57] The incentives to Spanish soldiers of war booty and the involvement of large domesticated animals were major contrasts to how Mesoamericans waged war. By the time of the final assault on Granada, gunpowder was used in battle, though even in the time of the Spanish-Mexica war a harquebus could only fire once every 10 minutes, making them more of a psychological than tactical advantage.

The conquistadors were something between entrepreneurs and mercenaries, not formal soldiers. Their arms and attire reflected a capricious mix of what was available at the time in Iberia, a simplified assemblage relative to formal armies used for fighting in Europe under the Spanish Crown.[58] Conquistadors used little to no armor, and what they did wear tended to be iron breastplates and an occasional iron helmet or shield, but these were more typically made from cheaper materials, such as fabric hats and caps or wooden and leather shields. They did carry swords, which were often made from the famously hard Toledo steel. These were far more durable and destructive than Aztec broadswords lined with obsidian blades (the *machuahuitl*), which were initially very sharp but would dull quickly and, following that, essentially be akin to hitting a foe with a cricket paddle.[59] Steel also tipped Spanish lances, pikes, crossbow bolts, and arrows, but would need to be recycled after battle or replaced with Mexican obsidian spear and projectile tips. During the wars of conquest, many Spaniards switched to Native cotton-quilted armor, since it provided better maneuverability while still offering defense from obsidian-tipped projectiles.

The Spanish used battlefield formations that were adapted to Iberia's mountainous terrain: heavy on infantry and supplemented by light cavalry and the artillery of crossbows and harquebuses. Historically, the most common battlefield progression around the globe has involved three sequential stages: first, volleys of missiles from a distance; second, close combat using shock weapons; and finally, pursuit of captives once the battle turned decisively for one side.[60] In early modern Europe, this sequence often involved artillery of cannons or muskets (heavier harquebuses) and volleys with bows and crossbows, close shock combat using swords and bayonets, and pursuit with cavalry. In Postclassic Mesoamerica, in contrast, it would involve volleys with bow, atlatl, or slings; a shock stage with stone-tipped broadswords and lances, wooden clubs, or stone knives; and pursuit on foot.[61] This last stage was critical since Mesoamerican warfare, though also aimed at conquest or political dominance, was closely entwined with a religious system that valued human sacrifice as the ultimate offering to the gods. The effect of this on battlefield tactics was that at the close-combat stage, warriors would often use striking blows to the legs to cripple but not kill an opponent, so that they could be taken captive. Aztec warfare was strongly meritocratic and warriors rose in rank according to the number of captives they took back alive, not those killed on the field of battle. These captives could be destined for sacrifice or to serve as laborers or, if elite, for extracting ransom. This meritocratic system provided the collective good of incentivizing bravery in battle but also made battlefield tactics highly individualized, and less cooperative, as warriors on the same side essentially competed for captives.[62]

Another significant material difference in warfare between early modern Spain and Aztec Mexico was in fortifications, which were massive for European powers but all but absent for Mesoamerican states. Spain's most powerful kingdom, Castile, encapsulates much of this history, since it took its name from its frontier castles built during the *Reconquista*, and the term derives from the Latin *castellum*, the derivative of *castrum* ("fort"), which appear all over the peninsula as testaments to the Roman and pre-Roman past. In contrast, fortified towns did not dot the Mesoamerican landscape, as the technologies and associated tactics of warfare were different.[63] The extended sieges of towns that led the Romans, Muslims, and Christians of Iberia to build heavy fortifications and ensure intramural water sources, such as *aljibe* cisterns constructed during Islamic rule and continued after the Christian *Reconquista*, did not characterize Mesoamerican warfare and urban planning.

Military organization intersected with religion in both societies, such as in the religiously based military orders that bestowed higher status on their members. The major Castilian military orders were Santiago, Calatrava, and Alcántara. Since non-military religious orders were monastic organizations tied to the Holy See, they enjoyed relative political autonomy from the Crown. Through the strengthening of the military orders under the Catholic Monarchs and Charles V, these social and religious institutions were brought more closely under the domain of the state, along with their powers to motivate fealty and create patron-client bonds to the Crown among the nobility.[64] Of the three orders, Santiago's became the most powerful and prestigious of early modern Spain. It had diverse roots in Old Castile and Galicia, associated with the pilgrimage route to Santiago reviewed in the previous chapter, but also in the Extremaduran city of Cáceres, which prided itself on having a high proportion of resident knights of the order. From that perch, the Order of Santiago was integral in overseeing territories of the central Guadiana Valley, including Mérida and Cortés's hometown of Medellín.[65]

In the Aztec system of warfare, warriors could rise in military rank through the number of captives taken in battle, many of whom were destined for sacrifice in the Sacred Precinct of Tenochtitlan. Higher military rank brought with it the ability to wear certain vestments and adornments, or to use certain arms or shield types, but did not result in higher social rank, such as a commoner moving to noble status. For instance, upon taking their first captive in battle, Aztec warriors could wear cotton rather than maguey-fiber garments; with three or more, they took on leadership roles on the battlefield and exhibited their elevated status through increasingly elaborate garments and shields woven with the feathers of exotic birds.[66] Warriors were able to rise in social rank through induction into two military orders: the Eagle and Jaguar knights. Both orders drew power through their association with these apex predators of the Mesoamerican world and with their associations with the sun: the diurnal eagle with the day sun high in the sky and the nocturnal jaguar with the night sun as it traveled through the underworld. The Eagle knights had a specially designated lodge in one or more of the palaces at Tenochtitlan, known only from colonial period texts. They were also likely part of the ritual complex excavated at the foot of Tenochtitlan's Great Temple that was furbished with stone benches decorated with sculpted friezes rendered in a neo-Toltec style, based on models from Tula (Figure 4.6).[67] This purposeful archaism linked the city's military to deep history in central Mexico, but they likely had deeper roots, as is clear from the murals of warriors garbed as eagles and jaguars at Cacaxtla and earlier still at Teotihuacan. Analysis of chemical residues from the floors of the complex recovered traces of blood that may have been offered along with incense and foods.

A remarkable architectural complex relating to the knights is perched still today at the mountain sanctuary site of Malinalco, located 70 miles (115 km)

Figure 4.6. Benches in neo-Toltec style drawing on early styles seen at Tula from the House of the Eagles next to Tenochtitlan's Great Temple with terracotta statues of (left) Miclantecuhtli, Lord of the Underworld, and (right) Eagle knight. Museo del Templo Mayor.

Photo by the author. Reproduction authorized by the Instituto Nacional de Antropología e Historia, Mexico.

Figure 4.7. Eagle House shrine carved from cliff-face at Malinalco.
Photo by the author. Reproduction authorized by the Instituto Nacional de Antropología e Historia, Mexico.

from the capital. The main shrine at Malinalco, called the Cuauhcalli ("Eagle House"), was fashioned as one monumental sculpture by carving into the living rock of the mountainside (Figure 4.7), while an adjacent structure once featured murals depicting warriors, which have now deteriorated. Aztec priests may have inaugurated Eagle and Jaguar knights at Malinalco, and they and/or others of noble status may have engaged in sacrificial rituals relating to sacred warfare and the regeneration of the cosmos.[68] On both sides of the Atlantic, military orders demonstrate one way in which the sociopolitical dynamics and material culture of conquest fused with particular systems of religion and philosophical worldview. These legitimated and perpetuated the existing order through socialization of new generations of Aztecs and Spaniards, but also provided opportunities to challenge political hierarchies and colonial endeavors throughout Mexico and Spain.

Religion and Philosophy

Within the heavily religious worldviews of the Aztecs and Spaniards of the early sixteenth century are both points of remarkable overlap and strong divergence. The military orders were one example of how religion imbued notions of warfare and conquest in both societies; the patron deities or saints that were petitioned for divine assistance in battle are another. During the *Reconquista* Castilians called on Santiago for such assistance, whereas the Mexica called on Huitzilopochtli, their patron deity linked with sacred warfare, the sun, and the ancestral migration from Aztlan. Other Aztec groups called on different patron deities, often associated with the ethnic migration narratives from this same mythistorical place.

Spain developed its empire under the Catholic Monarchs by drawing on the mythology of the Christian reconquest, mixed with a neo-Roman vision of a universal empire.[69] Spaniards celebrated the historic spiritual and political victory of the *Reconquista* in a new form of public spectacle, the dance of *Moros y Cristianos*, which was rare before 1492 but proliferated afterward as a way of affirming Christian identity.[70] People still hold multiday festivals of this sort today in Spain and its former colonies. One of the largest is at Valencia, the city indelibly linked to the mythistory of El Cid. *Moros y Cristianos* dances involve elaborate dress and ceremonial weapons set to music with a narrative that centers on the taking of a city by Islamic forces and its retaking by Christians. The pageant, of course, minimizes the actual religiously motivated violence of the period. Although Christian inquisitions had started in thirteenth-century France, the fervor with which Jews and Muslims were killed under the Catholic Monarchs and their grand inquisitor, the Dominican Tomás de Torquemada, has rightfully earned the Spanish Inquisition its infamy as one of the more terrible chapters in human history.[71] The first *auto-da-fé* ("act of faith") of the Spanish Inquisition was held in Seville in 1481, and between then and the expulsion of the Jews in 1492 some 2,000 individuals were executed and hundreds of thousands were tried and subjected to some form of penance.

A common comparison drawn regarding religious violence in both societies is one between the Spanish *auto-da-fé* and Aztec human sacrifice. In the *auto-da-fé*, individuals were charged with heresy and were often subjected to public humiliation or torture in the main plaza of a city, with the most severe punishment being the slow and painful death by burning at the stake outside of the city walls. In Aztec human sacrifice, which increased in frequency under the Tenochca-Mexica and is best known from them, victims were most often war captives who had been taken alive in battle to be marched up steps of a temple and killed through heart extraction—an almost instantaneous death.[72] Any sort of debate on this issue is unavoidably tied to divergent ideas on when killing is considered "just," including what physical settings and for what reasons taking of human life is justified. Commonly employed linguistic conventions bias the discussion by having one society "fighting wars" and "executing prisoners" while another conducts "human sacrifice" to "idols." Scholars who study these issues practice cultural relativism as a heuristic tool for better understanding the behavior of another culture or from centuries ago, but that does not mean we forgo a moral compass for life in the present. In order to understand any complex issue, such as violence in past societies, we need the complete cultural and historical context to figure out how different parts of a society fit together. In the case of Aztec human sacrifice, we cannot divorce the issue from the technologies and practices of warfare reviewed earlier, since the large majority of victims were captured in battle and sacrificed to the gods, rather than being killed on the field of battle. Not all were, however, and Mesoamerican societies also sacrificed women and children, but in much lower numbers than battle-age men. Neither was it all militaristic state theater; the Aztecs and other groups clearly believed in the efficacy of the practice as a debt payment to divine forces that recharged their energies and kept the Fifth Sun of creation in motion (Figure 4.8).

When people refer to Aztec sacrifice as a specific cultural practice, what they are mostly thinking of are Mexica rituals at the imperial capital of Tenochtitlan. Mesoamericans practiced human sacrifice throughout the pre-Hispanic sequence, beginning even before they settled into farming villages, but the scale was much lower than the thousands sacrificed annually at Tenochtitlan's Sacred Precinct. Inhabitants of rural and smaller urban centers of the Aztec world also engaged in human sacrifice on a greatly reduced scale, and public rituals tended to emphasize shared interests in ensuring agricultural fertility and keeping the cosmic order going.[73] As an imperial strategy, the higher scale of sacrifice undertaken at Tenochtitlan signaled the city's military prowess. Yet even the imperial version of Aztec religion did not impose an absolutist worldview, as did the Spanish Inquisition to the other monotheistic faiths and then to colonized peoples of the Americas. Aztec priests did not proselytize, and the religious system was incorporative rather than absolutist. A good illustration of this outlook is the temple called the *coateocalli* (literally "snake god's house," with the snake a metaphor for reciprocal back-and-forth). Located in Tenochtitlan's Sacred Precinct to the northwest of the Great Temple, it was used to house the images of the gods of conquered peoples. These deities were treated with respect and incorporated into the Aztec system, thus greatly expanding the pantheon

Figure 4.8. Center of Aztec Sun Stone from Tenochtitlan. Museo Nacional de Antropología.

Photo by the author. Reproduction authorized by the Instituto Nacional de Antropología e Historia, Mexico.

relative to earlier religions in Mexico. That would end with the conquest, as Mexican Catholicism of the early colonial period approached religion in absolutist terms.

Pilgrimage sites were vital parts of the sacred landscapes of both societies, including most notably Santiago de Compostela in Spain and Cholula's temple of Quetzalcoatl in Mexico. Pilgrims did not arrive to the monastery of the Virgin of Guadalupe in anything like the numbers they did for Santiago, but it was a favorite destination for Castilian monarchs following its founding in 1340 and was patronized heavily by Queen Isabela, greatly increasing the monastery's renown (Figure 4.9).[74] The Guadalupe monastery and cult of the Virgin provide more examples of Spain's deeply layered history. The image of the Virgin, carved from cedar and thus giving her a dark complexion, is believed to have been made in Roman Hispania. Christians fleeing the Muslims from Seville along the Ruta de la Plata took her to Guadalupe where, it is said, they hid the image in a forest until a

Figure 4.9. Monastery to Virgin of Guadalupe in Extremadura, Spain. Baptismal font is the one used by Columbus to baptize Taínos he brought from the Caribbean. Photo by the author.

shepherd found it centuries later. The monastery's *mudéjar* architecture mixes Christian and Islamic aesthetics. Columbus became very devoted to the Virgin of Guadalupe after praying to her during a storm that raged against his fleet. He returned in 1496 with Natives of the Caribbean to have them baptized in the font that is now in the main plaza in front of the monastery. The most sacred site in Extremadura, Guadalupe also had a major impact on Cortés and other conquistadors. She was adored for her protection of armies who fought infidels and invoked in converting them to Christianity.

Each new generation of Aztec and Spanish youth was educated and socialized into the particular worldview of their cultures and the code of logic undergirding it—drawing on historical predecessors as guides and sources of legitimation. In Chapter 3, we touched on the origins of medieval European universities in cathedral towns with general studies in theology, law, and medicine, including at the University of Salamanca in the Castilian heartland. We have less information concerning educational systems in pre-Hispanic Mesoamerica, but we saw in Chapter 2 that epigraphic and archaeological evidence demonstrates the operation of formal training in scribal arts, math, and astronomy within the courts of Classic period Maya cities. Early colonial period texts from central Mexico provide richer information and show that Aztec cities had a two-tier system of compulsory education: a school for the sons of nobility or select, non-elite candidates for the priesthood called the *calmecac* ("house of the cords"),[75] and a school for everyone else that provided civic and military training called the *telpochcalli* ("house of youth"). It is useful to consider this Aztec system in tandem with the pedagogy of late fifteenth and early sixteenth-century instruction at Salamanca and other Spanish universities. Whereas the latter provided some of the filter through which Cortés and other conquistadors and Sahagún and other mendicant chroniclers viewed the conquest and colonial endeavor, the former did the same for the Native and mestizo elites who produced hybrid Indo-American documents in colonial centers of learning.

In fifteenth-century Spain, university curricula expanded to include more of a liberal-arts education with instruction in philosophy and grammar, in addition to the earlier triad of theology, law, and medicine. The widening of curricula coincided with larger enrollments and attendance at university of more non-elite students who were trained as part of the incipient bureaucracy of the more politically centralized country.[76] Those students "of letters" (*letrados*) worked within a system of royal rewards and the possibility for advancement within the bureaucracy, particularly under the rule of the Catholic Monarchs (Figure 4.10). By attending the University of Salamanca

Figure 4.10. Carved façade from the University of Salamanca with Catholic Monarchs depicted in central rosette above doorways.

Photo by the author.

to study law for two years before dropping out, Cortés had some training as a *letrado*. While Cortés was studying there, Columbus came to Salamanca to lecture on his discoveries in the Americas, but it is not known how much this influenced the young future conquistador.[77]

It is clear that the curricula for *letrados*, typically concentrating on law, and for students of theology, which included many of the friars who went to the Americas or debated colonization from Spain, were quite different. An important primary-source document bearing on the curricula of Salamanca in the late fifteenth to early seventeenth centuries is a compilation of statutes for the university compiled in 1625, but incorporating earlier modifications to its bylaws and coursework.[78] By the fifteenth century, an earlier program of general studies was on the way to becoming more differentiated into fields of study, but it still emphasized Classical period Greco-Roman authors—for instance, Aristotle and Cicero for rhetoric, Hippocrates for medicine—who were elaborated on and Christianized by fathers of the Church, especially St. Augustine, and medieval theologians, especially St. Thomas Aquinas. The writings of these scholars were critical for debates regarding under what circumstances war could be justified, and the curriculum as a whole provided a broad base of scholarly knowledge, supplemented by other Greek, Hebrew, and especially Latin authors. Along with a deep immersion in the orations of Cicero, students in theology also studied rhetoric of the Hispano-Roman author Quintilian and the medieval Spanish theologian Durand of Huesca. This formed the base of knowledge for many of the friars who traveled to the Americas and later debated the colonial enterprise. As a student of law, Cortés had a much narrower vocational education. He would have been exposed primarily to Roman civil law in the *Digest*, compiled by the Eastern Roman emperor Justinian I in the sixth century, and to canonical law of the later Roman Catholic Church.[79] Cortés would have read some humanistic authors as well, but not to the degree pursued by aspiring theologians.

Instruction at Salamanca and other Spanish universities required knowing Latin well and ancient Greek and Hebrew less well, depending on course of study. For theologians, these three languages mattered greatly and were combined by Cardinal Cisneros in his Complutensian Polyglot Bible, in which he rendered the Old Testament texts in the three languages in parallel and joined them with an Aramaic version translated to Latin at the bottom of the page. Cisneros' bible allowed readers to semantically parse the different versions and interpret their significance. The bible takes its name from Complutum, the former Roman settlement at Alcalá de Henares, and

Cisneros' founding of a university in the town created a rival in prestige to Salamanca. Linguistic standardization was a hallmark of this period, which saw both the rise of the printing press and Castilian preeminence. An interesting linguistic convention that separated Castile from other parts of Europe was the production of texts in the vernacular at an early date, such as the catechism of Pedro de Cuéllar, written in 1325 in Segovia.[80] Spain's celebrated year of 1492 not only marked the fall of Granada and the launching of the Columbian invasions, it was also when Antonio de Nebrija, the Renaissance scholar we saw earlier extolling the virtues of Mérida and other parts of Roman Hispania, standardized the Castilian tongue. His *Gramática de la lengua castellana* represents the first grammar of a modern European language.[81] Nebrija hailed from Seville and taught at both Salamanca and Alcalá de Henares. He presented his work to Queen Isabela and in the prologue noted that language was the "companion of empire," implying that, as Latin had done for Rome, Castilian would frame nascent nationhood and aspirational empire. Castile's political ascendency and linguistic standardization combined to make Castilian Spanish, and not some other peninsular variant or language—such as Basque, Catalan, or Galician—the language of Spanish America.

The system of education in Aztec society was, like the Spanish one, connected to religion and physical places of worship.[82] It differed in being compulsory for boys and in the transmission of canonical knowledge through more oral means rather than through reading alphabetic texts, though the Aztecs did produce texts using instructive images combined with more sparse hieroglyphs than the Classic period Maya had used. Somewhat like the European model of university education, the Aztecs had a theological specialization (the *calmecac*) and training for a more bureaucratic career (the *telpochcalli*). These were more differentiated as two separate types of school, and the bureaucratic training was not for scribes and accountants, like a Spanish *letrado*, but for a base in civic and military duties.[83] Youths of the telpochcalli spent significant time undertaking public works projects on behalf of their community and training in the martial arts.

The mid-sixteenth-century Codex Mendoza provides rich pictorial and textual information on gendered socialization of boys and girls in Aztec society, including associated rites of passage, chores, personal decoration, and the allocation of boys to the calmecac or telpochcalli (Figure 4.11).[84] Aztec boys and girls circulated in different spheres for many parts of their education and socialization, but were combined for public rites of

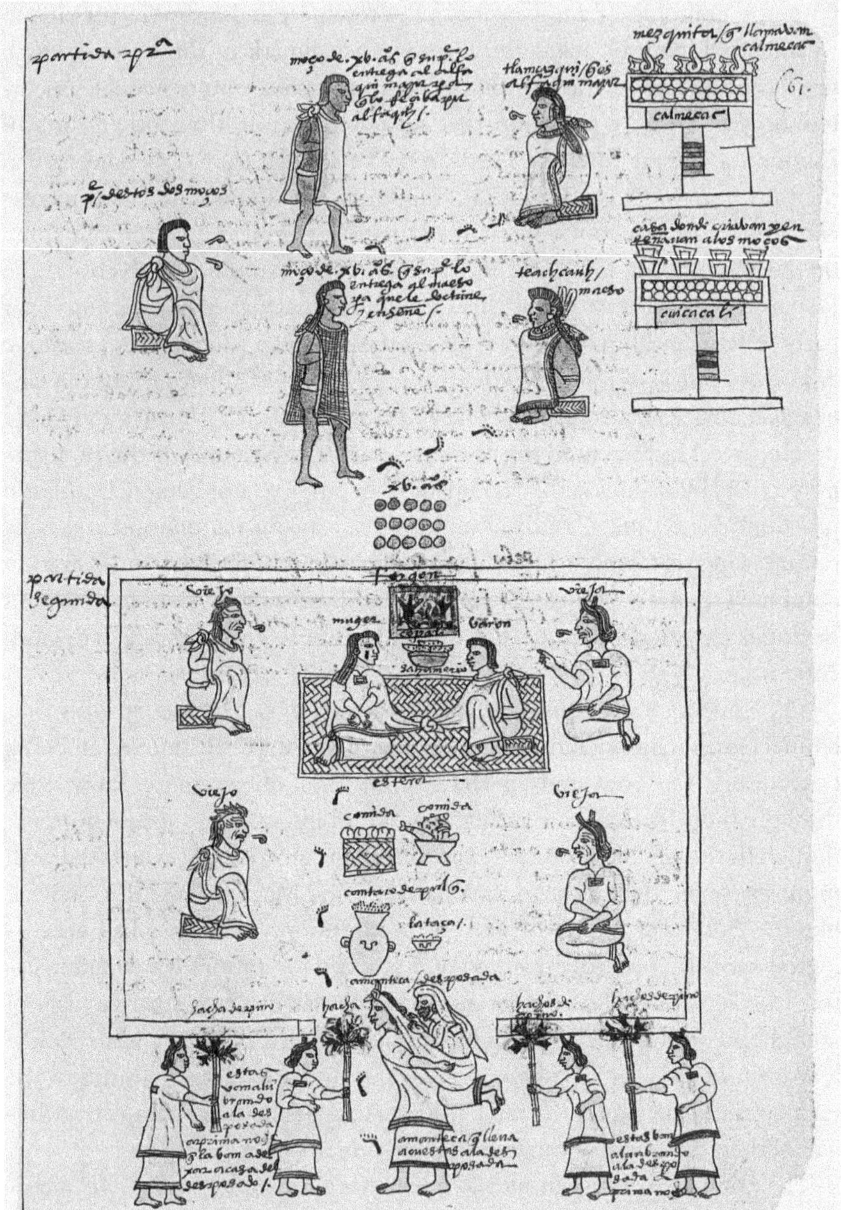

Figure 4.11. Aztec social life showing (top) dual educational system of calmecac and telpochcalli and (bottom) a marriage ceremony. Codex Mendoza, folio 61 recto.

passage and in a puberty-age school called the *cuicacalli* ("house of song"), which indoctrinated them in the songs and dances appropriate to Aztec religion. Recent excavations at the calmecac of Tenochtitlan uncovered large roof adornments from the building that depict the cross-section of a conch shell (*ehecailacocozcatl*), an emblem seen in the Codex Mendoza rendering and associated with Quetzalcoatl and his incarnation of the god of learning.[85] Aztec wisdom was thereby perceived as derived from divine and historical precedent, as it was in Spain. Sahagún and his Nahua scribes recorded a key component of Aztec philosophy in Book VI of the Florentine Codex, on rhetoric and moral philosophy, in a suite of poetic aphorisms called *huehuetlatolli* ("sayings of the elders").[86] Upending this richly textured view of the world and the institutions that undergirded it would be one of the major justifications on the part of the Spanish for the invasion of Mesoamerica and war with the Aztecs.

Comparative History and Society

A skeptical reader may observe at this point in our journey that we are at the midpoint of a book dealing with the Spanish invasion of Mesoamerica and there is only recent and scant mention of them having arrived to the Caribbean. This could be seen as overly elaborate stage setting for the "show" to come, namely the Spanish-Aztec war of 1519–1521. I hope, however, that the foregrounding of comparative deep history and cumulative cultural changes in the first chapters of this book has the effect of decentering any particular scene or actor in favor of a broader perspective that underscores how these disparate pieces fit together in social and historical processes that were both destructive and generative of something new.

The points of similarity and divergence between Aztec and Spanish society in ethnic affiliation; social organization into cities, economic networks, and empires; and relative understandings of the roles of technology, religion, and education contributed directly to decades of wars of conquest and the forging of the new colonial order of New Spain. Earlier civilizations of Mesoamerica and Iberia were drawn upon selectively by fifteenth- and early sixteenth-century Aztecs and Spaniards to frame their worldviews and to legitimate institutions of power. They were also contributors to the less conscious backdrop of cumulative cultural change that shaped particular types of agents of the era, including members of military orders drawing from conquering gods or saints, administrative bureaucrats, religious specialists, political leaders, long-distance merchants, and the base of farmers that supported both societies.

We have briefly encountered Cortés, Moctezuma, Queen Isabela, and Malinche as key actors in the historical narrative, and many more will emerge in chapters to come. Yet we will continue to deliberate the structural variables of broader societal organization and how it manifested on the physical landscape and in the world of things of conquest-era Mesoamerica and its transition to colonial New Spain. Differences between the nationalizing identity and direct territorial control strategies of Spain's empire and the micro-patriotism and indirect control strategies of Aztec Mexico were critically important in how wars of invasion and conquest unfolded. Likewise, the long trajectories that produced specific agricultural and economic systems on both sides of the Atlantic would come into conflict and shape colonial society, as would differences in the absolutist orientation to religion on the part of the Spanish compared with the incorporative orientation of the Aztecs. The meeting and mixing of the two worlds was strategically framed, debated, and negotiated by individuals schooled in the philosophies and cultural logic of these two traditions and the historical wellspring, grounded in an acute connection to the past, from which they drew.

5

Invasion of the Mesoamerican Coast

It especially made [Moctezuma] faint when he heard how the guns went off at [the Spaniards'] command, sounding like thunder . . . fire went showering and spitting out . . . it had a very foul stench . . . it turned a tree to dust; it seemed to make it vanish, as though someone had conjured it away. Their war gear was all iron. They clothed their bodies in iron, they put iron on their heads, their swords were iron, their bows were iron, and their shields and lances were iron. And their deer [horses] that carried them were as tall as the roof. . . . And their dogs were huge creatures. . . . When Moteucçoma heard it, he was greatly afraid.

—*Florentine Codex*, Book XII, Chapter 7[1]

Setting out from Cuba on February 10, 1519, Hernando Cortés captained the Spanish expedition to Mesoamerica that would result in the invasion and eventual demise of the Aztec Empire. It was not the first Spanish mission to Mesoamerica that featured battles resulting in Native and Spanish casualties. Earlier ones headed by Francisco Hernández de Córdoba and Juan de Grijalva had confronted Maya communities along the coast of Yucatan in the two preceding years. Key members of Cortés' expedition—such as Pedro de Alvarado and Francisco de Montejo, who would later lead their own invasions of the Maya highlands and lowlands—were part of these earlier voyages, but Cortés himself was not. Cortés remained in Cuba as a mid-level colonial administrator when the earliest encounters began. These three expeditions were not even the first arrival of Spaniards to Mesoamerica. Since the time of Columbus' voyages, Spaniards had charted portions of the Yucatan coast and Gulf of Honduras and even made exploratory incursions on the Yucatan peninsula in 1502, 1506, and 1508.[2] In 1511, Gonzalo Guerrero and Jerónimo de Aguilar were shipwrecked and ended up on the island of Cozumel, off the peninsula's northeast coast. Guerrero is a fascinating figure who illustrates the complexities of culture contact and colonization. He fully embraced his new surroundings, marrying the daughter of a local Maya chief, dressing and adorning himself as a member of his adopted tribe, and starting the first known mestizo family of children with one Spanish and one Mesoamerican parent. Aguilar, in contrast, remained an outsider among the Maya until members of Cortés' mission arrived and set him to work as a translator during the invasion of the Aztec Empire. Guerrero stayed with his family on Cozumel, declining to join the expedition.

The existence of these earlier encounters explains the fact that when, in 1519, scouts for Moctezuma informed him of the arms, armor, and animals of the Cortés expedition, witnessed along the Gulf of Mexico and relayed in this chapter's epigraph, the Spanish presence was not wholly novel to him. The text is nevertheless illustrative of Native Mesoamerican interest in foreign elements of material culture and how the sort of micro-patriotism that characterized pre-Hispanic politics was exploited by Cortés and other conquistadors during their invasions. This micro-patriotism constitutes a form of bias that needs to be taken into account when reading primary sources of the sixteenth century. The passage comes from Book XII of Bernardino de Sahagún's *Universal History of the Things of New Spain*, usually called the Florentine Codex for its current location in Florence. It was written beginning sometime around 1555, and the English text is a translation of the original Nahuatl in which authors from Tlatelolco, Azcapotzalco, and Cuauhtitlan wrote half of the document. The other half was written in Spanish and exhibits more editorial influence on the part of Sahagún.[3] Since Tlatelolco was the smaller Mexica sister-city to Tenochtitlan, located on the same island and annexed by the imperial capital in pre-Hispanic times, the colonial-period Tlatelolca who collaborated on the document exhibit their clear anti-Tenochca predisposition. Those authors from other *altepemeh* were likewise not from Tenochtitlan and go along in depicting Moctezuma as cowardly. Although it was not until November 8 that Moctezuma would meet Cortés, with the hundreds of Spaniards who traveled with him and the many thousands of Native warriors who constituted the main fighting force of the invasion, the passage portrays the Great Speaker as already cowering in his palace months before the fateful encounter.

Chroniclers and Their Agendas

An underappreciated fact of early colonial administration in early Spanish America was a culture of relatively free speech, at least when it came to matters not pertaining to religion. Documents from the early sixteenth century are rife with critique of administrators or even reigning monarchs themselves.[4] In 1509 King Ferdinand decreed that no official in the Indies could block the sending of letters and other information from the colonies back to Spain, and instructions in 1521 given by Charles V—by that time Holy Roman Emperor—were explicit in soliciting reports from the rapidly enlarging territories, whether the news was good or bad. As a result, the corpus of documents from the period is relatively rich but in need of judicious reading regarding the motives and intended audience of the authors and the veracity of the information they provide.

Relevant texts can vary in representing eyewitness accounts or secondary accounts: some written early but from outside Mexico, and others recorded within Mexico but later and by authors who were not alive for the events of 1519–1521.[5] Sources can also be separated by the ancestry of the authors and whether a particular account was penned by a Spaniard or by a Mesoamerican or mestizo who honors his or her indigenous ancestry. These two groupings are useful as an initial way of sorting types of sources, but we can parse them further until we get to the level of individual authors and their often personal reasons for writing. Other meaningful categories of bias in the sources include micro-patriotism to ethnic city-state (*altepetl*) on the part of Native authors, as well as a desire on the part of the same to extol the virtues and loyalties of their ancestors during the Spanish-Mexica war. In the case of Native and mestizo authors, the chronicles date to decades after the fall of Tenochtitlan and were typically written by individuals of noble lineage whose primary agenda was to retain their titles and prerogatives in the context of colonial New Spain. We should make another meaningful distinction between Spanish authors who were conquistadors or friars. In the case of conquistador sources, we can distinguish between those written in the midst of military actions—most notably Cortés for Mexico and Alvarado for Guatemala—and those by other conquistadors who wrote later to justify their titles and landholdings within the new colonial order, especially when they came under threat by the 1542 New Laws, which were passed to regulate the harsh labor requirements that early colonists had imposed on Native peoples of Spanish America. Conquistadors also wrote to rectify what they perceived to be undue attention to the actions of Cortés and Alvarado at the expense of other participants. This motivation is most apparent in the best known of the conquistador accounts, written by Bernal Díaz del Castillo. Documents authored by friars also range from being harshly critical of the conquistadors to complicit in their actions. All friars nevertheless authored accounts with shared motivations of promoting the spiritual conversion of Native peoples to Christianity.

The earliest eyewitness accounts of the invasion led by Cortés were five letters written by the conquistador himself—the first of which was written from Veracruz in 1519 and is lost, though a contemporaneous letter written by other members of the expedition is taken as a partial substitute.[6] The second was written from Tepeaca, Puebla, in 1520 during the Spanish-Mexica war, and the third was written at the conclusion of the war in 1522 from Coyoacan, south of Mexico City. The fourth and fifth letters were written from Mexico City in 1524 and 1526. Cortés addressed the letters to King Charles I—who by the second letter was also Emperor Charles V—with an eye to historical posterity and a more immediate motivation to justify his breach of protocol in invading Aztec Mexico when his direct superior, Diego Velázquez, the governor of Cuba, had only authorized reconnaissance and trading. The perception of continuity between the *Reconquista* of the Iberian peninsula against the infidels and the new *conquista* initiated by Cortés, or at least the framing of the justification for it, is clear in his letters and in accounts by other conquistadors in their characterization of Mesoamerican temples as "mosques," housing as in a "Moorish style," and the comparison of Mesoamerican cities to Granada and other former Islamic capitals of Al-Andalus.

After Cortés' own letters, the next most Cortés-centric account was authored in 1552 by his secretary and chaplain, Francisco López de Gómara, who never set foot in Mexico.[7] Gómara provides the most unabashedly great-man history of the "Conquest of Mexico" written in the sixteenth century. Later historians who follow a similar narrative arc draw heavily on Gómara, while the author himself drew primarily from Cortés' letters, conversations he had with the conquistador, and accounts of Native society culled from the chronicles of the Franciscan friar Toribio de Benavente, better known as Motolinia for the Nahuatl name the Tlaxcalteca bestowed on him. Gómara's portrayal of Cortés as the heroic primary agent of the conquest spurred Díaz del Castillo to write his own account, which he began soon after Gómara's was released and continued to revise until his death in 1584.[8] The aged conquistador also hoped to justify the encomiendas that he and other Spaniards had been awarded at a time they were in danger of being abolished as part of the New Laws and the sharp critiques levied by friars. The most complete version of Díaz del Castillo's text is known as the Guatemala manuscript. In it, and the many abridged translations since, we can clearly glean the expressed intent by the author to downplay the singularity of the exploits by Cortés in favor of recognizing the expedition and climactic war as a group endeavor with shared responsibilities on the part of many conquistadors, including of course the author himself. He proclaims: "With the historian Gómara it is always thus: Cortés did this, Cortés did that, Cortés was there, Cortés left there . . . [H]e could not possibly have been everywhere, and have done everything himself."[9] Though clearly biased, Díaz succeeded in authoring a compelling narrative that is one of the few books written in the sixteenth century that remains readable today—somewhat akin to Cervantes' *Don Quixote* minus the amusing satire.[10] His specific agenda is best encapsulated by the fact that Díaz wrote the only chronicle of the conquest to record his own participation in it. As a lowly foot soldier, he was overlooked by the mounted captains of the expedition.

Other eyewitness accounts written by some of the few horsemen who rode into battle are much shorter and drier than Díaz de Castillo's. They include Andrés de Tapia's brief account that preceded Gómara's as a Cortés-centric telling of events—de Tapia and Cortés grew up together in Medellín—and Bernardino Vázquez de Tapia's also brief account that preceded Díaz's in decentering Cortés. Like Díaz and other conquistadors, Vázquez de Tapia was motivated to write his account after the passing of the New Laws threatened his encomiendas. We also have his replies to questions posed by the Royal Audencia of Mexico regarding the conquest and Cortés's conduct within it, which was recorded following the founding of the Audiencia in 1528 and is more critical of Cortés. Other Spanish eyewitness accounts are provided by the chaplain Juan Díaz, who was also on the Grijalva expedition; Alonso de Aguilar, a conquistador who took the name Francisco when he joined the Dominican order at the end of his life; and one that was authored anonymously by "a companion of Cortés," which focuses on Native lifeways rather than the narrative of conquest, making it one of the earliest of several proto-ethnographic accounts.[11] An account of the conquistador Juan Cano de Saavedra is lost, but portions of it can be gleaned from the sixteenth-century histories authored by Gonzalo Fernández de Oviedo y Valdés and Alonso de Zorita, who used it and conversations with Cano as source material.[12]

Nahua (colonial Aztec), Maya, and other Mesoamerican societies are covered in greatest detail by the works compiled by friars such as Motolinia, Las Casas, and Sahagún, and by mestizo authors such as Diego Muñoz Camargo. Of these, only Las Casas was alive and in the Americas when the invasion of Mexico took place and he was far from the action, on missions taking him between Spain, South America, and the Caribbean. Francisco Cervantes de Salazar was a Salamanca-trained Spanish historian who immigrated to Mexico in the mid-sixteenth century, served as rector of the newly established University of Mexico, and left a mostly completed manuscript dealing with the conquest.[13] These secondary accounts contain some novel details relating to the conquest and were written or edited by people who approached the documentation of Native peoples during the early colonial period more ethnographically and sympathetically—sometimes working directly with Native authors in multilingual settings, most notably in the case of Sahagún.[14]

Secondary accounts written by Native and mestizo authors tend to exhibit the biases of micro-patriotism toward their altepetl and even more narrowly toward their family line. They were often authored as petitions for recognition of a city's or family's contributions as loyal allies, as well as to signal their full embrace of Christianity and their fidelity as colonial subjects. No group was more active in petitioning the Spanish Crown than the Tlaxcalteca, who sent five delegations to Spain between 1528 and 1585. Muñoz Camargo was part of the fifth and carried his history of the city and province of Tlaxcala with him to present to King Phillip II personally.[15] Over three decades earlier, Muñoz Camargo had overseen the production of a Native pictorial account of Tlaxcala's history and role as primary allies to the Spanish that was illustrated on cloth, giving it its name, Lienzo de Tlaxcala. As with certain Native-author texts, such as Book XII of the Florentine Codex, the Lienzo de Tlaxcala and other pictorial sources provide excellent information on what vestments, weapons, and other elements of material culture Native authors prioritized.[16]

In a somewhat similar vein to the Tlaxcalan sources is the early seventeenth-century account written by Fernando de Alva Ixtlilxochitl, of noble lineage from Texcoco, previously the second most important altepetl in the Aztec Triple Alliance.[17] Alva Ixtlilxochitl's account is intently focused on his own lineage and the role of his great-great-grandfather, who had the same Nahuatl name and was christened as Fernando, in the alliance and fall of Tenochtitlan. Another Native noble account is provided by the late sixteenth- and early seventeenth-century chronicler Hernando Alvarado Tezozomoc, also known by his Nahuatl surname. As a grandson of Moctezuma, Tezozomoc provides a balance to the scribes of the Florentine Codex in emphasizing the pre-Hispanic conquests of Tenochtitlan's earlier Great Speakers and portraying his uncle as a concerned but capable leader during the advance of the Cortés expedition on his capital city.[18] Whereas much of the timeline of the pivotal events of 1519–1521 is on firm historical footing, corroborated by multiple authors,[19] certain details can be parsed by reading critically a wider corpus of authors with the previously noted types of bias in mind. Doing so allows us to more accurately interpret the motivations of groups and individuals, or pivotal episodes that may have led to different historical outcomes had they gone another way.

The Pre-Invasion Setting of Early Spanish America

Spaniards and those navigating under the Spanish Crown sailed well beyond the Pillars of Hercules in creating the world's first global empire during the sixteenth century. The process took close to three-quarters of a century to unfold, and only saw true globalization with the colonization of the Philippines in 1565, which connected the established trans-Atlantic network with the trans-Pacific one first traversed by Ferdinand Magellan and Juan Sebastián Elcano contemporaneously with Cortés' invasion. In the first quarter-century, between the expeditions of Columbus and Cortés, there were significant changes in the administrative strategies for the Indies pursued by Spanish monarchs, courtiers, and church authorities. It was when the rift first developed between those who gained the most economically from their exploitation of Native peoples—the conquistadors, local administrators, and land-trusted encomenderos—and certain members of the clergy whose interests lay in saving souls and therefore criticized aspects of the colonial endeavor. This fight would only intensify with continued conquests in Mexico, Peru, and elsewhere.

One of the most important Spanish institutions of overseas administration was the House of Trade (Casa de Contratación) founded in Seville in 1503 by

Queen Isabela to regulate commerce and funnel revenues to the state from colonial enterprises along the Barbary Coast, on the Canary Islands, and in the Caribbean.[20] The House of Trade oversaw the outfitting and insuring of trading fleets and the regulation of their cargoes and payment of duties. It was the commercial and administrative hub of Spain's burgeoning maritime empire, but also served a role as a Catholic charity. Juan Rodríguez de Fonseca, the bishop to whom Juan de la Cosa presented his map depicting the New World, was instrumental in setting up the House of Trade and served as its first treasurer. He was also Queen Isabela's chaplain and later became president of the Council of the Indies, the legislative body that oversaw the administration of Spanish America. Originally located close to the docks of the Guadalquivir River, the House of Trade was later moved to the fortified Real Alcázar palace (Figure 5.1). It featured storage facilities, accommodations for administrators, a bureau for safeguarding navigational charts, a center for training pilots, and a jail. After Queen Isabela's death in 1504, the House of Trade was granted even more oversight under King Ferdinand, including better defined roles for judges, inspectors, and a chief navigator called the pilot-major (piloto mayor). In 1508, Ferdinand bestowed this last role on

Figure 5.1. House of Trade within Royal Alcázar of Seville.
Photo by the author.

Américo Vespucio (Amerigo Vespucci in the navigator's native Italian), who would eventually become the namesake of the Americas.

Seville was an appropriate city to oversee the Spanish imperial monopoly on trade. Situated in an agriculturally productive region with deep commercial ties dating back to Roman Baetica and the Tartesian-Phonecian trade network, Seville was one of the most, if not the most, historically significant urban centers of the peninsula. Even before the city gained the imperial trans-Atlantic monopoly, it was already one of the largest trading centers in Iberia with access to the sea, and the Guadalquivir Valley was the most urbanized and commercialized region.[21] Prevailing winds and currents made Seville a prime location for expeditions out into the Atlantic, and its location upriver from the Gulf of Cádiz meant it was somewhat protected from naval attacks. The inland setting also posed problems, since a major sandbar in the estuary at the mouth of the Guadalquivir at Sanlúcar de Barrameda could obstruct the passage of larger ships. This hydrology had the effect of making the constellation of ports stretching 50 miles (80 km) from the city to the Gulf of Cádiz (Figure 5.2). It attracted international merchants, including the

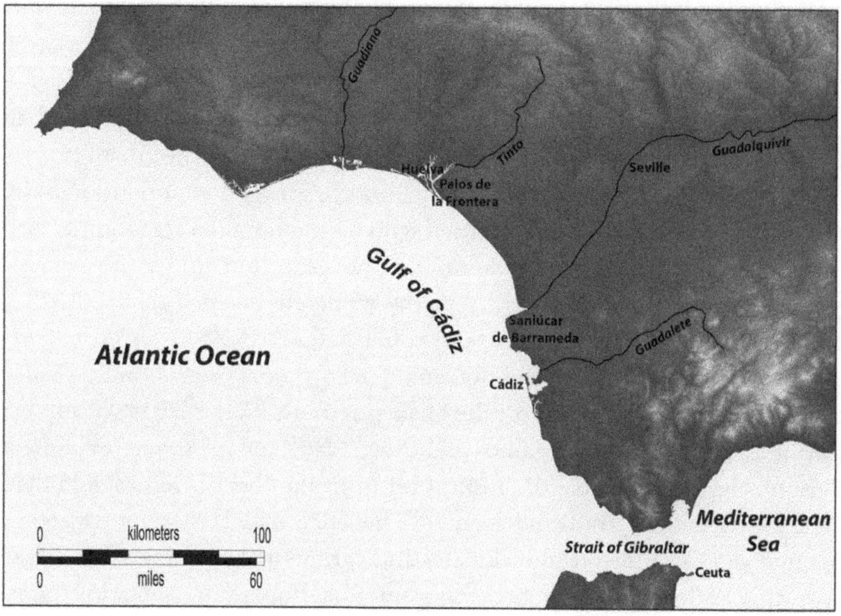

Figure 5.2. Map of greater Gulf of Cádiz port region with Seville and important entrepôts of the sixteenth century.

English, some of whom lived in Seville and exchanged at the House of Trade for goods such as sugar, tropical woods and fruits, and tobacco.

The Catholic Monarch's granting of Seville with the overseas monopoly stagnated the development of other Spanish ports, which became relegated to secondary roles within the burgeoning trans-Atlantic system. Towns in the Gulf of Cádiz served as anteports or entrepôts to Seville, as some goods were offloaded at Cádiz and moved by land to the House of Trade, whereas others served as anchorage while ships were outfitted prior to journeys. Other ports in the Canaries, especially Las Palmas and Santa Cruz de Tenerife, played the role of outports that were stopovers for gathering extra goods or crews on voyages from Spain to the Indies. Cortés's arrival to the Americas followed a fairly typical progression: at the age of 19 he joined the Caribbean expedition of Alonso Quintero, which had been authorized by the House of Trade and launched from Sanlúcar de Barrameda, stopping first at La Gomera in the Canaries before docking in Santo Domingo, Hispaniola.[22]

Upon his arrival to Hispaniola, Cortés joined a young colony that had been claimed for Spain by Columbus 12 years earlier and whose indigenous Taíno population had already been devastated by the introduction of Old World diseases previously unknown in the Americas, the attempts of Columbus and others to begin a slave trade in Native peoples, and the imposition of the encomienda system.[23] Columbus began returning enslaved Natives with him to Spain and Portugal with his first return voyage and transported between 400–600 individuals in 1495, many of whom died at sea.[24] From the onset, Spanish monarchs attempted to stem the tide of Native slaves from the Indies brought to Europe on religious and ethical grounds: in 1499 they granted those who returned with Columbus their freedom; in that same year they also retracted Columbus's governorship, under the suggestion of his rival, Fonseca; and in 1501 the monarchs decreed that all Native subjects of the Caribbean colonies were free peoples.[25]

The Catholic Monarchs did not simply take a moral stance on this issue; it also made economic sense for the Spaniards to use Native labor within the Caribbean itself. Here the Taínos and other Native peoples were exploited through the encomienda, the institution from the Iberian *Reconquista* that partitioned Islamic land and labor.[26] The encomienda system was then adapted and expanded to the climates and agricultural regimes of the New World, with local tobacco becoming another important plantation crop. Technically a "trust" to the Spanish encomendero, the encomienda shared structural similarities to systems of feudalism and servitude in medieval

Europe with the provision that the encomendero was obliged to protect and evangelize Native peoples in return. However, this trust was routinely abused and the institution as practiced in the distant colonies could look more like enslavement in all but name. African enslavement remained legal and intensified in inverse proportion to the granting of greater protections to Native peoples of the Caribbean.

True evangelization efforts did not begin until a group of 12 Franciscans, symbolically new apostles to the New World, arrived on Santo Domingo on April 15, 1502. A similar mission of Dominicans did not arrive on the island until 1509 or 1510, though the most famous eventual friar of the Order of Preachers within the Americas, Las Casas, also arrived in 1502 with his father as part of the encomendero class. In all, the archives of the House of Trade record the voyages of 140 Franciscan friars and 50 Dominican friars to the Indies between the years 1508–1521.[27] We have seen that whereas the Franciscans historically made their appeals more sentimentally, the Dominicans worked through institutions of colleges and seminaries. In many cases, this difference of the orders can account for the more personal, proto-ethnographic approach of some of the Franciscan chroniclers of Mexico, such as Motolinia, Sahagún, Mendieta, and Torquemada. Dominican accounts can seem more institutional or detached from the Native populations, with certain exceptions—Las Casas foremost among them in his advocate role as "Protector of the Indians."

Las Casas and Cortés led remarkably parallel lives before the first underwent a seismic shift in his perspective on the colonial enterprise. Both men were born in the mid-1480s—Las Casas in Seville—and were likely contemporaries at the University of Salamanca.[28] They both traveled to the Americas at the age of 18 and were certainly contemporaries on Hispanola and as participants in the invasion of Cuba. Following the conquest of Cuba, Las Casas was allotted Taíno workers for his encomienda; he also owned African slaves. Archaeologists have identified one of the encomiendas owned by Las Casas at the site of Loma del Convento, located on the island's south-central coast.[29] Artifacts from the site show the transformation from pre-Hispanic to Spanish colonial material culture with the introduction of items such as glazed pottery (majolica) and metal items, including a bronze compass needle. Las Casas renounced his role as encomendero and began critiquing the Spanish colonial enterprise in 1515. He was inspired to conversion after hearing a stirring 1511 sermon given by Antonio de Montesinos, a Dominican friar who had also studied at Salamanca. There is no known surviving copy of Montesinos's sermon, and we only know of its impassioned plea for Spanish colonists to reform their ways through the *Historia de las Indias*, written decades later by Las Casas. In that work, Las Casas writes that Montesinos preached to the assembled colonists of Santo Domingo: "I have to tell you that you are all in a state of mortal sin; you now live in it, and you will die in it, and this on account of the cruelty and tyranny you practice on these innocent Natives. Tell me, what gives you the right to subject these Indians to such an atrocious and horrible slavery? They once flourished in large communities, but a great many are now dead and forgotten as a result of your actions."[30]

Montesinos traveled to Spain to confront King Ferdinand with a document listing the legal and moral violations committed by Spanish colonists and an appeal for better treatment.[31] The appeal made an impact on the king and resulted in the 1512 Laws of Burgos, which nominally abolished enslaving Native peoples of the Indies and specified how encomiendas would be run, including establishing minimum standards for the quality of accommodations, diet, and education for the subject population of laborers. In the meantime, Spanish conquests in the Caribbean continued unabated. Christopher Columbus' son Diego was named governor of the Indies in 1508 and was the top regional authority at the time of Alonso de Ojeda and Diego de Nicuesa's 1509 invasion of the continental mainland between Honduras and Columbia (called Tierra Firme), Juan de Esquivel's 1509 invasion of Jamaica (called Santiago), and Diego Velázquez's 1511 invasion of Cuba (called Fernandina). Juan de la Cosa advocated on behalf of Ojeda to lead the mainland invasion and ended up paying for it with his life, being killed by poisoned arrows fired by Native archers in Columbia.

Cortés participated in the invasion of Cuba, which took three years to conquer due to strong Taíno resistance mobilized by a local chief named Hatuey. The experience of witnessing the colonization of Cuba soured Las Casas on the colonial enterprise even more and prompted him to journey to Spain and petition Ferdinand to outlaw the encomienda entirely. At this point in his conversion, Las Casas still advocated the use of African slaves on the grounds of its longer precedent among European powers and as part of a "just war" versus less civilized, heathen populations. With the death of Ferdinand, in 1516, Las Casas lost his audience on the encomienda issue, though as regent Cisneros appointed him Protector of the Indians.[32] The plan by Las Casas to encourage families of Spanish peasants to move to the Americas and work fields themselves never came to fruition, and instead the transfer of sugar plantations from the Canaries to Hispaniola, and the lack of a specially designated protector for Africans, led to increased reliance on African slaves in the Caribbean.[33]

Following the Laws of Burgos, further conquests in the Americas were also formalized by the Requirement (*Requerimiento*), a written summons designed to establish the legal legitimacy of Spain's subjugation of Native peoples and dictate the terms under which war and violence were acceptable courses of action. The Requirement, with roots in similar documents from the *Reconquista* era, was intended to be read aloud—a type of legal-religious performance—to Native peoples prior to any military engagement.[34] Its incarnation for the Americas was composed in four parts by Juan López de Palacios Rubios, totaling fewer than 1,000 words but with a Jekyll-and-Hyde-like character that mixed the language of pleas with requirements that could be backed by harshly punitive actions. The sections of the text cover (1) the European biblical vision of cosmogenesis and partitioning of the Americas between Spain and Portugal by the papal bull and Treaty of Tordesillas; (2) Spain's legitimate right to evangelize in the Americas by virtue of the first; (3) a plea that Native peoples submit to the king and pope; and (4) a promise of war and violence if they do not submit, including the enslavement of women and children. The proclamation was delivered in Castilian Spanish, frequently without any translation or with a muddled translation, casting doubt on whether it was actually intended for Native peoples or, alternatively, for other Europeans, the pope, or God. Las Casas famously remarked that he didn't know whether to laugh or cry at the document.

Across the Caribbean and Gulf of Mexico sat the Yucatan peninsula, which the Spaniards assumed to be an island. Yucatan has a very particular geology and hydrology that structured indigenous settlement on it and the manner in which early Spanish explorers interacted with these coastal populations. The peninsula is mostly limestone as it was once a sea floor. Its bedrock is therefore soluble and forms a karstic landscape, meaning that underground drainage has eroded caves and other cavities and in some spots created sinkholes where the surface has collapsed to reveal the water below. Rivers do not form on the porous surface, making these sinkholes essential to human occupation on the peninsula as sources of fresh water. The sinkholes are called *ts'onot* in Yucatec Mayan, a term that was Hispanicized to cenote. In the early sixteenth century, just about every cenote was the location of a Maya town whose inhabitants claimed the water. As the expeditions to Yucatan led by Córdoba and Grijalva carried limited water in the holds of their ships, they were forced to stop at cenotes and come into direct contact with Maya towns (Figure 5.3).[35] The hydrology of the peninsula changes at Champotón and Laguna de Términos to the west and Chetumal Bay to the east, each of which have sheltered harbors fed by rivers. The lagoon and bay became particularly important for portage for the caravels and other Spanish ships sailing the Yucatecan coast.

Cenotes have also been productive spots archaeologically since the Maya considered their water sacred and would deposit offerings of precious materials into them. The most famous of these is the cenote at Chichén Itzá, which archaeologists dredged in the early twentieth century to discover brilliant discs made of gold and turquoise, along with deposits of the aromatic sap copal, used as incense in Mesoamerican rituals. Cenotes often contain human remains as well, some of which likely fell in accidentally or posthumously and others that were parts of rituals of human sacrifice. An example of the former confirms the antiquity of humans on the Yucatan peninsula, as the remains of a girl from 12,000–13,000 years ago were encountered by underwater archaeologists in the Hoyo Negro cenote. The bones were preserved well enough to extract ancient DNA that exhibits a clear overlap

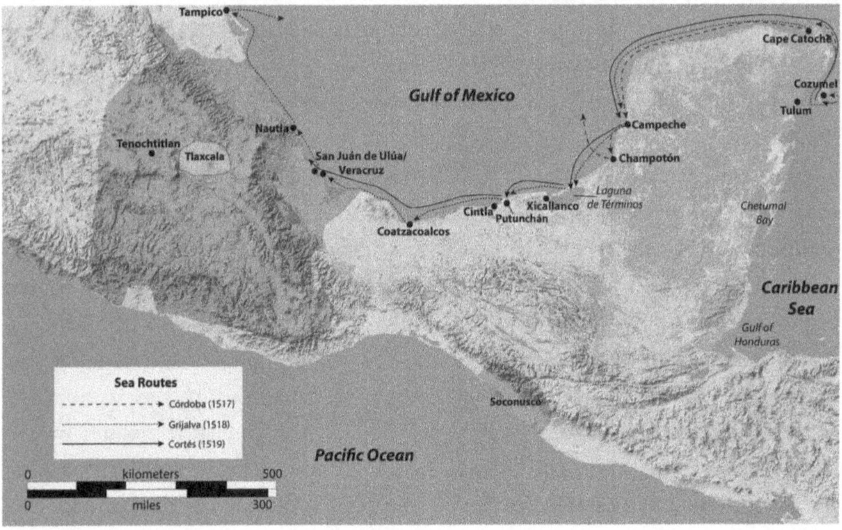

Figure 5.3. Map of Mesoamerica depicting sea routes of the expeditions captained by Córdoba, Grijalva, and Cortés, with Maya cities on Yucatan peninsula shading over area of Aztec Empire.

with genetic markers of contemporary Native American populations.[36] It is clear that by the first millennium BCE patterns of material culture, such as housing, art, and artifacts, are ethnically Maya and would exhibit cultural continuity with later peoples of the peninsula. Based on analysis of colonial-period documents and skeletal remains, it is possible to distinguish the Yucatec Mayan-speaking population of the northern peninsula from the Putun- or Chontal Mayan–speaking ones who had their base to the west in the modern Mexican states of Tabasco and Campeche. The second group have been called the "Phoenicians of Mesoamerica" in their capacity as traders circumnavigating the peninsula between the Gulf of Mexico and Gulf of Honduras.[37] One of the great trading centers was located on the western coast of Laguna de Términos at Xicallanco, the probable homelands of the people referred to in central Mexico as the Olmeca-Xicalanca, whose highland-lowland networks were critical to cities such as Cacaxtla and Cholula. The region was therefore the nexus of the Nahua and Maya worlds. It is important to keep in mind that Mayan is a language family comprising several languages as differentiated as ones in the Romance family—Spanish to Italian, for instance—meaning the Yucatan of this period should be considered a multicultural region.

Roughly at the midpoint of the coastal trading route along the Yucatan were settlements that served as entrepôts on the mainland, including the major contemporary tourist destination of Tulum (Figure 5.4), and others on the island of Cozumel, where the tallest temple was some 50 feet (15 m) high. To the west, Maya occupation around Champotón began at least as early as the late first millennium BCE and reached a Postclassic apogee with an urban population of approximately 25,000, consistent with the estimate of 8,000 houses made by Spanish sources.[38] Its original Mayan name was Hol Ha Chakan Putun, and the greater region was called Chochitan by Nahuatl-speaking merchants. When Spaniards encountered these sites as part of the Córdoba and Grijalva expeditions, they were struck by the urbanity of Maya culture, which contrasted with what they knew from the Caribbean islands and was instead reminiscent of historical cities of Iberia and the circum-Mediterranean region. For instance, when the approximately 110 Spaniards along with Córdoba made landfall in northern Yucatan after 21 days at sea—placing it around March 1, 1517—they saw a Maya town of stone pyramids covered in gleaming white plaster, prompting them to invoke what they thought of as the ancient Orient and Muslim lands, naming it the Great Cairo.[39] They arrived in three ships and designated the narrow strip of land

Figure 5.4. Maya port town of Tulum, on the Caribbean coast of the Yucatan peninsula.
Photo by the author. Reproduction authorized by the Instituto Nacional de Antropología e Historia, Mexico.

where they made landfall Cape Catoche, north of the contemporary resort city of Cancun. The Spaniards named the cape based on a phrase the Maya repeated to them and that they took as welcoming them to their home. When armed Maya warriors then attacked them in the town, the Spanish took it to be a deceptive ambush rather than a case of miscommunication. Córdoba took two Mayas hostage, whom he christened Julian and Melchor, in the hopes of their serving as future translators. Both men were part of the Grijalva expedition, but Julianillo died in 1519 and only Melchor continued with Cortés.[40]

Although they were run from Cape Catoche, the members of the Córdoba expedition had seen the trappings of urban society in Mesoamerica including, most crucially, some gold objects that would whet their and future conquistador appetites. The expedition continued westward for 15 days until needing to stop for water at Campeche. Here the Maya greeted them unarmed and used the phrase "Castilian," indicating that this ethnonym was known on the peninsula from previous encounters. Neither the Maya of Campeche nor the newly captured translators spoke Castilian, however, so communication was realized through hand gestures, a ceremonial burning of a bundle of reeds in the town center, and the whistles of Maya call to arms signaling that the Spaniards should take their water and leave. Córdoba sailed another 10 days before stopping for water at Champotón, where things did not go as well for the Spaniards. Under the leadership of Moch Couoh, the Maya of Hol Ha Chakan Putun put up a serious resistance, killing over 50 members of the Córdoba expedition and wounding nearly all the rest. Among the casualties was Córdoba himself, who died of his wounds soon after returning to Cuba on April 20, following another stopover for water in Florida. Before he died, the captain wrote an account to Velázquez, informing him of the finely made cities and gold jewelry he had seen and quickly turning the governor's attention to fielding a follow-up expedition to be led by Velázquez's nephew, Grijalva. Around the same time, across the Atlantic, on September 17, the young Hapsburg prince Charles I sailed from the Netherlands to land in Spain. Although only beginning to learn the native tongue (Castilian) of his mother (Juana "the mad") and grandmother (Queen Isabela), he negotiated for unified rule over all the Spanish kingdoms, including overseas possessions such as the Aragonese domains in Italy and the more distant Indies. As a result, the Spanish Empire grew more powerful in Europe and more expansionistic abroad.

Díaz de Castillo claims to have been part of the Grijalva expedition, but the lack of detail he provides gives reason to doubt this. The participation of Vázquez de Tapia is more certain, and we have his terse eyewitness impressions of having seen "large towns and stone buildings" on Cozumel, where the expedition first landed in early May 1518.[41] The conquistador also recounts the losses suffered by the Spanish at Campeche and their first hearing of a powerful empire to the west when the expedition landed at San Juan de Ulúa. Juan Díaz also was part of the Grijalva expedition as a chaplain. He likened a building on an island in the Gulf of Mexico, which the Spaniards dubbed Isla de los Sacrificios, to Old World antiquity, but by invoking the Roman ruins at Mérida.[42]

The Grijalva expedition was better prepared than the one led by Cordoba. It brought over 200 men, including the Maya translators, and a larger arsenal that featured canons, which were used to shock and awe the Maya at Campeche. These canons were a small variety called falconets that could be fired from caravels, brigantines, and other ships used by the Spanish in the Caribbean.[43] Falconets could shoot some 450 feet in a straight line and over 6,000 feet at an incline, but since they were not attached to wheels their use would have been confined to the initial, volley stage, and they were not easily mobile for the shock or pursuit stages of a battlefield sequence. As they proceeded along the coast of the Gulf of Mexico, the Grijalva expedition rested and secured fresh water at Laguna de Términos. Here they were followed by some 2,000 Maya of Putunchán in canoes who emerged from the Tabasco river, which today bears Grijalva's name.

The most significant occurrence of the Grijalva expedition was for the Spaniards to have learned of the existence of a powerful king named Moctezuma who ruled a great empire to the west. While on the Veracruz coast they were told of the dominion of the Culhúa of Mexico—the first term being the occasional ethnonym used by the Mexica for its connection to the migration narrative that took them through Culhuacan and bestowed on them some degree of Toltec pedigree. The Spaniard's mishearing of the term resulted in the misnomer Ulúa, which they applied to the island off Veracruz where they first heard it, rather than connecting it with the imperial core. During the colonial period, Ulúa became the fort complex defending the port city of Veracruz. This encounter also marked when the Mexica first learned for certain of the Spaniards, who had now reached the empire's periphery. We might envision a scene in Moctezuma's palace like this chapter's epigraph from Book XII of the Florentine Codex, but this particular passage relates to messengers from the time that the Cortés expedition passed through Ulúa. In the eyes of Alva Ixtlilxochitl, in contrast, news of the Grijalva expedition "did not trouble Moteczuma [*sic*], who found himself on the greatest throne that he or his ancestors had ever held."[44]

Moctezuma sent emissaries bearing gifts and hoped the Spanish would return from where they came. This was not a good strategy, exemplified by the lists of items obtained by the Grijalva expedition that were compiled by various conquistadors and recounted in detail by Gómara.[45] In emphasizing gold rather than iron, these lists present a Spanish juxtaposition with Aztec perspective recorded in the Florentine Codex. Gómara lists 71 types of items in descending order of European valuation, prioritizing objects made primarily of gold first, and then passing through gilded items to less significant items made without gold. He provides an estimated European monetary value for some items, such as 40 axes with an estimated worth of 2,500 ducats. Gómara contrasts the Native goods with 22 types of items that Grijalva traded in return, declaring the exchanges to have unfairly advantaged the Spanish. Significant among the Spanish trade items were 2,000 green glass beads that Gómara noted were particularly valued by the Natives, as these resembled the most precious Mesoamerican substance, jade, and its symbolic links to fertility and renewal. Gómara also mentions the gifting of a woman, and that several men were taken as captives by the expedition. The Grijalva expedition returned to Cuba, as Moctezuma had hoped, but these exchanges only ensured that Spaniards would hurry to return.

Launching of the Cortés Expedition

When Diego Velázquez designated Cortés as captain of the third expedition to survey the Yucatan, it was initially with the motive of retrieving Grijalva, who had been away longer than warranted. Yet the governor's official instructions came on October 23, 1518, two weeks after Grijalva returned to Cuba, and the conflicting motivations behind launching or detaining the Cortés expedition are difficult to sort out from existing documents.[46] Cortés paid close attention to the political climate of the Spanish court and of administrative apparatuses such as the Council of the Indies and House of Trade, and he clearly sought to leverage the ambiguities in colonial policy available to him.[47] What remained unambiguous, however, was that directly under Diego Columbus (governor of the Indies) were Velázquez (governor of Cuba) and Francisco de Garay (governor of Jamaica), all of whom outranked Cortés and were poised to gain adelantado titles. It was only people bearing this title, repurposed from its *Reconquista* roots to colonization of the Indies, who were authorized to lead further military actions in Mesoamerica. Cortés, in turn, was an encomendero who had Taíno laborers mining minor gold deposits on Cuba and tending cattle, sheep, and horses. His advancement in administrative duties increased from being notary of the town council in Azúa, Hispaniola, to the two-time mayor of Santiago de Cuba. Cortés and Velázquez had a mixed relationship, at times amicable and other times rivalrous, and Cortés had served as the governor's secretary. Nevertheless, he did not possess the military pedigree of Velázquez or Garay, both of whom he would come into conflict with by launching his own invasion before the Crown appointed them as adelantados.

We have previously traced the long-term development of Seville and the greater Gulf of Cádiz as a port region, the northern Meseta of Old Castile as a cultural core with established institutions, and Extremadura as a cultural frontier between these areas. Practically all of the conquistadors originated from these three regions, and more specifically from concentrated subregions within them, shaped roughly by triangles between the towns of Huelva-Cádiz-Córdoba in the Andalusian port region, Salamanca-Segovia-Burgos in the Meseta of Old Castile, and Badajoz-Medellín-Cáceres in Extremadura.[48] The two captains of the previous expeditions to Mesoamerica and the two friars who accompanied Cortés were from the more established core regions: Hernández de Córdoba was from the Andalusian city attached to his surname, and the friar Juan Díaz was from Seville; whereas Grijalva, like his uncle Velázquez, was from the Old Castilian town of Cuéllar, and the friar Bartolomé de Olmedo was from the town of his surname, also in Castile. In contrast, Cortés and a number of his captains hailed from Extremadura, and an estimated 16 percent of the expedition were *extremeños*. More participants of the Cortés expedition came from the two core regions of the Andalusian port zone and Old Castile, with a minority hailing originally from elsewhere in Iberia, including Portugal. There were also a number of non-Iberians, including Taíno and west African servants. One of the few named Black conquistadors was Juan Garrido, but others are mentioned or illustrated in chronicles as well.[49]

Although relatively few of the conquistadors came from Extremadura, the region has received disproportionate attention in histories of the conquest for how its environment may have shaped the ethos of Cortés and other central figures. Pedro de Alvarado hailed from Badajoz and became second in command in the mission. Gonzalo de Sandoval and Alonso Hernández Portocarrero were close confidants of Cortés, from the same hometown, where Portocarrero would have been the highest ranking among them as first cousin to the Count of Medellín. Andrés de Tápia was also from this relatively small town. Like other towns in Extremadura, Medellín projected its frontier identity and fighting spirit through architecture and veneration of patron saints. The town was anchored by its castle stronghold surveying the Guadiana River, and two of Medellín's three churches were dedicated to bellicose saints: Santiago "Matamoros" and San Martín, the latter being the sixth-century Roman legionnaire from what is today Hungary.[50] Cortés was baptized in the church of San Martín, also the namesake of his father, and his parents named him Hernando/Fernando after Fernando III, the *Reconquista*-era king who had converted the mosque at Córdoba into a church and founded the great cathedral of Burgos. The frontier ethos of the

Reconquista and new trans-Atlantic *conquistas* may have therefore been more palpable in Extremadura, compared to the more established core regions.

Cortés spent months outfitting the personnel and supplies for his expedition. With a force of at least 400–500 combatants and another 100 sailors and support staff, it was twice as large as Grijalva's. According to Díaz de Castillo, they sailed from Cuba on 11 ships with 13 musketeers, 4 falconets, and 16 horses aboard. The author even provides us with the behavioral traits of the horses and the colors of their coats, such as one "very good dark chestnut horse, a grand galloper" and another "dappled horse almost black, no good for anything."[51] Gómara reports the flagship of the expedition as a larger *nao* that weighed 100 tons, with three others likely classifiable as caravels weighing between 70 and 80 tons, and the rest smaller brigantines and open vessels.[52] Whereas Cortés-centric narratives paint this force as small in order to highlight its defeat of an empire of millions—ignoring or minimizing the tens of thousands of Native conquistadors who joined the Spaniards—it should be considered in the context of a total European population in the Caribbean at this time of some 5,000 people. In other words, it constituted 10 percent or more of the population and was therefore a considerable force for the colonial Indies of the time.

In charting a course to invade Mexico, Cortés drew on the collective knowledge of the men with him who had been on previous expeditions and anchored in locations where they had encountered fewer hostilities. It began with a return to the island of Cozumel, where the ships arrived staggered by a few days. Díaz, as part of the first group, remarked on encountering a Maya town with fine masonry architecture, whose inhabitants eventually appeared. It was a pacific reception, relative to the defensive posture taken by Maya towns on the peninsular mainland. The inhabitants of Cozumel were Putun traders who were accustomed to receiving strangers in their central location along the Gulf of Mexico–Caribbean exchange route.[53] Díaz reports that Alvarado had taken items from the abandoned town before Cortés reached Cozumel, including minor idols and adornments made with some gold.[54] Cortés objected to the theft and, using Melchor as a translator, had them returned to the Maya and presented them with European goods such as beads, bells, and shirts. The expedition spent a few days on Cozumel, during which Cortés erected a cross and statue of the Virgin in one of the temples. This particular temple was an appropriate location for a Marian image because it was dedicated to and housed a clay effigy of the Maya goddess Ixchel, a pre-Hispanic deity who served as an oracle for pilgrims to the island.[55] The substitution of statues and other effigies of Mesoamerican deities, which the Spaniards referred to as "idols," with this pairing of the Virgin and cross became standard practice for the expedition.

Cortés also sent a mission to the mainland near Cape Catoche in hopes of enticing Jerónimo de Aguilar and Gonzalo Guerrero to join the expedition. Since he had retained his Spanish self-identity after being marooned on the peninsula, Aguilar felt as if he had been saved at last and hurried to join his countrymen. He found his way to Cozumel by paying a Maya canoe team to bring him to the island. He used more green glass beads, which Cortés had sent with the mission, in order to pay the paddlers.[56] When Aguilar arrived, he reported that Guerrero no longer identified as a Spaniard—he was tattooed and wore earspools and a labret, typical adornments for Mesoamericans of status—and chose to remain with his Maya wife and three mestizo sons. Cortés sailed north and west around Cape Catoche to avoid the hostilities encountered by Grijalva, which Aguilar claimed had been initiated by Guerrero.

The expedition anchored for a couple of days off Isla Mujeres, and here de Tapia and Gómara provide brief narrative interludes in their accounts on the catching of a shark—*tiburón* in Spanish.[57] Early Mediterranean seafarers wrote about large sharks, but they disappear from medieval natural histories, giving good reason to believe that the terms for them in both English and Spanish come from the Caribbean. Gómara attempts an etymological linkage to the "gluttony" of the shark's appetite, but *tiburón* likely originated from a Carib term, while the English term was adapted from the Yucatec Mayan *xook* (where the *x* is phonetically sh-), providing us with a bit of linguistic linkage to these events and their environmental setting (Figure 5.5). The fleet then continued sailing to the coast of Campeche, where rough tides prohibited disembarking, and to safe harbor in Laguna de Términos, which brought the expedition in close proximity to the Tabasco/Grijalva River and city-state of Putunchán. The ships arrived at the mouth of the river on March 12, 1519, and the battles of Putunchán and Cintla would be the first two major military engagements between Cortés' forces and the Maya.

Figure 5.5. Ceramic vessel depicting a shark from the Maya city of Lamanai, Belize.
National Museum of the American Indian, Smithsonian Institution (9/1594).
Photograph by NMAI Photo Services.

War with the Maya

Quests to identify the ruins of Putunchán and Cintla date back to the nineteenth century and continue today.[58] Recent research combining the analysis of historical and satellite maps of the region with salvage excavations indicates that the Grijalva River has experienced significant sedimentation over the last five centuries and that Putunchán would have originally been closer to the coast, perhaps near a bridge that crosses the river south of the town of Frontera. The archaeological visibility of Putunchán is complicated by two facts: (1) this area of the Gulf coast has less available stone than the karstic limestone shelf of the Yucatan peninsula, so the Maya built using more perishable materials, such as earthen mounds with pole-and-thatch buildings; and (2) the Spanish established a colonial town in the area that likely involved the destruction of larger Maya structures. One way of estimating locations in dubious cases such as these is to use the distances reported by conquistadors, who used leagues as the unit of measurement. During the sixteenth century, the Spanish measured distance using a legal league of some 2.6 miles (4.19 km) and a common league of 3.46 miles (5.57 km).[59] Whereas the first was used in property claims, the second seems more likely for the sorts of rough calculations of linear distance given in conquistador accounts. So when, for instance, Gómara and Díaz report that Putunchán was located half a league from where the ships of the expedition anchored, we can estimate this being somewhere between 1.3 and 1.73 miles inland (and more likely to be closer to the higher value).

Cortés directed the expedition toward Putunchán because Grijalva's had experienced a peaceful reception there, though the Maya surveyed these earlier arrivals and displayed their large fighting force from fleets of canoes. While anchored at the mouth of the river, Cortés communicated through Aguilar with messengers from Putunchán, who were backed by armed warriors wearing headdresses made from the feathers of bright tropical birds. The accounts of the battles of Putunchán provided by Gómara and Díaz are similar on major details, but Gómara's narrative builds more dramatically and plays up the deceptive maneuvering of both parties in their initial encounters, which included requests by the Spaniards for food, water, and trade goods.[60] Cortés was of course deceptive in order to invade an autonomous kingdom, whereas the Maya of Putunchán, under their leader Tabascoob, were looking instead to defend their homeland. Yet the Spaniards did not view it in this manner and proceeded in what they considered to be a legitimate progression of international engagement: The Requirement was read aloud by the notary Diego de Godoy, translated into Yucatec Mayan by Aguilar at an unknown level of fidelity and audibility to a population of Chontal Mayan speakers. The inhabitants of Putunchán defended their town valiantly at the river from wooden barricades, and over the first night had sent women and children to safety while Cortés offloaded artillery from the ships and split his forces in order to be able to attack both from the river and land. Díaz claims the Maya numbered over 12,000 warriors, while Gómara only says there were many.

The battle of Putunchán and subsequent battle of Cintla present several firsts that would be repeated in remaining episodes of the invasion of Mesoamerica. The Spaniards used their artillery—canons, harquebuses, and crossbows—to break the wooden Maya barricades, a type of fortification suited to Mesoamerican raiding and hegemonic warfare, but not to these technologies that had developed as part of European systems of total war. The Maya nevertheless adapted quickly to the new battle tactics of the invaders by keeping their formations at a distance beyond Spanish infantry—primarily using swords and pikes—from which they could continue to fire their own projectiles of arrows, darts, and slingshot.[61] When the Maya retreated from the first day of conflict and the Spanish occupied Putunchán, Cortés undertook the first ritual act of possession by slicing with his sword into a sacred ceiba tree that was a central feature of the main plaza of the town. Ceibas are the largest trees on the Yucatan and were sacred to the Maya and other Mesoamerican peoples as manifestations of the axis mundi believed to connect the earth and heavens.[62] Through this performance and symbolic marking, Cortés was exceeding his authorization by Velázquez to explore and trade through an act of territorial possession. It was interpreted by the Maya as an attack on their religion and view of the cosmos.

Horses and European apparitions of divine intermediaries on horseback made their initial appearances on Mesoamerican soil in the battles of Putunchán and Cintla. We may be quick to assume that the battlefield advantage of actual horses was more consequential to the Spanish invasion, but should not minimize how the Spaniards framed warfare religiously, as Mesoamericans did, and that accounts of these apparitions could have motivated them to fight when they were outnumbered and their chances seemed slim. On the tactical side, Cortés' deployment of cavalry at Cintla and the devastating effect it had of breaking the formations of Maya warriors is well documented. Although there were only 13 riders, Mesoamericans had never encountered cavalry before and therefore never had the need to develop an infantry with anti-cavalry tactics and technologies.[63] Díaz reports that the Maya at Cintla thought that both horse and horseman represented a single animal, and the chapter's epigraph conveys Aztec fear of the Spaniard's "large deer." In later battles, the Spaniards would find ways of exploiting the advantage conferred by their cavalry by splitting it up into small groups in coordinated formations with their infantry.

The tactical advantage of having horses is clearer than what divine interventions, if any, the conquistadors perceived at the time. Eventually these crystallized in colonial-period literature as Santiago Mataindios, a recasting of the Moor-slayer to the Indian-slayer.[64] Gómara mentions Cortés calling on a holy triad of God, Santiago, and St. Peter, whereas Díaz mentions multiple conquistadors calling out "Santiago" as a battle charge. Vázquez de Tapia recounted witnessing a miraculous arrival of a heroic horseman galloping into the fray on a white horse when the Spanish chances looked bleak, which harkens to Santiago mythology from the battle of Clavijo and others of the *Reconquista*.[65] Whatever the exact details may be, the remaining invasion of Mesoamerica would likewise be characterized by fierce battles waged to conquer or defend territory using different military technologies and conceptualized through different worldviews that had developed over millennia on alternate sides of the Atlantic.

La Malinche and Early Alliances

In the aftermath of the battles of Putunchán and Cintla, the Chontal Maya of the region followed standard Mesoamerican protocol for defeat by making a peace offering to the Spaniards that included food, jewels, and 20 women. Women were exchanged in Mesoamerican societies to extend kin networks and cement alliances. The quantity of 20 reflected their vigesimal system of numeration. So began a process of mestizaje that was different from the earlier case of Gonzalo Guerrero and his Maya family. It was one in which Mesoamerican and Spanish understandings of such pairings were not aligned, resulting in the widespread sexual abuse and exploitation of Native women.[66] The Spaniards christened these women, with a greater interest in making them sexual servants than in saving their souls.

One was christened with the name Marina, but she is better known to history as Malinche.[67] Whether called by the honorific titles Doña Marina, Malintzin, or La Malinche, she had humbler origins than the titles bestowed on her later imply. Early chapters of Malinche's life are opaque, but the fact that she could speak courtly Nahuatl, which had a different grammar than the vernacular language, indicates that she was raised in proximity to a sphere of imperial power. She was born around 1500 in a village named Huiotlan or Olutla, which was situated between the coastal Gulf town of Coatzalcoalcos and the imperial Aztec garrison of Tochtepec, farther to the west. Malinche's father may have been a local lord, but following his death she was sold into servitude to Chontal Maya from the region of Putunchán and Xicallanco, eventually becoming a servant of Tabscoob, the leader who mobilized the resistance against the Spanish. Her ability to speak the Aztec imperial lingua franca and Chontal Mayan, intelligible by Aguilar through his grasp of Yucatecan, made Malinche one of the key figures during all subsequent events. The Spaniards did not yet know of Malinche's abilities as a potential translator at Putunchán. Cortés reserved her for Puertocarrero, his social superior from Medellín, based on her physical attractiveness rather than her latent intelligence.

Language diversity and translation involving multiple speakers were critical to enabling Spanish-Mesoamerican alliances and to mediating war and peace. In addition to courtly and vernacular Nahuatl, languages of the Aztec Empire included those in the Otomanguean family such as Otomi, Mixtec, Zapotec, Mazahua, and Pame, generally spoken in highland regions; Totonac and Mixe-Zoquean languages, found more on the coasts; and the Mayan language isolate Huaxtec, whose speakers were separated from the main Mayan group and had a home within the Sierra Madre Oriental.[68] Because Nahuatl was the imperial language, subject city-states employed their own translators (*nahuatlatos*, "those who speak Nahuatl").[69] After being gifted to the Spaniards, Malinche and other Maya women communicated with Aguilar on the ships. This journey, which coincided with the Christian Holy Week, departed from Putunchán on Palm Sunday, passed by Malinche's original home region around Coatzacoalcos, and landed at San Juan de Ulúa the Thursday before Easter, on April 21, 1519. At Ulúa, the expedition was first approached by emissaries of Moctezuma who spoke Nahuatl and, after Aguilar failed to understand what they were saying, Malinche stepped forward to translate. It was a strategic calculation made by Malinche, whose decision-making was severely limited by the conditions in which she found herself, and it would bring her renown among the Spaniards and Mesoamericans who bestowed on her the honorific titles we know her by today.

The next day being Good Friday, Cortés saw it fit to bestow the mainland across from Ulúa with the name Veracruz, meaning "true cross." In all, three locations along the coast were christened with this name, which is now mostly known for the state in Mexico and its major port city. Over the ensuing days, the expedition received Moctezuma's emissaries as well as provincial governors and local lords, whom they grouped as *caciques*, using the Taíno term they were familiar with from the Caribbean. The groups exchanged goods regularly throughout the stay in Veracruz. On Easter Sunday, Bartolomé de Olmedo and Juan Díaz presided over mass with the emissaries and caciques looking on, including a local governor named Teuhtlilli (also known as Tentlil and Tendile) who arrived with a larger delegation that Gómara claims numbered 4,000 (Díaz's estimate is lower). Cortés held the military parade that Moctezuma's emissaries recount to him in the epigraph to this chapter.[70] The Great Speaker of Tenochtitlan learned of the expedition through the emissaries and with regular updates arriving through teams of relay runners who carried news and goods between the coast and imperial core. The emissaries also made illustrations of the expedition that are now lost but presumably were either rendered on *amate* paper made from the pulp of a ficus tree typical for Aztec books, or cloth. In their illustrations, the scribes highlighted attributes that were foreign to them, such as the beards on the men, their armor and weapons, and the relatively large size of the boats, dogs, and strange "deer." The scribes also depicted Malinche as the crucial intermediary (Plate 4b).

Exchanges between the Spaniards and local groups continued for weeks and also included more distant contacts between Veracruz and Tenochtitlan. On behalf of his sovereign Moctezuma, Tehutlilli lavished extravagant gifts on Cortés, among which were a solar disc made of gold and a complementary lunar disc made of silver; elaborate vestments; masks depicting deities; and ornately feathered shields, fans, and staffs. Cortés opens his second letter to Charles V by noting that he had sent the lost first letter on June 16, 1519, with Puertocarrero and Montejo, who also carried the treasures gifted by Moctezuma. The date would have been 12 days before the king was elected as Holy Roman Emperor, though his official coronation ceremony in Germany would not be until October of the following year. The expedition made its way up the coast from Veracruz to Cempoala, the largest Totonac city-state and a tributary province of the Triple Alliance (Figure 5.6).

Figure 5.6. Totonac city of Cempoala.
Photo by the author. Reproduction authorized by the Instituto Nacional de Antropología e Historia, Mexico.

Although she did not speak Totonac, Malinche knew to request *nahuatlatos* from the delegation of Cempoalans who had journeyed to Veracruz to meet the Spaniards once Moctezuma's emissaries had left. Through Malinche and these translators, the Cempoalans invited the Spaniards to their city, which Cortés tried unsuccessfully to rename Seville. In these discussion Cortés learned that the Cempoalans were dissatisfied with their overlords.

The events and individual motivations that drove the Cortés expedition during the time spent on the Veracruz coast, from late April to the middle of August, are disputed. Three key episodes include the founding of a town council (*cabildo*) at Villa Rica de Veracruz as a means of authorizing the invasion; the Spanish-Totonac alliance made at Cempoala, which added hundreds of Native porters and scouts who provided knowledge of the physical and political landscape ahead; and Cortés' scuttling of the ships to ensure that no faction of the expedition could mutiny.[71]

Cortés wrote his second letter to Charles V on October 30, 1520, at a midpoint in the invasion. Throughout it, he framed Native groups as generally willing vassals to the Holy Roman Emperor, and his own actions earlier in Veracruz as a means of quelling rebellion on the part of those men loyal to Velázquez and in the service of gaining for the emperor what was rightfully his. In the very first line of the letter, Cortés used the term "New Spain" for the first time in recorded history. This branding served to bestow legitimacy on his actions and to veil the yet-to-be established colony in an aspirational name. It is possible that Cortés had used New Spain earlier in his lost first letter as well, but it was not used in the town council petition from Veracruz. Cortés and Gómara both foreground the conquistador as the instigator of the founding of Villa Rica de Veracruz and its town council, which dutifully designated Cortés as capitan general, thereby providing the legal legitimacy for invasion. Any claims to such legitimacy are based on medieval Castilian law known as the Siete Partidas (Seven Part Code), established by King Alfonso X in the thirteenth century and printed in Seville in 1491.[72] As part of Cortés' legal training at Salamanca, he was likely aware that the legal code allowed for some autonomy from the chain of command if it was in the interests of the "common good" of the kingdom. Yet it is clear that other members of the expedition understood the ambiguities inherent to their campaign. They were situated at an unprecedented distance from the Spanish Crown and its administrative institutions, and Díaz presents the decision to invade, rather than explore and trade, as jointly made by Puertocarrero, the Alvarado brothers, and many other members of the expedition, including lowly foot soldiers such as himself.[73] As the captain closest to Velázquez, Montejo had to be convinced of the legitimacy of the action before he sailed with Puertocarrero, the letter, and treasure to present to King Charles. Because of the prevailing winds, voyages between the Gulf of Mexico and Spain took at least four and a half months, and this was when winds were favorable in May and June; voyages across the Atlantic in the other direction were half the duration.[74]

The shipment brought to Spain by Puertocarrero and Montejo was an important part of the protracted political negotiations of the expedition, whose members made their case for invasion through the written word and through the presentation of Mesoamerican goods and peoples, as Totonacs from Cempoala were also aboard.[75] Items were listed in detail in the town council petition that has become substituted as Cortés' lost first letter. The gold and silver discs and other finery are also recorded by Gómara and were corroborated by the German artist Albrecht Dürer, who viewed them at court in 1520. When Puertocarrero and Montejo docked at Seville in early November 1519, their timing was unlucky because they coincided with a visit to the city by Velázquez's chaplain, Benito Martín, who promptly convinced the customs officials of the House of Trade to embargo the ships and their precious cargo. Undeterred, Puertocarrero and Montejo set out with Cortés' father, Martín, to track down the king at Barcelona, but by the time they arrived, Charles and his entourage had left for Castile. The conquistadors finally caught up with the king at Tordesillas, where the partition of the Americas between the Spanish and Portuguese had been decided a quarter of a century earlier.

Following contested negotiations with individuals loyal to Velázquez and critical of Cortés, including Fonseca of the Council of the Indies, Moctezuma's treasure and other items collected along the Gulf of Mexico were released from the House of Trade and reached Valladolid in early April 1520. By this time, Cortés and the allied forces were already in Tenochtitlan, and Puertocarrero and Montejo were akin to overseas diplomats arguing for the king's legitimation of the expedition. They petitioned the king once more following the impactful display of the Mesoamerican goods and before he was set to sail from A Coruña to be crowned as Holy Roman Emperor at the German cathedral of Aachen. A part of the treasure remained in Castile while other pieces journeyed with Charles to Flanders. Europeans valued the gold and silver only for their potential as coinage, not as objects of art, and they were smelted into bullion. But composite objects, especially those involving elaborate featherwork that Aztec artisans excelled at, helped to materialize a notion of a New Spain across the Atlantic. Although King Charles did not legitimate the Cortés expedition, neither did he order that it cease. The expedition fit with his official motto *plus ultra* ("further beyond") that as Holy Roman Emperor he began to affix to his imperial coat of arms, also featuring the Hapsburg eagle, the royal arms of the unified kingdoms of Spain, and the critical flanking elements of the Pillars of Hercules—which, unlike the ancients, including even the Romans, his kingdom now extended further beyond.

Over their months stationed at Veracruz, it had become clear to the Spaniards that any future success of the expedition required the committed participation of a large number of Native allies. Alliance building began at Cempoala when a joint army of the Cortés expedition plus a Totonac force that Díaz estimates as 2,000 battled to the north around the towns of Nautla and Quiahuitzlan, where the Cempoalans looked to reassert their dominion over lands claimed by the Triple Alliance. Totonac leaders, including the ruler of Cempoala referred to by Díaz as the "fat cacique," appear to have strategically directed alliance formation, perhaps proposing a new triple alliance among themselves, the Spaniards, and powerful city-states of the highlands hostile to the Aztec Empire, such as Tlaxcala.[76] Other Totonac polities remained loyal to the Triple Alliance or were reined in by the captains of imperial forces in the region around Quiahuitzlan and Nautla. Approximately a month later, when the group led by Cortés had headed inland, Moctezuma sent a force to the coast, under the command of Qualpopoca, which killed several Spaniards. This would prove important later, as Cortés used it as a pretense for his actions in Tenochtitlan.

Cortés also confronted the prospect of rebellion among his own ranks, as some members loyal to Velázquez were reported to have plans to mutiny. In order to punish the leaders of the potential rebellion, Cortés had two executed, flogged the others, and declared that the ships should be destroyed on the basis of being "unfit to sail."[77] Writing in the later sixteenth century, historians such as Cervantes de Salazar elaborated a myth that Cortés ordered the boats to be burned to signal a Caesar-crossing-the-Rubicon-type moment for the expedition. This romanticized notion became pervasive in later histories but is a myth. The ships had been at sea for six months without maintenance, and Díaz notes that Cortés wanted the decision to look consensual among the expedition. If it looked like the unilateral decision of a fearless leader, Cortés alone could have been asked to recompense the loss of property at a future date.[78] In disassembling and sinking the ships, Cortés kept all of the important hardware—such as sails and metal fittings—and maintained the flagship intact, along with a few small skiffs. The expedition was not cut off from the Spanish Caribbean, as there were other expeditions along the coast, including one to the north captained by the governor of Jamaica, Franciso de Garay. Another ship also arrived at Veracruz from Cuba, bringing the expedition a few more men and horses, as well as the news that Velázquez and Garay had been granted adelanto status and were authorized by the Crown to establish settlements. Finally, the Cortés expedition had its own expert shipbuilder, Martín Lopez, who could assemble new ships whenever necessary. The sinking of the ships nevertheless presents a dramatic moment in the narrative and remains compelling because of the implications of this purposeful act of destruction. A Mexican-led underwater archaeology team is currently surveying the coast of Veracruz for any preserved remains of the ships.[79] They have so far discovered three anchors that are stylistically consistent with Spanish use in the early sixteenth century, one of which incredibally has preserved wood. The wood has been radiocarbon dated to the fifteenth century and identified as a species from the forests of Cantabria. If the anchors or other discoveries are verified as from Cortés' lost fleet, they will provide yet another tangible link to this foundational chapter of Mexico's past.

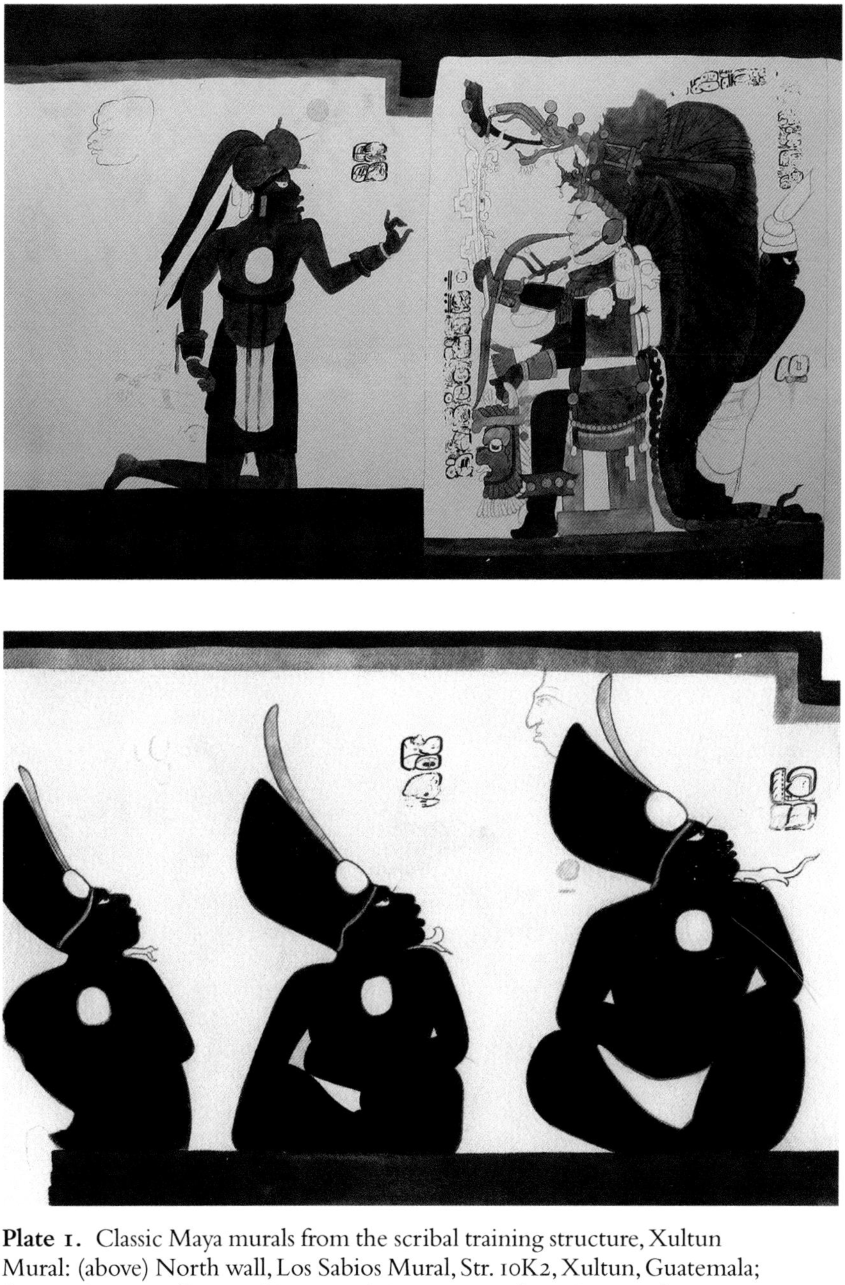

Plate 1. Classic Maya murals from the scribal training structure, Xultun Mural: (above) North wall, Los Sabios Mural, Str. 10K2, Xultun, Guatemala; (bottom) West wall, Los Sabios Mural, Str. 10K2, Xultun, Guatemala.

Illustration by Heather Hurst ©2014; used with permission.

Plate 2a. View of Teotihuacan looking south from the Moon Pyramid to the Sun Pyramid and Street of the Dead.

Photo by the author. Reproduction authorized by the Instituto Nacional de Antropología e Historia, Mexico.

Plate 2b. Mural depiction of an Eagle Warrior standing on a Feathered Serpent from the site of Cacaxtla.

Photo by the author. Reproduction authorized by the Instituto Nacional de Antropología e Historia, Mexico.

Plate 3a. Anthropomorphic landscape of Las Médulas, León, once the most productive gold mine in the Roman Empire.
Photo by the author.

Plate 3b. Seville and Guadalquivir river with Islamic tower (the Tower of Gold) in foreground and minaret in background, both with later Christian additions.
Photo by the author.

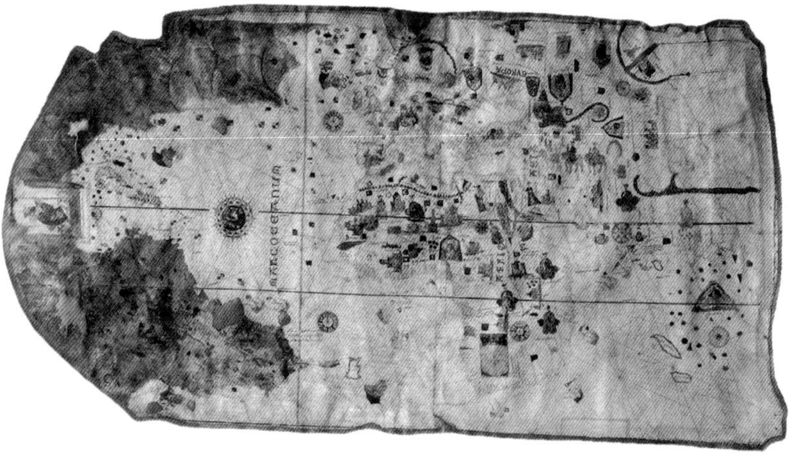

Plate 4a. Juan de la Cosa's *mappa mundi* of 1500, the first European one depicting the Americas.

Public domain. https://commons.wikimedia.org/wiki/File:1500_map_by_Juan_de_la_Cosa-North_up.jpg

Plate 4b. Illustration of Malinche (labeled as Marina) and Cortés (labeled as Marques) with Spanish boats from Durán.

Alamy Stock Photo.

Plate 5a. Tlaltecuhtli stone found at base of Great Temple. Museo de Templo Mayor.

Photo by author. Reproduction authorized by the Instituto Nacional de Antropología e Historia, Mexico.

Plate 5b. Plaza of the Three Cultures at Tlatelolco: site of Cuauhtemoc's surrender, the church of Santiago erected above the pre-Hispanic precinct, and Imperial College of Santa Cruz college where Sahagún worked with Mexica scribes.

Photo by author. Reproduction authorized by the Instituto Nacional de Antropología e Historia, Mexico.

Plate 6a. Tiles from Charles V's pavilion in the garden of the Alcázar, Seville, commemorating his marriage to Isabela of Portugal and displaying his motto *plus ultra*.

Photo by the author.

Plate 6b. Conquest of Michoacan from *Lienzo de Tlaxcala*, with Native depiction of richly garbed Tlaxcalteca in the vanguard against local Purepecha (Tarascans).

Alamy Stock Photo.

Plate 7. Class at the University of Salamanca, 1614.
Alamy Stock Photo.

Plate 8. El primer milagro ("the first miracle") depicting the Virgin of Guadalupe healing a Nahua actor after an accident in a September 26, 1531, mock battle between Toltec-Mexica and Chichimecs as part of the procession up the causeway between Mexico City and Tepeyac.

Attributed to the workshop of José Júarez (1653). Museo de la Basilica de Guadalupe.

6

Old Foes, New Allies

> [W]e saw so many cities and villages built in the water and other great towns on dry land and that straight and level Causeway going towards Mexico, we were amazed and said that it was like the enchantments they tell of in the legend of Amadis, on account of the great towers and cues [temples] and buildings rising from the water, and all built of masonry. And some of our soldiers even asked whether the things that we saw were not a dream.
>
> —Bernal Díaz del Castillo (1576)[1]

On August 16, 1519, the joint Spanish-Totonac forces began their ascent from the humid Gulf coast to the Aztec core on the temperate Altiplano. A Cempoalan named Tlacochcalcatl led the way as a guide and Totonac-speaking translator. Cortés and Díaz report that 400 Cempoalans accompanied them in all, primarily serving as scouts and porters. These Native allies thereby doubled the size of the expedition, since Cortés left some 150 men, mostly sailors from the now-ruined boats, behind at Veracruz under the command of Juan de Esclante. By joining the bearded foreigners, the Totonacs were gambling that they would not be judged harshly by their Aztec overlords; yet, they may have also been hedging their bets on the eventual outcome of the expedition by purposefully assuming less of a military role. The Cempoalans vowed to lead the Spaniards to the Tlaxcalteca, whom they promoted as better allies, renowned as fierce warriors and bitter rivals of the Mexica.

Over two weeks of travel between Cempoala and Tlaxcala, the expedition stayed in the town of Jalapa and then meandered southward on the eastern flank of the Sierra Madre Oriental, which is a fertile coffee-growing region today around the towns of Coatepec and Xico, formerly Xicochimalco (Figure 6.1). The detour south was a strange decision given the eventual progression of the route, as they could have continued west from Jalapa to

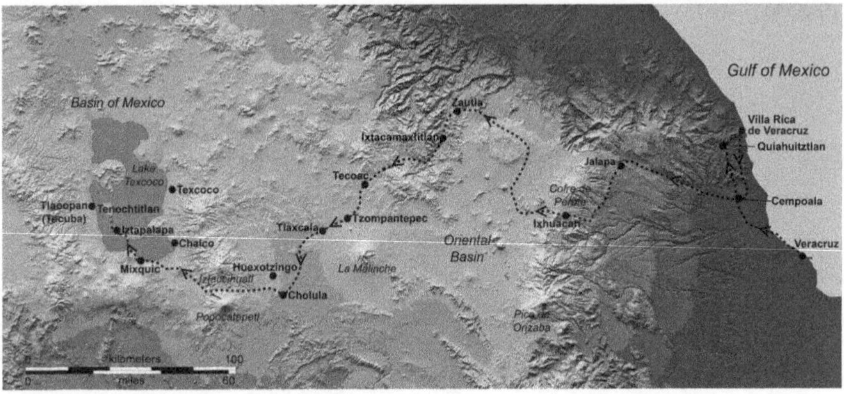

Figure 6.1. Map of route inland from Cempoala to Tenochtitlan.

the Altiplano. Instead, they cut through a mountain pass via the town of Ixhuacan south of Cofre de Perote, a dormant volcano with a boxy peak over 14,000 feet above sea level (4,280 m). Looming in the distance farther south was Pico de Orizaba, a majestic volcanic cone called Citlatepetl ("star mountain") in Nahuatl. At 18,491 feet above sea level (5,636 m), Orizaba's is the highest point in Mesoamerica and one of the tallest in North America. It is snowcapped year round. Cortés and Diáz comment on the impressive peaks and the change to arid and cold landscapes when they first reached the high plains at the eastern Oriental Basin and headed northward.

Motivations for the tack north in the Oriental Basin are also not completely clear. The expedition made a loop to pass through the lands of Tlalquaquitepec and Zautla (previously Tzauhtlan or Xocotlan) before returning south to enter Tlaxcala, when they could have entered more directly by continuing in a westerly direction through the Otomi city-state of Huamantla. The decision to enter from the north may have been made after receiving news that the Tlaxcalteca were skeptical of the motivations of the foreigners, especially since they were in frequent contact with emissaries of Moctezuma's, and were determined to resist them at the border. The Cempoalans may have therefore charted a course into the mountains bordering Puebla and Veracruz, where populations were subject to the Triple Alliance and had contacts with Totonacs from the coast. Alternatively, the Spaniards may have wanted to search for gold mines to the north, or they may have considered a salt lake and arid landscape of the Oriental Basin as obstacles to charting a route westward.[2] Whatever the case may be, the expedition headed north and eventually arrived at Zautla and then Ixtacamaxtitlan, both located along a natural corridor of communication cut between the Altiplano and Sierra of Puebla by the narrow Apulco River.

It is here that the sources get more specific regarding the route and entry into Tlaxcala. When Cortés referred to three to four leagues of settlement lining the canyon lands cut by the Apulco at Ixtacamaxtitlan, he surely groups a number of towns and villages that could have been subject to the altepetl over some 10–12 miles (15–20 km). Prior to its conquest by the Triple Alliance, Ixtacamaxtitlan was a powerful polity that benefited from its location on a corridor of communication and the natural defensibility offered by the canyon. Some of the Portuguese members of the expedition dubbed the town Castilblanco because it reminded them of a fortress town of that name in their country (Castelo Branco). Architectural remains visible today at Ixtacamaxtitlan are not as large as other towns on the route, but the site still maintains ruins of domestic terraces along the slopes of the canyon and sculpture that local inhabitants discovered primarily on hilltops such as Cerro Acolhua. The late eighteenth-century French explorer Guillermo Dupaix illustrated some pyramidal platforms that were still visible when he visited, but were dismantled to make use of the stone since then.[3] Sculpture from the site includes a statue of a coyote on top of two serpents and a skull rack (*tzompantli*) where stylized skulls are rendered on tenons that were inset to a wall. There is no archaeological confirmation of a skull rack made from 100,000 actual human skulls, as Díaz dramatizes,[4] but a smaller one may have once existed. Cortés mentions that the ruler of Ixtacamaxtitlan resided on this hill and, although a vassal of Moctezuma's, lodged the expedition for three days (August 28–30) while they awaited news from messengers sent to Tlaxcala. He also provided 300 additional warriors, bringing the total size of the expedition's forces close to 1,000, divided among soldiers, scouts, porters, and other supporting roles. Though larger, this force was poised to face a much more formidable foe in the Tlaxcalteca, who possessed greater numbers and a more cohesive state than any the Spaniards had encountered thus far among the Maya and Totonacs.

The Battle of Tecoac

Entering Tlaxcala in early September near the end of the rainy season, the Spaniards and their allies, now from Cempoala and Ixtacamaxtitlan, would have encountered a relatively green highland landscape with valleys and plains partitioned by bluish-green sierras and a volcano with the Nahuatl name Matlacueye ("she of the blue-green skirt") towering in the distance (Figure 6.2). The volcano has been dormant for the last 3,000 years, and its Nahuatl name is evocative of its gradually sloping sides converging on a peak, like the silhouette of a skirted woman.[5] Its feminine associations continue today, as it was eventually renamed La Malinche in honor of Malintzin and the critical role she played in translating the encounter.

Being the tail end of the rainy season, nearing harvest, the entry into Tlaxcala was not during the typical war season on the Altiplano, which was in the dry season when there were no fields to tend. Northern Tlaxcala would have been seen as arid by the coastal Totonacs, but it receives substantially more rain than the entry point the expedition took through the Oriental Basin and through Ixtacamaxtitlan. To the eyes of Castilians from the Iberian Meseta, it would have been an intelligible landscape, similar to the better-watered parts of that region. In fact, the anonymous conquistador

Figure 6.2. Tlaxcalan landscape at the point of initial encounter near the exit of the Apulco Canyon leading from Ixtacamaxtitlan, with La Malinche volcano. Photo by the author.

began his account by drawing this very comparison: "This land of New Spain is similar to Spain, and the mountains, valleys, and plains are almost the same, except that the sierras are more fearful and rugged; so much so, that they cannot be scaled without infinite work."[6]

Artifacts from the contact era in northern Tlaxcala exhibit a division between what archaeologists have designated the Tlaxco culture, named for the largest town in the region, and the widespread stylistic horizons known as Aztec IV–V. Among the differences in material culture are the white or cream color of some pottery diagnostic of the Tlaxco sphere, which may have been made locally in northern Tlaxcala or imported from the Huaxtec region to the northeast. In either case, it differs from the dominant black-on-orange pottery of Aztec serving wares. Here once again, general ethnonyms like Aztec prove problematic, but it is apparent that stylistic differences reflect some ethnic differences and variability in social networks. Whereas Tlaxco materials may have more Otomi and possible Huaxtec ethnic markers, Aztec horizon materials show closer affiliations with the Nahua sphere of interaction, be it by actual Nahuatl speakers or Otomis who were more closely connected with the commercial and stylistic networks of Aztec cultural core, even if politically independent from the Triple Alliance.[7]

Among the Otomi polities mentioned most in historical sources, Tecoac and Hueyotlipan contributed valued warriors to the Tlaxcalteca army and were both located on trade routes that would have integrated these populations more into the Nahuatl-speaking sphere.[8] Hueyotlipan's name signifies "on the great road" in Nahuatl, as it was situated on the natural footpath between the Basin of Mexico and Gulf of Mexico, which was of enduring strategic importance ever since Teotihuacan's apogee, centuries prior to the Aztecs. Tecoac was situated along a secondary route to the northeast, following the Apulco River into the Sierra Madre Oriental and down to the Gulf coast. In contrast, the Tlaxco sphere likely coincides with the Otomi domains of Tliliuhquitepec and Atlangatepec, which were not as integrated into the core of the Tlaxcallan confederation, though warriors from Tliluhquitepec also allied with the Spaniards. It remains unclear whether they joined from their homeland to the north or whether they were residents in the city of Tlaxcala as refugees following their recent conquest by the Triple Alliance.

Some debate exists regarding the exact route the Spaniards and their allies from Cempoala and Ixtacamaxtitlan followed, as well as the stops along the way listed in the chronicles, on their way to Tlaxcala. One opinion situates the initial encounters with Otomis and Nahuas of Tlaxcala in the vicinity of Huamantla.[9] It can be dismissed, however, since a second route involving entry to Tlaxcala via the Apulco River is much more supported by textual and archaeological evidence. The Apulco originates in the continental divide at the northern Tlaxcala-Puebla border, where it is also known as the Xalneneque, and increases in flow passing Ixtacamaxtitlan before eventually joining the Tecolutla River and draining in the Gulf of Mexico.[10] It is the route that the expedition had followed since Zautla. Lines of evidence that converge on this entry point into Tlaxcala include pre-Hispanic settlement patterns, place names from the early colonial period up to the early twentieth century and, most convincingly, the distances that Cortés and others mention for the route.[11]

Soon after setting out from Ixtacamaxtitlan, Cortés and other eyewitnesses recount coming to an abandoned defensive wall made of stone cemented with lime, standing nine feet high, and stretching across the valley to mark the boundary with Tlaxcala. Earlier scholars claimed to have located sparse remains of the wall, but the area has not received systematic archaeological survey.[12] Wherever it may have been within the canyon, Cortés estimates progressing four leagues beyond the wall before encountering armed warriors, who were primarily or exclusively Otomis rather than Nahuas. Díaz estimates having traveled two leagues from Ixtacamaxtitlan before arriving at the wall, and then an unspecified but short distance before the location of the first battle the expedition faced within the Mexican highlands. Both Cortés and Díaz relate having camped next to a stream, and their accounts of distance are consistent with a journey up the canyon cut by the Apulco. Cortés' estimate of four leagues past the wall is equivalent to some 14 miles (22.5 km), and Díaz's estimate of two leagues plus some undetermined but short interval would be a similar or shorter distance. Given a little extra travel to the wall in Cortés' account, the distance is much more consistent with the 19 miles (30.5 km) between Ixtacamaxtitlan and the contemporary town of Lázaro Cárdenas, where the Apulco begins to descend toward the Gulf from northern Tlaxcala, than the 44 miles (71 km) separating Ixtacamaxtitlan from a town named Tecoac near Huamantla.

Tecoac is significant as the first large battle between Cortés' forces and people from Tlaxcala, who would become the critical allies in toppling the Aztec Empire. The altepetl is also referred to in chronicles as Tecohuactzinco, Tecoatzingo, or Tehuacingo. Muñoz Camargo, the sixteenth-century mestizo historian of Tlaxcala, identifies Tecohuactzingo as an Otomi polity of Tlaxcala's northern frontier, as do the scribes of the Florentine Codex, but using the name Tecoac.[13] Tezozomoc refers to the inhabitants of Tecoac as both Otomi and Chichimec, the latter intended to convey their less "civilized" nature relative to the Mexica.[14] These frontier Otomis were respected within highland Mexico as great warriors, including the legendary figure Tlahuicole who is said, by Muñoz Camargo and others, to have been captured by the Mexica prior to the Spanish arrival in one of the "flowery wars" against Tlaxcala. The Mexica took Tlahuicole to Tenochtitlan to be sacrificed in gladiatorial combat, but he succeeded in killing seven warriors who fought him sequentially. For this, Tlahuicole was spared his life and incorporated into the Mexica army. Though small, the Otomi population in northern Tlaxcala was therefore a force to be reckoned with.

The initial battle of Tecoac occurred on September 2, but it began a period of over 20 days of fighting and uneasy diplomatic forays. The hostilities began somewhere in the exit from the Apulco Canyon with Cortés and some 6 to 11 other horsemen, who had advanced half a league ahead of the rest of the expedition, confronting a couple dozen warriors who "fought so fiercely with us that they killed two horses and wounded three others and two horsemen."[15] The initial group of scouts was part of a strategy to entice the Spaniards out of the Sierra of Ixtacamaxtitlan to face the main fighting force, which Díaz estimates at 3,000, Cortés estimates at 5,000, and de Tapia inflates unrealistically to 100,000—much too high for even the full Tlaxcalteca army. The rest of the Spaniards and Native allies did not arrive at Tecoac until sunset, when they established camp.

Mesoamericans typically started battles early, and at daybreak the next morning the Tlaxcalteca had already assembled in the valley below, which at this time of year would have been milpa fields of fully grown maize, beans, and squash, interspersed with spiky maguey plants (agave). Other warriors were better hidden within ravines bisecting the terrain. Whereas the small initial group of the previous day may have been only Otomis, this larger group was surely a mix of Otomis and Nahuatl-speaking Tlaxcalteca, with more of the latter. Díaz recounts Cortés' invocation of Castile's conquering saint in shouting "Santiago—and at them!" before the assault.[16] Cortés ordered the cavalry be in the vanguard for the battle, which proved decisive in this initial victory. Other sources provide hyperbolic statements about the battle, such as Gómara claiming that Tlaxcalteca broadswords lined with obsidian (the *machuahuitl*) could "slice cleanly through the horses' necks, reins and all"—a clear impossibility based on experimentation with the weapon.[17] Nevertheless, the fact that Otomi and Tlaxcalteca warriors were successful at targeting and taking down cavalry clearly made an impression on the Spaniards, as did their taking the horses' heads as war trophies, possibly to display on the skull rack in the capital city of Tlaxcala.[18]

The Codex Huamantla provides a pictorial account of the battle of Tecoac rendered by Otomi scribes in a strongly pre-Hispanic style. It depicts two Spaniards, one representing Alvarado, leading cavalry charges against defeated and bleeding Otomi warriors—a grizzly scene flanking a central one depicting the Otomis bringing food and jewels to the Spaniards. The descriptive illustrations that accompanies Muñoz Camargo's text were drawn in a much more European style. In one associated with the battle of Tecoac, the caption states that once the Otomis realized that the expedition was not allied with Moctezuma they brought the Spaniards and Totonacs food to make amends, and that this took place in the mountains of Ilihuca, which likely translates as "place of alder (*ilitl*) trees."[19] The image depicts Cortés and Juan Díaz on horses with Malinche on foot next to an alder tree and two Tlaxcalteca carrying turkeys (Figure 6.3). These sixteenth-century Native

Figure 6.3. Entry into the Tlaxcala's northern frontier, depicting Cortés and Juan Díaz on horses, Malinche next to tree, and Otomis bringing turkeys.
Illustration by Pedro Cahuantzi Hernández based on Muñoz Camargo (1584/2000: cuadro 29).

accounts therefore portray the Spaniards as camped at the forested edge of the sierra, rather than the plains of northern Tlaxcala. They also depict both the Nahuas and Otomis of Tlaxcala as loyal allies from the inception, but this narrative was concocted within a context of colonial negotiation with their new Spanish overlords; alternate lines of evidence point to fierce initial Native resistance. The Tlaxcalteca resistance made an impression on the Spaniards, who had gathered from the Cempoalans that these rivals to the Triple Alliance would be amicable and disposed to form an alliance of their own to topple the empire.

The Spanish-Tlaxcalteca Alliance

The altepetl of Tlaxcala, or Tlaxcallan, is proving through recent research to be one of the most interesting political formations of the pre-Hispanic world: a Native experiment in pluralistic governance. Although all central Mexican city-states incorporated some elements of shared decision-making, including systems of co-rule involving two or four leaders, or single rulers elected by a noble council they were somewhat beholden to, the confederated political entity centered on the city of Tlaxcala took these institutions in new directions.[20] It provides yet another example of where colonial period texts have to be read critically with reference to what has been found archaeologically.

In the post-conquest period, the Tlaxcalteca presented themselves as having been a confederation between four city-states or *altepemeh* (the plural of altepetl): Tizatlan, Tepeticpac, Quiahuitzlan, and Ocotululco. If so, the arrangement may have had some similarities with other confederations in central Mexico, including the Aztec Triple Alliance, or perhaps other Native American confederacies like the Iroquoian (or Haudenosaunee) League of upstate New York. Yet when archaeologists recently mapped the pre-Hispanic occupation of Tlaxcala systematically, they found it to be one contiguous urban agglomeration comprising interconnected residential terraces and plazas, with these four place designations more akin to urban wards or districts, except for a detached ceremonial center at Tizatlan (Figure 6.4). Cortés and other conquistadors likened Tlaxcala to the Renaissance republics of northern Italy, with Cortés writing in his second letter: "The orderly manner in which, until now, these people have been governed is almost like that of the states of Venice or Genoa or Pisa,

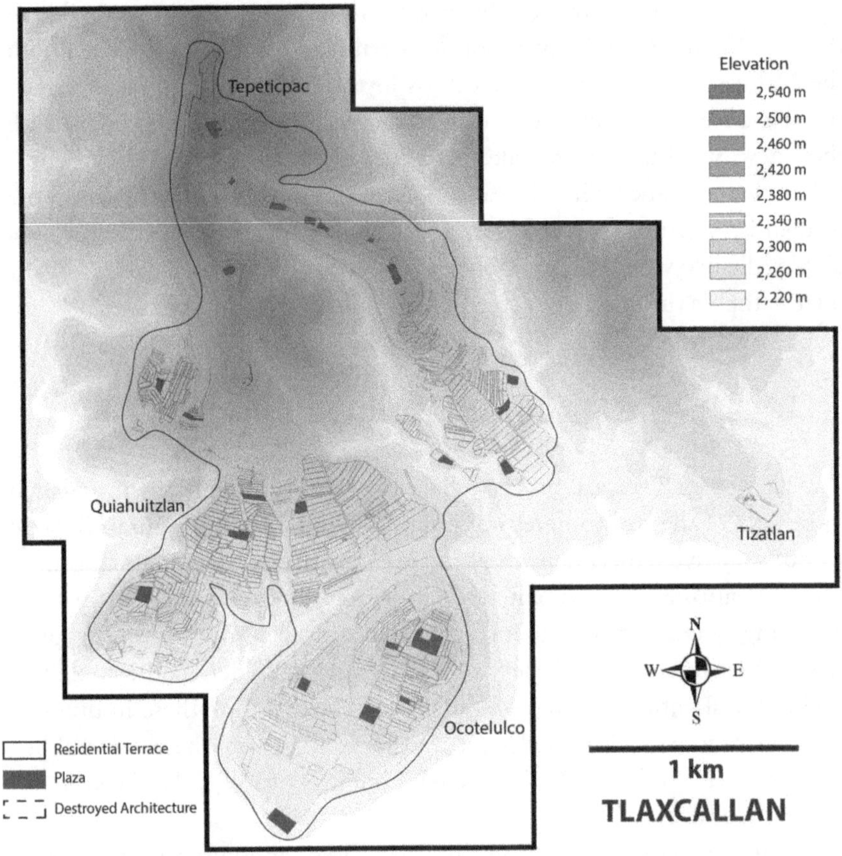

Figure 6.4. Map of the city of Tlaxcala, or Tlaxcallan, based on archaeological survey showing a single urban agglomeration of terraces and plazas, with detached ceremonial precinct at Tizatlan.

Modified from map made by Fargher and colleagues (2011a), and used with permission.

for they have no overlord. There are many chiefs, all of whom reside in this city, and the country towns contain peasants who are vassals of these lords and each of whom holds his land independently; some have more than others, and for their wars they join together and together they plan and direct them."[21]

The Tlaxcalteca combined collective sociopolitical organization and active military resistance in holding off the Triple Alliance during the century prior to the arrival of the Spaniards. In a political system that permitted common people of non-noble rank to ascend to the ruling council, and which held its multiple rulers accountable in pursuing the collective good, the Tlaxcalteca used pluralistic governance as a means of motivating their citizenry to defend against the external threat posed by the Triple Alliance. The Tlaxcalteca also framed their collective identity within the shared traditions of central Mexican religion. They claimed Tetzcatlipoca-Camaxtli as their patron deity in opposition to the focus on Quetzalcoatl among city-states that were more noble-centric in their political organization (Figure 6.5). The Tetzcatlipoca suite of divine entities is a complex one, consisting of several avatars and the powerful animal spirit (*nahual*) of a jaguar. In Mexica myths, he is depicted as a trickster or dark sorcerer and is associated with the chaotic and barbaric Chichimecs in juxtaposition to Quetzalcoatl's connotations of Toltec civilization and noble-kingship.[22] The defining accoutrement of Tetzcatlipoca (meaning "smoking mirror") is an obsidian mirror that can reveal the true nature of things, including one's soul. In a pivotal myth, Tetzcatlipoca holds the mirror before Quetzalcoatl, who is horrified by what he sees and flees Tollan. This side of the dualistic opposition was all the more appropriate for the Tlaxcalteca,

Figure 6.5. Statue of Tlaxcalan patron deity Tetzcatlipoca-Camaxtli holding his iconic mirror. Museo Regional de Tlaxcala.
Illustration by Pedro Cahuantzi Hernández.

where Tetzcatlipoca-Camaxtli symbolized the complement to the imperial order—a patron of its indifagitable resisters.

Tlaxcalteca resistance to the Triple Alliance compelled them to construct a fortified stronghold in the mountains north of the city at Tepeticpac (Figure 6.6). While the site's prominence and thick fortification walls are impressive, Tepeticpac, like other parts of Tlaxcala, has no major stepped-pyramid temple or conspicuous palace typical of more hierarchical Aztec cities of the time. Rather, the Tlaxcalteca designed Tepeticpac as a place from which they could surveil the entire Puebla-Tlaxcala Valley, including their allies turned rivals at Cholula and the mountain passes that Triple Alliance forces would have crossed through from the Basin of Mexico. Although it is possible that the Aztecs could have conquered Tlaxcala had they more intently focused their attention on that goal, as Moctezuma eventually proposed to Cortés, the mix of a more pluralistic and egalitarian social organization and the banding together to resist the empire certainly increased the costs of

Figure 6.6. Fortifications of Tlaxcalan stronghold at Tepeticpac, located in the hills north of the city.

Photo by Aurelio López Corral; used with permission. Reproduction authorized by the Instituto Nacional de Antropología e Historia, Mexico.

conquering their rivals. Being culturally very similar to the Aztecs and geographically so close, the independent Tlaxcalteca seem a clear example of the fractious nature of Mesoamerican politics.

When the Tlaxcalteca and their Otomi allies first learned of the Cortés expedition, they were right to be wary and to mobilize a strong resistance to the new threat at their border. Through the messengers who communicated between the two groups before their encounter, the Tlaxcalteca learned that heading their way was an army of foreigners in continual contact with emissaries of Moctezuma and who were growing in force by adding allies from Cempoala and Ixtacamaxtitlan, both subjects of the Triple Alliance. None of this would have seemed promising to the Tlaxcalteca. In their major battles at Tecoac and then one league farther to the south at Tzompantepec, the Tlaxcalteca fought intensely with the goal of defeating the Spanish-led forces. Yet they would have observed a different style of warfare than what they were used to: one of total war with the primary intent to defeat the foe on the battlefield, rather than force a surrender and take captives for sacrifice back at the temples.[23] A vivid example of this difference is how the Tlaxcalteca brought provisions to the Spaniards between battles, as defeating a weakened foe would have been viewed as cowardly.

It is possible that the Tlaxcalteca used early battles, especially in the first few days in the northern Otomi territory, as a way of testing the foreigners. It is also possible that Tlaxcalteca from the confederation were fighting alongside the Otomis in the early contest at Tecoac but strategically downplayed their involvement decades later in colonial documents to appear as having been loyal to Spain from the start.[24] Even Gómara noted, "The Tlaxcalteca always excused themselves by saying it was not they who were annoying the Spaniards, but the scoundrelly Otomí, acting without their permission."[25] By the time of the battle of Tzompantepec, however, there was an army of tens of thousands of Tlaxcalteca under the command of Xicotencatl the younger. This was a larger, better trained, and more organized fighting force than any the Spanish had encountered previously anywhere in the Americas.

Among Tlaxcala's leaders were the military commander Xicotencatl the younger, who, like Cortés, was in his thirties, and his aged and blind father of the same name, differentiated as Xicotencatl the elder. Together they represented the Tizatlan faction of the confederation. In their travels throughout Mesoamerica, Cortés and other Spaniards consistently looked to identify a single leader to deal with diplomatically, both because this was simpler than consulting with multiple individuals and because it better matched their monarchical vision of European petty kingdoms. In the case of Tlaxcala, Spanish texts single out Xicotencatl the elder and Maxixcatzin, who represented the Ocotelulco faction of the confederation. Leading figures of other important factions are also named by chroniclers, including Temilotecutli of Tepeticpac and Chichimecatecle of Quiahuitzlan, but it is clear that within this pluralistic system decisions were made by the ruling council, not a single individual. Certain named figures were merely authorized as more prominent speakers for the community; they were not paramount rulers. Díaz lists a fifth ruler named Guaxoban and says that all five commanded 10,000 warriors: "Each company had its device [battle standard] and uniform, for each Cacique had a different one, as do our dukes and counts in our own Castile."[26]

Major hostilities between the two forces began the morning of September 5 in the open plain near the hilltop settlement of Tzompantepec. The town is adjacent to the northwestern flank of the La Malinche volcano and some 11 miles (18 km) from the city of Tlaxcala, which the Spaniards could glimpse from the hilltop. Cortés' claim of a Tlaxcalteca fighting force of approximately 150,000 warriors is higher than other accounts and almost certainly inflated, as this seems more in line with the population for the entire altepetl at the time.[27] Something like Díaz's estimate of tens of thousands seems more likely, keeping in mind that warriors also came with support personnel who may have been included in these counts. Their roles were to replenish the quickly exhausted obsidian-tipped weapons and coordinate the movement of battle regiments with standards and banners, rather than actual fighting. Cortés' forces, in contrast, were in a weakened state after having traveled for over two weeks from Veracruz and was as low as 250 Spaniards, 10 wounded horses, and a few hundred Native warriors and porters.[28] Much of Cortés' military strategy would be to conceal his weakened forces and present a veneer of strength by accentuating his cavalry and superior artillery, and by riding across the Tlaxcalan countryside to periodically attack small settlements.

The Tlaxcalteca confronted the Spaniards with artillery waves of slingshot, arrows, and darts launched by atlatl. Díaz recounts being wounded in the head by the first and in the thigh by the second.[29] In addition to the men and horses they had lost since making landfall in Veracruz, the Spaniards were also conscious of conserving their limited supplies of artillery fire. Still, the cavalry and artillery provided big advantages to the Spanish in open-field conflict. When fighting moved to the more uneven terrain of deeply incised streams and ravines, such as the *barranca* Amomoloc west of Tzompantepec,[30] the arrows, lances, and macuahuitls of Xicotecatl the younger's forces were more effective. We still lack material remains of this pivotal conflict, which could be recovered through systematic survey and battlefield archaeology in the future.

Military engagements between the Spaniards and Tlaxcalteca lasted for almost two weeks but varied in their intensity and were broken up by diplomatic efforts to call a truce and forge an alliance. Through this interval, Cortés boasts of having burned 10 nearby settlements and ordering the hands cut off 50 Tlaxcalteca who had delivered food but, as was determined after an interrogation mediated by Malinche and Aguilar, were suspected as spies. Cortés also sensed dissent among his men. He recounts a rumor among them analogizing him to Pedro Carbonero, the legendary *Reconquista* captain who led bold but reckless attacks on the kingdom of Granada.[31] Spanish accounts state that the Tlaxcalteca taunted them across battle lines, yelling to the invaders that they would sacrifice them and cannibalize their remains, but Native and mestizo sources make no mention of this. Although resistance to the Spanish could be marshaled by a significant faction of Tlaxcalteca, Xicotencatl the younger was the leader who most objected to surrendering. This delayed enacting the developing majority opinion to join the foreigners in order to conquer their Triple Alliance foes by a few days.[32] It appears to have taken the visit by another group of Moctezuma's emissaries to Cortés' camp at Tzompantepec to convince Xicotencatl the younger and the Tlaxcalteca opposition that the Mexica were equally concerned and that the Spaniards were therefore the enemy of their enemies.

The Spaniards and their Native allies entered the city of Tlaxcala on either September 18, according to Gómara, or September 23, according to Díaz. In his second letter, Cortés continued his allusions to the city of Granada, declaring Tlaxcala's market to be grander, and invoking the republics of northern Italy in describing its political organization. These would have been salient, if somewhat overstated, referents for his intended audience of Charles V and his court. Cortés also began scapegoating Cholula as a city that was antagonistic to his new allies. He claimed a Choluteca had stolen gold from a Spaniard and the Tlaxcalteca summarily executed this individual.[33] As one way of cementing their alliance to the Spaniards, the Tlaxcalteca leaders presented Cortés with their daughters. There were five in all, and each came with her own female servant.[34] The rulers and their daughters were all baptized by the priest Juan Díaz, and a daughter of Xicotencatl the elder, christened with the name Doña Luisa, was held in highest esteem among the Tlaxcalteca. She was betrothed by Cortés to Alvarado, whom Luisa would accompany on later invasions of Guatemala and as far as South America.

While staying in Tlaxcala for some 20 days, the Spaniards heard the grievances of their hosts against the Aztec Triple Alliance, including the existence of an economic embargo that deprived the Tlaxcalteca of common imports such as cotton, which only grew in warmer lowlands, and salt, which could be processed on the coast or along saline lakes of the highlands. Chemical analysis of obsidian artifacts from Tlaxcala nevertheless indicates that the Tlaxcalteca had continued access to the stone for their basic tools and weapons, even though no source existed within their realm.[35] This suggests that interregional trade continued up to the time of Spanish arrival, but investigations of the topic are complicated by the fact that the few decades of possible Aztec embargo are difficult to distinguish archaeologically.

Cortés had temple effigies in Tlaxcala replaced with crosses and representations of the Virgin. He also requested that Tlaxcalteca rulers halt their practice of human sacrifice, but they demurred, contending they would lose the support of their people by not properly honoring the gods. Thus began processes of negotiation and selective acculturation that would characterize Tlaxcala and other parts of rapidly transforming Mesoamerica. Even while in Tlaxcala, Cortés remained in contact with Mexica emissaries—six nobles with a support staff of a couple hundred—through whom he messaged to Moctezuma that he wished to continue onward to Tenochtitlan without fighting.[36] Moctezuma's recorded replies typically involved messengers presenting the Spaniards with more gifts while obliquely suggesting that they turn around instead of continuing to the capital. Cortés sent Alvarado and Vázquez de Tapia ahead with Mexica emissaries and a contingent of Mesoamerican allies to survey the route to Tenochtitlan and attempt to receive an audience with the Great Speaker. Whereas Díaz records this advance team as having left from the city of Tlaxcala, Vázquez de Tapia himself states that they left from Tecoac, weeks before the Spanish-Tlaxcalteca alliance was made.[37] The conquistador notes that Cortés was unwilling to part with any horses, so the group proceeded on foot past the city of Tlaxcala, where they were threatened for being accompanied by Mexica and Triple Alliance provincials. The advance team continued to Cholula, Huexotzingo, and followed a route passing south of the Popocatepetl volcano via the modern state of Morelos to enter the Basin of Mexico through the mountain pass at Amecameca. They then skirted the lake system of the Basin of Mexico to the east and arrived at Texcoco. Although the group did not make it to Tenochtitlan, these Spaniards were now in the heart of the Triple Alliance core and in negotiations with the rulers of the second-largest altepetl of the empire.

Only following the vital alliance with the Tlaxcalteca did the company led by Cortés constitute a formidable military force with the shared objective of toppling the Aztec Empire. It now comprised an army some 10,000 strong, the large majority of whom were Nahuatl-speaking Tlaxcalteca and Otomis from Tlaxcala. The decision by these indigenous Mesoamericans to ally with the foreigners was a fateful one because, unlike other city-states that joined the Spaniards from the Triple Alliance—as provinces in the cases of Cempoala and Ixtacamaxtitlan, or even from the second most powerful altepetl of Texcoco—the people of Tlaxcala were the primary antagonists of the empire. Whereas Texcoco or subject provinces of the Triple Alliance could more easily have made amends should the Mexica turn back the threat and reassert their hegemony, Tlaxcala would have likely faced harsh retribution. In allying with the Spaniards against their traditional foes, the Tlaxcalteca were therefore risking everything. While it is difficult to project the motivations of all the rulers of Tlaxcala and the will of its large ruling council based on manuscripts written in a colonial context, it is apparent that a majority perceived the Spanish arrival as an opportunity to tip the balance of power in their protracted conflict with the Triple Alliance and the Mexica of Tenochtitlan in particular. The Tlaxcalteca shared with the Spaniards that they counted on the people of Huexotzingo as their allies, but those of Cholula had betrayed them by turning to the Triple Alliance and were now foes. The Tlaxcalteca also provided critical information regarding the layout of Tenochtitlan, both in words and also rendered on painted cloth *lienzos* depicting its system of defenses and the fact that the city was connected to, but could also be cut off from, the mainland through causeways, bridges, and the aqueducts that carried the city's water from Chapultepec.[38] This information would be of great value to eventually laying siege to the city. Cortés and the Tlaxcalteca leadership plotted a route to Tenochtitlan, but Cortés first turned his attention to cementing their alliance by attacking the long-lived city of Cholula.

On the Road to Ruin

Few places in contact-era Mesoamerica could challenge Cholula as a source of historical, political, and religious legitimacy. In addition to being one of the oldest more-or-less continuously occupied cities, it was also a vibrant market center and the major pilgrimage center for the god Quetzalcoatl.[39] Mesoamericans considered Cholula an archetypal city—a Tollan—and in the Postclassic period it became the locus of investiture ceremonies associated with noble Toltec rulership. Rulers of other city-states would journey to Cholula to have their nasal septum perforated in order to wear adornments marking high office. The city therefore assumed a politico-religious function in central Mexico similar to the one Teotihuacan had served centuries earlier. The Great Speakers of Tenochtitlan did not travel to Cholula to be endowed with the trappings of high office, but Díaz records that Moctezuma dined every day off Cholula pottery (Figure 6.7), which he likened to the highly regarded Spanish pottery made at Talavera.[40] The region around Cholula had

Figure 6.7. Polychrome cup from Cholula. Museo Regional de Cholula.
Photo by author. Reproduction authorized by the Instituto Nacional de Antropología e Historia, Mexico.

been prized for the quality of its clays and high artisanal standards since the glory days of Teotihuacan, but Moctezuma's choice of tableware was surely also based in Cholula's enduring prestige and its association with the god of creation, civilization, and kingship.

Cholula did not have a single sovereign, and its political organization may have been more theocratic than other city-states of the time, though political and religious power were always entangled in Mesoamerica. The two individuals charged with external affairs, the *Aquiach* and the *Tlalchiach*, are generally referred to as high priests of the priesthood of Quetzalcoatl, while a noble council with six members elected a speaker, or "cacique," who oversaw internal affairs (Figure 6.8, bottom).[41] The city's urban organization was similar to other great Aztec-period centers in possessing a major temple, minor temples, a *calmecac* school, and the partitioning into calpolli districts. These are better known from historical texts than from archaeological remains because the colonial-period center was overlaid by the Spanish directly on

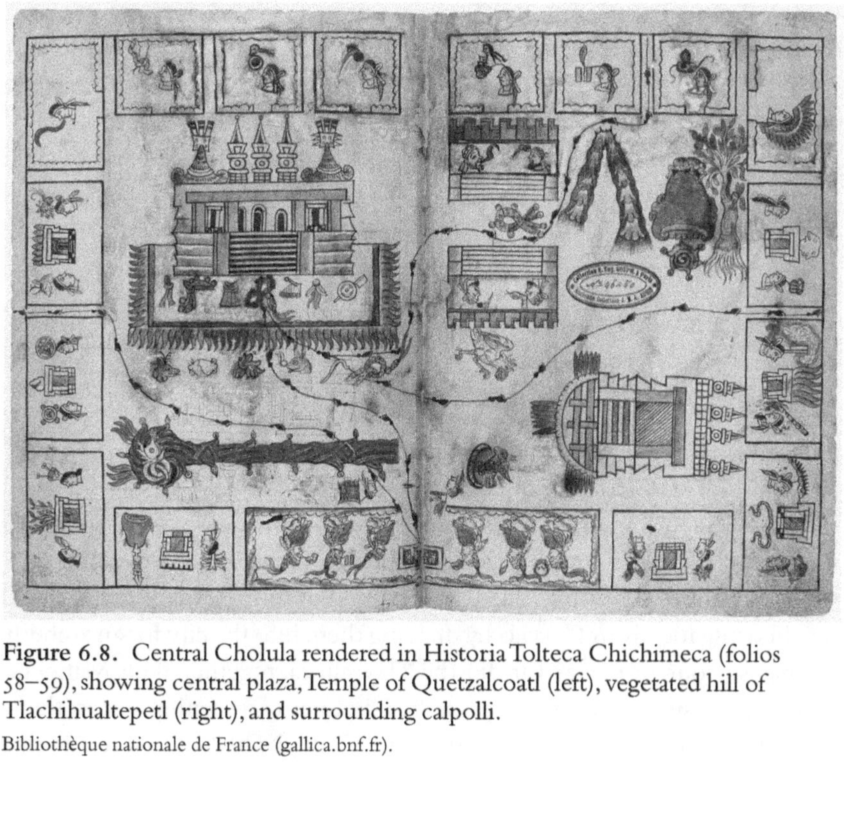

Figure 6.8. Central Cholula rendered in Historia Tolteca Chichimeca (folios 58–59), showing central plaza, Temple of Quetzalcoatl (left), vegetated hill of Tlachihualtepetl (right), and surrounding calpolli.

Bibliothèque nationale de France (gallica.bnf.fr).

top of the Postclassic one and involved the destruction of the Temple of Quetzalcoatl and other religious and civic buildings. According to Díaz, Cholula's Temple of Quetzalcoatl stood even taller than the Great Temple at Tenochtitlan, but archaeological explorations have been restricted by the wealth of colonial-period buildings that sit on its foundations.[42] Excavations have nevertheless recovered the remains of stucco-covered floors, painted adobes, roof adornments, large braziers, human burials, and the diagnostic polychrome pottery Cholula was famed for during the contact era. Native maps rendered in the *Historia Tolteca Chichimeca* and other documents depict urban Cholula as laid out orthogonally, with four major avenues leading from the sacred precinct and main plaza dividing the city into quadrants and orderly calpolli districts (Figure 6.8). This urban plan follows Mesoamerican conceptualizations of the cosmos being ordered into four cardinal directions and a center.

The razing and burial of contact-era Cholula under the colonial city means that population estimates are problematic. An estimated 40,000 inhabitants, presented in Table 4.1 in Chapter 4, splits the difference between reasonable ranges of plus or minus 10,000. Estimates provided by Cortés, always eager to exaggerate his achievements, must be viewed skeptically. He writes that 100,000 Tlaxcalteca originally set out with him toward Cholula on October 10, but he convinced all but 5,000–6,000 to turn around and return home.[43] Cortés claims this force faced Cholula's 20,000 urban houses—a potential population of over 100,000—with the looming threat of 50,000 warriors sent by Moctezuma who were garrisoned two leagues away. Díaz places the assembled Mexica force at 20,000, and in his reply to the questions of the Royal Audencia, Vázquez de Tapia stated that some 5,000–6,000 Choluteca were massacred by Cortés and his forces, while 20,000 or more died in the invasion of Cholula as a whole.[44]

Motivations for the detour to Cholula and impetus for the sacking of the city and massacre of thousands of its unarmed citizens are matters of historical debate. There is a lack of consensus on why the invaders saw the need to pass through the city on their way to Tenochtitlan, as it was not along the most direct route from Tlaxcala and could have been avoided. Did the Choluteca and their Triple Alliance allies attempt to trick the foreigners and neighboring foes from Tlaxcala by drawing them into the city for an ambush, as Spanish sources relate? Or did the Tlaxcalteca, together with Malinche, guide the mission to take revenge on the Choluteca for turning against them, as the Tlatelolca claimed in the Florentine Codex? The fact that it is even a debate illustrates that the Tlaxcalteca should be considered as conquistadors in their own right, of equal consequence to the assault on the Triple Alliance order as the Spaniards. Yet in the instance of the sack of Cholula, the preponderance of the evidence points toward Cortés' guiding of the mission and the later Spanish invention of the ambush plot as a means of justifying their belligerence.

The Spanish take on the massacre is encapsulated by Gómara, who states that the Choluteca welcomed the Spaniards into the city while the Tlaxcalteca were made to remain outside it. He claims that the Choluteca plotted to kill the Spaniards, who watched them sacrifice 10 children to Quetzalcoatl, making the massacre a justifiable retribution.[45] Gómara likely drew his account from de Tapia, though the conquistador wrote that the man-god Quetzalcoatl founded Cholula with the explicit commandment that its inhabitants sacrifice quails and other game animals, rather than humans. While they looted the city, the Spaniards grabbed gold and silver, but the Tlaxcalteca are purported to have taken the cloth and salt they lacked access to on account of the Triple Alliance embargo. In Cortés' telling, the detour to Cholula on the way to Tenochtitlan was made on the recommendation of Moctezuma's emissaries and the Tlaxcalteca were very reluctant to go.[46] The plot against the Spaniards was exposed by Malinche—the first time (in the second letter) Cortés refers to her role as translator—and after the conquistadors observed barricades, stores of slingshot ready to fire, and holes dug into the city streets. Díaz also claims the Tlaxcalteca wanted to pass through the lands of their allies of Huexotzingo rather than through Cholula, and elaborates on the narrative of ambush by claiming that Cempoalan scouts identified the holes in the streets as trap-holes with sharpened stakes at their bases, positioned point-up to kill the horses.[47] This last bit is pure fabrication because the Choluteca and other Mesoamericans had never seen horses prior to the Spanish arrival, so would not have fashioned Eurasian anti-cavalry defenses. It undermines the Spanish narrative through its clearly implausible embellishments.

What the Spaniards almost certainly did not understand were the political dynamics of factions within the altepetl of Cholula. Although the faction ruling the city-state in mid-October 1519 was loyal to the Triple Alliance (though semi-autonomous from the empire), there were also dissenters concentrated in the calpolli district of Tenanquiahuac, who had close ties to Tlaxcala. The Tlaxcalteca stayed in Tenanquiahuac when the Spaniards and allies from Cempoala and Ixtacamaxtitlan spent a first night in the city.[48]

This faction of Choluteca supported an alliance with the Tlaxcalteca and Spaniards, and their early colonial-period descendants emphasized the loyalty of their ancestors in order to receive favors from the Spanish Crown. When thousands of Cholula's unarmed nobles, priests, and other inhabitants were killed by the Spaniards in the city's main plaza, the Tlaxcalteca do not appear to have been present. Rather, they arrived two hours later and partook in their own looting and revenge against those who supported the ruling faction not allied with them. Tellingly, de Tapia records that hostilities between the Tlaxcalteca and "certain lords" from Cholula continued months later, as he was sent back from Tenochtitlan to quell them.[49]

We can therefore isolate certain related motivations for the sack of Cholula. From the perspective of Cortés and the Spaniards, it laid waste to the only serious challenger that stood between the ultimate goal of Tenochtitlan and their lifeline to the Spanish Caribbean at Veracruz. From the perspective of the Tlaxcalteca, it restored the system of alliances that, with Cholula and Huexotzingo to the south and west and Otomi groups to the north and west, buffered them against their foes. From the perspective of both groups, it solidified their alliance with one another and proved their willingness to jointly conquer the Triple Alliance.[50] Regardless of what individual motivations were at play, the result was a bloody conflict that left thousands dead, with physical remains that tell more of the story. Archaeologists have uncovered over 600 burials from the precinct of San Gabriel, formerly the location of the Pyramid of Quetzalcoatl, with attributes of having been some of the victims of the massacre.[51] The bodies were laid to rest following conventions of a Christian burial, lying on their backs with heads toward the East, but were adorned with pre-Hispanic jewelry and many had cosmetic cranial deformation—a practice that was abandoned after the conquest. Dozens of the skeletons show the victims had been decapitated or dismembered, while others exhibit bodily wounds from the conflict, such as cut marks on bone from steel weapons. The Spanish-Mesoamerican force spent a week or two in Cholula after conquering it, perhaps having buried these bodies during that time, and then set out for Tenochtitlan sometime between October 25 and November 1.

Over Mountains and Causeways

Although the guides who led Alvarado and Vázquez de Tapia to the Basin of Mexico had charted a course circumventing the sierra of tall volcanoes, Cortés was quite taken with the majesty of Popocatepetl and Itzaccihuatl. He sent 10 Spaniards, captained by Diego Ordaz but led by more Mesoamerican guides, on a reconnaissance mission to investigate the high mountain pass. Ordaz had distinguished himself earlier in the battle of Cintla and would later go on to search for the fabled El Dorado in what is today Venezuela. The guides were familiar with the route since it was used by traders and they would have also known the mythology associated with the two volcanoes: that Popocateptl embodied the soul of a brave warrior who returned from battle to find his beloved betrothed princess dead, and so lay her white silhouette down on the northern mountain range while he remained smoldering in rage by her side. The advance team witnessed a minor eruption of "Popo," also known today as Don Goyo for his association with Saint Gregory. There they encountered more Mexica scouts, who informed the group that they could continue to Tenochtitlan along the route—memorialized afterward as the Paso de Cortés. At over two miles above sea level (11,150 feet, 3,400 m) the pass is as high as the summits of the tallest mountains of Iberia, and the peaks of the two volcanoes, thousands of feet higher still, soared above anything the Spaniards would have known from Europe or North Africa. Spanish accounts note their amazement in encountering icicles and falling snow.

When the full force set out along this route, it required passing through the southern territory of the altepetl of Huexotzingo but not through the urban center itself. Mexica emissaries in the group were initially reluctant to go through the lands of another hostile polity, but the large contingent of Tlaxcalteca convinced their Huexotzinca allies to greet the foreigners warmly and provide food, shelter, gifts, women, and more warriors. Cortés lists 4,000 Mesoamerican allies as accompanying him across the mountains, originating from Tlaxcala, Huexotzingo, Cholula, and Cempoala—apparently passing over those from Ixtacamaxtitlan and grouping the Otomis from Tecoac and Tlilihquitepec with the Tlaxcalteca.[52] With porters from Mesoamerica and the Caribbean, African slaves and servants, and Native and Spanish women, the total group that crossed the sierra into the Basin of Mexico could have numbered close to 10,000.

During the descent from the volcanoes into the southeastern basin and province of Chalco, the group encountered other delegations, including more Mexica from Tenochtitlan, as well as Acolhua from Texcoco. Texcoco did not actually enjoy peer polity status with Tenochtitlan, since the latter was many times larger, and through the common Aztec practices of noble polygyny and hypogamy, Texcoco's ruler Cacama was outranked in lineage by Moctezuma, who was his uncle.[53] Following the death of Nezahualpilli in 1515, a dispute for succession in wearing the turquoise diadem on behalf of Texcoco erupted between a faction loyal to his eldest legitimate son, Cacama, backed by Tenochtitlan, and another that supported Ixtlilxochitl, his half-brother by another mother, who later adopted the surname Cortés and was the great-great-grandfather of the Native chronicler Alva Ixtlilxochitl. Unsurprisingly, the chronicler plays up the noble pedigree and skilled diplomacy of this ancestor, who would forge another key alliance with the Spaniards, Tlaxcaltecas, and others following the death of Cacama in 1520. The courtly intrigue and romantic liaisons of Texcoco presented by Alva Ixtlilxochitl stand up to those from early imperial Rome and good Mexican *telenovela* soap operas of today.[54]

Why exactly Moctezuma awaited the allied Spanish-Mesoamerican force at Tenochtitlan and welcomed them into the city, rather than sending the full Mexica army to confront them coming out of the mountains, is one of history's conundrums. Whether or not there was a Mexica plot against the foreigners at Cholula, their approach was decidedly nonconfrontational. November was the tail end of the harvest season on the Altiplano, which may have made it difficult to mobilize the many tens of thousands of warriors that would have been necessary—in addition to the much smaller corps of permanent soldiers—to mount a serious resistance against the invaders. Alternatively, a willingness on the part of Mexica leadership to allow the foreigners to continue advancing may have been the result of not sensing a direct threat, along with a desire to begin with diplomacy, imagining that any hostilities could be crushed within the capital city. Another possibility is that they were reluctantly willing to nominally acknowledge a foreign sovereign, Charles V, as a legitimate ruler to whom tribute was due, but otherwise the Triple Alliance would remain intact.[55] This logic is consistent with common Mesoamerican norms of hegemonic politics, not European ones of territorial conquest through total war.

The Tlatelolca author-informants of the Florentine Codex, always quick to critique the actions of the Great Speaker, relate Moctezuma as sending to meet the invaders not only emissaries, but also sorcerers to cast spells on them.[56] In this episode, the Mexica ritual specialists encounter a ranting drunkard who speaks ill of Moctezuma and presents them with a foreboding vision of Tenochtitlan engulfed in flames. The omen is in the tradition of others presented at the beginning of Book XII and in different colonial-period documents that fuse biblical narratives of the plagues of Egypt with the arrival of the Spaniards, likely originating with the friar Motolinia as a way of teaching central Mexicans the Old Testament. Yet this particular episode ends with the Tlatelolca noting that the character of the drunkard was in fact Tetzcatlipoca, once again projecting his mirror of insight to foretell what was to come. Alva Ixtlilxochitl, in contrast, provides a much more practical explanation for Moctezuma choosing diplomacy over war. He says that even though Moctezuma's brother Cuitlahuac favored war, Cacama of Texcoco returned from meeting the foreigners in Ayotzingo, within the altepetl of Chalco, to council the Great Speaker to receive them peacefully.[57] Doing so also followed another prevalent cultural norm in Mesoamerica of hospitality toward strangers.

From a perspective grounded in European notions of conquest warfare and politics, the apparent timidity with which Moctezuma awaited a force of foreigners allied to his major rivals has often been portrayed as intelligible only on the grounds that he considered the Spaniards to be gods and/or Cortés to have been some sort of returning king. This possibility has been offered since the sixteenth century, with Cortés most often cast in the role of the returning man-god Topiltzin Quetzalcoatl.[58] While possible, there are several reasons to be skeptical about the notion, or to problematize it to the point at which it loses any real explanatory value.[59] Most notably, Cortés himself did not record having been viewed as a god; nor did de Tapia, who relates Moctezuma addressing Cortés as a returning lord.[60] The earliest eyewitness account that mentions Spaniards as gods was likely provided by Aguilar: "They regarded us as immortal men and called us *teules*, which means gods."[61] The narrative proliferated in later sources written by Díaz and Spanish friars, as well as in Native-author ones such as the Florentine Codex and Alva Ixtlilxochitl's account. Confounding the issue are Mesoamerican notions of sacredness, which were broad and could be applied to a range of animate essences without characterizing an individual as divine. A relevant parallel example is that the Tlaxcalteca and Mexica referred to Alvarado by the name of the solar deity Tonatiuh, but this was due to his fiery temperament and bizarrely foreign blond hair, not because they conceived him to be the sun in human form. Also at play were Mesoamerican speech conventions of formalized status inversions, which were practiced in situations such as when warriors took captives in battle or ruling sovereigns greeted social inferiors. This would account for miscommunication along the route that Cortés was a returning king, particularly during the iconic meeting with Moctezuma on the causeway leading from the Iztapalapa peninsula to the island city of Tenochtitlan.

The Iztapalapa peninsula stretches approximately 20 miles (32 km) westward from the eastern lakeshore in separating the large and brackish Lake Texcoco from freshwater lakes to the south, which took their names from the largest altepetls in their regions, Chalco and Xochimilco. These two southern partitions were bisected by narrow causeways connecting through the island of Tlahuac. The southern basin was the breadbasket of the Triple Alliance because of the high productivity of the chinampa field systems around Chalco and Xochimilco. The landscape would have therefore been very green, with rows upon rows of these field beds, bisected by canals and growing all sorts of produce from the fertile mud of the lake floor. It is also the area with the deepest urban tradition in the Altiplano, where Cuicuilco had developed as the largest city two millennia earlier. The joint Spanish-Mesoamerican forces crossed onto the peninsula via Tlahuac and were received by local lords, including from the altepetl of Culhuacan, the source of the alternative ethnonym Culúa for the Mexica. They were lodged in a palace in Iztapalapa that made a great impression on Díaz, whose memory of setting out on the causeway the following day is captured in this chapter's epigraph. Díaz invokes the wonders of the best-selling chivalric romance of the day, *Amadís de Gaula*, written in his hometown of Medina del Campo, in comparing the view from the causeway with the settings for the exploits of this fictional knight.[62] The cities ringing the lake system would have looked like some Mediterranean cities at a distance, in having gleaming white buildings covered in a lime plaster or stucco and with roof adornments that presented profiles akin to the crenellated battlements of European castles, but did not share their defensive function. Aztec buildings were also embellished with colorful highlights painted with natural pigments, mostly of turquoise blue and blood red.

On November 8, 1519, the Iztapalapa causeway was the setting for the momentous meeting between Moctezuma and Cortés. Setting out from the peninsula onto a much longer and wider causeway than they had used in the southern lakes through Tlahuac, the Spaniards clearly felt some apprehension about the mission. This is registered in comments by Cortés, Aguilar, Vázquez de Tapia, and others about the defensibility of the island city and how easy it would be for them to be trapped within it. Aguilar observed, "The Indians could raise the bridges and give us battle, or even if they did not fight us we could all die here, since there was no way out because the lake was so deep; and even if any of us did get out we could be killed by arrows shot from the canoes that swarmed on the water."[63] The lake setting negated the advantage the Spanish had been exploiting in open battlefields with their cavalry, and the lakeshore cities that Díaz waxed poetically about all represented potentially hostile forces. Yet the arms and armor clearly made an impression on the scribes of the Florentine Codex, who in Chapter 15 of Book XII spent nearly 100 lines of Nahuatl text describing them and the sequence of procession up the causeway, compared with a brief 16 lines that were translated and edited into Spanish by Sahagún.[64]

The Iztapalapa causeway stretched approximately eight miles (13 km) in a straight shot to Tenochtitlan, giving plenty of time for Cortés and his captains to ponder the utility that boats would serve in the lake setting.[65] Iztapalapa was the grandest of Tenochtitlan's causeways, but other large ones connected the island city to the mainland, including west via Tacuba, the smallest altepetl of the Triple Alliance, and north via Tepeyac, a sacred spot associated with fertility goddesses, including the Earth goddess Tonantzin.[66] The causeways were engineered with rows of pylons driven in the lakebed interspersed with bridge segments that could be opened or closed for canoes to pass and to regulate overland movements to and from the island. It is difficult to speculate exactly when Cortés and the other captains formulated their eventual military strategy, but it may have become apparent during the entry march that Tenochtitlan's sense of impregnability came from a context of pre-Hispanic warfare. Its defenses would be vulnerable to Spanish siege tactics and naval assault borne of millennia of total war in Europe.

If thoughts of eventually laying siege to Tenochtitlan were in the minds of the Spaniards, the full group marching up the causeway had the veneer of a diplomatic caravan because also traveling with them and their Native forces were the speakers of Texcoco, Tacuba, Iztapalapa, and Coyoacan. These were some of the most powerful political actors of the Triple Alliance, with oversight of councils and offices that decided internal and external affairs. Yet as Great Speaker, Moctezuma represented the highest authority in foreign relations. He was dutifully carried from his palace in a litter to the entrance into the city from the causeway, accompanied by 200 nobles. When Moctezuma's feet touched the ground, people swept the path before him as he walked, making sure not to look at his face directly. Spanish sources describe him as approximately 40 years old, with hair that covered his ears, and with a stately but jovial manner. The Great Speaker was elaborately garbed in his turquoise diadem—analogous to wearing a crown in Europe—with gold-soled sandals on his feet and shaded by a canopy of resplendent quetzal feathers. Malinche performed her essential translation duties, and Cortés presented Moctezuma with a necklace of pearls and glass beads, which he placed around the Great Speaker's neck. But when Cortés went to embrace Moctezuma, he was blocked by the nobles surrounding him, as such physical contact would have been taken as an indignity. The Tenochca ruler led the party to the palace of his father Axayacatl, a previous Great Speaker who reigned 1469–1481. He addressed Cortés: "Malinche, you and your brethren are in your own house, rest awhile."[67] This "while" became an eight-month stay in Tenochtitlan, culminating in its destruction.

7
The Spanish-Mexica War

> Nothing but flowers and songs of sorrow
> are left in Mexico and Tlatelolco,
> where once we saw warriors and wise men.
>
> —*Cantares Mexicanos*[1]

Over years of more sporadic initial encounters since the Cortés expedition made landfall on Yucatan, both Spaniards and Mesoamericans had viewed the foreign other with a mix of horror and amazement. This experience culminated with the entry into Tenochtitlan on November 8, 1519. The wonder expressed in Aztec sources describing the Spanish boats anchored on the coast of Veracruz, their steel weapons and armor, their hairiness and other physical attributes, and their large horses and dogs was reciprocated with how the Spaniards took in the sights and sounds of the imperial capital (Figure 7.1). Not all accounts were equally evocative, however, and Vázquez de Tapia again proves a master of understatement in writing: "We entered Mexico and were there for eight months, more or less, until Pámfilo de Narváez arrived, during which time significant things happened but, so as not to dwell, I ignore."[2] While it is true that the eight-month stay represents a sort of standoff or "cold" war before hostilities erupted, they are central to the historical documentation of contact-era Tenochtitlan, a slow unfolding of important events before tensions suddenly and violently erupted.

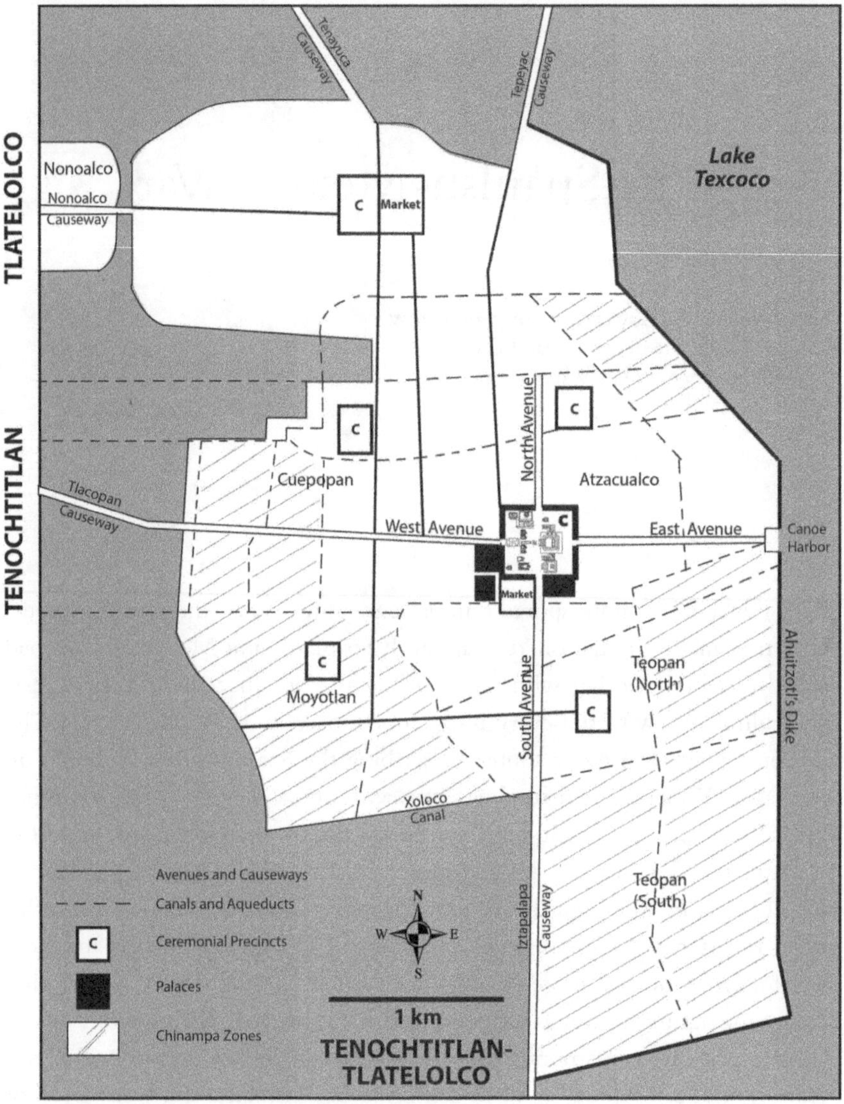

Figure 7.1. Map of Tenochtitlan-Tlatelolco.
Based on Calnek (2003) and Smith (2008).

La Gran Tenochtitlan

After graciously receiving the party of foreigners, provincial subjects, and rival Tlaxcalteca, Moctezuma led them to his father's palace just outside the walls of Tenochtitlan's sacred precinct. The precinct covered approximately 400,000 square feet (122,400 m^2) and featured the central temples, shrines, altars, ballcourt, calmecac school, other ritual training facilities, and skull rack (*tzompantli*) for exhibiting the skulls of vanquished foes and sacrificial victims, while the major palaces, royal zoo, and market surrounded the precinct (Figure 7.2).[3] While the specific locations of many buildings in the city remain unclear, being buried under Mexico City, those that have been fully or partially unearthed by the Templo Mayor Project, Urban Archaeology Program, and other salvage operations can prove or disprove urban

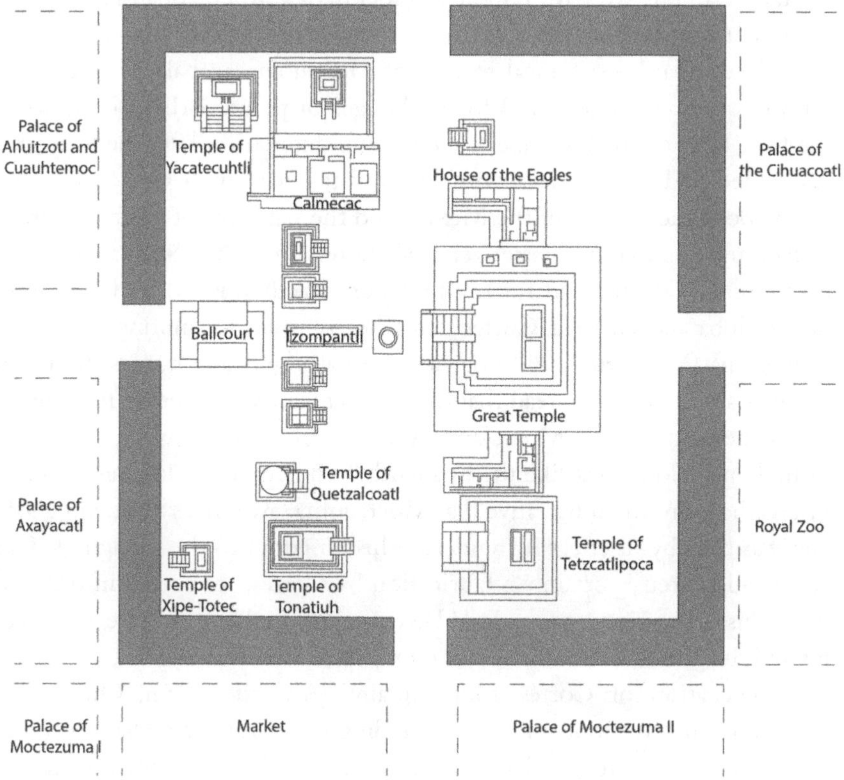

Figure 7.2. Sacred precinct at Tenochtitlan.
Based on Matos (1988) and Aguilar-Moreno (2006).

reconstructions based on colonial-period texts. Moctezuma's own palace was located just south of the sacred precinct, and its foundations are still present under Mexico's National Palace, whereas Axayacatl's stood somewhere to the west of the precinct and was occupied by previous Great Speakers, likely beginning with the empire builder Itzcoatl and Moctezuma Xocoyotzin's earlier namesake, Moctezuma Ilhuicamina.[4] Like other Mesoamericans, the Aztecs viewed the universe as a quincunx, divided into four quadrants that converge on a central axis connecting the underworld to the heavens. For the Mexica of Tenochtitlan, this conceptualization was rendered in microcosm in the layout of their city, which was divided into four urban quarters (*nauhcampa*), with the sacred precinct serving as the hub or navel (*tlalxico*) around which the city and empire revolved.[5]

Most of the thousands of Native allies with the Spaniards must have been lodged elsewhere, since they could not have possibly fit in the palace of Axayacatl, but we have few details identifying where. Spanish accounts comment on the fine construction of the *tecpan* palaces and their large central courtyards—a typical feature of Mesoamerican palaces in general, serving to receive guests and for exchanges of political rhetoric between the host, local council members, and foreign dignitaries. After the Spaniards had rested and dined, Moctezuma arrived to speak with Cortés. He told them about the origins of the Mexica and the narrative of migration from Aztlan, and also that his messengers had alerted him to the Spanish presence on the coast, as they had for the previous expeditions led by Hernández de Córdoba and Grijalva. Cortés states clearly in his recounting of the exchange that Moctezuma did not view him as a god, and quotes the Great Speaker as remarking instead that the Spaniards may have heard from other Mesoamericans that he, Moctezuma, was a god, but that he was in fact made of flesh and blood, just like the Spaniards.[6] The conquistador, nevertheless, inserts the convenient narrative that Moctezuma saw him as a returning lord and was thereby in effect surrendering his kingdom to the foreigners. This last detail is pretty certainly a fabrication by Cortés, concocted in order to justify his later actions to Charles V. Before taking his leave, the Great Speaker invited the guests to visit him at his own palace the following day.

A delegation of Cortés, four captains (Alvarado, León, Ordaz, and Sandoval), and five foot soldiers—including the chroniclers Díaz, de Tapia, and Aguilar—was received by Moctezuma. Aguilar describes his amazement at the splendor of the palace and details the foods on Moctezuma's table: dishes, warmed on charcoal braziers, of roasted turkey, quail, and other fowl; fish from the surrounding lakes, but also from the Gulf coast, two to three hundred miles away; and a variety of tortillas and other maize products, which he liked. He noted: "The kinds of bread they brought were greatly varied—kneaded and very tasty, so that the bread of Castile was not even missed."[7] Díaz adds yet more detail: the large volume of jars filled with a frothy cacao beverage; that Moctezuma smoked tobacco, another New World domesticate, after eating; the Great Speaker's strange, to European eyes, practices of personal hygiene, including daily baths and regular changing of clothes; and that the palace housed storerooms of fine adornments, a library, and armories.[8] The Native scribes of the Florentine Codex also registered their nostalgia for past Mexica grandeur in the 17th chapter of Book XII, where the Nahuatl passage on foods, tableware, and jewels in the palace is over 50 percent longer than the version translated into Spanish.[9] Many of the finest jewelry and other forms of bodily adornment were crafted by expert artisans who worked shell, turquoise, and other lapidary materials in the *totocalli* ("bird house") within the palace. Mexican archaeologists have replicated the production of such adornments discovered in excavations at the sacred precinct and have determined various steps in the manufacturing sequence, showing there to be a high degree of standardization in finished products, consistent with production by palace artisans.[10]

During this first week in the city, the Spaniards were also admitted to the sacred precinct and took in the vista from its highest point atop the Great Temple. From this vantage, they could survey the urban expanse and its connection to the mainland by the system of causeways and aqueducts—of strategic value to plotting a way off the island. They were summarily impressed by the gridded order to Tenochtitlan's urban plan, which was unlike the spiral or hub-and-spoke-like layouts of most cities of medieval Europe. They commented on the Venetian quality to the city in being bisected by canals, including one that ran south of the sacred precinct so that goods could enter the palaces and plazas on canoe. The size of the city was also remarkable to the Spaniards. Most population estimates for the twin city of Tenochtitlan-Tlatelolco vary from a low of 60,000 to a high of 300,000. Even 60,000 would have been larger than Seville or any other Spanish city, and a midpoint between the high and low estimates would have been larger than any European city except perhaps for Paris, which had somewhere between 150,000 and 250,000 residents.[11] Tenochtitlan was the most consequential capital of a polity that ruled more subjects than the conquistador's own Castile did. Equally impressive was the royal zoo and aviary located east of the precinct, where successive Great Speakers had collected every species of their known world and which predated European zoos. On visiting the marketplace at Tlatelolco, Díaz reports how impressed the Spaniards were with the range of products bought and sold, its orderliness, and its size, which was deemed to have been larger than those of Rome and Constantinople in the judgment of men who had visited those cities.

From atop the temples of Tenochtitlan and Tlatelolco, the Spaniards also saw things that unsettled them and that they cited continually in justifying their invasion and imposition of their own religion. The altars, shrines, and staircases of the Tenochtitlan's Great Temple were washed in blood from human sacrifices; sculptures depicting fearful-looking deities surrounded them; and in the plaza below, the *tzompantli* of severed heads supported skulls in different stages of decomposition glaring outward—de Tapia reports 136,000 of them (Figure 7.3).[12] Ongoing discoveries at and around the temple corroborate parts of these accounts, while adding a depth to our understanding of how the Mexica imbued the precinct with sacredness and projected their authority to control life in their perceived sacred duty to keep the cosmos going and repay human debts to the gods for creation. At the foot of the Great Temple sat not only the large sculpted stone disc depicting

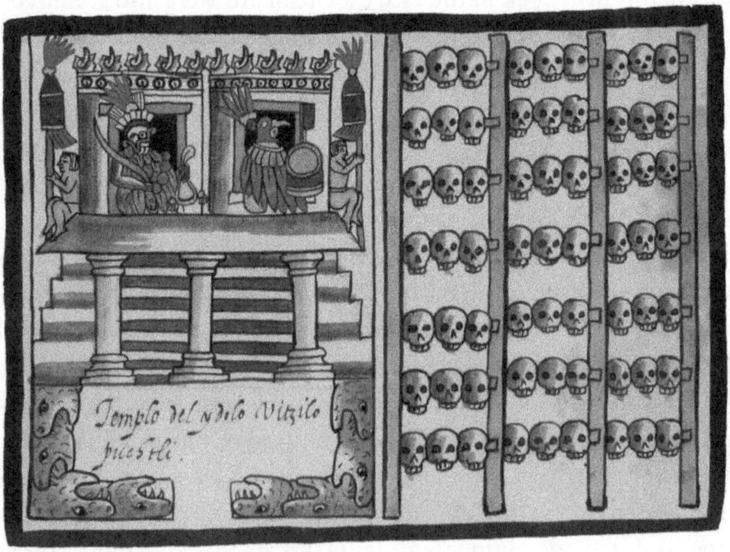

Figure 7.3. Rendering of Great Temple with *tzompantli* skull rack. Codex Tovar. Public domain.https://commons.wikimedia.org/wiki/Tzompantli

Huitzilopochtli's dismembered sister, Coyolxauhqui, memorializing and sacralizing the southern half of the temple as a symbolic Coatepec of the Mexica migration narrative, but also a larger sculpture of the Earth goddess Tlaltecuhtli (Plate 5a).[13] The Tlaltecuhtli monolith is even larger than the iconic Sun Stone and was similarly sculpted in the highly ornate style of the late empire. It likely covers a final resting spot for Moctezuma's predecessor and uncle, Ahuitzotl, who died in 1502, but to date no remains of the cremated Great Speaker—the standard mortuary practice for rulers—have been identified. Nevertheless, the base of the temple is pockmarked with rich offering complexes that are now safeguarded, along with the temple's sculptures and statuary, in the Templo Mayor museum.

Other major recent finds include the circular platform likely used to cremate Ahuitzotl and as a setting for other important rituals (the *cuauhxicalli*), the trunk of a massive tree that once stood in the plaza, and the *tzompantli*—this last covered in hundreds or even thousands of skulls.[14] Not discovered thus far are statues depicting Huitzilopochtli and Tetzcatlipoca, described by Díaz and others, but different monumental sculptures have been unearthed over the years at the temple and adjacent areas, including depictions of Tlaloc and Coatlicue. Depictions of the first two deities may have been the target of Spanish iconoclasm, because the conquistadors and priests identified them most strongly with sacrificial practices and characterized them as incarnations of the devil. While on top of the temple, Moctezuma rebuffed a plea by Cortés to have a cross and statue of the Virgin installed in place of the "idols."

For the Aztecs and other Mesoamerican peoples, life and death were integrated parts of a duality, with one necessitating the other. The practice of preferentially taking captives in battle in order to ritually kill them and display their skulls, rather than killing them outright on the battlefield, was wholly strange to norms that had developed over centuries of Eurasian total war, even though heads sat on spikes at the Tower of London and in other European capitals. The scale of ritualized violence at Tenochtitlan was much greater than anywhere else in the contact-era Americas, and the Mexica used sacrifice both to renew the cosmos and to strike terror in the hearts of their adversaries. The fact that individuals who were not war captives were also sacrificed, though in lower numbers, demonstrates that the practice was part political theater but was also believed to be efficacious in the context of a religious system. Cortés and his captains were, of course, not attuned to or concerned with the broader societal context of Mexica human sacrifice.

They were concerned with their own survival in a metropolis they hoped to conquer and reported on sacrifice as a convenient justification for doing so. In contrast, the Tlaxcalteca and other Mesoamerican allies understood the practice but sensed the strategic opportunity to topple the Mexica and upend the political order in their favor.

Moctezuma did consent to the wish of the Spaniards to construct a Christian chapel within Axacayatl's palace. While searching for a suitable spot, a Spanish carpenter discovered a hidden room in the palace whose blocked doorway Cortés had broken to reveal a royal *totocalli* treasury. The Spaniards claim to have resealed the room but soon began plotting to take Moctezuma prisoner, using any pretense to do so, such as that the Mexica may be hatching a plot themselves.[15] A better reason soon presented itself when messengers arrived from Veracruz with news that a Triple Alliance force had been sent by Moctezuma in October, under the command of a provincial administrator named Qualpopoca (also spelled Cuauhpopoca and Cohualpopocatzin). They battled with the Spaniards stationed at Nautla (christened as Almería by the Spaniards), which resulted in the death of the commanding officer Juan de Escalante, six other soldiers, and a horse. Díaz relates that an apparition of the Virgin Mary prevented the casualties from being worse. Cortés and another contingent went to confront Moctezuma in his palace about this perceived hostile act, demanding that Qualpopoca and other Mexica commanders involved in the conflict be brought to Tenochtitlan to be executed by being first mauled by dogs and then burned at the stake—a form of ritualized violence that horrified the Mexica.

Cortés also took the hostile actions on the coast as grounds to hold Moctezuma prisoner in his own palace. What could have motivated the Great Speaker to be so pliant to foreign invaders in his city? Within the highly factional politics of the Aztec world, he may have worried that refusing Cortés' request would have created a power grab on the part of other Mexica claimants to the speakership and that, following Mesoamerican political logic, being a vassal to a king across the ocean would still allow him to hold power locally. Alternatively, he may have wanted to delay the looming conflict in order to observe what the Spaniards were up to before acting more decisively. The accuracy of various accounts of Moctezuma's strategy during this key episode are hotly debated, but the end result was the factionalization and destabilization of the Triple Alliance.[16] Moctezuma's confinement not only put his status as Great Speaker of Tenochtitlan in question, it also set off a chain of successional dispute in Texcoco, where the speakership soon passed from Cacama, who had plotted with the leaders of other cities to attack the Spaniards, to contested loyalties on the part of factions supporting half-brothers Coanacoch, Tecocoltzin, and Ixtilxochitl. The mix of micropatriotism to the altepetl and factional disputes within them generated by noble polygyny fostered a political landscape of shifting Aztec alliances that was one of the strongest determinants of subsequent events.

Although he adhered to some notion of house arrest, Moctezuma still went about typical daily activities of making offerings to the gods within his palace; receiving chiefs and emissaries from other city-states; presenting gifts to the Spaniards, including jewels, elaborate vestments, and women—one of them his daughter; leaving the palace to visit the Great Temple, with the proviso that his venerations would not involve human sacrifice; and even hunting and gambling with the Spaniards. Cortés turned his attention to searching for gold and building boats to launch on the lakes. He sent expeditions out to reconnaissance imperial provinces containing gold deposits, as well as the independent Mixtec kingdom of Tututepec, located over 250 miles (400 km) away on the Pacific coast of Oaxaca. Moctezuma and rulers of Texcoco continued gifting adornments containing gold to the Spaniards, but these came as composite pieces with blue-green feathers, turquoise, and other materials that Mesoamericans valued as highly as gold. The gold contained in the treasury at the palace of Axacayatl was valued at 600,000 Castilian pesos, but after Cortés reserved the royal fifth for Charles V and distributed the rest among the soldiers, none of the Spaniards was content with his allotment. The metal was smelted down on site, yet other finds from the sacred precinct give us a sense of the style of composite adornments including gold.[17] The fact that Triple Alliance rulers continually gifted Cortés goods of the highest value in their system shows the Mesoamerican strategy of gift tribute as a means of recognizing a foreign hegemon with the assumption that the Spaniards would be satisfied and would leave the imperial core more or less alone. But this was not the Spanish model of conquest, which built directly on earlier systems of territorial control, from the Iberian metal extraction of the Carthaginians and Romans in antiquity to the *Reconquista* battles between Christians and Muslims.

Cortés devised a plan to have boats built under the guise of being "pleasure" ships and had fittings delivered that had been salvaged from the destroyed ships that landed the expedition at Veracruz. Over four to five months, master shipbuilder Martin López led carpenters and teams of Spanish and Mesoamerican laborers in acquiring wood and assembling four brigantines that Cortés claimed were capable of holding 300 men plus horses and that López stated were 25–26 cubits each—approximately 40 feet (12 m).[18] The carpenters used a combination of oak from a forest four leagues from Tenochtitlan, perhaps located east of Texcoco, and cedars from around Tacuba. López later testified, in seeking compensation, that he financed the construction of the ships. Once completed, they were launched on the lakes and took a group including Moctezuma and one of his sons to royal hunting grounds south of the city. Although Díaz and other Spanish accounts report Moctezuma as being marveled by the speed and maneuverability of the brigantines, he certainly would have also felt trepidation when seeing and hearing the successful discharges of their mounted cannons. These were not the only ships on the landscape, as in April 1520 two successive messengers arrived to Tenochtitlan to tell Moctezuma of news, visually rendered on cloth paintings as well, of 18 new Spanish ships plying the coast and their eventual anchoring near San Juan de Ulúa.[19] This was the arrival of Pánfilo de Narváez, sent by Velázquez from Cuba to arrest Cortés.

Narváez, Disease, and Mexica Resistance

With more than 1,000 men, the Narváez expedition was twice the size of Cortés' initial group. Velázquez gave orders to seize the rebellious captain and continue the invasion in his name, prompted by learning of the rich cargo that Montejo and Puertocarrero carried with them during their stopover in Cuba on the way to Spain to petition the king, and after Velázquez had sent his own representatives to petition Charles V and Fonseca, president of the Council of the Indies, that Cortés be stopped. As Velázquez saw it, he was the authorized *adelantado* with official decrees to conquer Mesoamerica. Yet the matter of authorization was not so cut-and-dried because after Montejo and Puertocarrero's petition the council did not rule for either side and sent a judge, Lucás Vázquez de Ayllón, to prevent fighting by the two Spanish factions.[20] Velázquez could have captained the expedition against Cortés himself, but as governor of Cuba he was occupied with the outbreak of a disease epidemic, likely involving smallpox. The epidemic entered the Caribbean in October 1519 and possibly originated from Sanlúcar de Barameda, the same Spanish port town Cortés and many others had left from, devastating the Native populations of Hispaniola and Cuba.

Diseases with symptoms of pustular rashes consistent with smallpox are registered in some of the earliest written histories of Afro-Eurasian civilizations. Recent genetic research on the variola virus that causes smallpox suggests an origin in Africa tens of thousands of years ago, prior to the domestication of farm animals, and the breakout of major epidemics in which newer and more lethal strains replaced earlier ones up through the period of colonization of the Americas.[21] Paleopathology, the study of ancient diseases, is a rapidly developing field that promises to unravel the suite of pathogens from Europe, Africa, and Asia that swept through Native American populations. New research is confirming the large-scale death tolls that afflicted Native peoples in the sixteenth century, and is identifying traces of less commonly discussed diseases, including salmonella.[22] For our purposes here, it is sufficient to highlight the role that the introduction of a suite of diseases into Mesoamerica had on the ability of the Aztecs and other Native peoples to resist the invasions and colonization of the Spanish.

The Narváez expedition followed the coastal route charted by earlier expeditions along Yucatan and to the central Gulf of Mexico, making landfall at San Juan de Ulúa and eventually an encampment at Cempoala. Cortés had sent Andrés de Tapia to the coast on a reconnaissance mission and installed Gonzalo de Sandoval, his friend from Medellín, as commander of the region, stationed at Villa Rica de Veracruz. This appointment followed the dubious claim that Villa Rica was a legitimate town within Charles's domain and required protection against the usurpers with Narváez. Weeks of politicking between the two Spanish groups followed, with delegations sent by Narváez to Tenochtitlan and by Cortés to Veracruz. Of the new arrivals who journeyed to Tenochtitlan in late April and early May, some appear to have been in contact with Moctezuma about forming an alliance against Cortés and his loyalists, whereas others were propositioned by Cortés to switch sides, with the justification that they stood a better shot of gaining booty through conquering the rich city under his lead. In writing to Charles V only a few months after these events, Cortés claims that his initial reluctance to journey to the Gulf was because he wanted to safeguard all of the gold he had acquired for the king, but he eventually needed to go there in person because the Cempoalans and other Totonac groups had begun siding with Narváez.

Cortés records leaving 500 men behind in Tenochtitlan under the command of Alvarado, whereas de Tapia writes there were only 50 and Vázquez de Tapia places the remaining force at 130.[23] This last figure may be the most accurate because Vázquez de Tapia was one of those who remained in the city. He also mentions there was a Spanish woman with them, though this passage is ambiguous. Vázquez de Tapia may have been referring to one of the few women on the expedition, the female *conquistadora* María de Estrada, who fought in ensuing battles. She was from Seville and was the sister of the conquistador Francisco de Estrada; the two siblings likely arrived in Mexico via Cuba with the Narváez expedition. Alternatively, Vázquez de Tapia may have been alluding to the statue of the Virgin that was installed in the Great Temple, as he recounts how the amazing beauty of the woman awed the Mexica.[24] The return journey to the Gulf went through Cholula, where Cortés began negotiating with Narváez by couriers exchanging letters, while Sandoval undertook most of the face-to-face negotiations in order to assemble a Native army and convince a faction of Narváez's group to defect to Cortés' side.[25]

Many of the Spaniards were familiar with one another from years stationed in the Caribbean, meaning that the members of Cortés' group could convince individuals they knew of the better prospects offered by alliance with the Tlaxcalteca and a track record of successes. Mesoamerican guides directed Cortés to the Gulf plain via the more frequently used pass south of the Orizaba volcano. Cortés, through a mix of persuading a number of the men with Narváez to turn, offering his own men a bounty for capturing Narváez, and attacking Cempoala at night, not only turned back the threat to the expedition, but also emerged with an even stronger military force. He could not have done it alone, and relied on significant aid from Sandoval and thousands of Mesoamerican allies. The decisive surrender on the night of May 28 was staged dramatically atop the main temple of Cempoala, where Narváez had lodged himself. He was struck in the eye by a pike atop the temple, but survived, while Martín López, the shipbuilder, burned the thatch roof of its shrine.[26] Following Narváez' defeat, Cortés commanded over 1,300 Spanish and other European or African soldiers, with 80 crossbowmen and 80 harquebusiers, and nearly 100 horses. Another one of the new arrivals was Juan Cano de Saavedra, only 18 at the time, who came from a distinguished family of Extremadura and was the son of the commander of the fort in Cáceres. He would later marry Moctezuma's elder daughter, who had the best claim to her father's wealth and title.

Following the conflict with Narváez, the Spaniards learned of inflamed tensions back at Tenochtitlan. Stated reasons for the unrest include that Narváez and Moctezuma had been conspiring at a distance; that a faction of Mexica were seeking to liberate Moctezuma, who had in actuality been keeping the peace; and that the Mexica resented the crosses, statues of the Virgin Mary, and images of Saint Christopher that the Spaniards had installed in their temples, replacing sculptures of their own divinities.[27] Yet clearly the primary cause that directly precipitated fighting and the Mexica destruction of all four Spanish brigantines was Alvarado's massacre in Tenochtitlan's sacred precinct on May 22, during the festival month of Toxcatl ("Dry Thing") that honored Tetzcatlipoca and Huitzilopochtli at the end of the dry season. The Native scribes of the Florentine Codex go into great detail regarding the preparations for this festival in Chapter 19 of Book XII, including the assembly of an effigy of Huitzilopochtli made from amaranth seeds, decorated in feathers, gold and turquoise adornments, darts and a shield, and a hummingbird headdress—details that are skipped over in the much shorter Spanish translation. It is likely that this description actually corresponds to the festival for the month of Panquetzaliztli, the principal one honoring Huitzilopochtli's regeneration during the winter solstice, but the deity complexes of the Mexica patron god and Tetzcatlipoca often overlapped, and Spanish sources make clear the Mexica honored both deities during Toxcatl.[28] Tetzcatlipoca served as patron deity of many earlier Aztec city-states, and when the Mexica elevated Huitzilopochtli he could be paired in images with Tetzcatlipoca or have that entity's iconic smoking mirror for a foot. The most sacred offering of the festival was the sacrifice of a youth who for a year prior had been feted and treated like Tetzcatlipoca incarnate, and who was given a fortified pulque (fermented beverage of agave sap), referred to as "obsidian medicine," before being sacrificed.

Whatever the exact rites of the ceremonies, we have already seen that the Spaniards considered these two deities the most diabolical in the Aztec pantheon, and Alvarado took the festival as an opportunity to block the exits to the central courtyard and slaughter hundreds of nobles, priests, and elite warriors while they danced to honor their gods. Thousands of non-elite spectators were also killed. The scribes of the Florentine Codex provide grizzly details of the violence, with Mexica being hacked apart, dragging their entrails as they tried to flee, and a "stench of sulfur" from the carnage.[29] As a Spanish eyewitness who was at least in the city, if not in the sacred precinct itself, Vázquez de Tapia was equally damning regarding Alvarado's brutal conduct, and claims he spoke out against the mobilization for the massacre. His testimony also provided the pretense that the Mexica wanted to reinstall the statue of Huitzilopochtli to his shrine atop the Great Temple, removed by Cortés.[30] Even Gómara depicts the massacre negatively, noting that Alvarado was covetous of the gold jewels the nobles adorned themselves with for the ceremony, and the killing as cruel, but that Cortés did not punish his captain.[31] It is conceivable that Cortés had in fact ordered the massacre from Veracruz because he either feared some sort of alliance between Moctezuma and Narváez's men, or because it gave him the opportunity to greatly reduce the ranks of elite eagle and jaguar knights assembled at the ceremony.[32] The rationale for the massacre as motivated by witnessing sacrificial rituals is unconvincing, because the Spaniards had seen them before without taking to arms. This possibility would also explain the failure to reprimand Alvarado for disobeying orders, which Cortés typically did. A final explanation offered by both Spanish and Native author sources, such as Alva Ixtlilxochitl, is that the Tlaxcalteca, remembering earlier sacrificial ceremonies in which their compatriots who had been captured in "flowery wars" were killed, spread the rumor to their foreign allies that the Mexica were planning to sacrifice Alvarado and other Spaniards.[33] Following the massacre, Alvarado and his forces rightfully feared for their lives and garrisoned themselves in the palace of Axacayatl.

On their return to Tenochtitlan, the larger combined force of Cortés' and Narváez' men, with their Mesoamerican allies, passed through Tlaxcala and were joined by another 2,000 Tlaxcalteca warriors before continuing to Texcoco. Spanish accounts relate having received a cold reception in both Texcoco and Tenochtitlan, but Alva Ixtlilxochitl portrays his Texcocan ancestors as continued loyal allies in greeting the Spaniards. One month after the Toxcatl massacre, on the feast day of Saint John the Baptist (June 24), Cortés re-entered the ominously quiet imperial capital. Moctezuma greeted him, but their relations were strained because of the massacre and due to Cortés' belief that the Great Speaker had conspired with Narváez. Hostilities first erupted along the Tacuba causeway into Tenochtitlan, led by Moctezuma's brother Cuitlahuac, and it was in that third Triple Alliance city that Mexica warriors captured one of Moctezuma's daughters, whom Cortés kept as a concubine. She may have been the elder daughter Tecuichpochtzin, baptized Doña Isabel, or one of Moctezuma's younger daughters baptized Doña Ana and Doña Inés.[34] Cortés sent Diego de Ordaz with 400 men to pacify the uprising along the causeway, but they were besieged by Mexica warriors, who killed several Spaniards and injured Ordaz. In their retreat, the fighting moved to the center of the city with Ordaz's forces battling on the streets while Cortés' forces fired cannons and muskets from Axacayatl's palace, which the Mexica set ablaze. Days of fighting ensued on the streets of the city and within the sacred precinct itself. In one battle, the Spaniards and Tlaxcalteca fought the Mexica from the top of the Great Temple, where they burned the shrines to Huitzilopochtli and Tlaloc—a form of iconoclasm understood by all Mesoamericans as symbolic of military conquest.

When the Spaniards made it back to the palace, many of the new arrivals who had come with Narváez made their sentiments clear that they wished to retreat from Tenochtitlan. The city was in open war and not the bargain of easy booty they thought they had signed up for. Cortés attempted to use Moctezuma to calm the uprising by receiving Cuitlahuac and other Mexica nobles and by addressing crowds from atop the palace of Axayacatl. Yet, by this time, the Great Speaker had already lost the confidence of most the city's inhabitants. The Mexica resistance continued to shower the palace with projectiles, and when Moctezuma went out to address the crowd he was struck down, most likely by a slingshot. He died three or four days later, at the end of June. Vázquez de Tapia notes the Mexica suspected the Spaniards killed Moctezuma while in custody. This introduces a compelling counter-narrative to the official Spanish story that the Great Speaker died from wounds suffered from a projectile thrown by his own people, and after telling Cortés to look after his children and possessions.[35] The Mexica perspective seems probable, as Moctezuma no longer offered much political value to Cortés. His remains were taken by Mexica priests to be cremated, and the Tlatelolca scribes of the Florentine Codex register one last indignity in claiming that Moctezuma's pyre produced a stench and that witnesses verbally condemned him as he burned, whereas their own speaker, Itzquauhtzin, was sent by boat back to Tlatelolco to be cremated with great splendor and no harsh words.[36]

The majority of sources are in agreement that Tenochtitlan's ruling council elected Cuitlahuac, who had been tlatoani of Iztapalapa and a consistent critic of appeasing the Spaniards, to succeed his brother Moctezuma as Great Speaker.[37] Cortés sought to prop up another puppet ruler among the ranks of Moctezuma's children, and the minority narrative that one son named Axayacatl was the rightful successor via European notions of primogeniture found favor, particularly in sources that drew from Juan Cano, whose agenda was to legitimate his wife, Doña Isabel Moctezuma, as the heir to the Great Speaker's land and titles following the death of her brother.[38] When this succession scheme failed, Cortés quickly changed strategy and decided to leave the city. He addressed Mexica nobles from atop a temple in hopes of a truce that would allow them to depart. The Mexica suggested to Cortés that he exit the city via the Tacuba causeway, as it was the shortest route out. Cortés accurately gauged the suggestion as signifying that his men would be ambushed by Mexica forces while attempting to leave. He therefore set about trying to clear the path through attacks targeting the destruction of houses lining the planned escape route to the causeway. In preparing for the flight, Bernal Díaz claims he had the foresight to fill his pockets with jade rather than gold, as he knew this would better serve him in paying Mesoamerican communities along the escape route back to Tlaxcala for food and assistance.[39] The Mexica made escape more difficult by removing the bridge segments from the causeways and widening canals along the route. Cortés had a portable bridge built, but it proved inefficient to transport thousands of people as they attempted to flee at night. The route out followed a progression from the palace of Axayacatl to Tecpantzingo, Tolteacalli, and the large canal at Toltecaacalopan (each segment about 1.25 miles or 2 km); then to the Ahuehuete tree at Popotla that legend states Cortés cried under (another 2.25 miles or 3.6 km), to the city of Tacuba (1 mile or 1.6 km); and from there north to a fortified resting spot at Otoncalpolco, christened later as Los Remedios (4.5 miles or 7.25 km).

The image of Cortés sobbing under a tree provides the Spanish perspective on what is conventionally termed *La Noche Triste* ("the night of sorrow") for the Mexica resistance and successful expulsion of the invaders from Tenochtitlan (Figure 7.4). The Spaniards, Tlaxcalteca, and other Mesoamerican allies were now engaged in an outright war with the Mexica, who likely realized at this point that they would have to wage the sort of European style of total war, yet they also continued to take Spanish and Native captives to sacrifice at temples in addition to killing in pursuit of their foes. Casualties from the expulsion of the invaders from Tenochtitlan were high on both sides. They included Cacama of Texcoco, Moctezuma's son Chimalpopoca, and hundreds of Spaniards, many of them Narváez's men, whom Cortés may have viewed as expendable for their dubious loyalties and perceived cowardly response to the days of fighting within the city. Cortés wrote to Charles V that he had attempted to save all of "the king's" gold that he could, dividing the load among Spanish horsemen and Tlaxcalteca porters, and also to escape with two of Moctezuma's daughters and Chimalpopoca. Mesoamerican guides were once again essential. Cortés noted in leaving Otoncalpolco: "We knew no road nor where we were going, save that an Indian from Tlascalteca [*sic*] led us, saying that he would take us to his land."[40] Díaz recounts that among the survivors, "how

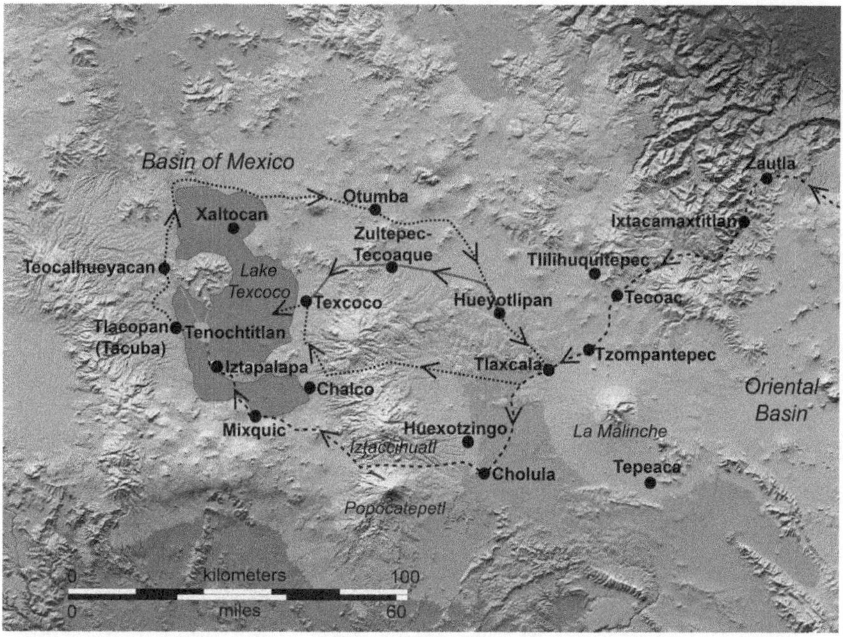

Figure 7.4. Map of route of retreat from Tenochtitlan back to Tlaxcala, and return via Texcoco. Solid line indicates alternate route taken by the brigantine caravan.

happy we were to see Doña Marina [Malinche] still alive, and Doña Luisa the daughter of Xicotenga [Xicotencatl of Tlaxcala], whose escape at the bridges was due to some Tlaxcalans, and also a woman named Maria de Estrada, who was the only Spanish woman in Mexico."[41]

The joint Spanish-Mesoamerican force received an amicable reception when they reached Teocalhueyacan, an Otomi community that had connections to the Otomis of Tlilihuiquitepec, on Tlaxcala's northern border, who were part of the group.[42] The people of Teocalhueyacan provided them all with food and rest, and an opportunity to dredge nearby canals for bodies, gold, and armor. The retreat to Tlaxcala continued in a counterclockwise progression around the northern Lake Xaltocan until the group skirted the Teotihuacan Valley to the north of Cerro Gordo. This route is likely because Spanish accounts make no mention of the ruined city, which had transformed from its role as a Classic-period capital to being a province of Texcoco, but was also hallowed ground for the Mexica, whose Great Speakers made regular pilgrimages to Teotihuacan. The Mexica had constructed altars for performing rituals at the base of the

Sun Pyramid—which stood, covered in vegetation, as a testament to an earlier golden age—and excavated the ruined city to recover artifacts that they offered in consecration of their own Great Temple. Surrounding the ruins were small towns of primarily Nahuatl speakers, while the more arid northeastern valley had a larger proportion of Otomis, including the altepetl of Otumba (Otompan or "place of Otomis").[43] Otumba had a population of some 4,000 in its urban core and close to 40,000 in surrounding areas of the city-state. It was a major center for craft production and exchange, with resident *pochteca* traders and specialists who manufactured obsidian tools, lapidary adornments, and products derived from the maguey plant.

On the plain near Otumba, bordering the hill of Cerro San Lucas, the joint Spanish-Mesoamerican force encountered a large Triple Alliance army, comprising primarily Mexica with assistance from Texcoco, the Otomi altepetl of Xaltocan, and from Otumba itself. The assembled Aztec force was almost certainly not the 200,000 warriors that Gómara claims, and the author's casting of Cortés in his typically heroic light makes no mention that, according to Aguilar, Cortés was "in tears" before rallying his troops for battle.[44] The account of Díaz seems more evenhanded in describing the battle, which he places on July 14, 1520, approximately two weeks after leaving Tenochtitlan. The Spaniards were outnumbered and had lost all of their cannons and gunpowder in the flight from the city. Yet they retained 23 horses and used these to their advantage on the open battlefield outside of Otumba. Gómara has Cortés calling on Saint Peter, whereas Díaz claims the Spaniards were rallied by appealing to Santiago, whose spirit appeared on the field of battle, and that the Tlaxcalteca fought alongside them "like lions." In the decisive charge, Cortés led other horsemen into enemy lines and Juan de Salamanca killed the Aztec general, who held a feathered battle standard. The charge led to an Aztec retreat and Salamanca's subsequent incorporation of feathers on his colonial-period coat of arms to memorialize his role in the battle.

The victory at Otumba left a relatively unimpeded route back to Tlaxcala, but one of the most significant archaeological discoveries relating to the conquest era provides a vivid illustration of the strong Aztec resistance that is glossed over or only ambiguously referenced in textual sources. The site of Zultepec-Tecoaque is located in the modern state of Tlaxcala, but during the contact era was on the fringe of Texcoco's domain. Extensive excavations at the site conducted by Mexican archaeologists since the 1990s have documented a community of the contact era and the capture and sacrifice of a caravan of foreigners that would best coincide chronologically with the chaos following the expulsion from Tenochtitlan.[45] Zultepec-Tecoaque features an intriguing mix of typical Aztec material culture, European glazed pottery, a European-style oven, and Aztec-style terracotta figurines that depict Europeans rather than typical pre-Hispanic subject matter. Yet the most fascinating evidence comes from the bones, which include European animals such as cows, chickens, sheep, goat, and horses—some of these likely from the early colonial period—but also Europeans and at least one African, some of whom were sacrificed and their skulls displayed on the rack in the town's central plaza (Figure 7.5). The most likely explanation is that inhabitants of Zultepec-Tecoaque captured one or more stray caravans during the flight from Tenochtitlan and sacrificed some of the individuals to the gods.

Whomever this unfortunate faction recovered from Zultepec-Tecoaque were, the main group with Cortés first began mending themselves at Hueyotlipan, the Otomi community of a few thousand residents allied with the Tlaxcalteca and situated on the great road eastward. While stationed there for three days, Xicotencatl the elder, Maxixcatzin, and other rulers of Tlaxcala

Figure 7.5. Central plaza at Zultepec-Tecoaque with round temple to Ehecatl-Quetzalcoatl and altar where tzompantli (skull rack) held the skulls of Spaniards and allies from captured caravan.

Photo by author. Reproduction authorized by the Instituto Nacional de Antropología e Historia, Mexico.

journeyed from their capital city with thousands of warriors to welcome the Spaniards (Figure 7.6). Here, then, was another crucial moment of the Spanish-Tlaxcalteca alliance that now revolved around mutual survival. The Tlaxcalteca could have abandoned the Spaniards, and this surely would have doomed Cortés's mission, but it also would have left them vulnerable to a resurgent Mexica seeking for revenge on their traditional foes. Xicotencatl the younger, in the traditional Spanish narrative, was the only dissenter to renewing bonds, but there are grounds to dispute this, based on his later participation in leading tens of thousands of Tlaxcalteca warriors for the final assault on Tenochtitlan.[46]

While once again hosted in Tlaxcala for approximately 20 days, Cortés stayed with Maxixcatzin while Alvarado stayed with Xicotencatl the elder—who was his father-in-law in the reckoning of Mesoamerican bride exchange by having been paired with Xicotencatl's daughter Doña Luisa.

Figure 7.6. Tlaxcalteca providing food and more warriors at Hueyotlipan.
Illustration by Pedro Cahuantzi Hernández based on Muñoz Camargo (1584/2000: cuadro 55).

Cortés faced initial reluctance from many of the men in his plan to continue with the mission of conquest, but this was somewhat alleviated by the arrival of reinforcements from the group stationed at Veracruz and from expeditions captained by other Spaniards who continued to arrive to the Gulf coast.[47] These new arrivals brought soldiers, horses, and supplies to Tlaxcala and reconstituted the collaborative conquering army. The fact that some of these caravans setting out from Veracruz for Tlaxcala were also attacked by Triple Alliance forces prompted Cortés to invade Tepeaca, located in southern Puebla along the natural corridor toward the Gulf south of Orizaba.[48] He brought some 4,000 Tlaxcalteca warriors with him, who were aggrieved by damages to agricultural fields within their own province by the Tepeyacans and the Triple Alliance. Díaz records intense fighting around August 1 and the harsh retribution inflicted by Cortés, who dismissed the Tepeyacans as "cannibals" in enslaving and branding women and children. It is from Tepeaca, which he fortified and christened Segura de la Frontera, that Cortés penned his second letter to Charles V.

Late autumn was the beginning of the dry season—the typical time for war—and the Mexica began with an offensive aimed at regaining territories south of Tlaxcala, which prompted Cortés to counter. He claims to have led the army to fight Triple Alliance forces at Quauhquechollan, located in southwestern Puebla, four leagues from Cholula, but Díaz is emphatic that Cortés did not go and rather sent an army under the command of Cristóbal de Olid. The Spaniards and Tlaxcalteca emerged victorious, and Quauhquechollan provided more Mesoamerican allies who assisted in later conquests. They next pushed southward into the warmer and lower *tierra templada* around Izúcar, Puebla, and from there received representatives from the Mixtec kingdom of Coixtlahuaca, a gold-rich province of the Triple Alliance, who pledged their loyalty to the Spanish-Mesoamerican alliance, rather than their traditional overlords. Their allegiance could have in fact been prompted by the independent efforts of the Native conquistador Gonzalo Mazatzin Moctezuma of Tepexi de la Seda, in southern Puebla, who may have been the grandson of the earlier Tenochca Great Speaker Moctezuma Ilhuicamina. In the late sixteenth century, Mazatzin Moctezuma's grandson, Joaquín de San Francisco, testified vehemently that his grandfather had led a mission south through Oaxaca to conquer or coerce Native polities to ally with the Spaniards against the Triple Alliance.[49] This episode once again highlights the role of Native peoples as conquerors in their own right, not merely allies along for the ride.

It is important to emphasize not only the role of micro-patriotism in stimulating Native people to actively shape the dynamic political landscape of 1519–1521 and beyond, but also the sustained arrival of Spanish forces to the Gulf of Mexico. The continued waves of expeditions to Mesoamerica underscores some of the inevitability of conquest and colonialism, even if Cortés' mission had failed. The other critical factor was disease. While the Spaniards were regrouping at Tlaxcala and consolidating areas to the south, an epidemic swept across the Altiplano from mid-October to mid-December, with dire consequences for Mesoamerican populations. It took the lives of thousands of Tlaxcalteca, including Maxixcatzin, and other groups allied with Cortés, but also devastated the Mexica, including Cuitlahuac, who had only served as Great Speaker for some 80 days. Smallpox seems the most likely candidate for the epidemic, but a suite of pathogens may have been involved. The scribes of the Florentine Codex described and illustrated the "great rash" of 1520 that saw people's bodies covered in pustules and large bumps (Figure 7.7).[50] Although individuals on both sides of the war were affected—Díaz recounts a bout with fever that had him vomiting blood—the epidemic largely skirted the Europeans and Africans on Cortés' side, as their genetic ancestries conferred advantages to fending off diseases that had evolved in Afro-Eurasia.[51] Providing one of the few eyewitness estimates, Vázquez de Tapia gauged that the epidemic killed approximately one-quarter of the Native population of Mexico. It decimated the Mexica demographically and destabilized its political leadership, thereby providing another historical pivot in the forging of New Spain.

The Siege and Fall of Tenochtitlan-Tlatelolco

Cortés closed his second letter to Charles V in articulating the term "New Spain" for the first time, while also mentioning to the king that he was having a dozen brigantines—other sources say there were 13—constructed in Tlaxcala in order to mount a large-scale naval assault on Tenochtitlan. He opened his third letter, written after the fall of the city, by picking up the same thread.[52] The fittings for the ships arrived from Veracruz in December 1520, and Cortés oversaw their partial assembly in Tlaxcala for a couple of weeks before heading to Texcoco, from where he planned to launch them. Under Conancotzin, however, Texcoco was still the second-largest member of the Triple Alliance. It is likely that plans to splinter Texcoco's loyalties were

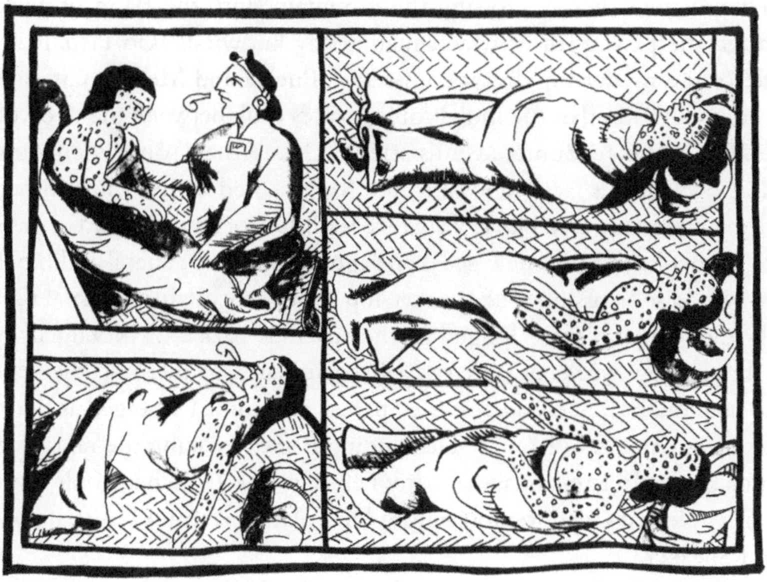

Figure 7.7. Epidemic of 1520 that Tlatelolca of the Florentine Codex called the "great rash."
Illustration by Pedro Cahuantzi Hernández.

not only Cortés', based on his diplomatic encounters while at Tenochtitlan, but also were prompted by Xicotencatl the elder and other Tlaxcalteca and Otomis from Tlaxcala. They had been on opposite sides of a political divide for decades, but in an earlier era Texcoco and Tlaxcala had amicable diplomatic relations. The early colonial Nahuatl document called the *Annals of Cuauhtitlan* details pre-Hispanic political history and recounts an episode in which Nezahualcoyotl, who became the greatest of Acolhua speakers, went into exile in the altepetl of Tliliuhquitepec during a factional dispute over succession in Texcoco, creating an alliance with that altepetl, Tlaxcala, Huexotzingo, and Atlangatepec prior to the wars that overthrew the Tepanec and created the Triple Alliance.[53] Nezahualcoyotl sired children with noblewomen from Tlaxcala, and the Tlaxcalteca and Otomi from Tliliuhquitepec were right to express faith in the existence of a faction within Texcoco predisposed to ally with them and the Spaniards to reclaim rulership and emerge from under the thumb of the Mexica.

A force of Spaniards and Tlaxcalteca set out for Texcoco on December 28, 1520, and spent a first night in Texmelucan, within the former domain of Huexotzingo, before crossing the mountains into the Basin of Mexico through the pass north of Itzaccihuatl, today known as Río Frio. It is the route of the modern highway connecting Puebla and Mexico City, and is lower in elevation that the initial route Cortés took between the two volcanoes. The group encountered emissaries of Coanacotzin somewhere outside of Texcoco, but his faction, loyal to the Mexica, fled to Tenochtitlan before Cortés entered the city. The key alliance with Texcoco was instead cemented with Tecocoltzin as the new speaker, supported by his general Ixtlilxochitl, who would soon assume the speakership after Tecocoltzin's death.[54] Cortés and other captains were lodged in the spacious palace of Nezahualcoyotl for the first few weeks of January. At Tenochtitlan Cuauhtemoc, the general who had fought fiercely against the Spanish at Otumba emerged as the new leader. His name translates as "Descending Eagle," evoking the raptor's dive to attack prey. In late January or early February, the Tenochca noble council officially elected Cuauhtemoc, whom Díaz placed at around 25 years old, as Great Speaker.

The addition of the Texcoca to the Spanish-Mesoamerican alliance was perhaps of equal significance to the more frequently noted alliance with the Tlaxcalteca.[55] Not only did it remove the second most powerful altepetl from the Aztec Triple Alliance, it also provided a strategic location across the lake from Tenochtitlan to serve as a base of operations from which to strike. Ixtlilxochitl became a conquering general as well, and beginning in February he led an army possibly as large as 60,000 in campaigns that progressed counterclockwise along the lake system over three months through Xaltocan, Tenayuca, Azcapotzalco, and Tacuba.[56] These were part of a grand strategy aimed at encircling the island city and cutting the Tenochca and Tlatelolca off from food, water, and allies—tactics of European total war that had not been employed previously in Mesoamerica. The Spaniards planned to assault the island city and those mainland cities that still remained loyal to it by land and water, and most of the violent battles took place on causeways. Cortés and Sandoval led campaigns into the Aztec breadbasket of the southern Basin of Mexico by taking Iztapalapa, Chalco, Xochimilco, and Coyoacan by force or threat of it. While at Iztapalapa, emissaries from Otumba came to apologize for their role in the earlier battle and agree to a voluntary alliance. Cortés established a camp in the south at Coyoacan and sent Sandoval and Alvarado to do the same, following campaigns to secure the causeways leading to Tacuba, the shortest access to Tenochtitlan, and Tlatelolco, with its valuable marketplace. Cervantes de Salazar, Díaz, and other mid- to late sixteenth-century sources also claim that Sandoval created a garrison at Tepeyac, significant as the terminus of the northern causeway and the future spot for the adoration of the Virgin of Guadalupe.[57]

While the Spaniards, Tlaxcalteca, Texcoca, and other allies were occupied with encircling Tenochtitlan by land, the brigantines were prefabricated in Tlaxcala in order to be transported to Texcoco for launching. These ships were built to be slightly longer than the original four constructed while in Tenochtitlan. One or more of them were likely fully assembled in Tlaxcala and tested on the Zahuapan River but then disassembled prior to transport. The massive freight dictated a flatter route than those that had been used to cross the sierras for the initial entry into the Basin of Mexico, between the tallest peaks, or to Texcoco through Río Frio. The caravan instead journeyed along a similar inter-montane corridor used in the return to Tlaxcala after the Noche Triste following the "great road" with a stopover in Hueyotlipan before continuing north of the sierra to enter the basin.[58] This same flatter route is where Mexico's first railroad line was constructed to connect Mexico City to Veracruz. Several Tlaxcalteca nobles, and thousands of warriors, accompanied Martín López and the partially assembled ships to Hueyotlipan, where they waited for Sandoval with cavalry and reinforcements to accompany them the rest of the way. The total force comprised tens of thousands of warriors, distributed to protect the precious cargo in the front and rear, and with a couple thousand porters carrying provisions. Cortés gave Sandoval orders to sack Zultepec-Tecoaque in retribution for the capture of the earlier caravan and to ensure secure passage through the frontier between the territories of Tlaxcala and Texcoco.[59] The massive caravan of this hybrid army, featuring Spaniards, Tlaxcalteca, horses, warriors adorned with feathered headdresses and shields, swords of Toledo steel and machuahuitls lined with Pachuca obsidian, accompanying a dozen ships overland, would have been a remarkable sight in the annals of military history. Boisterous chants of "Castile! Castile!" and "Tlaxcala! Tlaxcala!" became a rallying call for the army as it marched west toward the basin.

At the end of February the brigantine caravan arrived in Texcoco, where large teams of Native laborers excavated a long canal to make the city a protected port from which to launch the ships onto Lake Texcoco. Alva Ixtlilxochitl gives a sense of the scale of the undertaking, which may be somewhat inflated in celebrating the aid provided by his ancestors. He suggests that teams of 8,000–10,000 labored for 50 days in excavating a canal over half a league long (1.7 miles or 2.7 km) connecting the city of

Texcoco to the lake.[60] Like the four earlier brigantines, the newly assembled ships possessed European artillery, including falconets, harquebuses, and crossbows. Accompanying them for the naval assault on Tenochtitlan were thousands of canoes supplied by Texcoco and other lakeshore communities; these were armed with archers. With a grand strategy of controlling the lakes and invading Tenochtitlan by land, the Spaniards, Tlaxcalteca, and Texcoca set to laying siege to the island city by destroying certain bridges on causeways to restrict escape while repairing others they planned to use for entering by land; breeching dikes so that their boats could pass; and cutting off the freshwater supply by severing its aqueducts, particularly the primary one from Chapultepec, which they did on May 13. The Mexica were left with a dwindling supply of drinking water from springs and wells on the island, and the destruction of the dikes left it exposed to floods that later plagued colonial Mexico City.[61]

By May 1521, the regular afternoon and early evening rains had returned to the Altiplano. Normally this would mean Mexica warriors returning from distant battlefields to plant their agricultural fields; yet everything had changed, and they now faced a battle for their city and their survival as a people. As was the case in the earlier battle of Tenochtitlan that expelled the invaders, the Mexica were fighting a different sort of war than they were used to, staged in their own city and encircling lake. They adjusted by constructing wooden barricades and taking to the roofs of buildings to shoot at the invaders on the lake or entering through the causeway. The Spaniards, in turn, combined European martial tactics of naval assault using projectiles with land attacks from the garrisoned camps at the mainland termini of the causeways. Cavalry provided the Spaniards little advantage on the causeways and on the urban streets of Tenochtitlan-Tlatelolco, so they fought to take control of large open spaces in the city where horses were useful, which included the sacred precincts and marketplaces of both sister cities. Cutting off marketplace exchange also exacerbated the famine the Mexica were experiencing from the interruption of their normal agricultural cycle and system of imperial taxation. They had to rely on limited storehouses of dried foods and what they could fish or forage around the lakes, including small reptiles, amphibians, and birds. Cortés also gives a sense of wartime subsistence in noting the Spaniards' own food shortages and that Aztec communities of the southern basin supplied them especially with "fish and cherries," the last being the *capulín* or Mexican chokecherry.[62]

Although they were deprived of food and water, encircled by hostile forces, and decimated by disease, the Mexica continued to mount a strong-armed resistance. Francisco de Aguilar admired Mexica grit in the face of Mediterranean-style naval battle previously unknown to them. He observed: "The Indian canoes, which covered the water, boldly attacked the brigantines. As soon as the Spaniards took any of the houses, which were all on the water, they had the Tlaxcalan Indians demolish and level them, for this gave more freedom to maneuver. And so they fought bravely, and the Indians defended themselves and killed or wounded some of the Spaniards."[63] The Mexica sank one of the brigantines by driving wooden spikes into the shallow lake bed to run it aground and attack by canoe. Yet the most significant Mexica victories occurred at the end of June, when they fended off various attacks from the northwestern causeways, especially those leading from Tacuba and Nonoalco. On June 30, they handed the Spaniards and Native allies a major defeat on the Tacuba causeway in which Cortés was surrounded and almost taken captive—highlighting again the Aztec system of battlefield conduct in which taking the captain captive was preferable to killing him outright. Cortés claims the Spanish captain Crístobol de Olea saved him, whereas Alva Ixtlilxochitl claims it was his own great-great-grandfather.[64] The Mexica resistance on the Tacuba causeway cost the lives of some 35–40 Spaniards during the battle and over a thousand Native allies, whom the scribes of the Florentine Codex record as Tlaxcalteca, Texcoca, Chalca, and Xochimilca.[65] The Mexica also took men and horses captive to be sacrificed at Tlatelolco in a ceremony that terrified the Spaniards, as they could see the activities on top of the temple in the distance and hear the ominous sounds from the drums and shell trumpets. The Tlatelolca report that 53 Spaniards and still more Mesoamericans were sacrificed, and that their heads were fastened to the skull rack, including those of the horses.

The Mexica resistance on the causeway and subsequent sacrifice provide another illustration of how the violence of the war was framed through two different religious traditions and ideologies of battle. In sequential passages of his third letter, Cortés writes that during the sacrificial ritual the Mexica "offered up to their gods as a sign of victory many perfumes and incense of a gummy substance" (the tree resin copal), and that the Spaniards would have taken the great marketplace of Tlatelolco, "if God, on account of our sins, had not permitted such a great disaster."[66] Cortés thereby attributes his temporary defeat in a protracted war of conquest with massive battlefield casualties to the Christian notion of original sin, while claiming that the Mexica conducted their sacrifices to scare the Spaniards and their Native allies, even after noting how the ceremony was conducted in the manner typical of Aztec religion. Díaz provides more details in recording that certain sacrificial victims were first adorned with feathered headdresses and fans and made to dance before a statue of Huitzilopochtli before being offered to the god.[67]

We have seen that Mexica sacrifice can rarely be separated from its political and military context, and though during the siege of Tenochtitlan it was still practiced to appease Huitzilopochtli or other divinities, it also had the effect of instilling fear in the invaders. Following the defeat, scores of Mesoamerican allies abandoned the Spaniards and returned home. Cortés later charged Xicotencatl the younger with defection prior to this exodus and had him executed, which is inconsistent with how Cortés responded to these other defections and may have really been an effort to strengthen the political position of Maxixcatzin's son, whom he could better control, relative to Xicotencatl. Many Native allies remained throughout, including Ixtlilxochitl, since his legitimate claim to Texcoco required defeating Coanacotzin, who was still alive in Tenochtitlan. When other groups saw that the Mexica had not routed the Spaniards, who still maintained their land bases encircling the island city and controlled the lakes through their fleet of brigantines and canoes, these Native allies returned to the field of battle. The Spaniards also benefited from the timely July arrival in Veracruz of a ship from the failed expedition of Juan Ponce de León. Ponce de León had first landed in Florida in 1513, and in 1521 he attempted to establish a colony in the southwest of the peninsula, but met fierce resistance from the local Calusa and died from his battle injuries upon returning to Cuba. The failed expedition resulted in a boon to Cortés, as it supplied hundreds more men, horses, and gunpowder and crossbows.[68] Cortés placed the force of the final assault on Tenochtitlan-Tlatelolco with 900 Spaniards and more than 150,000 allied Tlaxcalteca, Texcoca, and other Mesoamericans.

The final assault of Tenochtitlan transpired over July 20–25, with the last stand of the Mexica occurring at Tlatelolco on August 1, and the official surrender of Cuauhtemoc on August 13. The Tlatelolca recount the days spent by the invaders filling gaps in the causeways while the Mexica would reopen them at night, bravely guarding the women and children lodged in the city.[69] The Spaniards constructed a catapult to launch stones into Tlatelolco, but it misfired badly. However valiant their resistance, the effects of the siege and continual attacks had left the Mexica starving and short of weapons with which to defend themselves. Cortés painted the bleak picture: "I had commanded Gonzalo de Sandoval to sail the brigantines in between the houses in the other quarter in which the Indians were resisting. . . . In this way they would be surrounded and so hard pressed that they would have no place to move save over the bodies of their dead or along the roof tops. They no longer had nor could find any arrows, javelins or stones with which to attack us; and our allies fighting with us were armed with swords and bucklers, and slaughtered so many of them on land and in the water that more than forty thousand were killed or taken that day. So loud was the wailing of the women and children that there was not one man amongst us whose heart did not bleed at the sound."[70]

When Cuauhtemoc came to Tlatelolco's marketplace to surrender in the shadow of the city's Great Temple, Cortés took him prisoner rather than killing him, as he claims the Great Speaker requested (Plate 5b). Days of

Figure 7.8. Ruins of Tenochtitlan's Great Temple in foreground, with colonial period cathedral and Zócolo plaza in background.

Photo by author. Reproduction authorized by the Instituto Nacional de Antropología e Historia, Mexico.

massacre and rape of the population of Tenochtitlan-Tlatelolco followed, as did the looting of the city and melting down of gold objects. The Tlatelolca recount the plunder and sexual violence: "The Spaniards took things from people by force. They were looking for gold; they cared nothing for greenstone, precious feathers, or turquoise. They looked everywhere with the women, on their abdomens, under their skirts. . . . And picked out the beautiful women."[71] Women covered their faces with mud and dressed in ragged clothes in attempts to escape the assaults. Cortés and other Spanish captains ordered the razing of the city's buildings, especially those linked to sources of pre-Hispanic politico-religious power (Figure 7.8). Tenochtitlan was no more, but it was from this tragic violence and erasure of tangible memory that the Aztec city was reborn as the capital of New Spain.

8

Forging a New Spain

> Although humans from the beginning have sought tirelessly to expand themselves throughout the universe, never in their vanity could they imagine that there was anything left to discover—as we see with Hercules who, when he reached where he placed his columns, understanding there to be no more world, put that bravest of blazons "no more," thinking he had reached the end of all the land. And in this delusion, how many kings and monarchs have fallen, as well as philosophers and cosmographers, and how many errors can be found regarding what they said and wrote.
>
> —Diego Muñoz Camargo (1584)[1]

Among the enduring myths of the Spanish invasion of Mesoamerica is that the 1521 defeat of the Mexica capital of Tenochtitlan marked a definitive completion of "the conquest of Mexico."[2] Due to the size of the Triple Alliance empire—some 5–10 million subjects—and its eventual role as the heart of New Spain with a renewed capital at Mexico City, the Spanish-Mexica war can certainly be seen as the most momentous of the military actions that took place in sixteenth-century Mesoamerica. It created the first established European colony in the continental Americas and served as a base of operations and tactical blueprint for later colonial endeavors. Yet, as we shall see, the notion of a neatly completed conquest is a myth. A related misconception today is that the rapid fall of the Aztec Empire must have been due to an imbalance in military and transportation technologies. Comparative historical cases provide evidence to the contrary, since many other premodern empires fell just as quickly without great technological disparities, including the Achaemenid or First Persian Empire to Alexander the Great; successive Chinese dynasties to more nomadic groups from the north: the Xiongnu, Mongols, and Manchu; and large portions of the Arab Abbasid dynasty and the Byzantine Empire to the Turks.[3]

The Spanish-Mexica war was similar to these other examples in its tempo, but differed in the outsized role played by Native combatants on the offensive side. The forging of New Spain unfolded over decades or even close to two centuries, as the last independent Maya kingdom, Tayasal or Nojpeten, was not defeated until 1697. It was a co-creative process that left tangible marks on the natural and sacred landscape, in the field systems and buildings of a new political and economic order, in multivalent art and architectural styles, and in personal possessions that defined Spanish, Native, mestizo, and other identities in a New World.

On October 15, 1522, a little over a year after the fall of Tenochtitlan, Hernando Cortés received a Real Cédula (Royal Warrant) from Spain that decreed him governor, captain general, and supreme justice of New Spain. In addition to constructing palaces for himself in Mexico City, Coyoacan, and Cuernavaca, overseeing his vast encomiendas, and siring a son with Malinche—christened Martín after his own father—Cortés led new invasions of northeast Mexico's Panuco region, in 1522, and a 1524–1526 expedition to Honduras (Las Hibueras). Both were motivated by the missions of other conquistadors that Cortés viewed as threats to his authority: in Panuco against Francisco de Garay's attempt to conquer and settle northeast Mexico, and in Honduras to counter an alliance made between his rival Velázquez and Cristóbal de Olid. Cuauhtemoc, the last independently elected Great Speaker of the Mexica, accompanied Cortés on the mission to Honduras, during which he was executed by the conquistador. Joint Spanish-Mesoamerican wars of conquest and Native counterinsurgencies continued in the decades that followed, and two of these produced new colonial provinces that would receive their own *audencias*, the highest tribunal in Spanish America, under the viceroyalty of New Spain: Guatemala to the southeast and New Galicia to the northwest. The captaincy general of Guatemala took nearly a decade to subdue, and the kingdom of New Galicia was only realized two decades after the close of the Spanish-Mexica war (Figure 8.1).

The creation of New Spain was a protracted process that generated new forms of social, political, economic, and religious institutions and relations, all with global consequences. Colonial studies grapple with the notion of hybridity as a way of characterizing the merging of different cultural traditions in a context of disparate power relations and the ability of the colonized to resist or set the terms for new forms of cultural creation. A shortcoming with the term "hybrid" is that the deeper in time one looks, the clearer it

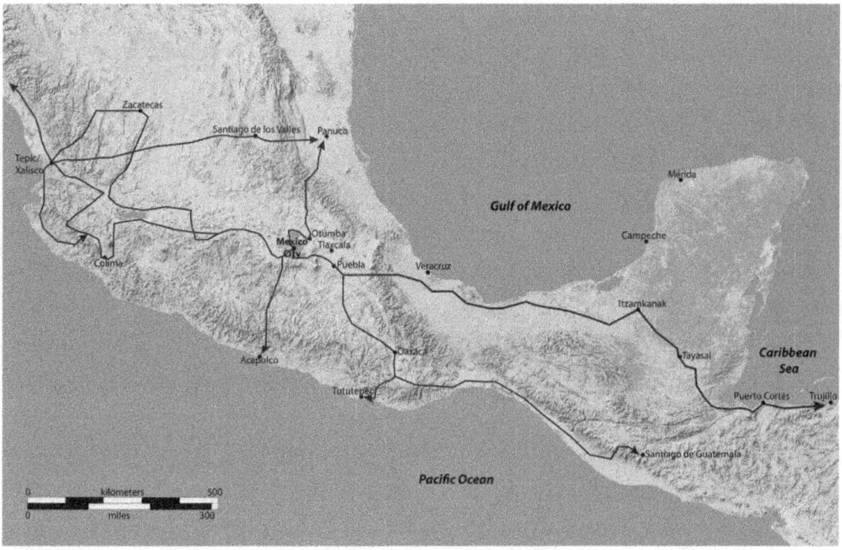

Figure 8.1. Map of continued invasions from Mexico City, including those led by Cortés to Panuco and Honduras, the Alvarado brothers in Guatemala, and by Francisco Cortés and Nuño de Guzmán in west Mexico.

becomes that all of human history involved some level of hybridity. Our species regenerates culture through interaction and accepting, rejecting, or modifying the existing culture around us. Just as sixteenth-century Castilians combined legal intuitions of Roman Hispania and *mudéjar* architecture of Islamic Al-Andalus, sixteenth-century Aztecs combined Olmec and Maya artistic traditions from lowland Mesoamerica with Teotihuacano urban planning and neo-Toltec architecture from their direct predecessors in highland Mesoamerica. All culture is therefore composite, but in the context of colonial encounters, terms like "hybridity" can productively encapsulate the qualities and creative actions that accentuate instances of cultural adaptation within a newly established colonial hierarchy.[4] Out of the conquests that followed the Spanish-Mexica war, New Spain was created, a hybridization of cultural traits that had evolved over millennia on different sides of the Atlantic. Colonial hybridity and syncretism developed through cultural exchanges that could be termed mutual accommodation, selective acculturation, subjectification and resilience, or negotiation within domination.[5] All of these convey that culture is not imposed monolithically from a donor to a receptor culture. The last two best capture the power dynamics inherent to relations between the colonizers and colonized, but we will see how Native peoples exercised agency within certain social arenas to shape their lives and the course of the new societal and religious order.

Colonial institutions and their accoutrements in styles of architecture and portable material culture were transposed from old Spain to New Spain, but the result was the creation of something different that fused elements of the deep histories of both places. As an example, at the apex of power of this new colonial regime was the emperor Charles V, who emblazoned his motto *plus ultra* on his imperial crests in conjuring Iberia's geo-history as peninsular hinge and legitimizing its expanding imperial reach beyond the legendary Pillars of Hercules, depicted as two columns separated by water (Plate 6a).[6] But this new order was also one in which the mestizo Diego Muñoz Camargo, who had been schooled in classical Greco-Roman literature on these same pillars and the origins of the motto, could incorporate it into part of his own history, alongside the traditions of his homeland—the "Indian Republic" of Tlaxcala—rendered in this chapter's epigraph. Sixteenth-century New Spain was a dynamic hub for novel forms of cultural creation that combined elements of Mesoamerican, European, African, and eventually also Asian ways of doing and knowing into new forms of cuisine, artisanship, spectacles, ceremonies, religious belief, and notions of race and ethnicity. Further, this exchange was not unidirectional, as Mesoamerican products, practices, and people were introduced to Eurasia, changing the course of its history as well.

Spaniards and Mesoamericans Continuing in Conquest

A year after the fall of Tenochtitlan, Maya emissaries trekked from the highlands of Guatemala to the new colonial capital rising from the ruins of the old to have an audience with Cortés. They were K'iche' and Kaqchikel, from the two dominant but rivalrous Maya polities of the region. Cortés recounts that the delegations came to swear loyalty to the Spanish Crown, but they likely were also acting to strategically gather information about the new overlords of central Mexico and to either dissuade them from coming south or to assess whether an alliance with the Spanish would help them to prevail over their local rivals.[7] The visits prompted Cortés to organize a conquest company headed by his trusted captain, Pedro de Alvarado, who eventually would be authorized as *adelantado* for the expedition. The company also included Pedro's wife Doña Luisa Xicotencatl of Tlaxcala, who gave birth during the expedition to their daughter, baptized as Doña Leonor de Alvarado, as well as Pedro's brother Jorge, two other brothers, and three cousins of theirs.[8] Jorge de Alvarado also brought with him Doña Lucía, who was Luisa's sister. There were some three to four hundred Spaniards in the first mission to Guatemala and more than 3,000 Native allies, around a third of whom were Tlaxcalteca who recognized Xicotencatl's daughters as nobility who brought legitimacy to the mission. Other participants included Nahuatl-speaking Mexica, Xochimilca, and Quauhquecholteca, as well as Mixtec and Zapotec speakers from Oaxaca, who had largely allied with the Spaniards. The multiethnic conquest company set off from Mexico City on December 6, 1523.

During the expedition, Alvarado wrote four letters back to Cortés, including two on route from Tehuantepec and the Soconusco, which did not survive but are referenced in the later ones sent from Guatemala. The letters were addressed to Cortés but were written with a joint audience of both him and Charles V in mind. Native accounts of the invasion have also survived, including two pictorial ones: the *Lienzo de Tlaxcala* and the *Lienzo de Quaucquechollan*.[9] Alvarado exaggerated the grandeur of the expedition to his intended audience, likely including his estimate of an opposing force of more than 30,000 warriors confronted outside of Quetzaltenango (Xelajub' in K'iche' Mayan).[10] A more egregious exaggeration was that he had succeeded in subduing the entire population of highland Guatemala as well as Izcuintepeque (Escuintla) in the piedmont heading to the Pacific Ocean, and continuing along the coast as far south as today's El Salvador. These regions were inhabited by Nahuatl speakers known as Pipil, and Escuintla had been linked to central Mexico since the Classic period, when Teotihuacanos traded with local inhabitants and exerted some influence over its lands, which like the adjacent Soconusco were rich in cacao. The smaller and more decentralized political landscape of highland Maya and Pipil kingdoms proved easy to defeat militarily but very difficult to administer, since no unifying political structure such as the Aztec Triple Alliance existed. After returning to Mexico, Jorge de Alvarado needed to go back to Guatemala with a force two or three times larger than the original to actually subdue the Kaqchikel, K'iche', and other populations over 1527–1529. Jorge's mission included re-establishing the Spanish capital named for the conquering patron saint—a first settlement named Santiago de los Caballeros followed by a second, relocated after an earthquake, named Santiago de Guatemala (today known as Antigua). The younger Alvarado's campaign was as or more important than Pedro's but the latter, as *adelantado*, assumed the credit.

Native sources vary depending on whether they were part of the victors or vanquished. In texts and in the pictorial lienzos of the Tlaxcalteca and Quauhquecholteca, these Nahua (Nahuatl-speaking) allies projected a sense of having been true conquerors, either richly adorned in Native battle attire or wearing European armor (Plate 6b). Less elaborately attired highland Maya were depicted as the losers, and the documents were created to convey Nahua loyalty to the Spanish Crown in an effort to reduce their tax or tribute burdens. The Maya did the same, but on the premise that they were being overly exploited under the new colonial order, beginning with Pedro de Alvarado's thirst for gold and continuing as tax in labor, precious materials, and utilitarian goods and food. The Kaqchikel also referred to Alvarado as Tonatiuh, following the Nahua association with the Aztec sun god, and one account quotes Alvarado/Tonatiuh as exclaiming: "Why won't you give me precious metal? Do you want me to burn you, to hang you? You have five days to give it up."[11]

Shortly after Alvarado had set out for Guatemala, Cortés led the expedition to Honduras in order to prevent Cristóbal de Olid from establishing his own autonomous colony. Cortés had sent a fleet captained by Francisco de las Casas first, but then decided to lead his own expedition by land, unaware that Olid had already died, making the whole mission pointless. Bernal Díaz accompanied Cortés, as did Malinche, Ixtlilxochitl of Texcoco, and other Mesoamerican nobles, warriors, and porters.[12] By this time, Malinche had learned enough Castilian to do all the translating from Nahuatl and Mayan herself. At Orizaba, on the way to Honduras, Cortés oversaw her marriage to the Spaniard Juan Jaramillo, also awarding her the encomiendas of Huilotlan y Tetiquipac. Díaz oversaw an encomienda in the Coatzacoalcos region of Veracruz, near Malinche's hometown. The conquistador-chronicler had two daughters with a Mexica woman granted to him by Moctezuma, whom Díaz renamed Doña Francisca. Coatzacoalcos was the last Spanish settlement the expedition would stay in before trekking across the Yucatan peninsula through still independent Maya city-states. Díaz's account mentions the welcoming of Cortés to the town with Roman-style triumphal arches and *Moros y Cristianos* performances, the first documented for the Americas.[13]

Native perspectives on the mission to Honduras can be found in Alva Ixtlilxochitl's relation of the contributions of his great-great-grandfather and a brief account written in Chontal Mayan in 1612 (but narrating events of 1524–1525), which describes an intriguing exchange between the captive Great Speaker Cuauhtemoc and the local ruler Paxboloncha. The city-state of Acalan was in the same general emporium crossroads of the Aztec and Maya cultural spheres where Malinche came from, between the modern states of Tabasco and Campeche. Acalan's capital, Itzamkanac, possibly corresponds to an archaeological site in western Campeche called El Tigre, which has evidence of some two millennia of occupation.[14] The account written in Chontal Mayan relates that Cuauhtemoc informed Paxboloncha about the dire threat posed by Cortés and the Spaniards. The king demurred and informed Cortés, who had Cuauhtemoc beheaded and impaled on a ceiba tree. The Maya of Itzamkanac assisted the Spaniards in constructing various bridges in an attempt to create a land route through the region, and the Chontal account also makes mention of Montejo's later conquests in northern Yucatan. Alva Ixtlilxochitl disputes the claim that Cuauhtemoc had plotted an uprising. He tends toward the hyperbolic in writing about the mission, including that one of the bridges erected was "the most impressive thing in the world."[15]

As with the Alvarado invasion of highland Guatemala, the decentralized nature of lowland Maya city-states made their incorporation into New Spain a more protracted affair, as each needed to be conquered or coerced independently, unlike the imperial structure that characterized the former Aztec world. After returning to Mexico from his mission to Spain with Puertocarrero to petition the king on behalf of Cortés, Francisco de Montejo tried in vain to conquer Yucatan between 1528 and 1535. His son of the same name, and known as "el Mozo" or the Younger, had better success in the early 1540s, when he founded the cities of Campeche and Mérida—the latter named for the Roman ruins in Extremadura and constructed on the ruins of the Maya city of Tiho.[16] The Spaniards found the rainforest environment of the former Classic-period core of Maya civilization in the southern lowlands particularly inhospitable and did not establish any large colonial towns there.

Upon returning from Honduras in June 1526, Cortés was welcomed with more pageantry, including canoes full of Mexica warriors who may have engaged in mock battles as entertainment. He soon authorized his nephew Francisco Cortés de San Buenaventura to conquer territories west of Mexico City in what are primarily today's coastal states of Colima and Nayarit. The

Spanish bestowed place-names appropriate to the namesake pilgrimage region of northwestern Spain, such as the Santiago River, which drains from the large Lake Chapala to the Pacific and today divides the states of Nayarit and Jalisco, and an intended coastal capital at Compostela, which lost out in the preference of Spanish colonists of New Galicia for the city of Guadalajara.[17] Compostela was founded by Nuño de Guzmán, the governor of Panuco and rival to Cortés, who had been sent to Mexico by Charles V to counterbalance the conquistador's influence in New Spain. Guzmán set off from Mexico City in 1529 and waged a more violent invasion in 1530–1531 that saw the fall of the Purépecha or Tarascan Empire, previously the second-largest Mesoamerican state to the Triple Alliance. The invading army crossed north-central Mexico to found Santiago de los Valles in the Huaxtec region of San Luis Potosí. Campaigns in the northwest during the mid-1530s mobilized Native resistance among various Chichimec tribes, including the Caxcans, Zacatecas, Coras, and Guachichiles. The uprising culminated in the Mixtón war (1540–1541), named for a hilltop stronghold near what became the colonial town of Zacatecas. Pedro de Alvarado was diverted from a planned trans-Pacific expedition to assist in the Mixtón conflict. Alvarado's zeal for conquest is exemplified by his efforts to first conquer Andean South America, making it to Quito in 1534 with Doña Luisa Xicotencatl and an army, only to discover that Pizarro had already conquered the region, and then his plan to cross the Pacific believing he could eventually conquer China. Alvarado met his end in the Mixtón war after being injured when another Spaniard's horse fell on him while in retreat from Native forces who successfully held the hilltop stronghold at Nochistlan. His death was registered by a Native scribe in the Codex Telleriano-Remensis, identified by a pictograph of the sun to label Alvarado as Tonatiuh.

Many other invasions of formerly autonomous peoples created New Spain and broader Latin America. The preceding cases only provide some illustration, yet they highlight the essential role played by Mesoamerican peoples in expanding this new sociopolitical order, whether through the actions of Native warriors and porters or women who legitimated new power relations. Alvarado relied on Mesoamerican armies in campaigns that traveled as far south as the northern Andes of South America, and the Tlaxcalteca and other Native peoples were essential components of missions to the present-day US-Mexico borderlands as north as Santa Fe and west across the Pacific Ocean to the Philippines.[18] This trans-Pacific link was the start of what we today call globalization, and it was made possible through the participation of Native Mesoamericans.

Administration and Economy

New Spain's political and economic institutions provided much of the social structure that was imposed on Native peoples, which they either adapted to or contested in various ways. In this section and the next, focusing on religious and educational institutions, we examine these first in terms of what was enacted by the Spanish state, and next how this was negotiated by Mesoamericans in constructing norms and institutions that diverged from idealized state templates. By understanding these social structures and the possibilities of variable action within them, we can appreciate the strategies pursued by smaller groups or individuals, be they Spaniards, Natives, mestizos, elites, non-elites, or along other intersecting spectra of identity.

Spanish oversight of the American colonies became increasingly bureaucratized over the course of the sixteenth century, beginning with single governors like Columbus or members of the court like Cisneros and Fonseca, and evolving into more formal institutions such as the House of Trade and Junta of the Indies. Charles V referred to his Council of the Indies earlier but established it formally in 1524 to keep him regularly updated on affairs pertaining to Spanish America. The council was also tasked with upholding a state monopoly of the trans-Atlantic economy run through the House of Trade in Seville, and to stimulate exchange by sending utilitarian products to the Americas. Goods with strict regulations included steel products, as the extraction of iron ore was highly centralized and manufacturing was concentrated in select guilds, and European foods that did not grow well or had not yet become established crops in agrarian regimes of the Americas, such as wheat, olive oil, and wine. Extracted goods flowed back to Spain, especially precious metals and somewhat later the plantation crops that had been introduced to Iberia under Islamic rule and first developed in the encomiendas of the Canary Islands. Charles V also founded Consulates of Commerce on both sides of the Atlantic, which in Mexico were overseen by the viceroyalty of New Spain beginning in the 1530s.[19]

Spain centralized its imperial economy through the House of Trade, Flotilla of the Indies, and Manila Galleon in a manner not seen in Europe since the height of Rome, though there also existed a certain amount of leakage to alternate ports along the Iberian Atlantic, including Lisbon and along the Galician coast. During much of the sixteenth century, an average of 80 boats a year arrived annually to Seville from the Indies. They were filled with approximately 2,200 lbs (1,000 kg) of bullion per year in the first half of the century, followed by a boom that saw four times this figure in the first decade of the second half of the century.[20] In the initial decades of the colonial period, the viceroyalty of Peru provided the highest quantity of gold from Spanish America, but it was superseded beginning in the 1560s by the output exploited from New Granada, corresponding to today's Columbia, Ecuador, and Venezuela. The proportion of silver extracted from New Spain and Peru was similar throughout the sixteenth century, with Peru's output representing a larger proportion during the seventeenth century, succeeded by Mexico's mines during most of the eighteenth century up to independence. Dyes, timber, hides, and foods represented some of the more mundane goods crossing from Spanish America to Europe.

As the hub of Spain's trans-Atlantic economy, Seville's population tripled to more than 100,000 residents during the late sixteenth century, making it significantly larger than the recently established imperial capital of Madrid. As had been true over a millennium earlier in Roman Baetica, the greater Gulf of Cádiz port region was the most urbanized in Iberia, with over 10 urban centers having populations in excess of 10,000 inhabitants. For comparison, Portugal had four of this size and Catalonia only one. As we saw in Chapter 4, the reclamation of the Roman past was part of Castilian-Spanish nation building of the early sixteenth century, made explicit in the works of Antonio de Nebrija and the political rhetoric of the day. Spanish imperial administration also more closely matched the direct control and territorialism of Rome's, rather than the more indirect or commercial-hegemonic model of fifteenth- and early sixteenth-century Portugal, the seventeenth-century Dutch, or the mid-first-millennium BCE Phoenicians, for that matter.[21] Charles V made a minimal attempt to diversify port locations by decreeing on December 24, 1522, that the Galician port of A Coruña would be the location of a second House of Trade dealing exclusively in spices (Casa de Contratación de Especiería).[22] Coruña was the same port he had left from two years earlier to be crowned Holy Roman Emperor. It was well situated for trade with northern Europe, and its deep harbor could accommodate large Portuguese ships arriving from the Moluccas (the "Spice Islands"). Yet Coruña had only approximately 3,000 inhabitants at the time, and this House of Trade shuttered in 1529 before Charles had it revived in 1552.

The emperor's vision of global empire, realized in the symbols on the tiles of Plate 6a, was bolstered by his marriage to Isabela of Portugal on March 11, 1526. The tiles adorn the garden pavilion in the Royal Alcázar of Seville built to commemorate the historic union consecrated there between Charles and his first cousin, who was also the granddaughter of Isabela and Ferdinand. Having been born and raised in Iberia, Isabela of Portugal was the peninsular soul of the pair, and all evidence points toward Charles' deep and genuine affection for her; after her death in 1539 during the birth of their seventh child, he remained a widower in mourning and never remarried. Charles also confided in Isabela, and she occasionally served as regent when he was abroad. Their marriage pavilion provides an architectural and iconographic exemplar of sixteenth-century Spanish hybridity (Figure 8.2).[23] The building shows a continued appreciation of Islamic or *mudéjar* styles in its interior pool and glazed tilework with decorative elements that highlight Renaissance fixation on the classical Greco-Roman world. Neoclassical styles can be seen in the figurative decoration on gesso friezes and the *plus ultra* motto between the columns representing the Pillars of Hercules. The interspersed political emblems represent medieval Christian kingdoms: the

Figure 8.2. Interior of Charles V's pavilion in the garden of the Alcázar, Seville, showing mix of Islamic and European Renaissance styles.
Photo by the author.

crests of Castile and Leon and the Hapsburg double-headed eagle. Clutched in the talons of the eagle is an orb that harkens to Isidore of Seville's T-O map of the world and Hapsburg ambitions for global hegemony.

Certain administrative and economic institutions of New Spain had deep roots that can be clearly traced to the imperial structure of Roman Hispania—what brought the "Latin" to Latin America—including language, laws, land tenure, mineral extraction, and physical infrastructure applied to urban centers and their rural hinterlands. These had been modified by medieval Christian and Muslim kingdoms of Iberia and especially by the institutions that developed during the centuries of the *Reconquista*, such as the encomienda and the negotiated political arrangements between the Spanish Crown and nobles, town councils (*cabildos*), or the semi-autonomy offered by legal privileges (*fueros*) granted to frontier regions and for the purposes of alliance building. These layers of Iberian history are evoked in the architecture and styles of adornment of New Spain. An impressive example still stands in the massive aqueduct complex stretching for 21 miles (34 km) from springs near Zempoala, in southern Hidalgo, to Otumba, where the battle after the expulsion of the Spanish from Tenochtitlan took place.[24] Construction of the massive hydraulic work lasted almost two decades (1554–1571) and is today a UNESCO World Heritage Site that bears the name of Padre Tembleque for a friar involved in its oversight. We saw that impressive hydraulic works including aqueducts were built by the Aztecs, but the Tembleque aqueduct presents a uniquely fused style of New Spain: Roman-style arch sections and bridges, distribution tanks and other hydraulic engineering of Islamic Al-Andalus, Christian shrines, and support structures made using techniques of Mesoamerican adobe construction by the Nahua and Otomi laborers who assembled the monumental public work (Figure 8.3).

As we saw in Chapter 4, and as the Spaniards continually noted in their initial encounters along the Yucatan and all through the uneasy stay in Tenochtitlan before its destruction, Mesoamerica was highly urbanized prior to Spanish arrival. Colonial urban centers therefore continued as the administrative nodes of New Spain and were often erected directly on top of the ruins of pre-Hispanic ones or, more rarely, created anew in locations that had sparser Native populations. The clearest overlaying can be appreciated in how Tenochtitlan-Tlatelolco served as the direct foundation of Mexico City,[25] but similar superposition characterizes Cholula, Texcoco, Tlaxcala, Cuernavaca, and other cities of central Mexico. It can also be seen outside of the central Mexican core, such as the construction of

Figure 8.3. Tallest portion of Tembleque aqueduct, at Tepeyahualco, with mix of Roman-arch bridge construction, Christian shrines, and Mesoamerican adobe support structures.

Photo by author. Reproduction authorized by the Instituto Nacional de Antropología e Historia, Mexico.

Mérida on top of the Yucatec Maya city of Tiho. This layering of urban plans in many Mesoamerican cases contrasts with other colonial towns of Spanish America, where urban layouts were novel and saw the imposition of a city-wide grid where none had existed previously.[26] Such examples are prevalent throughout the Caribbean or other areas with lower density pre-Hispanic settlement and also in regions that possessed indigenous urban centers but not the large ports the Spanish maritime economy required, which were developed in places like Lima-Callao and Veracruz near former provincial centers of the Inca and Aztec Empires. These and other mainland Spanish American ports were the first stop for African slaves, who did not arrive in the same numbers as they did to the Caribbean or Brazil, but some 100,000 are estimated to have arrived in New Spain between 1521 and 1650.[27] Black Africans were also moved from ports like Veracruz, Acapulco, and Campeche to Mexico City and other interior cities, where they worked as artisans and domestic servants or labored in silver mines. In contrast to the systems of slavery among northern European colonial powers, systems in Spanish America had precedent in Roman law and its translation through the medieval Siete Partidas, which offered greater, but still limited opportunities for slaves to buy their freedom.[28]

Colonial urban centers of Spanish America were strongly regimented by a series of instructions dictated by Spain's successive kings—Ferdinand, Charles V, and Phillip II—with the most exacting stipulations provided by Phillip II's 1573 "Ordinances Concerning Discoveries, Settlements and Pacification of the Indies" (*Ordenanzas de Descubrimiento, Nueva Población y Pacificación de las Indias*).[29] This list of 148 ordinances, by sixteenth-century Spain's most bureaucratic emperor, compiled, augmented, and codified the decrees made by his predecessors, including a few sent in 1523 by Charles V to Cortés. It included stipulations to find locations that could be constructed on "without damage to the Indian population" (Ordinance #5); that square or rectangular plazas serve as focal points of settlements and be located at the center of inland towns and near the waterfront of port towns (Ordinance #112); that principal streets lead to and from all four sides of these plazas (Ordinance #114); and a number of stipulations regarding the types and relationships of structures, including arcades along the main plaza for merchants (#115), secondary plazas and temple complexes (#119), buildings for the *cabildo* and other administrative entities (#122), the zoning of noxious industries like slaughterhouses and tanneries (#123), and the presence of a commons with shared use rights for grazing and recreation (#129–130).

Rather than viewing the late sixteenth-century Ordinances as a purely Spanish imposition on its American colonies, it is worth probing what planning principles already existed in Mesoamerica and considering how colonial urbanism was generated through co-creative processes.[30] We saw in Chapters 3 and 4 that although plazas were characteristic of Iberian urban centers, gridded plans were very rare. Citywide grids or orthogonal plans were present in Roman Hispania but then fell out of use in medieval Christian and Islamic cities, only to reappear in the later thirteenth century, particularly along the pilgrimage route to Santiago and in the south associated with the *Reconquista*.[31] The gridded plan therefore had administrative associations with ordered settlements in the context of religion and conquest. Yet, as we saw in Chapter 2, plazas were also at the center of Mesoamerican towns and cities (Ordinance #112) since their inception, and gridded urban plans dated back to at least the first millennium BCE, likely making them older in Mesoamerica than in Iberia.[32] Larger pre-Hispanic Mesoamerican cities such as Teotihuacan, Tenochtitlan, and Cholula also conformed to the patterns of scaled spatial replication featuring a central plaza-temple precinct and smaller secondary plaza-temple precincts dispersed among residential neighborhoods (Ordinance #119), whereas Tenochtitlan and probably Cholula featured principal streets emanating from the four sides of their central precincts (Ordinance #114) as well. The coexistence of these pre-Hispanic urban designs plus Spanish ordinances are clearly evident in a mid-sixteenth-century map of Mexico City by Alonso de Santa Cruz depicting the superposition of the colonial *traza* (grid plan) on the foundations of Tenochtitlan-Tlatelolco (Figure 8.4). Relationships between a primary sacred precinct at Tenochtitlan, a secondary one at Tlatelolco, and distributed district precincts were closely retained in colonial Mexico City, and these were partitioned into a grid that followed the major Mexica causeways to the island (labeled "Calz." for "calzada" in the map) and by streets to the plaza and temple complexes. Formal planning principles of a grid and scalar spatial replication of plaza-temple precincts were not adhered to in laying out the Hapsburg section of Madrid on top of its Islamic predecessor. Phillip II's Ordinances for Spanish America seem instead to have been significantly influenced by Tenochtitlan and other pre-Hispanic cities that were ordered around a central plaza-temple precinct and orthogonal plan. In other cases pre-Hispanic urban plans underwent major alterations with the transformation into colonial cities, such as at Tlaxcala, where the earlier model of multiple-nuclei made way for a defined central plaza and secondary plaza abutting the large San Francisco church and monastery complex.

As with urban planning, the provincial administration of the viceroyalty of New Spain was largely configured using the skeleton of the Triple Alliance empire and its broader sphere of interaction. Remarkable continuity is apparent with the Postclassic Mesoamerican world system in the division of early New Spain into similar zones: (1) core zones—central Mexico above all, but secondary ones that developed around key ports and certain smaller inland cities as well; (2) affluent production zones, such as the cacao-rich Soconusco coveted by the Teotihuacanos and Aztecs, areas of concentrated nopal cacti favorable for cochineal production, and the Maya mercantile centers with salt deposits along the Yucatecan coast; (3) unspecialized peripheries throughout more rural regions; and (4) contact peripheries including the Chichimeca desert of the northern frontier extending to the present-day Southwestern United States.[33] Many of these zones continued to play a

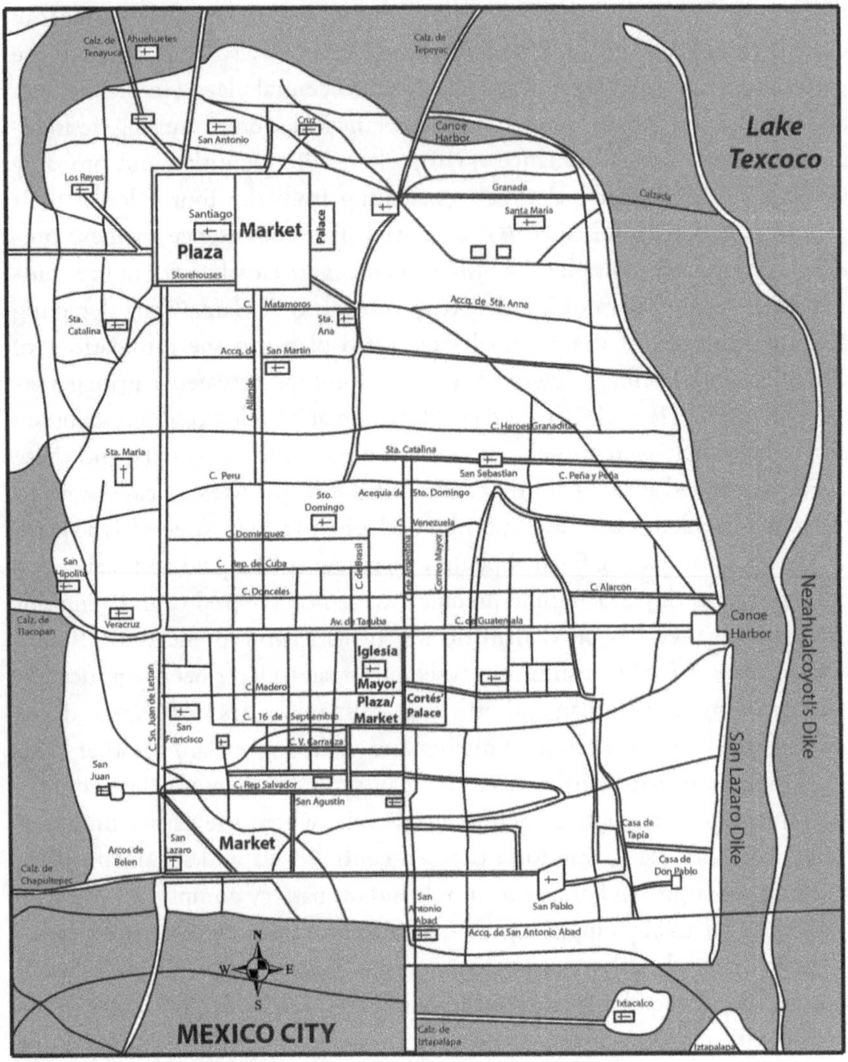

Figure 8.4. Map of Mexico City in the mid-sixteenth century, based on map of Alonso de Santa Cruz.

Redrawn and modified from Calnek (2003).

similar role in the early colonial Mesoamerican world system, while others diverged due to changes that came with the trans-Atlantic economy, particularly the development of important ports and mining towns. The flow of goods and labor was directed toward colonial urban centers through systems of tax and tribute reconfigured to flow primarily to Spanish coffers, and with the greatest concentration moving to Mexico City or crossing the Atlantic to Seville. Administratively, urban centers were ranked following a Spanish system that designated cities, villas, town, villages, and hamlets in decreasing order of significance but kept much of the pre-Hispanic political system in place by designating former city-states that had their own speakers as head settlements (*cabeceras*).[34]

Commerce became truly global through the highly centralized Manila Galleon exchange linking Spain and the Philippines through New Spain using convoys of ships referred to as *naos de China*. The expanded maritime economy required major port cities at Veracruz on the Gulf and Acapulco on the Pacific. These two ports were connected by an overland transshipment route passing through Mexico City and Puebla, a town primarily of Spanish settlers. In the decades after the conquest, the marketplaces of Mexico City simply continued in their pre-Hispanic locations but featuring a mix of products from Mesoamerica, Europe, and eventually Asia.[35] For this last, the Parían market in the city's main plaza specialized in goods from the galleon trade and took its name from the neighborhood in Manila where Chinese merchants resided. Before this, however, were decades of colonial institutional development, beginning with the very loose structures provided by the encomienda and earliest missionizing friars.

After the fall of Tenochtitlan, Cortés rewarded his men by allocating them land and resident labor as encomiendas. Cortés claimed 22 towns for himself, Otumba among them, comprising the labor of 23,000 resident Natives, but he was stripped of most of these by 1528, prompting his return to Spain to petition the king.[36] The encomienda was the first form of administration in New Spain, and because it was in private hands, it was easier for individual Spaniards to exploit. Though the trust theoretically gave the encomenderos Native labor and tribute in return for protection, certain benchmarks for standard of living, and a Christian education, the distance from Spain and lack of developed imperial bureaucracy in the first decade after the Spanish-Mexica war meant that encomenderos could circumvent laws established by the Spanish Crown and Council of the Indies. Notable differences between the encomiendas of old and New Spain were that in New Spain the encomenderos did not own the land, as they could in Spain, and women and Natives of noble birth could also be entrusted with encomiendas, which they could not in Spain. The arrival of the *audencia* to New Spain at the end of 1527 and the 1535 establishment of the province as a viceroyalty served to reign in the encomiendas. The 1542 passage of the New Laws established additional checks on the encomenderos and the former conquistador class, and following that date the system of *repartamiento* grew while the encomienda declined. Natives were not allocated to Spanish colonists under the *repartamiento* and instead worked on a rotational basis somewhat akin to the pre-Hispanic *tequitl* system, and later for fixed wages.

As a reward for their key contributions to the conquests of Tenochtitlan, Guatemala, and elsewhere, the Tlaxcalteca were not subject to the encomienda and were instead granted the status of Indian Republic directly under the Spanish Crown.[37] This legal privilege (*fuero*) had a precedent from the colonization of the Canary Islands, whose indigenous occupants petitioned successfully for semi-autonomy in 1514. The Tlaxcalteca were successful in many of their petitions throughout the sixteenth century and prohibited Spaniards other than certain friars and administrators to settle in their city. Petitions were typically made by the cabildo, a form of collective Native advocacy and litigation we will explore later. Although the term and configuration were of Iberian origin, in New Spain many cabildos mimicked noble councils of the pre-Hispanic era, and this was especially true in Tlaxcala because of its greater autonomy in governance. Tlaxcala's cabildo records were written in Nahuatl, and processes of deliberation varied from Spanish protocols.[38] A cabildo member was termed a *regidor* in Spanish, but cabildos across central Mexico often referred to them using the Nahuatl term *tlatoque* (speakers) and in cabildo documents from Tlaxcala even the viceroy in Mexico City—the first being Antonio de Mendoza y Pacheco (1535–1550)—was referred to as *tlatoani*. *Corregidor* was the title of the early office held by Spaniards that evolved over time into equivalents of mayor (*alcalde mayor*) and governor (*gobernador*). A few years into the colonial period, Charles V began permitting the participation of a few Nahua nobles in the cabildo of Mexico City as a means of integrating them into political life. Viceroy Mendoza called for the establishment of Indian cabildos and the nomination of Native mayors and regidores in other cities. Even Puebla, the city founded for Spaniards, had a Native cabildo member by the 1560s.

Economic changes within early New Spain led to many of the disputes recorded in cabildo archives. Groups and individuals negotiated new concerns involving the encroachment of Eurasian grazing animals on Native lands; the introduction of new European products, market demand, and currency; and the persistence of disputes over land allocation and taxes, which carried over from the pre-Hispanic economy but were now monetized and saw conflicts between Native and Spanish systems of inheritance and taxation. Changes in practices of agriculture and consumption—from basic subsistence to symbolic marking of one's identity through diet—were profound with the Columbian exchange.[39] Like the Caribbean, lowland Mesoamerica's environment was hostile to many Mediterranean crops, but these were more successfully cultivated in the semi-arid highlands of the former Aztec core and regions to the north. Lowland regions saw the introduction of tropical plantation crops, including in the Soconusco, where cacao production continued for local and export markets and was joined by fields of sugarcane, bananas, rice, and coffee.[40] Spaniards and Mesoamericans both favored the foods they knew but also integrated novel ones into their diets. The Spaniards planted wheat for baking bread, but local production of the wine and oil of the Mediterranean diet lagged because grapes and olives did not fare as well. Mesoamericans preferred maize as their primary grain and were also deprived of the second most important pre-Hispanic highland grain when the Spanish suppressed the cultivation of amaranth on the grounds that the Aztecs also used it ceremonially in rituals to their gods and ancestors.[41] This included rituals of consumption of amaranth seeds held together by honey, today called *alegrías* but previously formed into figures of Huitzilopochtli, as was described for the ceremony before the Toxcatl massacre, and other deities or family ancestors—this last akin to the sugar skulls made today during Day of the Dead.

When pigs arrived to New Spain from the Caribbean they were embraced as a source of meat by Mesoamericans to the point that the rapidly multiplying swine population of Mexico City necessitated the passage of an ordinance to keep the streets free of them. Yet pigs were merely an inconvenience compared with the considerable impacts that new grazing animals had on the Mesoamerican landscape. Although pasturing animals was new to Mesoamericans, they had for millennia supplemented growing crops with tending to lacustrine resources and by cultivating maguey—called the "green cow" of Mexico, as it requires daily extraction of its milk-like sap and also provides secondary products in fiber and cloth (*ixtle*).[42] Through their cabildo, the Tlaxcalteca petitioned the Crown to stop the encroachment of Spanish settlers passing cattle through their lands, whereas the north of the province was becoming crowded with sheep, as shepherding was much more embraced by Nahua, Otomi, and mestizo populations. Early in the colonial period, Mesoamericans were not interested in herding cattle, though Spanish ranchers did in places like Ixtacamaxtitlan, which became an early center of cheese production.[43] For

Native populations, sheep offered a more manageable animal, with wool that could be spun using traditional techniques and fashioned into hybrid Native-Spanish garments. Large textile plants (*obrajes*) manufacturing wool cloth soon sprung up in the Tlaxcalan town of Apizaco and elsewhere nearby good pasture. A major difference in the behavior of the newly introduced grazing ungulates was that, whereas cattle mostly posed a nuisance by trampling fields and eating ears of maize off the stalk, unregulated sheep could strip the grass cover that kept the relatively thin soils of more arid regions of the highlands in place. The result was large-scale soil erosion in areas such as the Mezquital Valley, north of the Basin of Mexico. Overgrazing sheep may have also contributed to erosion in northern Tlaxcala, but an alternative explanation is that it was caused by soil-conserving agricultural terraces falling into disuse as a result of population decline and the pursuit of new niches within the economy.[44]

Massive population decline is documented through multiple lines of evidence, especially Native and Spanish texts, archaeological settlement survey, and paleopathology.[45] Disease was clearly the major culprit, but the exact pathogens involved and the increased death toll caused by exploitative labor, quality of life under the encomienda, or an apparent prolonged drought in the mid-sixteenth century are issues that require more investigation. We saw in the previous chapter that Vázquez de Tapia estimated 25 percent of the Native population died in 1520 because of the first major epidemic that swept through Mesoamerica. Two other major epidemics, referred to as *cocolitzli* ("the pest") in Nahuatl, struck in 1545 and 1576. Historical figures from Tlaxcala suggest the population declined by half during the mid-sixteenth century, from approximately 500,000 to 250,000, and that the decline reached between 80 and 90 percent by the 1630s. Based on systematic archaeological survey of surface architecture in the Basin of Mexico, the Late Postclassic period apogee of 1.6 million occupants in 1519 was reduced to 250,000 by the early seventeenth century—a similar decline of 84 percent. The Otumba subregion seems even harder hit, with only between 6 and 9 percent of its 1519 population surviving. Peripheral areas were also heavily impacted, with the population of the northern Yucatan declining to 60 to 80 percent of its contact-era figure of almost one million, and the Soconusco region declining from a peak of close to 80,000 to between 5 and 10 percent of this value in the early seventeenth century. If analogous values were applied to the whole of Mesoamerica, the devastating decline of Mesoamerican populations during the sixteenth century would approximate the chart in Figure 8.5, whether or not the total population estimates are precise. What exact pathogens were involved—smallpox, salmonella, plague, measles, typhus, or others—and which may have originated in the Americas rather than in Afro-Eurasia, perhaps a strain of syphilis, will be clarified through future studies. More research is also needed to better understand the differential impacts of mosquito-borne illnesses that evolved in Afro-Eurasia such as malaria, which current genetic evidence suggests arrived with the trans-Atlantic slave trade in a least two different waves corresponding to Spanish and Portuguese colonialism, and how these may have resulted in greater population decline in lowland environments relative to highland ones.[46] Whatever the resolution to these issues proves to be, it is clear that disease-based demographic decline had dire consequences for the Native population. Without it, we may ask if the colonial transition from Mesoamerica to New Spain would have looked more like European colonial endeavors in Asia, such as British India or French Indochina, rather than the more prolonged territorial control of Spanish America.

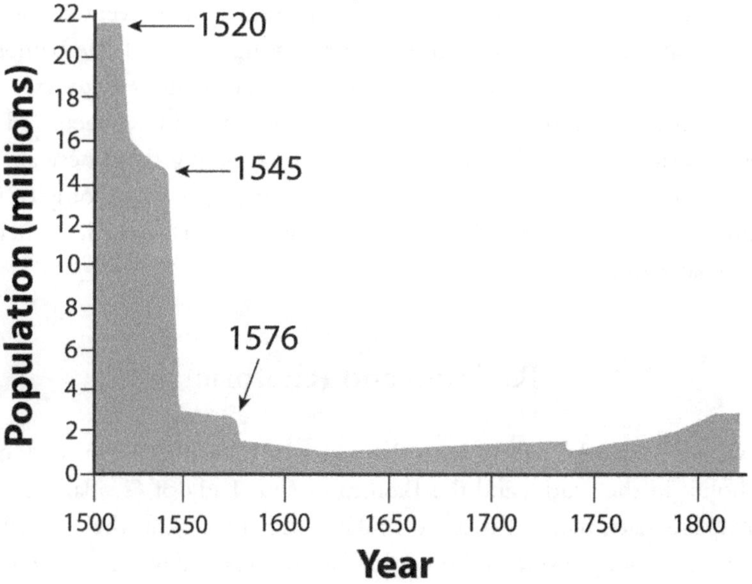

Figure 8.5. Estimated decline in population in New Spain during the sixteenth century, noting years of specific disease epidemics.

Modified from Acuna-Soto et al. (2002).

The response of the viceroyalty to the massive decline in Native populations of the mid-sixteenth century was to forcibly resettle people so as to congregate them into denser towns and villages like those that existed in Europe—a policy called *congregación*. This sort of European settlement pattern, featuring nucleated and typically walled urban centers with largely vacant fields surrounding them, was the product of centuries of total war in which walking great distances to one's agricultural fields was the price people paid for defense. Pre-Hispanic Mesoamerican patterns of warfare and land tenure had developed a more dispersed settlement distribution, except in certain large cities like Teotihuacan and Tenochtitlan. In many regions, such as in the Yucatan, *congregación* had the negative consequences of leaving many farmers distant from their agricultural fields and fracturing existing social networks.[47] Native communities varied in their responses, but commonly drafted maps of land claims and marked community space with crosses and monumental architecture in larger settlements, which exhibited greater demographic stability than did rural areas. In a document drafted in 1560 by the Cabildo of Tlaxcala, council members registered their displeasure at *congregación* by raising practical concerns of distant fields going fallow and who was going shoulder the burden of building new houses in the more concentrated settlements.[48] The petition also includes a nice inventory of crops and animals of the mid-sixteenth century, listing a mix of Mesoamerican domesticates such as maize, maguey, nopal, sweet potato, sapote fruit, chayote squash, chia, and turkey, and European peach, quince, sheep, and pigs. Mesoamericans pursued varied strategies in navigating these new agricultural and dietary regimes, as well as the broader political economy of New Spain and the newly introduced religion that framed worldview, rhetoric, and socialization in new ways.

Religion and Rhetoric

Mexico is today the nation with the second largest population of Roman Catholics in the world, and the Basilica of Our Lady of Guadalupe, north of Mexico City, receives over 20 million pilgrims a year, the most in the Americas, making it one of the world's largest sites of devotional peregrination. Religious conversion and accommodation of sixteenth-century New Spain was thereby profound and an example of how Christianity has been successfully translated to other cultures across the globe. Priests journeyed with the conquistadors, and we saw that Cortés throughout his invasion of Mesoamerica had crosses and statues of the Virgin Mary or saints erected in pre-Hispanic temples, while conquistadors called out to Santiago, Mary, or other saints for divine assistance on the battlefield. Tlatelolco, the site of Cuauhtemoc's surrender, was renamed Santiago de Tlatelolco and the conquering saint was recast in religious imagery from being a Moor-slayer to an Indian-slayer.[49] At one level, we may therefore talk of a "spiritual conquest" that unfolded beginning with the broader Spanish-Mesoamerican war and gathered steam with the arrival of mendicant friars in the first decades of the colonial period. The term follows the title of the classic book by Robert Ricard, *The Spiritual Conquest of Mexico*, which was first published in the mid-twentieth century.[50] Ricard documented variability in the proselytizing methods of the different orders and their spatial distribution within New Spain, which involved clear spatial clustering of Dominicans in south, Franciscans in the west, Augustinians in northeast, and all three orders in the central Mexican core. Like with other elements of New Spain, however, Mexican Catholicism did not simply assume the sacred spaces, devotional art, and ritual practices of Spain. It combined elements of the diverse cultural traditions of both Iberia and Mesoamerica

Historians of religion and art, anthropologists, and scholars from other fields have grappled with how to characterize the co-creative processes of religion in New Spain. Instead of spiritual conquest, alternative ways of framing the processes include ritual substitution, selective acculturation, mutual accommodation, guided syncretism, or subjectification and resilience, in increasing order of how centralized one envisions the institutional roles of Church and Crown to have been. Another term was coined in the context of colonial art, but can also transfer to architecture and even to ritual practices. The Mexican art historian José Moreno Villa introduced the Nahuatl term *tequitqui*, meaning "tributary" or rotary laborer under the Native system of labor tax, co-opted by the Spaniards during the colonial period for the sort of hybrid art and architecture that was produced by Native peoples as a synthesis of pre-Hispanic and Hispanic models.[51] The term emphasizes that Mesoamerican artisans and construction workers, whether called by the Nahuatl term *tequitqui* or an equivalent term in another Native language, were the people who actually sculpted the stone and painted the frescos of New Spain and participated directly in materializing its religious tradition. We will look first at the efforts at conversion by Spanish institutions and rhetorical debates within and among mendicant orders and then consider

Native responses in *tequitqui* art, architecture, and other forms of hybrid materials used in ritual spectacles and ceremonial dramas.

As soon as Europeans learned of a mainland Indies near the Caribbean islands, they started planning its church. It began in Mesoamerica even before the Cortés expedition with the creation of the Diocese of Cozumel in 1518. After the Spanish-Mexica war, Charles V and Pope Clement VII transferred the diocese to Tlaxcala in 1525 and next to Puebla in 1539. They created the See of Mexico in 1528 with Fray Juan de Zumárraga as its first bishop.[52] Cortés had two Mercedarian friars accompanying him, but he, members of the House of Trade and Council of the Indies, and the king himself considered the Franciscans and Dominicans to be better evangelizers.[53] Three Franciscans from the Low Countries were sent by Charles V in 1523, led by his cousin Pieter van der Moere, widely known as Peter of Ghent. The king then requested Pope Hadrian VI to authorize sending 12 "new apostles," all Franciscans, who arrived in New Spain in 1524. The missionizing force was led by Martín de Valencia, whose official title was Saint Evangelist in New Spain and Yucatán, but Cortés preferred the less mystical and more proactive proselytizing of Toribio de Benavente. Toribio's original surname was Paredes, which he rarely used, and he appropriated the Nahuatl name Motolinia ("he who afflicts himself with poverty") as the term the Tlaxcalteca and other Nahuatl speakers used for all friars in indexing their vows of poverty and humble dress in opposition to the gold-lusting conquistadors. Motolinia was the quickest to learn Nahuatl, and he adopted the name as a badge of honor. His accounts are some of the earliest proto-ethnographies of the Native peoples of New Spain. He often advocated for them against the predations of bureaucrats, but also sided with the encomienda against the critique of the institution levied by Las Casas.

The first group of Dominicans arrived in 1526 shortly after the Franciscans, followed by the Augustinians in 1533. Many of the friars hailed from the established core of Old Castile and had ties to the University of Salamanca, particularly the Dominicans, or to the province of Santiago and its cathedral town honoring the patron saint. Among the 12 Franciscans, Martín de Valencia was from León, not the Mediterranean city of his surname, but he had been Provincial of Extremadura and thrice on missions to convert Muslims;[54] Martín de Coruña was, as advertised, from that Galician town; and Motolinia was from Benavente, province of Zamora. As the leader of the group, Martín de Valencia was stationed in Mexico City and eventually retired to the more rural town of Amecameca. Motolinia spent much of his ministry in Tlaxcala and Martín de Coruña was stationed primarily in New Galicia. Their journey to New Spain was similar to Cortés' in originating from Sanlúcar de Barrameda, stopping over in the Canaries, arriving sequentially in the three large islands of the Caribbean, and finally disembarking at San Juan de Ulúa to march inland to Mexico City, after first stopping in Tlaxcala.[55] In addition to its commercial functions, the House of Trade also had a Catholic charity arm that supplied goods such as chalices and sacred texts for the mendicant friars in their proselytizing missions and also provided food and lodging for Amerindians brought to Spain.[56]

The years 1525–1540 saw the determined efforts of the friars to destroy the temples, sculptures, and texts they considered idolatrous. It was common practice for Mesoamericans to continue venerating effigy images of pre-Hispanic deities. Motolinia recounts several instances of encountering "idols" on mountain shrines or hidden among altars and other Christian devotional spaces. He visited Cholula's Great Pyramid in 1535, where the Spaniards had erected a cross on its summit that the Cholulteca were venerating, only to discover they had buried pre-Hispanic effigies and conch shell trumpets at the base of the cross.[57] The shrine and now church on top of the pyramid is dedicated to the Virgin of the Remedies (see Figure 1.2 in Chapter 1), whose cult originated in Seville. Conversion fervor peaked with the Indian Inquisition in Mexico City, 1536–1543, when Don Carlos Ometochtzin of Texcoco was burned at the stake for idolatry on the orders of Bishop Zumárraga.[58] He was accused of venerating a sculpture of Tlaloc and conducting rituals in the hills east of the city, where the former Great Speakers of Texcoco did the same and had their royal bath and garden complex. This event underscores the limitations of referring to religious syncretism in balanced terms, as doing so minimizes the domineering stance taken by the Church and Crown in many matters pertaining to religion: Mesoamericans could continue to prefer maize tortillas over wheat bread, or use adobe bricks in fashioning European style architecture, but they risked execution for certain religious transgressions.

The Indian Inquisition can be seen as the result of a crystallization of the rivalry between the Franciscans and Dominicans into heated arguments about whether Native peoples were capable of converting to Christianity and, if so, what the best methods of conversion were. As we saw in Chapter 3, different approaches characterized the two orders from the time of their founders, with the Franciscan strategy of connecting with laypeople more sentimentally and the Dominicans more intellectually. These contrasting approaches continued in New Spain, as the Franciscans preached sermons directed at less educated audiences and explained scripture using more audio-visual pedagogies, whereas the Dominicans incorporated Aristotelian rhetoric directed at wealthier audiences on both sides of the Atlantic to guide them to their own spiritual revelations. To generalize these groups, the different approaches meant that the Franciscans acted more like what anthropologists call participant-observers as a method of understanding a culture by learning the language and participating in it—a reason why texts written by Motolinia and compiled and edited by Sahagún read so ethnographically, at least in matters not pertaining to religion. The Dominicans, in turn, were often addressing a different audience that included the highest tiers of the Spanish bureaucracy. Dominican friars like Las Casas criticized the mass-baptisms and sermons of Franciscans like Peter of Ghent and Motolinia as superfluous and at the root of continued idolatry. Las Casas argued for a unitary, true method of conversion that needed to be sincere and not rushed.[59]

Although the Dominicans were the great educators of medieval and early modern Spain, many of the first schools in New Spain were established by the Franciscans. Peter of Ghent founded the first one in Texcoco, San José de los Naturales, where he began learning Nahuatl and developed pictographic catechisms as a means of teaching scripture, particularly to noble children.[60] Instruction ranged from how to manufacture certain crafts to grammar and basic Latin. By the 1530s, hundreds of Mesoamericans were literate in the European alphabet, with many able to read and write in Castilian Spanish, Latin, and Nahuatl. Native indoctrination accelerated with the founding of the College of Santa Cruz in Tlatelolco on top of where the city's central calmecac had once stood (see Plate 5b). When formally opened in 1536, Santa Cruz trained 80 students from different parts of central Mexico in the *trivium* (grammar, rhetoric, and logic) and *quadrivium* (arithmetic, geometry, astronomy, and music) of European higher education. Although the Florentine Codex, Molina's Nahuatl dictionary, and other critical colonial-period works came from the college, Ricard was correct to note its shortcomings, particularly its failure to produce a single Native bishop.[61] When Pedro de San Buenaventura, one of Sahagún's Native scribes, returned home from Santa Cruz to Cuauhtitlan, he likely authored or oversaw the compilation of the *Annals of Cuauhtitlan* with the objective of presenting his perspective of history, which was opaque even to Sahagún.[62]

The Dominicans, in the meantime, made their arguments in print and at the University of Salamanca (Plate 7). These included critiques of the Franciscans and both critiques and defenses of Native peoples. We saw in Chapter 5 that Las Casas had been a vocal critic of the colonial endeavor from the Americas since 1515; yet his major adversary in what is known as the Valladolid debate, Juan Gines de Sepúlveda, was also a Dominican and drew on the same foundational texts of Aristotle, Thomas Aquinas, and others to counter Las Casas by arguing that indigenous peoples of the Indies were natural slaves and the encomienda and other colonial practices were justified. Before this famous showdown, however, were the arguments put forth by the second Salamanca school, led by Francisco de Vitoria.[63] Others participated in the intellectual undertaking, such as Friar Pérez de Oliva who authored a Socratic dialog in the 1520s arguing that all people are dignified under God, including the Indians. Vitoria wrote a series of lectures that he gave at the university and his students assembled as the book *De Indis* in 1539. He drew particularly from the *Summa Theologiae* of Saint Thomas Aquinas in addressing the issue of the colonization of the Americas and in arguing that Native peoples lived ordered lives with urban centers and social institutions. Vitoria also argued that Natives of the Americas had less developed agriculture and education, but he had never crossed the Atlantic and based his arguments on early chroniclers—ignorant, for instance, of the complex symbiosis of milpa agriculture, the Aztec chinampa field systems, or calmecac schools.

It is important to note the historical context of Vitoria's arguments, as he made them during a time of increased unrest in northern Europe. Vitoria was interested in refuting the Lutherans, who argued that people living in mortal sin, like the pagan Natives, could not be responsible for their possessions; and it was also the same year as a rebellion against Charles V in Ghent.[64] The Holy Roman Emperor responded to the latter by a show of brute force that included torturing and executing leaders of the rebellion; stripping the city of rights, public property, its coat of arms, and church bells; seizing documents dealing with the issue of rights within the Indies from the Dominican's San Esteban monastery in Salamanca, and prohibiting further discussion on the matter unless licensed by the Crown—as claims for autonomy anywhere in the empire were considered a threat. Las Casas returned to Spain in 1540 to petition his sovereign. The friar's efforts were successful in seeing the establishment of the 1542 New

Laws, which succeeded in abolishing the encomienda for a few years. Las Casas also wrote *A Short Account of the Destruction of the Indies* in that same year, but it was not published until after the 1550–1551 Valladolid debate with Sepúlveda.[65] Drawing from the same general corpus of sources, the two presented contrasting arguments: Sepúlveda argued that indigenous peoples of the Indies were barbaric, unreasoning, and cruel so should be punished and governed by civilized Spain, whereas Las Casas countered by noting ways in which the Natives should be considered civilized, that the gospel of Paul does not allow for the sort of just war that Aristotle discussed, and that there were no grounds for Spanish punishment or wars of conquest. In drawing from Iberia's Classical history, Las Casas astutely noted that Pompey and other Romans had viewed the Celtiberians as barbaric just as some Spaniards viewed the Indians, and ultimately both assessments were incorrect. Díaz and Gómara both claim to have witnessed the debate in person. Although the arguments of Las Casas were influential, they merely created more laws that conquistadors could skirt and resulted in what was primarily a semantic shift as power transitioned to Phillip II and new generations of adelantados "pacified" rather than "conquered" new lands.[66]

Given these strong control mechanisms of Crown and Church, in matters pertaining to religion especially, in what ways could Native peoples resist or take a co-creative role in guiding syncretism? Documented infractions of what the Spaniards viewed as idolatry were not tolerated, but other fusions or substitutions of Mesoamerican language, thought, and material styles presented room for accommodation. In the realm of language, Mesoamericans referred to Christian churches using the same terms they had used for their temples, such as *teocalli* in Nahuatl and *kuna* in Mayan, translating as "sacred house" or "god house."[67] Likewise, God, the Virgin Mary, and the panoply of saints could have Native terms added or substituted to their Spanish designations, with the result that certain pre-Hispanic conceptualizations endured and the logic of an incorporative cosmovision could simply continue to add more divine essences. Material manifestations of New Spain's sacred houses and symbols convey these fusions particularly well in *tequitqui* art and architecture. Nahua and Otomi artisans employed a visual language that linked to the pre-Hispanic antecedents with symbols such as water-mountains, solar discs, and toponymical pictograms to render Christian concepts intelligible with Native conceptualizations of mythistory and landscape.[68]

Peter of Ghent is responsible for many of the accommodations that dictated the now iconic architectural plans of sacred architecture in New Spain: the open chapels, atria, and quadripartite *posa* ("resting spot") shrines with central crosses. Preaching outdoors was not completely unknown in Europe, where it could be done in market settings, during disease epidemics, or for other purposes of expediency. Yet Christian mass, baptisms, and other rituals were clearly indoor affairs in early modern Europe, and Mesoamericans were accustomed to practicing religion outdoors. Peter of Ghent designed the first open chapel, also called San José de los Naturales, next to the Franciscan monastery in Mexico City. In front of the open chapel was a large enclosed atrium—*atrio* or *patio*—that served as a forecourt and presented a completely new organization of sacred space without direct precursors in Europe.[69] The paired open chapel and atrium complexes were often built directly on top of pre-Hispanic sacred precincts, and in central Mexico often followed the millennial long tradition of being located east of the main plaza. With the combination of four chapel-like *posas* in the corners and a central atrial cross-altar, they followed the quincunx organization Mesoamericans perceived in the cosmos and encoded in microcosm into urban centers like Tenochtitlan (Figure 8.6). The Tlaxcalteca referred to the atrial cross as Tonacaquahuitl ("the tree that sustains our life"), following the axis mundi trees of pre-Hispanic faith. The Maya also linked the Christian cross to the tree of life and communities in the highlands today created foliated crosses by attaching pine boughs.

Colonial atria could therefore continue to fulfill the functions that large palace courtyards and central plazas of sacred precincts served in pre-Hispanic times, including politicking and rhetorical exchanges or orations. They also allowed for ritual processions through quincunx patios that merged Mesoamerican conceptions of the cosmos with Christian theology, and were of an appropriate scale for presenting mass and baptizing large groups. Two excellent examples are preserved from Tlaxcala and Izamal (Figure 8.7). The Monastery at Izamal was designed by Diego de Landa, who arrived to the Yucatan in 1549, and was constructed on top of a former temple to the Maya god Itzamna in 1553–1561.[70] The large atrium is one of the best encapsulations of the quincunx ideal, with four *posa* chapels located at the corners and an atrial cross marking the sacred center. The church and monastery complex in Tlaxcala was dedicated by Motolinia and the resident Franciscans to Our Lady of the Assumption, but is now referred to as

Figure 8.6. Syncretism in world directions of colonial atrium layout from Codex Osuna, depicting Peter of Ghent in center with hieroglyph for Tenochtitlan and four quadrants of the city: San Sebastian, San Pablo, San Juan, and Santa Maria.

Public domain. Bibilioteca Nacional de España.

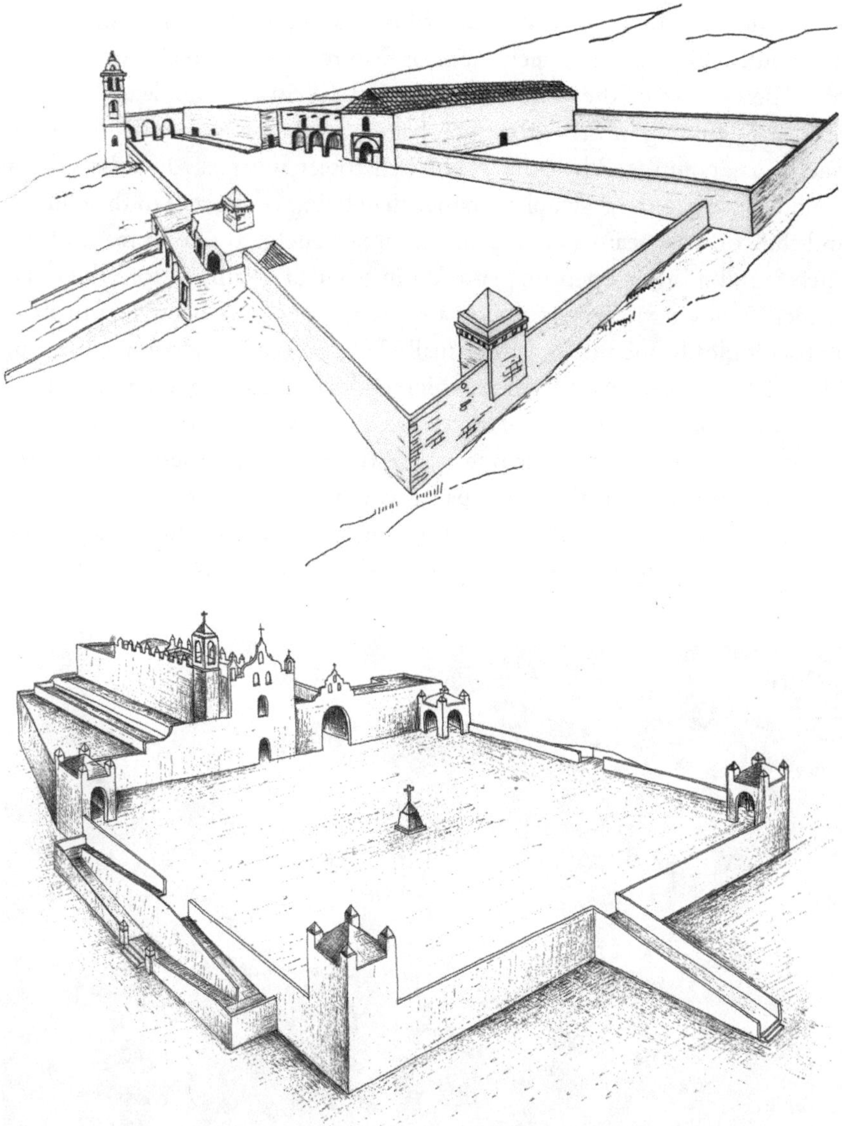

Figure 8.7. Franciscan open chapel and atria complexes: (a) the complex of Our Lady of the Assumption in Tlaxcala, featuring two atria and open chapel before ramp; (b) the complex to Saint Anthony of Padua in Izamal, featuring a quincunx patio with four *posa* chapels, central atrial cross, and open chapel to the right of the church.

Redrawn from McAndrew (1965).

San Francisco. Muñoz Camargo described it and provided an illustration of its layout, which has an eclectic mix of features that are likely the product of its being one of the earliest constructed Christian complexes of New Spain—beginning in the early 1530s, halted for the disease epidemic of the mid-1540s, completed by 1564.[71] The bell-tower was placed to the side of the hill closest to the town plaza, rather than being connected to the church, and the complex features two atria: an upper enclosed one in front of the church and a lower open one situated in front of a ramp before the open chapel (Figure 8.8). Two atria plans are rare but have also been documented archaeologically, including at the small church-monastery complex at San Miguel Axaloapan, near Otumba, which is also early, dating to about 1540.[72] Thousands of Tlaxcalteca could have filled the two atria of San Francisco, but it is likely that the upper one was restricted to the priests and indigenous nobility, whereas the lower patio would have been for mass assembly of everyone else. This partitioning was not part of the original plan, however, as another open chapel next to the church was illustrated by Muñoz

Figure 8.8. Open chapel and bell-tower from Tlaxcala.
Photo by the author. Reproduction authorized by the Instituto Nacional de Antropología e Historia, Mexico.

Camargo without the dividing wall that reduced the size of the upper atrium and created a garden next to the church. A marvelous example of colonial hybridity can be seen in the ceiling of the church, whose gilded rosettes are in *mudéjar* style, developed in Spain from Islamic architecture but embraced by the time of its construction as a fully Iberian and Christian style (Figure 8.9).[73] Cholula's chapel for the city's indigenous inhabitants, the Capilla de los Naturales, likewise sits before a huge quincunx atrium, but its interior is a vast arcade reminiscent of a mosque.

Decorations on atrial crosses also illustrate *tequitqui* syncretism where instruments relating to the Passion of Christ are sculpted in glyphic elements reminiscent of Aztec writing.[74] A fascinating juxtaposition of pre-Hispanic and Christian imagery comes from certain atrial crosses in regions of central and west Mexico with obsidian mines, where polished obsidian mirrors were placed in the center of the cross, sometimes framed by Christ's crown of thorns (Figure 8.10).[75] We saw in Chapter 2 that inset obsidian discs could serve as the eyes in sculptures of Mesoamerican deities, such as the heads on Teotihuacan's Feathered Serpent Pyramid, or for adorning other sculptures and relief carvings. The association with the Aztec deity Tetzcatlipoca and his Tlaxtalteca counterpart Camaxtli is also clear, as his name references the mirror he used for revealing the true nature of things and could substitute for one of his feet (see Figure 6.5 in Chapter 6). It is unclear why the Spaniards did not consider the inclusion of obsidian mirrors on atrial crosses as problematic, but they may have not minded a shining or solar association with Christ, and the mirrors were objects of interest in Europe—Phillip II owned at least one himself.

Not only were the physical atria and their crosses manifestations of religious syncretism, but devotional practices around them, such as dance, processions, ritual battles, and dramatic spectacles, could also be arenas for hybrid practices. A decree written in Nahuatl by the cabildo of Tlaxcala in 1550, perhaps prompted by the Franciscan friars, levied a fine of 80 pesos on anyone who danced around the cross with precious feathers.[76] The steep fine suggests that Indians continued to practice such rituals, even after the inquisition ended in 1543. Another example from the end of 1531 is only known through later texts and images, but it is associated with the most famous instance of syncretism within Mexican Christianity: the apparition of the Virgin of Guadalupe to Juan Diego Cuauhtlatoatzin on the hill of Tepeyac. Devotion to the Virgin was mostly restricted to Mexico City and smaller communities in the Basin of Mexico during the sixteenth and early seventeenth

Figure 8.9. *Mudéjar* ceiling in church of Our Lady of the Assumption, Tlaxcala.
Photo by the author. Reproduction authorized by the Instituto Nacional de Antropología e Historia, Mexico.

Figure 8.10. Atrial cross with central obsidian mirror from Ciudad Hidalgo, Michoacán.

Photo by Nicholas J Saunders. Used with permission.

centuries, but then spread widely through the 1648–1649 publications on her written in Spanish and in Nahuatl. The Virgin revealed herself four times to Juan Diego, but it was not until the last, when her image miraculously appeared on his maguey fiber (*ixtle*) cloak—a sign of his low status as an indigenous peasant from Cuauhtitlan—that Bishop Zumárraga believed him and had a chapel built at Tepeyac to house the image. The image was moved from Mexico City to Tepeyac in a great procession up the causeway linking the two on December 26, joined by Cortés and his second Spanish wife, Juana Ramírez de Arellano de Zúñiga.[77] The procession is described as celebratory and having featured mock skirmishes in which Nahuas dressed the part of civilized Toltec-Mexica and barbaric Chichimeca, enacting battles on the lake from canoes. During the pageant, one actor was accidently killed by an arrow, but before the image of the Virgin he was healed, marking her first attested miracle. It is difficult to say for certain whether this mock battle took place, but the chronicles record similar processions for the years 1556, 1566, and 1595, meaning they would have been part of more recent historical memory when the texts were published. Shortly following the publications, a magnificent 1653 painting depicting the procession and first miracle was commissioned, attributed to the workshop of José Juárez (Plate 8). The painting shows a deep knowledge of pre-Hispanic material culture, likely possessed by the *tequitqui* Nahuas or mestizos who helped to execute it. It includes the differentiation of the bow-and-arrow wielding, nearly naked Chichimecs and the machuahuitl-wielding, richly garbed Toltec-Mexicas, as well as jaguar warriors and musicians playing pre-Hispanic instruments.

If Cortés did in fact participate in the procession, it would have been a year and a half after returning from Spain, where he journeyed to petition the king and pay his respects to the Virgin of Guadalupe at her monastery in Extremadura, as Columbus had also done before him.[78] Cortés arrived in Spain in May 1528 with Sandoval and a sizable contingent of Mesoamericans. They disembarked at Palos de la Frontera and first stayed at that town's Friary of Santa María la Rabida, located in the ancient Phoenician core around Huelva and possibly constructed on top of a former Temple to Melqart. During their stay, they overlapped with Pizarro, who was bound for Peru. Columbus had also lodged at the friary over three decades earlier while petitioning the Catholic Monarchs to fund his expedition, and brought the first goods from the Americas back to them upon his return.[79] The role of Mary as patroness of navigators was also commemorated in Seville by the chapel that Charles V established in 1526 at the House of Trade, decorated a decade later by a painted altarpiece that depicts the Virgin sheltering prominent explorers and conquistadors as well as Indians within her shroud. As his grandparents had done, Charles continued the royal patronage of the monastery at Guadalupe, though not with the same devotion as Isabela. Fray Gabriel de Talavera recounted in 1597 that Cortés had been bit by a scorpion in Yautepec and survived a bout of fever after praying to the Virgin of Guadalupe.[80] In thanks, Cortés commissioned a golden *ex voto* fashioned by a *tequitqui* artisan with a scorpion as its central element, which he offered at the monastery along with featherwork "paintings" made by Native artisans. The whereabouts of the golden scorpion is unknown, but a color illustration of it from the monastery's inventory of 1778 shows the hybrid style with what looks to be an Aztec or Mixtec date glyph linking the two halves of the chain.

The Virgin's clear associations with navigators and the conversion of Spanish America explain some of the prominence that Guadalupe achieved in New Spain. Yet her apparition at Tepeyac required merging with Nahua ontology. In Nahuatl documents, such as the one known as *Nican Mopohua* for its beginning lines, she is referred to as *Tonantzin* Guadalupe, meaning "our revered mother."[81] *Nican Mopohua* was published in 1649, helping to disseminate the cult, but it was likely first written in the mid-sixteenth century by Antonio Valeriano. The educated Nahuatl prose of the manuscript suggests that its author had been trained at the Colegio de Santa Cruz. Its delay in publication of nearly a century may be attributable to the fact that Franciscans had started the chapel at Tepeyac, and by the time *Nican Mopohua* was written the archbishop was the Dominican Alfonso de Montúfar, who granted it less importance to their order. The Nahuatl prose of a version compiled by Luis Laso de la Vega, titled *Huei tlamahuiçoltica*, employs a mix of Hispanic and pre-Hispanic metaphors in describing the Virgin's resplendence as making the stones of Tepeyac like "precious emeralds and jeweled bracelets" and the plants like "green obsidian, and their foliage like fine turquoise" with thorns of gold.[82]

Tepeyac was the appropriate setting for the apparition because the hill and those around it had been the sacred ground of Aztec fertility goddesses.[83] Two sculptures from Tepeyac itself survived the colonial period demolition of pre-Hispanic imagery and depict Cihuacoatl-Tonantzin (Figure 8.11) and Chicomecoatl—translating to "our mother snake woman" and "seven-snake," respectively. Directly behind Tepeyac, on Zacahuitzco hill, were pre-Hispanic relief carvings depicting two fertility goddesses that are

Figure 8.11. Sculpture of Cihuacoatl-Tonantzin from Tepeyac, now in Museo Nacional de Antropología e Historia.
Illustration based on López-Luján and Noguez (2011: Figure 8).

now destroyed but were rendered in the early eighteenth-century *Codex Teotenantzin*. The pair may represent Tonantzin and either Chicomecoatl or Toci-Teteoinnan ("our grandmother, mother of gods"). Whatever the exact identifications, the images certainly marked Tepeyac and surroundings as a sacred landscape imbued with feminine divinity and a place where Native and Spanish ontologies could be mutually accommodated, providing New Spain and, later, independent Mexico with its enduring patroness.

Colonists and Subjects of New Spain

Political, economic, and religious institutions of colonial New Spain provided the boundaries within which groups and individuals operated to advance their interests, some of which we have already considered. We now turn to this issue more specifically to look at how people negotiated their place in the colonial order and the variable strategies relating to intersecting identities of race, ethnicity, class, and gender. Dominant structures of power have resulted in a bias in textual documentation toward the individual actions of males of Spanish descent—the conquistadors, encomenderos, friars, and administrators. Yet documents also shed light on the efforts of Mesoamerican nobles to retain or enhance their titles: cabildo records that reveal collective actions of particular municipalities and class or racial tensions within them, and accounts of public spectacles that provide an idea of how power and identity were reified and contested. Valuable insights into colonial life comes from the archaeological record, which is especially informative about non-elite colonial subjects and their expression of social relations through personal adornment, food, and other patterns of consumption. We look at the strategies of colonial elites, both Spaniards and Native nobility; those of the much larger population of non-elites, primarily Native peoples and mestizos, but also Africans and others of mixed ancestry stationed along a racialized colonial hierarchy; and the dramatic enactment in pageants of historical memory and negotiated identity.

Spanish appropriation of Native labor and its associated social transformations can generally be marked by three chronological stages: the introduction of the encomienda beginning in 1521, its substitution by the repartamiento in the mid-sixteenth century, and the shift to greater individual wage labor in the second quarter of the sixteenth century. Labor relations of the first two stages possessed rough equivalencies in the pre-Hispanic era, making them intelligible to Nahuas, Otomis, and other former subjects of the Aztec Triple Alliance. The encomienda was somewhat analogous to an entire altepetl being run as a noble estate (*tecalli*), and the repartamiento was somewhat analogous to work parties delegated for rotary labor tax in the service of the state and noble class (*coatequitl*).[84] Market exchange continued but saw the introduction of European coinage to pre-Hispanic systems of equivalencies, scheduling based on the seven-day week, changes in market niches prompted by new global trade demands, and the later proliferation of cash wages. Other than the political-economic change under the encomienda and religious conversion pursued by the mendicant orders, other elements of Native culture and social relations were less affected during the first half of the sixteenth century. The second half of the sixteenth century marked a period of broader sociocultural change in domains of language, kinship, religious syncretism, and the power of Native cabildos.

Immediately following the fall of Tenochtitlan, the conquistadors, Mesoamerican nobility, and allies who had assisted and continued to help in wars of conquest all scrambled to gain or retain power. Although Cortés made a pilgrimage to the monastery at Guadalupe in Extremadura, his top priority in returning to Spain in 1528 was to petition the king against the loss of many of his encomiendas and to defend himself before ongoing investigations into his conduct as governor brought by Nuño de Guzmán and other administrators. Cortés retained titles but lost power, as he was stripped of his governorship and made to settle for the titles Marques of the Valley of Oaxaca and Captain-General of the South Sea (Pacific Ocean), thereby removing him from oversight of the core of New Spain.[85] Cortés did earn induction into the Order of Santiago, however, and married the noblewoman Doña Juana Zúñiga with a ceremony in the cathedral of Toledo. He took the logo for his coat of arms based on an account of the siege of Jerusalem by Roman Jewish author Titus Flavius Josephus, implying he had taken a second Jerusalem: *Judicium Domini apprehendit eos, et fortitudo ejus corroboravit bracchium meum* ("The judgement of the Lord overtook them, and His might strengthened my arm"). He brought his son with Malinche to Spain, called Martín "the mestizo" to distinguish him from another son named Martín with his Spanish wife. This mixed-race son of the conquistador and the translator was raised in Spain, received a European education, and became a page for the prince and future King Phillip II. He corresponded with chroniclers such as Las Casas and Zorita, and would not see his father again until 1541, when Hernando Cortés and his mestizo son fought together against Muslims in an unsuccessful expedition against Ottoman-controlled Algiers.

In the aftermath of the 1542 New Laws, a number of other conquistadors whose accounts we have relied on were prompted to justify to the king why they should retain their encomiendas, titles, and other trappings of power. Vázquez de Tapia wrote while serving as a regidor in Mexico City seeking to defend encomiendas of his in Tlapa, Churubusco, and Cuametitlan, plus a mine at Ayoteco.[86] He began his appeal by exalting his lineage and noting that a paternal uncle was a professor at Salamanca and a maternal uncle was an inquisitor. Many of the Native accounts of the conquest made similar appeals, such as Alva Ixtlilxochitl's pairing of his noble ancestry with accounts of the assistance his ancestors had provided the Spaniards. Polygyny among Mesoamerican nobles had left large numbers of elite offspring—Xicotencatl the elder of Tlaxcala had 90 wives when he died in 1522—who had grounds for making similar claims in the early colonial period.[87] The scarcity of Spanish women in early New Spain and the respect the Spaniards granted noble titles set the grounds for elite mestizaje, but they looked to impose Spanish, particularly Castilian, norms of male-preference primogeniture as the legitimate form of succession. This had not been the case in the pre-Hispanic era or when the speakership of Tenochtitlan passed from Moctezuma to Cuitlahuac to Cuauhtemoc during the Spanish-Mexica war, never going from father to son. Succession throughout central Mexico had followed a male preference but was decided by a council among candidates of noble brothers or nephews.

Some of the more enduring elements of Native lifeways during the early colonial period were in kinship, household organization, and land tenure. A carryover from the pre-Hispanic era was the institution of communally held land where use rights were delegated to certain families who allocated them among heads of households, but that would return to the community if left uncultivated.[88] The practice is particularly well illustrated in Tlaxcala, since their status as Indian Republic kept the infiltration of Spanish systems of kinship and land tenure at bay for decades. Documents from Tlaxcala also show that noble women could inherit land, retain control of it even after marriage, and pass it on to their children. The introduction of Spanish kinship norms imposed a more patriarchal system while also banning noble polygyny, but we see from census accounts recorded two decades into the colonial period that it could still be practiced in more rural areas. Male-preference primogeniture in the inheritance of physical houses was the prevalent though not universal pattern in Spain, differing from the widespread practice of the youngest son looking after his parents and inheriting the house (ultimogeniture) that survived in many Native communities.[89] Another source of conflict was in competing notions of tax and tribute. Whereas in the pre-Hispanic system, nobles were expected to contribute more to their altepetl reflective of their means, in a graduated tax system, Spanish nobles were a wholly extractive elite class exempt from paying taxes.[90]

Axes of identity defined by kinship, gender, class, and ethnicity—in the micro-patriotic sense of Native city states—all intersected with one another and with race in a colonial setting, and racial reckoning went beyond the *español-indio* (Spanish-Indian) distinction and most prevalent form of mestizaje. The combination of large Amerindian populations with Europeans, Africans, and Asians made for racial mixture in New Spain that was much more fluid than in Anglo North America, but also saw strong attempts to characterize and hierarchize a system of racially based social stations.[91]

Notions of race and ethnicity are culturally and historically contingent and intersect strongly with social class and political hierarchy. The caste system of New Spain did not produce endogamous groups that would not intermarry, like those of South Asia, but they carried clear notions of racial purity and status. Although the term *mestizo* has Latin roots and originated with more neutral connotations, in New Spain during the mid-sixteenth century it began to be used more in the sense of "illegitimate" rather than general mixing of socially defined racial constructs. Racially based notions of legitimacy could nevertheless be superseded by class and upbringing. For instance, the son of Isabel Moctezuma (formerly Tecuichpochtzin, the Great Speaker's daughter) and the conquistador Juan Cano was considered a Spanish *castizo*, or culturally "white." Although we have been considering Fernando Alva Ixtlilxochitl's chronicle as a Native source, in his time he was considered a Spanish castizo based on class and upbringing. The social construct of Alva Ixtlilxohitl's racial classification prioritized his education at Santa Cruz de Tlatelolco and, more important, his pedigree within the lineage of Triple Alliance rulers—his mother was the colonial Nahua ruler (*cacica*) of the town of San Juan Teotihuacan, built on the Aztec period settlement on the western side of the ruins of the earlier great capital.

Common racial types, such as mestizos, indios, *negros*, and *mulatos*, carried legal ramifications for non-elites, but the opaqueness of less common castes such as *moriscos, castizos, coyotes*, and *lobos* shows the porousness of the system. Castes became more defined later in the colonial period and were used to highlight difference, whereas by the time of incipient independence movements of the early nineteenth century, mestizaje was embraced as a shared identity of racial hybridity put to use for projects of national unity. The iconic colonial genera of *casta* paintings express Spanish and white creole (Spaniards born in the Americas) notions of racial purity that were not embraced by Nahuas, who never adopted the Spanish category "indio" as an ethnic moniker and made strategic calculations regarding when to emphasize or downplay their Native identity.[92] Micro-patriotism with regard to Native ethnic designations often continued as well, and it is clear that some groups resented the preferential treatments granted the Tlaxcalteca. In one cabildo petition of 1560 from Huexotzingo, signed by all 16 of its members, the emphasis is on their assistance to the Spaniards following the Cholula massacre and continuing with the invasions of Guatemala and west Mexico.[93] The Huexotzinca mark a contrast with the Tlaxcalteca in claiming that their conversion to Christianity was peaceable, whereas friars had been pushed out of Tlaxcala and nobles there had been executed for idolatry. Naturally, the Tlaxcalteca claimed no such thing and emphasized their enthusiastic embrace of the new faith.

Individuals in early New Spain reflected and negotiated their identities through dress, insignia, arms, and even animals. An example of the latter is in the late colonial Mexican saying, "a donkey for an Indian, a mule for a mulato, and a horse for a gentleman."[94] It reads better in Spanish ("el burro para el indio, la mula para el mulato, y el caballo para el caballero") because the animal terms, and associated notions of purity or hybridity, are embedded in terms mulato and caballero. All three animals were in fact important economically in New Spain, but the saying captures associations of race, status, and personal possessions. The highest-ranking Native elites looked to ride horses and mark their bodies with Spanish dress and weaponry, especially swords and daggers made from Toledo steel. They were granted permission to do so more than non-elites, but commoners could also petition for such symbols of power.[95] Similar strategies were also pursued by people of African descent. For instance, in 1636–1637 Lorenzo de Zúñiga, described as having brown (*pardo*) skin, successfully petitioned the court in Mexico City for the privileges of wearing a Spanish-style cape and using a dagger and sword by claiming the status of "white mulato" and freed slave.[96]

Household archaeology, in turn, reveals how lower status Mesoamericans adopted alternate strategies of using Spanish pottery such as tin-glazed majolica in feasts, with the goal of forging collective bonds within household settings, rather than the public spaces that the higher-ranked insignias were employed in. A local variant of majolica named Talavera, after the Spanish town in the province of Toledo, developed in southern Puebla-Tlaxcala and fused styles and techniques from Spain—which themselves combined Islamic and Italian traditions—with those of the region, and then saw the introduction of Chinese influences from porcelain that was transshipped overland though Puebla as part of the Manila Galleon trade.[97] Many other pottery forms continued pre-Hispanic manufacturing techniques but saw subtle stylistic changes, such as Aztec black-on-orange wares that are often difficult to distinguish from those prior to Spanish arrival, except for the hybridization of Native and European conventions for depicting flowers or other motifs (Figure 8.12). Generally speaking, vessel forms that were already part of the pre-Hispanic repertoire continued to be made using primarily Mesoamerican techniques, including using molds to form the vessel, whereas novel forms introduced from Europe or Asia, such as candleholders or oil

Figure 8.12. Colonial Aztec V period black-on-orange dish from Tlatelolco. Tlatelolco site museum.

Photo by author. Reproduction authorized by the Instituto Nacional de Antropología e Historia, Mexico.

jars, were made on potter's wheels and using more Old World techniques. These shifts in forms and styles were more pronounced in urban centers, whereas rural pottery production continued Native traditions even later into the colonial period.[98]

Within urban centers in particular, Mesoamerican elites drew on a mix of material culture with pre-Hispanic antecedents and Spanish introductions in proclaiming their continued place atop the social hierarchy. They built houses that continued many of the conventions of earlier palaces, especially large central courtyards and disc-friezes at their rooflines that had indexed the preciousness of jade beads for millennia. One example called the Casa de la Cacica stands in Teposcolula, Oaxaca, and was constructed for the female Mixtec ruler of the town in the 1560s.[99] She resided in the central structure and held semi-public gatherings, including bullfights, in the central courtyard. Another example was built on Cholula's main square, which had been transformed in the decades following the infamous massacre. The House of the Eagle Knight was constructed primarily in a Spanish plateresque style, but its designation comes from the relief carvings of that pre-Hispanic military order flanking the entrance (Figure 8.13).[100] Archaeological excavations below the house discovered elaborate pre-Hispanic Cholula polychrome pottery vessels, indicating its enduring locale as an elite space.

Non-elites pursued strategies for increasing their wealth and prestige through new niches in the colonial economy. A fascinating window is provided by a document from the cabildo of Tlaxcala dating to 1553 in which the nobles complain of commoners harvesting cochineal, the red dye made from the dried exoskeletons of female *Dactylopius coccus*, a parasitic insect that flourished on the prickly pear cacti.[101] Cochineal is one of the most colorfast natural red dyes—coloring textiles such as the jackets worn by British Red Coats—and this niche in a newly globalized economy caused friction within Native society by providing commoners with a new market outlet that at the time was bringing in some 100,000 ducados a year. The cochineal industry, plus the growing of wheat for Spanish markets, upset the Tlaxcalteca elites, who argued that commoners should be continuing

Figure 8.13. Relief flanking entrance of late sixteenth-century House of the Eagle Knight in Cholula's main plaza.

Photo by the author. Reproduction authorized by the Instituto Nacional de Antropología e Historia, Mexico.

their traditional maize agriculture, thereby maintaining traditional hierarchical relations. Economic changes meant that whereas certain trades diversified, and Mesoamericans could earn good wages manufacturing Spanish garments, swords, gloves, and glass, others saw deskilling, such as the substitution of obsidian by metal tools.[102] This process was much slower than might be expected because, though Spanish steel and iron tools were superior in their durability, they were rare and expensive in the early Colonial economy, and obsidian provided a sharper and more abundant alternative. Obsidian was also put to new uses such as hide working and silver mining. Archaeological survey and excavations at the Sierra de las Navajas mine near Pachuca demonstrated that Native artisans continued to fashion obsidian tools in great quantities, especially scrapers for working leather and maguey. The Franciscans constructed a *visita* chapel, one lacking a resident friar, to evangelize the obsidian miners in the decade after the 12 new apostles arrived in New Spain. Some of these miners likely moved to mine silver at Pachuca and Real del Monte in the 1530s, but others continued in the obsidian trade for many decades.

No social arena better captures the intersections of New Spain's material culture, mythistory, and identities better than the festivals and pageants of the early colonial period. Some drew on Roman traditions such as the circus, others on the *Reconquista* era *Moros y Cristianos* dances, and all were inflected by Mesoamerican traditions and recast by Native peoples to negotiate their place and sense of history in the new colonial order. In one of the final chapters of his history, Bernal Díaz recounts a Roman-style circus of 1538 in Mexico City organized by Viceroy Mendoza, Cortés, and the Royal Audencia in commemoration of Charles V's peace treaty with the king of France.[103] For the event, the Mexica constructed a mock forest in the main plaza, stocked with felines, which Díaz refers to as lions and tigers but were likely pumas and jaguars, to be ceremonially chased. He marvels at Mesoamerican animal taming, which we saw began in the pyramid offerings at Teotihuacan over a millennium earlier than Tenochtitlan's zoo. On the following day of the festival, half the plaza was converted into a simulacrum of the historic city of Rhodes for a mock battle between Ottoman Turks and Christian Crusaders. Festivities also included bullfights and horse races in Tlatelolco's central plaza. Not to be outdone by their former foes, the Tlaxcalteca next held a *Moros y Cristianos* pageant centered on the mock conquest of Jerusalem.[104] It is worth distinguishing here the official transcript promulgated by Spanish colonial authorities versus the hidden transcript that Native Mesoamericans could promote more subtly, but whose symbolism would have been communicated within the community. In staging the conquest of Jerusalem, the Tlaxcalteca followed the lead of Viceroy Mendoza, who had juxtaposed the forces he led against those of Cortés in the pageant in Mexico City, to cast Cortés as the Great Sultan. Tlaxcalteca actors played his role, as well as those of Alvarado, Mendoza, and other Spaniards, and could thereby theatrically recreate a scene of poetic justice in which they, as Christian allies, participated in the conquest of Cortés and his forces.

Other than the elaborate scenery and costumes, these festivals contained hybrid material culture, such as using sunbaked clay balls packed with red pigment—likely the hematite or cinnabar that Mesoamericans used previously to adorn murals and burial remains—to act as special effects of artillery drawing blood during battle. These were also venues for elaborate feasts, and Díaz gives a sense of a New Spanish smorgasbord in listing Mesoamerican turkeys and beverages such as fruit wines (perhaps one being pulque), mead, and frothy cacao, along with Old World wines and foods such as hams, quail and pigeon pies, beef, garbanzos, cabbage, olives, cheese, artichokes, and almond cake. People use food to define their ethnicity, class, and other dimensions of identity today as in the past, and in early New Spain there existed a range of culinary choices with which to do so—beyond the maize for Natives, wheat for Spaniards divide. Mesoamericans adopted more pork and chicken as meat sources relative to grazing animals, as the first two were easier to manage and similar to peccary, turkey, and quail already present in the Americas.[105] Mesoamericans of lowland regions helped to create major new centers of production for Old World sugar and citrus fruits, and Africans in New Spain embraced local maize, chiles, and peanuts, which were then introduced into continental African cuisines. Cortés profited directly from the new agricultural economy, as among his territories was a large sugar plantation at Cuernavaca.

Many of the diverse identities and conflicting strategies in New Spain came to a head in the mid-1560s, with a crisis and failed revolt in Mexico City. Like many other historical crises, this one involved disputes over power and taxes. First, however, we should start with the death of Cortés, which occurred in 1547.[106] The conquistador had returned to Spain a second time and, following the battle against the Ottomans with his son Martín "the mestizo," planned to return to Mexico but was struck with dysentery and died as a result. Cortés was buried outside Seville in the town of Santiponce, adjacent to the former home of Hispano-Roman emperors at Italica. Not even a year later, Charles V denounced the conquistador for his massacres during the invasion and treatment of Native peoples as governor of New Spain. Two decades later the conquistador's remains were exhumed and shipped to Mexico City in what was planned as a grand affair but had been sullied by the complicity of his three sons—Martín, Martín "the mestizo," and Luís—in a plot to make the first Martín, who as legitimate heir had inherited his father's title of Marques of the Valley of Oaxaca, the king of New Spain. The planned rebellion came about in a power vacuum following the death of Viceroy Luís de Velasco, and it oddly joined the Mexica, who did not want to pay taxes, and the Spanish encomenderos, who wanted to keep their holdings.[107] Since the fall of Tenochtitlan, the Mexica had not paid taxes to the Crown in coin or goods because they labored to build the colonial capital and supply its clergy with goods. Franciscan friars and Viceroy Velasco agreed with the Mexica that they should continue to enjoy tax exemption, but by 1564 the Crown demanded 14,000 pesos annually plus maize from the Native population, causing significant unrest.

The planned rebellion was hatched by encomenderos, who sensed popular support that Martín "the mestizo" was sent to quell by colonial administrators, addressing a crowd in broken Nahuatl. The lead organizers were discovered and executed, but the Cortés brothers were charged with conspiring against the viceroyalty, resulting in the torture and imprisonment of Martín "the mestizo" and the exile of his fully Spanish half-brothers. Because of the conflictive backdrop, the remains of their conquistador father did not return to Mexico City for a gala reburial and were instead quietly interred in Texcoco. In 1629 they were moved to a Franciscan monastery in Mexico City and next, to commemorate 275 years since the meeting of Cortés and Moctezuma at the end of the Iztapalapa causeway, the Count of Revillagigedo ordered them moved to the Church and Hospital of Jesús Nazareno in the same area. The church and hospital had been commissioned by Cortés and are relatively austere, with a *mudéjar* ceiling adorning the nave (Figure 8.14). Following Mexico's independence from Spain, the mausoleum honoring Cortés was removed from the church and the presence of the conquistador's remains there was kept inconspicuous until the mid-twentieth century, when they were once again exhumed to be studied and authenticated.[108] The remains of Hernando Cortés are still there today, and have survived plots to steal and destroy them, as a means of Mexican national recompense.

Figure 8.14. Church and Hospital of Jesús Nazareno in Mexico City, where the conquistador Hernando Cortés is buried.

Photo by the author. Reproduction authorized by the Instituto Nacional de Antropología e Historia, Mexico.

From America to Europe and the World

Throughout this book, we have examined deep histories at the intermediate geographical scale of Mesoamerica, Iberia, and New Spain, but the creation of the last had undeniably global implications. New Spain became the hinge between the trans-Atlantic and trans-Pacific exchanges that created a truly global world system. We have primarily considered how Mesoamerica was transformed by these exchanges, but how did Mesoamericans contribute to changing the world order? It was not merely through cultivating many of the products of the Columbian exchange that would forever alter world cuisines and trade, though this of course was significant. Mesoamericans also traveled to Europe in greater numbers than did any other Native Americans. Some mestizo nobles created new elite lineages in Spain at the same time that New Spain provided a place to which Europeans could migrate. Not only did American gold and silver finance the religious wars of Europe, but syncretic traditions of Mexican Christianity also inflected counter-Reformation theology.

The relatively large numbers of Mesoamericans who traveled to Europe in the sixteenth century reflect a mix of the centrality of New Spain to the colonial Americas and the fact that Mesoamericans had a strongly established tradition of pilgrimage to exotic locations, which in a trans-Atlantic context included new "Tollans" (prestigious, archetypal cities) such as Seville and Madrid.[109] Matching the route of Cortés' invasion, a first group in 1519 consisted primarily of Totonacs from Cempoalla. In later journeys, however, the highest percentage of Mesoamerican travelers were Nahuas, particularly from Tlaxcala, Tenochtitlan, Texcoco, and Culhuacan. Europeans were struck by the physical characteristics, material culture, and dances and acrobatic feats performed in Spain by Mesoamericans.[110] The ambassador of Venice records seeing a 1522 performance in which Nahua warriors branded shields adorned with jaguar skin and feathers and machuahuitls stripped of their obsidian blades. A group of ballplayers had demonstrated the hip-ball game to Charles V in 1526, and two years later, the German author Christoph Weiditz illustrated a delegation that traveled with Cortés in a work that includes one of the few prime-of-life portraits of Cortés. Most of Europe was seeing elements of the New World for the first time. This group included some 70 to 100 Mesoamericans, with ballplayers, jugglers, and dwarves who performed for Charles V at Valladolid and later for Pope Clement VII. Europeans marveled at their athleticism but also at the previously unknown substance of rubber, which moved like nothing they had ever seen before (Figure 8.15). Mesoamericans had converted sap from the rubber tree into an elastic industrial product 3,500 years earlier, and the substance would change the global industrial age a couple of centuries later. Most of the members of the 1528 delegation returned home to Mesoamerica, but some may have stayed in Spain. Imitation team ballgames continued to be played decades later in Toledo and Burgos. A hybrid form of the *Moros y Cristianos* dance also developed in Spain to mythologize the conquest of Mexico.[111]

The Spanish Crown legalized free migration of mestizos in 1524 and generally welcomed Native elites until 1575, when migration was temporarily halted. Existing mestizo elites in Spain formed a new type of aristocracy, whereas non-elites often became an urban poor who took up trades and could occasionally ascend to a middle-class existence.[112] The Tlaxcalteca were the most avid petitioners of rights and titles and in 1535 were successful in elevating their capital settlement to the status of Loyal City of Tlaxcala, which came with its own set of privileges. In 1547, four K'ekchi' Maya rulers traveled from highland Guatemala to make a parallel petition to the ones

Figure 8.15. Mesoamerican ballplayers in Spain demonstrating the hip-ball game and elastic properties of rubber, previously unknown to Europeans.
Illustrated by Christoph Weiditz. Alamy Stock Photos.

being put forward by Las Casas and Vitoria to end the abuses of the encomienda. They presented Phillip II, serving as regent, with 2,000 feathers from quetzals and other colorful birds of their homeland. Phillip II became an avid collector of materials from his domains. He housed objects in vast reliquaries and storerooms in the Royal Alcazar in Madrid, which burned in the early eighteenth century, losing much of that collection, and in the Escorial north of the capital, which still maintains its collections.

Among the Mesoamerican objects that Phillip II owned were obsidian mirrors, which were also collected by the Elizabethan mathematician Dr. John Dee, who used one to divine a successful political union between England and Spain through the marriage of the king and Mary Tudor.[113] Phillip may have given Dee the mirror, or Dee may have acquired one through English or French pirates who intercepted an earlier treasure ship sent by Cortés to Spain. In either case, both of these men viewed themselves as pious Christians and do not seem to have been troubled by the pre-Hispanic connotations of Mesoamerican mirrors, just as friars in New Spain permitted obsidian mirrors to serve as symbols of Christ's resplendence on atrial crosses. Another potential way in which Mesoamerican Christianity affected Europe was in the new emphasis on Christ's heart in devotion to the Sacred Heart and its artistic depiction during the Counter-Reformation, which grew in popularity within the syncretic milieu of New Spain and returned reinvigorated across the Atlantic to Europe.[114] Imagery of the Sacred Heart reflected a baroque religious sensibility and was spread particularly by Mexican Jesuits beginning in the late seventeenth and early eighteenth century before Charles III called for the order's expulsion from Spanish America in 1767. The idea that the New World opened up new forms of spirituality and healing is also supported by the fact that plants with purported medicinal properties spread more quickly in Europe than those considered wholly as foods.[115] Europeans were particularly wary of nightshades, so the dramatic transformation that potatoes and tomatoes had in European cuisine took longer to develop, whereas Europeans more quickly embraced non-staples such as chiles, chocolate, and tobacco.

The forging of New Spain saw transplanted species, styles, and people who drew from millennia of history on two sides of the Atlantic and contributed to shaping our globalized world. Transplanted species often thrive in new environments when they escape the plagues and parasites that evolved with them in their homelands. This explains why today 98 percent of the world's rubber is produced outside of the Americas, even though no one outside the Western Hemisphere had seen it until Mesoamerican ballplayers played in Spanish courts, and half the world's sugar and coffee, both Old World crops, are grown in the Americas.[116] When for the quincentennial of the Columbian exchange Carlos Fuentes framed the metaphor of mirrors in reflecting this trans-Atlantic encounter, from Aztec obsidian mirrors to Velázquez's painting *Las Meninas*, he pondered the construction of Spanish-American identity within this early period of global connectivity. It is apparent throughout that masterpiece of Spanish Golden Age painting: in the red curtains of the background that were dyed with Mexican cochineal and especially in the foreground, where the Infanta Margarita in the center of the painting is presented with a Mexican-style cup, perhaps containing a chocolate drink, on a silver platter whose ore was doubtless mined somewhere in the Americas.[117]

Deep histories of the new global world order are also apparent in murals that are much less well known than *Las Meninas*, painted in Cáceres, the former Roman town and home of the conquistador Juan Cano (Figure 8.16). The Palace of Toledo-Moctezuma was initially constructed in the fifteenth

Figure 8.16. Murals from two rooms of the Palace of Toledo-Moctezuma in Cáceres, Spain, celebrating the line of Mexican nobility by depicting Mexica emperors and the line of Castilian nobility by depicting Roman emperors.
Photo by the author.

century, but the hybrid elements of a mestizo aristocracy date from the late sixteenth century.[118] Juan de Moctezuma Cano, the son of Doña Isabel de Moctezuma (Tecuichpochtzin) and Juan Cano, married the Extremaduran noblewoman Elvira de Toledo from Cáceres and returned to his paternal family home. The noble titles of these lineages were celebrated by the couple and their descendants in the murals, crests sculpted on the sides of the palace, and by other furnishings. In depicting parallel sequences of Roman emperors and Mexica emperors in adjacent rooms, the family projected claims to their trans-Atlantic pedigrees, as well as the deep and entangled layers of Spanish and Mexican history.

Notes

Chapter 1

1. Fuentes (1992: 313) was commenting on the murals of José Clemente Orozco in this quote.
2. Michener 1968: 77.
3. Celestino Pérez and Rodríguez González 2017; Edmondson 2011; Rodríguez González 2018; Rodríguez Gordillo 2015.
4. Marquina 1979; Solis et al. 2006; Uruñuela et al. 2009.
5. Plunket and Uruñuela 2017, 2018; Townsend 2017: 17–52.
6. Camelo 2001; McCafferty 2000, 2016; Nicholson 2001b; Rojas 1985; for an eyewitness account on the high end of mortality figures, the conquistador Bernardino Vázquez de Tapia (1972: 82) answered to one of the questions in a series of them on Cortés' conduct that 4,000–5,000 unarmed Choluteca were massacred in the city's sacred precinct and over 20,000 total died in the fighting.
7. Martínez 1990: 147–201; Mora Rodríguez 2013.
8. Wright 2008.
9. Prescott (1843) provided a canonical great-man history for an Anglophone audience.
10. Barlow 1945.
11. Lockhart 1993; Oudijk 2012; Oudijk and Restall 2007, 2008; Restall 2003; Rojas 2011.
12. Brian et al. 2015; Lee and Brokaw 2014.
13. Schwartz 2000; Townsend 2017: 121–123.
14. Dietler 2009; Glick et al. 2018.
15. On the New Conquest History, see Restall (2003, 2012) and Townsend (2003).
16. Foster 1960; see also Vicens Vives (1972) for a compilation that includes Spain and the Americas, but is not explicitly comparative.
17. Fuentes 1992.
18. For an overview of big history or macro-history as a field of study, see Christian (2017). For archaeology as big history, see Fagan (2020). Some examples of popular "big histories" written in the last few decades include *Guns, Germs, and Steel: The Fates of Human Societies* (Diamond 1997); *Why the West Rules—For Now: The Patterns of History, and What They Reveal about the Future* (Morris 2010); *Why Nations Fail: The Origins of Power, Prosperity, and Poverty* (Acemoglu and Robinson 2013); and *Why Did Europe Conquer the World?*

(Thompson 2015). Among these authors, only Morris is a specialist in ancient history and archaeology (see also Morris 2015). He emphasizes certain long-term economic and technological processes similar to portions of the first half of this book, but with a Eurasian focus, rather than the more intermediate and comparative scale I employ here. I use the term "deep history" most similarly to its use by Shryock and Smail (2011) and their contributors in that I seek to emphasize temporal depth studied through interdisciplinary means, rather than the "thick description" or "close reading" of textually based historians, though I use these methods somewhat more for later chapters in which much of the evidence is text-based. My emphasis on material culture also overlaps with the notion within archaeology of sites as metaphorical palimpsests (see Bailey 2007). For other deep histories of two key bodies of water in this story, the Mediterranean and Atlantic, see Abulafia (2003, 2011), Braudel (1972), and Winchester (2010). And for well-researched and highly readable overviews of the Americas before and after Columbus, see the books *1491* and *1493* by Charles Mann (2005, 2011).

19. See contributions in Alexander and Kepecs (2018) for an archaeology of the *longue durée* in Mesoamerica attempting to mitigate such elite bias.
20. Recent conquest histories focused specifically on Aztec Mexico include Thomas (1993), Hassig (2006), and Restall (2018).
21. Scheidel 2016.
22. Mahoney (2000: 507–508) provides a cogent argument for defining path dependence in historical development of forms of social organization as, "specifically those historical sequences in which contingent events set into motion institutional patterns or event chains that have deterministic properties. The identification of path dependence therefore involves both tracing a given outcome back to a particular set of historical events, and showing how these events are themselves contingent occurrences that cannot be explained on the basis of prior historical conditions."
23. Key translations of these Native perspectives, especially Book XII of the *Florentine Codex*, have been provided by López Portilla (1966), Anderson and Dibble (1975), Lockhart (1993), and Restall et al. (2005: 23–61).
24. Cummins 1995: 56.

Chapter 2

1. Wolf (1959: 1), who titled his book *Sons of the Shaking Earth*, the inspiration for a section head in this chapter.
2. Tylor 1861, 1867. Tylor was a leading cultural evolutionist of the nineteenth century who classified societies into categories such as savagery, barbarism, and civilization, based on criteria exhibiting a strong northern European bias and racialist overtones. Contemporary usage, which I follow in the title and content of this chapter and the next, strives for neutrality in regard to terminology and the valuation of cultural traits, but retains the term "evolution" for describing

broad processes of change through time and what mechanisms may drive them. In this broad sense it includes major societal transformations such as a shift from foraging to farming and smaller scale societies to larger scale ones, but can also include cases of political collapse, demographic decline, and specific divergences in the lifeways of groups of people, in language, thought, or other cultural norms.

3. The crumpled paper ball story is likely apocryphal, but illustrates the Spanish recognition of Mexico's mountainous terrain. Cortés 1519/1986: 29; Melville 2000: 215–216.
4. Sanders (1956) termed this the "Mesoamerican Symbiotic Region."
5. Kirchhoff 1943; see Runggaldier (2014) for the history of the term "Mesoamerica" and the problems and potentials in its usage.
6. Oudijk and Restall 2007, 2008.
7. Carballo 2012; Maldonado 2017; Thibodeau et al. 2015.
8. The broadly shared cosmovision of Mesoamerican peoples is known as its *nucleo duro*, or "hard nucleus" (Carrasco 2014: 5, 2017; López Austin 2001; López Austin and López Luján 2009: 19).
9. Kaufman and Justeson 2009.
10. See Wright-Carr (2015) for an analysis of central Mexican loan translations (calques), which underscores the broadly shared cultural concepts between Nahuatl and Otomi in particular.
11. Plunket and Uruñuela 2012.
12. Cucina 2014; Morales-Arce et al. 2019; Spence et al. 2005.
13. Bierhorst 1992: 142–149.
14. Gamio et al. 1921; see also Carballo 2017.
15. For a general overview, see Bellwood (2014: 83–93).
16. The best chronological treatment and synthetic overview of pre-Hispanic Mesoamerica is provided by Evans (2013).
17. For an overview, see Bellwood (2005).
18. Marcus and Flannery 1996: 64–65.
19. Piperno 2011.
20. Jaenicke-Després and Smith 2006; Kennett et al. 2017.
21. Shady Solis 2006.
22. Lesure 2008.
23. Piperno and Smith 2012.
24. Robin 2006.
25. Parsons 2010.
26. López Austin 1997.
27. Lesure 2011.
28. Tarkanian and Hosler 2011.
29. Cyphers and Di Castro 2009.
30. Favila Vázquez 2016: 36–43.
31. Cyphers and Hirth 2016.
32. Grove and Gillespie 2009.

33. Wendt 2009.
34. Blanton et al. 2005. In this discussion I use a broader, functional definition of the term "urban" to designate settlements where certain activities take place that do not occur in more rural settings, necessitating that populations from those settings travel to the urban center. I use a more restrictive definition of the term "city" to designate urban centers with densely nucleated populations numbering in the tens of thousands and serving many more social functions than towns or other smaller urban centers.
35. Ramírez 2012; Sanders et al. 1979.
36. Carballo 2016.
37. Serra Puche et al. 2001.
38. Serra Puche 2005.
39. Plunket and Uruñuela 1998, 2005, 2008, 2012, 2018.
40. Pastrana and Fournier 1997; Ramírez 2012.
41. Marcus and Flannery 1996: 172–191.
42. Freidel 2010.
43. Aveni 2001.
44. Rossi 2018; Saturn et al. 2017.
45. McKillop 2010.
46. Golitko et al. 2012.
47. Budar 2017.
48. Cowgill (2015) presents the most recent book-length synthesis of Teotihuacan.
49. Carballo 2016: 127–140, 180–195.
50. Teotihuacan and other sites in central Mexico covered by systematic archaeological survey have sound population estimates, when not obscured by modern occupation, because the semi-arid landscape makes for good visibility of artifacts and the low rises of buried structures. For the Teotihuacan Mapping Project, see Millon (1973). For the latest population estimate for the city, based on GIS analyses of the map and currently excavated apartment compounds, see Smith et al. (2019).
51. Aguirre-Samuido et al. 2017; Spence et al. 2005.
52. Millon 1988; Cowgill 2015.
53. Levine and Carballo 2014; Saunders 2001.
54. Pastrana and Domínguez 2009; Carballo 2013a.
55. García-Des Lauriers 2008; Carballo 2011.
56. Hassig 1992: Ch. 4.
57. Sugiyama et al. 2015; Sugiyama 2005.
58. Hirth et al. 2019.
59. Smith 2020.
60. Sugiyama 2005.
61. Millon 1988: 153.
62. For the Moon Pyramid, see Sugiyama and Cabrera (2007); for the Tlajinga district, see Carballo et al. (2019).
63. See Cowgill (2012) for a comparison.
64. Parsons and Sugiura 2012.

65. See Webster (2018) for a comprehensive overview of Classic Maya populations. He has more conservative estimates than many of his colleagues and posits that approximately one million people resided in the Classic period Maya lowlands. Perhaps five times this figure resided in Classic period Mesoamerica as a whole.
66. Brittenham 2015.
67. See Piña Chan (1998) for sources on Cacaxtla, and Plunket and Uruñuela (2005, 2008, 2018; Uruñuela et al. 2009) on Cholula.
68. Smith 2000.
69. Andrews and Hirth 2006: 252–256.
70. Barba and Cordova 2010.
71. Helan and Cobean 2012.
72. Boone 2000.
73. Nicholson 2001a, 2001b; for native Mesoamerican and Spanish blending of mythic and historical narratives into "mythistory," see Tedlock (1985) and Restall (2003).
74. See López Austin (1993) for the concept of *hombre-dios* in Mesoamerican mythology.
75. López Luján and López Austin 2009.
76. Plunket and Uruñuela 2016.
77. Smith and Montiel 2001.
78. Hosler 1995; Maldonado 2012.
79. Hassig 1992; Helmke 2019.
80. Carballo 2012, 2013b.

Chapter 3

1. Trend 1967: 1.
2. For the original see Stesichoros in Davies (1991: 154); see also Celestino and López-Ruiz (2016: 26).
3. Celestino Pérez 2008: 98–103; Celestino and López-Ruiz 2016: 71, 96–104; Cunliffe 2001: 41, 2017: 19; Turnquist 1974.
4. I use a somewhat larger designation of western Iberia than Fernández (2017) in including the southwest to the Strait of Gibraltar.
5. Gracia Alonso 2008.
6. Harrison 1988: 19; Ruiz 2007: 6–13.
7. Foster 1960: 24–25, 51.
8. Glick 1996, 2005.
9. Runnels et al. 2014.
10. Richerson et al. 2001.
11. Agricultural origins in the Fertile Crescent and its spread through the Mediterranean are summarized by Zeder (2008, 2011); for its beginnings and later spread through Iberia, see Zilhão (2001) and Buxó (2009), respectively.

12. See Kohler et al. (2017) and contributions in Kohler and Smith (2018) for comparative studies of social inequality in early societies that highlight the greater levels of inequality in Eurasian societies relative to those of the Americas, and the likely contribution of the presence in Eurasia of large domesticated animals to these differences.
13. Gilman 1987.
14. Calvín Velasco 2014.
15. Lozano et al. 2014.
16. Cunliffe 2001: 64–70; 2017: 259–285.
17. See Celestino and López-Ruiz (2016); Celestino Pérez and Rodríguez González (2017); contributions in Dietler and López-Ruiz (2009); Ruiz Gálvez (2015).
18. Dietler 2009: 5.
19. Cunliffe 2001: 296; González-Ruibal 2004, 2008: 900.
20. Celestino and López-Ruiz 2016: 131–133; Cunliffe 2017: 223–224; Hoyos 2010: 1.
21. Alternatively, the allusion to red may have had something to do with the land of the setting sun in the West (see Celestino and López-Ruiz 2016: Ch. 4).
22. Harrison 1988: 124.
23. Celestino and López-Ruiz 2016: 228. Baal translates generally as "lord" and possessed attributes that appear to have inspired the Hebrew understanding of Yahweh (Day 2002; Kugel 2004).
24. Herodotus Book 4.8 (1987: 282).
25. López-Ruiz 2009; Turnquist 1974.
26. Maya Torcelly et al. 2015.
27. Calero et al. 2015; Gener Basallote et al. 2014.
28. Celestino and López-Ruiz 2016: 21, 302.
29. Eshel et al. 2019.
30. Harrison 1988: 54.
31. See also Celestino Pérez (2008); Delgado Hervás (2008); contribution in Dietler (2009); Harrison (1988: Ch. 4).
32. Cunliffe 2001: 302–310.
33. González-Ruibal 2004: 287.
34. González-Ruibal 2004: 289; Ruiz Gálvez 2015: 2004. Cunliffe (2017: 207) wonders whether the depiction could be of Mycenean Greek origin instead of Phoenician, but this is a less accepted identification. In any case, galleys of the eastern Mediterranean and Aegean were technologically similar at this time.
35. Arruda 2009.
36. Celestino and López-Ruiz 2016: 147–148; González-Ruibal 2004.
37. Cunliffe 2001: 84–90; Hoyos 2010: 51–55.
38. Cunliffe 2017: 283–288, 306–307; González-Ruibal 2004.
39. Celestino and López-Ruiz 2016: 163–170; Celestino Pérez 2009: 233–238.
40. Celestino Pérez 2008; Celestino Pérez et al. 2017; Rodríguez González 2018.
41. Celestino Pérez 2009: 241–245; Celestino Pérez and Rodríguez González 2017; Celestino and López-Ruiz 2016: 244–253.
42. Deamos 2009: 199; Hoyos 2010: 8; Rodríguez González and Celestino Pérez 2017.

43. Harrison 1988: 136.
44. Rodríguez-Corral 2012.
45. González-Rubial 2006.
46. Gracia Alonso 2008: 890–896; Hoyos 2010: 194–210.
47. Almargo Gorbea 2014.
48. Pérez García and Sánchez-Palencia Ramos 1992: 861; Villalibre 2005; Wilson 2012.
49. Dietler 2009: 30; Pohl and Lyon (ed.) 2016; Rouillard 2009 135–136.
50. Westner et al. 2017.
51. Edmondson 2014 (especially pp. 38–39 on *mestizaje*); González-Ruibal 2008 (for the northwest); Scullard 1982: 252–253.
52. Cunliffe 2001: 365–384; Leveau 2007.
53. Edmondson 2011: 38; Scullard 1982: 86–89.
54. Olivares Pedreño 2006.
55. On the late Roman importance of Lugo within northwest Iberia, see Fernández (2017), Pérez Macías et al. (2013), and Sánchez Pardo (2012).
56. Cunliffe 2001: 374–377; Pérez García and Sánchez-Palencia Ramos 1992; Villalibre 2005; Wilson 2012: 137.
57. López-Merino et al. 2014.
58. Edmondson 2011, 2016a.
59. Maya et al. 2015.
60. Beard 2015: 67, 418–420.
61. Everitt 2009: 3–10, 55–56.
62. Boatwright 2002: 268.
63. Boatwright 2000: 12, 206. This book provides a comprehensive perspective of Hadrian's projects and urban legacy. Some of the discrepancy between Trajan and Hadrian is surely sample bias, but the shift in attention from military conquest to building programs is clear.
64. Futrell 1997: 55–58, 249n20; Futrell makes the case that the spectacle of gladiatorial combat (the *munera*) can be productively analyzed as an institution of human sacrifice in honor of the state and imperial cult.
65. Jiménez and Carrillo 2011.
66. Scheidel 2007.
67. Webster's (2018) reconstruction of Classic period Maya population would suggest a total Mesoamerican population approximately half as large as in Roman Hispania.
68. Marciniak et al. 2018; Sallares 2002: 242.
69. Quiroga and Lovelle 1999; Valdeón Baruque 2008: 39.
70. Edmondson 2016b.
71. Through the Gothic power struggles, Iberia was partly conquered by Vandals after 409, then to a greater degree by the Suevi after 439. Next the Visigoths invaded and pushed Suevi to northwest after 456. They controlled much of the peninsula by 483, when King Euric records in an inscription that he had a bridge at Mérida repaired. The early Visigoths were based mostly in Gaul, however, and when the Ostrogoths in Italy (led by Theoderic) established a regency for the Visigothic king Amalaric, Spain was effectively ruled from the Italian peninsula until Theoderic died in 526 (see Wickham 2009: 131).

72. The term *Reconquista* is problematic, which is why I present it italicized throughout. Although the Iberian peninsula was unified as Roman Hispania, and more weakly under the Visigoths, various Muslim forces ruled over half of it for five centuries. The term *Reconquista* therefore implies more cultural and political continuity and a shorter duration than what was actually the case. Likewise, the traditionally used term "Moor" is rarely used in contemporary scholarship because it gives the false impression that most Muslims were foreigners (Catlos 2018: 3) and being derived from Mauritania does not account for Arabic influence. I restrict it to the festival of *Moros y Cristianos*, which was exported to Spanish America.
73. Fernández provides a detailed treatment of western Iberia from late Roman to Visigothic times, which I rely on heavily for this section.
74. Reynolds 2015.
75. Fernández 2017: 180.
76. Di Sciacca 2008: 3–15.
77. Ford 1970: 18–21.
78. Stevens 1980.
79. Williams 1997.
80. Catlos 2018; Miteva 2015.
81. Fletcher 1989: 12–16.
82. Wickham 2009: 343–345.
83. Cunliffe 2017: 10.
84. Cunliffe 2017: 477–510.
85. Dunmire 2004: 13–20.
86. Glick 1996, 2005: 974–986.
87. Foster 1960: 27.
88. Sayahi and Thomas 2005.
89. Sánchez Pardo 2012; Williams 1997: 18.
90. Suárez Otero 2014.
91. Ruiz 2007: 18.
92. Calleja Puerto 2017; Fernández Gallardo 2005; Moral García 2015.
93. Fletcher 1989; Smith 1983.
94. Laredo Quesada 2018: 35.
95. Ruiz 2007: 169.
96. Jay 2002: 1–10.
97. Corzo Sánchez 2004.

Chapter 4

1. Scheidel 2016: 29.
2. Valdeón Baruque 2008: 94.
3. Following Smith and Peregrine (2012) on methods of comparison, this chapter would be classified as an intensive comparison, with two cases and multiple variables, but one that is more qualitative than quantitative.

4. On migrations, see Smith (1984). The term Aztlan is usually glossed following the clearly identifiable suffix translating as "place of abundance" and the disputed prefix that could be "herons/egrets" or "whiteness." The first would suggest a place near water, but perhaps could serve both ways, as egrets are white. The color association is interesting because west and north are the directions most associated with the color white in Native cosmologies. For the Aztecs and contemporary Nahuas, West is more typically white (e.g., Ferrer 2000), but either may index a northwestern place of origin.
5. Aguilera 1984.
6. Overholtzer and De Lucia 2016.
7. See Dugan Iverson (2017) for the strategic employment of Toltec to be both unspecific ("civilized") and historically centered on the Early Postclassic inhabitants of Tula, and Smith (2008: 71–89) on the Aztec fusion of Toltec and Chichimec identities and the founding rituals for Aztec urban centers.
8. Smith 1984. The Michoque are also known as the Tarascans, who formed the largest rival empire to the Aztecs with its core in Michoacan, but are better known by their self-identification Purépecha.
9. Hassig (1992) reviews the development of Mesoamerican weaponry and debates for the introduction of the bow and arrow throughout the volume (see, e.g., 235–236). Many of these debates revolve around art and imagery, which may have been conservative in depicting atlatls and darts as the more prestigious projectile technology, and considerations of the size of points—larger for spears, smaller for arrows, intermediate for darts. We currently lack a systematic study of breakage patterns on smaller projectile points that could be large arrowheads or small dart points in order to estimate their velocity on impact, which should be higher for arrows.
10. Carrasco 2000; Nicholson 2001. Because of the dates, the narrative is most typically associated with Tula, but one wonders if the earlier desecration of the Feathered Serpent Pyramid at Teotihuacan was part of this historical memory.
11. Boone 2017: 121.
12. Matos Moctezuma 1988; López Austin and López Luján 2009.
13. Galindo Leal, Sarukhán Kermez, and Wright Carr 2017. These authors favor an etymology for the term Mexico as having derived from the Nahuatl word for moon (*metzli*), and signifying something like "in the heart of the moon," involving a lunar association for Lake Texcoco, in which Tenochtitlan was situated. Tenochtitlan, in turn, translates as "near [-*tlan*] the stone [*tetl*] pricky-pear cacti [*nochtli*]."
14. Umburger 2015. Another illustration of this substitution is that the dual temple of Tenayuca, predating Tenochtitlan's, appears to have been dedicated to Tlaloc and Tetzcatlipoca (Rojas 2012: 19)
15. Rojas 2012: 190.
16. Edmondson 2016: 71; see also Dietler (2009) on the preferred model of Rome versus earlier colonizers, such as the Phoenicians and Greeks.
17. Though the play was written decades after the Reconquista, see Simerka (1998) on the ambiguities between imperial glories and freedom in *La Numancia* by Cervantes.

18. Ruiz 2007: 119; Torró 2018.
19. Fernández Gallardo 2005.
20. Alibhai 2008.
21. Ruiz 2007: 193.
22. Remensnyder 2014: 89.
23. Trend 1967: 50–52; Ruiz 2007: 139–163.
24. Tarradell 1972: 122.
25. Hirth (2016) and Nichols et al. (2017) provide recent syntheses on the Aztec economy; for Spain, see Lader Quesada (2017: 99–118) and Ruiz (2007).
26. Smith and Hicks 2017.
27. Fargher et al. 2017a.
28. For population estimates of the Late Postclassic Basin of Mexico, Tenochtitlan, and other Aztec cities see Calnek 2003; Rojas 2012: 50–53; Sanders, Parsons, and Santley 1979; Smith 1994, 2008, 2017a, 2017b.
29. Charlton et al. 2000, 2018; Smith et al. 2013.
30. O'Flanagan 2008: 182–183.
31. Contributions in Sánchez Gamero (2017) commemorate the life and impact of Cisneros on the quincentennial of his death.
32. Hirth 2016: 11–12.
33. Rius 1972: 369–375.
34. For Aztec luxury goods and systems of value, see Berdan (1992); Maldonado (2012); Richter (2017).
35. See Gutiérez (2013) for a nicely documented example from the province of Tlapa, and on the shared linguistic roots between tribute (*tequitl*) and to negotiate (*tequiti*), p. 163.
36. Hicks 1999.
37. Hassig 2016a; Lockhart 1992: 106–107; Rojas 2011.
38. López Luján 2018.
39. Scheidel 2016.
40. On the populations of Iberian kingdoms, compare Ladero Quesada (2018: 43) and Ruiz (2007: 32).
41. Mayoral et al. 2012
42. Ladero Quesada 2018: 238–250; Ruiz 2007: 77–78, 97.
43. Sabloff 2019.
44. Glick 1996: 6, 15.
45. Baucells Mesa 2013; Cunliffe 2017: 510–513; Ladero Quesada 2018: 480–497.
46. Restall and Fernández-Armesto 2012: 25.
47. Heywood and Thornton 2007.
48. Townsend 2006: 19–28.
49. Klemm 1964: 79–107.
50. Cunliffe 2001: 77–78, 2017: 506–510; McGrail 2004: 243–248; O'Flanagan 2008: 34–35; O'Scanlan 1831/2003.
51. See Cañizares-Esguerra 2004 on Iberian science of the period; Winchester 2010: 112.
52. Cunliffe 2017: 531–534; Ladero Quesada 2018: 497–500.

53. Davies 1956; Laredo Quesada 2008: 29; Smith 2014.
54. McGrail 2009: 395–430.
55. Biar and Favila Vázquez 2016; Conway 2012.
56. Cervera 2011: 142–147; Favila Vázquez 2014.
57. González Arévalo 2018.
58. Bruhn de Hoffmeyer 1985; Hassig 2006: 11; Restall and Fernández-Armesto 2012: 52–55.
59. Pastrana and Carballo 2017: 337.
60. Quigley 1983: 43.
61. Cervera 2011; Hassig 1992, 2016b; Helmke 2019.
62. Clendinnen 1991a: 115–116.
63. Restall (2018: 317) comments: "By and large both urban and rural populations did not need to live in fear of sudden attack, slaughter, and enslavement—not until 1519, that is."
64. Postigo Castellanos 1985; Torró 2018.
65. Ladero Quesada 2018: 33.
66. Cervera Obregón 2011: 72–78.
67. López Luján (2006) favors a broader function of the House of the Eagles at the Great Pyramid than other scholars who link it wholly with the Eagle knights. He considers it as a combined ritual-military space (a *Tlacochcalco* or "House of Darts"), which we have seen also likely has earlier analogs at Tula and Teotihuacan.
68. Mendoza 1977.
69. Pohl and Lyons 2016; Restall 2003: 68.
70. Harris 2000.
71. Murphy 2012: 9–10.
72. See Carrasco (1999, 2008b) on Aztec sacrifice, better termed debt payment (*nextlaoalli*), and Innes (1969: 20) and Restall (2018: 89–90) for other comparisons with Spanish and other European societies.
73. Carballo 2018.
74. García 1991: 55–69; Peterson 2014; Remensnyder 2014: 82–83.
75. Scholars debate whether the term *mecatl* ("rope" or "cord") has the sense elite lineage or actual cords used as whips in rituals of penance.
76. Ruiz 2007: 170.
77. Pagden (1986: xlvi–xlviii) raises some doubt that Cortés even studied at Salamanca for the two years usually ascribed to him and concludes that if he did, he was only exposed to terse legal texts and not classical historians and rhetoricians that students of theology, or perhaps even more advanced students of law, encountered as part of their curricula.
78. *Estatvtos hechos por la Vniversidad de Salamanca 1625* (Rodríguez-San Pedro, ed., 1990); for school of law curriculum, see especially pp. 156–158; for school of theology curriculum, see especially pp. 170–174; for key authors such as Aristotle, Cicero, Quintilian, and St. Thomas Aquinas, see pp. 267, 314.
79. For secondary sources on the Salamanca curriculum of the time, see Barrientos García (2006) on theology; Codoñer Merino (2006) on Latin humanities; and Peset and Alonso Romero (2006) on law.
80. Ruiz 2007: 185.

81. Abbott 1996: 6–9; Ladero Quesada 2018: 27; Trend 1967: 54.
82. Calnek 1988; Rossi 2018.
83. Hassig 2016.
84. Joyce 2000; see Torquemada (1995: 137–147) for coeducational training in ceremonial life.
85. Barrera Rodríguez and López Arenas 2008.
86. León-Portilla 2003.

Chapter 5

1. Lockhart 1993: 80.
2. Amaya Topete 1958.
3. Townsend 2017: 121–123.
4. Hanke 1965: 8–10.
5. See Cortés (2008), Oudijk and Castañeda de la Paz (2017: 161–163), and Townsend (2003) for succinct overviews of sixteenth- and early seventeenth-century sources.
6. Cortés 1986. Cortés' second and third letters were first published in 1523 from Seville and have been reproduced numerous times since. A mixed-author account of the petition by the town council (*cabildo*) that Cortés convened at Veracruz is often substituted as the first letter (see Schwaller 2014).
7. López de Gómara 1969, 1988. Cortés and Gómara first met in 1541 when both were part of Charles V's failed invasion against the Ottomans at Algiers. I follow common usage in referring to Cortés' biographer as Gómara, his second surname, but list him in the bibliography using both surnames.
8. Adorno 2008; Díaz del Castillo 1844/2017, 1956, 2008. Díaz de Castillo channels the argument of Juan Gines de Sepúlveda, the major adversary of Las Casas in a trans-Atlantic debate regarding whether Spain's wars of conquest in the Americas were morally defensible, arguing that the invasion of Mesoamerica and other formerly autonomous regions complied with Classical and Christian notions of "just war."
9. Díaz del Castillo 1844/2017: 131.
10. Carrasco 2008: xiv; Simpson 1969: xviii.
11. A number of these accounts are assembled by de Fuentes (1963).
12. Martínez Barcas 2006. Cano's account provides an interesting perspective that straddles the Spanish and Aztec worlds because he married the Mexica princess Doña Isabel Moctezuma and wanted to legitimize claims to land and titles for his mestizo family. Cano first journeyed to Mexico with the mission led by Pánfilo de Narváez to stop Cortés, but later joined him for the Spanish-Mexica war. Cano was also less deferential to Cortés as within Extremadura his family, from Cáceres, outranked Cortés'.
13. Cervantes de Salazar 2006.
14. Villella (2016) covers a number of Mesoamerican elites who served as informants for chronicles authored by Spaniards.

15. Muñoz Camargo 2000; Taladoire 2017: 52–56. All the original versions of the *Lienzo de Tlaxcala* have been lost, but later copies present rich, hybrid imagery depicting the Tlaxcalteca alliance with the Spanish and the invaluable aid they provided during decisive battles in wars against the Aztecs, Mayas, and other groups.
16. Boone 1998.
17. Brian et al. 2015. Alva Ixtlilxochitl's account is similar to the Tlaxcalteca appeals to the Spanish Crown on the basis of having assisted in the conquest, but the Texcocoan alliance with the allied Spanish-Tlaxcalteca forces came later, when the war of conquest became exclusively versus the Mexica twin cities of Tenochtitlan and Tlatelolco.
18. Alvarado Tezozomoc 1878.
19. Hassig (2006) and Restall (2018) provide accessible timelines of the Aztec conquest.
20. Laredo Quesada 2008; McClure, n.d.; O'Flanagan 2008: 46–47.
21. O'Flanagan 2008: 21–22, 43, 117.
22. López de Gómara 1988: 8.
23. See Keegan and Hofman (2017) on Precolumbian cultures of the Caribbean, including pp. 11–15 on peoples and the problematic nature of ethnonyms. The Taíno were the largest group of the Greater Antilles, but the Macoris were another language group on Hispaniola, and the Carib, with more recent origins in northern South America, were concentrated primarily on islands of the Lesser Antilles.
24. Burkholder et al. 2018: 21–23; Taladoire 2017: 96–102. Isabela and Ferdinand originally granted Columbus wide leeway to govern the Indies during his first two voyages, making no prohibition of enslaving the Native population. This changed with the third voyage (1498–1500), when they directed him to abandon the model of a trading settlement to follow the *Reconquista* model of autonomous free towns with elected councils, and sent a new governor, who had Columbus arrested. He never governed again, but his son did.
25. Laredo Quesada 2008: 29, 59.
26. Glick 1996, 2005; Himmerich y Valencia 1991.
27. Laredo Quesada 2008: 46–48. Based on his analysis of the House of Trade archives, the author argues the first Dominicans to Hispaniola may have arrived in 1509, rather than the oft cited date of 1510, provided by Las Casas.
28. Restall 2019.
29. Knight 2010.
30. Jay 2002: 18.
31. Altamira 1938; Jay 2002: 29–30.
32. Vizuete Mendoza 2017.
33. Dunmire 2004: 95–105.
34. Faudree 2013.
35. Clendinnen 2003: 3–19.
36. Chatters et al. 2014; Cucina 2014; Cucina et al. 2008.
37. Sabloff and Rathje 1975; Townsend (2006: 25) notes that the ethnonym Chontal comes from the Nahuatl term *chontalli*, meaning "foreigners"—Putun is a Mayan designation.
38. Folan et al. 2012.
39. Díaz 2008: 3–4.

40. Díaz 2008: 5; Taladoire 2017: 28. These names are alternatively given as Julianillo and Melchior or Melchorejo.
41. Vázquez de Tapia 1972: 25–27.
42. Díaz in de Fuentes 1963: 11.
43. Hassig 2006: 50–53.
44. Brian et al. 2015: 19.
45. López de Gómara 1964: 15–18.
46. Pagden 1986; Restall 2018: 167–191.
47. Elliott 1967, 1986.
48. Thomas 1993: 150–154; a notable exception was Garay, the adelantado and governor of Jamaica, who was Basque, and Parilla (1992: 18) contends that the friar Juan Díaz was originally from Galicia, before going to Seville.
49. Restall 2003: 54–63.
50. Alberro 2015.
51. Díaz 1956: 38–39, 2008: 29–30 (quotations from 1956: 39).
52. López de Gómara 1964: 23. Total European population in the Caribbean at this time is reported by Townsend (2006: 38).
53. Sabloff and Rathje 1975.
54. Díaz 2008: 28–29.
55. Lothrop 1924; Remensnyder 2014: 240–242.
56. Díaz 2008: 34–36.
57. de Tapia in de Fuentes (1963: 22); López de Gómara (1964: 36–37); see Castro (2002) on the etymologies of "shark" and *tiburón* and Newman (2016) on shark fishing and mythology.
58. Brinton 1896; Chávez Jiménez 2007.
59. Chardon 1980.
60. Díaz 2008: 36–47; Gómara 1964: 38–52, who writes, "Each side thought to deceive the other" (p. 39).
61. Hassig 2006: 61–62.
62. Carrasco 2008c.
63. Daniel 1992: 189; Díaz 1956: 58–59.
64. Moral García 2015.
65. Vázquez de Tapia 1972: 29.
66. Hassig 2016a; Karttunen 1994: 1–23; Powers 2005; Restall 2018: 305–311.
67. I draw heavily on Townsend (2006) and Bueno Bravo (2019) in this section. Townsend argues convincingly that the name Malinche comes not from a corruption of the Nahuatl name Malinalli (meaning "grass"), but rather a Nahuatl rendering of the Spanish "Marina," where Nahuatl speakers would have substituted the *r* with *l* and added the honorific suffix *–tzin* (giving Malintzin) when the status of this woman grew among native communities over the course of the conquest (see Townsend 2006: 12, 36). The more well-known name Malinche may, in turn, come from a Spanish corruption of the Nahuatl term Malintzin or, as Díaz (2008: 116) states, related to a Nahuatl term for Cortés as "Marina's Captain." In that case, usage should be gendered masculine and the title La Malinche clearly refers to the woman.

68. Hill 2017.
69. Townsend 2006: 41–43.
70. Díaz 2008: 52–62; Gómara 1964: 57–67.
71. Restall (2018) probes these events and the mythology surrounding the first two in particular.
72. Elliott 1967; Frankl 1962.
73. Díaz 1844/2017: 88–93; see also Restall 2018: 185–188.
74. Hassig 2006: 69.
75. Elliott 1986; Russo 2011; for a list of the Aztec treasure sent to Spain recorded by the Veracruz town council, see Cortés (1986: 40–46).
76. Oudijk and Restall 2008.
77. Cortés 1986: 52.
78. Díaz 1956: 109, 2008: 85; Restall 2018: 189–190.
79. INAH 2018, 2019; Junco et al. 2019.

Chapter 6

1. Díaz 2008: 156.
2. Ramírez de Alba 2013: 39; Thomas 1993: 230.
3. López Luján 2015: 60; Ramírez de Alba 2013: 45.
4. Díaz 1844/2017: 121.
5. Castro-Govera and Siebe 2007; Muñoz Camargo 2000: 72.
6. Account of anonymous conquistador rendered in Motolinia (2007: 360). Author's translation of original Spanish reading, "Esta tierra de la Nueva España es semejante a España, y los montes, valles y llanos son casi de la misma manera, excepto que las sierras son más terribles y ásperas; tanto, que no se pueden subir sino con infinito trabajo. . . ."
7. On ceramic styles and possible ethnic affiliations in Tlaxcala, see Fargher et al. (2010), García Cook and Merino Carrión (1988, 1989), Heath-Stout (2019), and Merino Carrión (1989: 93–125).
8. Contreras 2015: 33; García Martínez 2001: 47; Muñoz Camargo 2000: 92.
9. Angulo Ramírez 2004: 75–76, 110–112; Thomas 1993: 236.
10. Cortés 1986: 57–59; Díaz 2008: 90–97; Gibson (1967: 6–19) summarized much of the literature favoring the Apulco route into northern Tlaxcala from Ixtacamaxtitlan. I update his discussion with my own observations, including having excavated at the La Laguna site, then thought to possibly correspond to the historical Tecoac/Tecohuactzinco, but now clearly a much earlier (Formative period) site with a sparse Postclassic occupation, likely named Hueyactepec, that was on the rural outskirts of that Otomi center (see also Borejsza [2013: Figure 1]; García Martínez [2001]; Trautmann [1981: Map 2]).
11. For pre-Hispanic settlement patterns, see García Cook and Merino Carrión (1977, 1988), Merino Carrión (1989), and Carballo and Pluckhahn (2007); for Colonial place names, see Borejsza (2013), Trautmann (1981), and García Cook and Merino Carrión (1989).

12. Angulo Ramírez 2004: 105; Cervera Obregón 2019.
13. Lockhart 1993: 90–91; Muñoz Camargo 2000: 239–240, painting 29 (252r).
14. Alvarado Tezozomoc 1878: 701.
15. Cortés 1986: 58; de Tapia in de Fuentes 1963: 28–29.
16. Díaz 1956: 125, 2008: 93.
17. Quote from Gómara (1964: 99). For experimentation with the machuahuitl, see Cervera Obregón (2006, 2011). A blow from the weapon could do significant tissue damage but not disarticulate large limbs. Importantly, the obsidian would lose its edge quickly and then function more as a blunt club.
18. Cervera Obregón 2019.
19. Vázquez Galicia 2008: 96–97.
20. Fargher et al. 2010, 2011a, 2011b, 2017b; López Corral et al. 2016.
21. Cortés 1986: 68.
22. Fargher et al. 2010, 2017b; López Corral et al. 2016.
23. On Tlaxcalteca versus Spanish battle tactics, see Contreras (2014, 2015), Hassig (2006: 79–88), and Martínez Barcas (2008).
24. Gibson (1967: 18–19) favored the possibility that blaming the northern Otomis of Tecoac and elsewhere, should they not be able to turn back the Spaniards, had been agreed upon by the general council of the Tlaxcallan confederation before engaging them.
25. Gómara 1964: 108.
26. Díaz 2008: 97.
27. Cortés 1986: 60.
28. Hassig 2006: 86.
29. Díaz 1956: 130–132.
30. Carballo and Lesure 2014.
31. Cortés 1986: 63.
32. Gibson 1967: 21.
33. Cortés 1986: 68–72.
34. Díaz 2008: 119–122; Muñoz Camargo 2000: 57, 252.
35. Millhauser et al. 2015; see Pastrana and Carballo (2017) on Aztec obsidian industries.
36. Cortés 1986: 69–71.
37. Vázquez de Tapia 1972: 34–38.
38. Díaz 1884/2017: 152, 2008: 123.
39. Plunket and Uruñuela 2005, 2017, 2018; Solís et al. 2006; Uruñuela et al. 2009.
40. Díaz 2008: 143, 168.
41. Lind 2012; Plunket and Uruñuela 2017: 525–529.
42. Díaz 2008: 143; Plunket and Uruñuela 2018: 209.
43. Cortés 1986: 70–72. The conquistador's estimate of 20,000 urban houses in Cholula and a similar figure of rural houses surrounding it are similar to the late sixteenth-century value in the *Relación de Cholula* by Gabriel de Rojas. Díaz (2008: 130, 133) has 1,000 Tlaxcalans going to Cholula and places the Mexica forces near the city at 20,000.
44. Vázquez de Tapia 1972: 82.
45. Gómara 1964: 123–130; de Tapia account in de Fuentes (1963: 34–36).

46. Cortés 1986: 70–73.
47. Díaz 2008: 135.
48. Plunket and Uruñuela 2017: 530, 2018: 242–244; see also Camelo (2001) on incongruities between native and mestizo sources along the Mexica/Choluteca and Tlaxcalteca/Texcoca axes.
49. de Tapia in de Fuentes 1963: 44.
50. Hassig 2001: 40–41, 2006: 96–97; Restall 2018: 201; Thomas 1995: 256.
51. Castro Morales and García Moll 1972; McCafferty 2000, 2016.
52. Cortés 1986: 79; Restall 2018: 210–211.
53. See contributions on Texcoco by Lee and Brokaw (2014), including Townsend (2014) on polygyny and factional disputes.
54. See Evans (1998a) on sex and politics in the Aztec world.
55. Clendinnen 1991b: 69–70; Hassig 2006: 100–101; Restall 2018: 16, 36–37, 127–128.
56. Lockhart 1993: 100–105; the Nahuatl description in Chapter 15 fills 113 lines of text, whereas the Castilian version is 16 lines.
57. Alva Ixtlilxochitl in Brian et al. 2015: 21.
58. Carrasco 2000; Nicholson 2001a, 2001b; Oudijk and Castañeda de la Paz 2017; Restall 2018.
59. For critiques and revisions of the Cortés as Quetzalcoatl narrative, see Clendinnen (1991b); Rabasa (2008: 55–56); Restall (2003: 112–113, 2018: 100–101, 127–128); Thomas (1995: 264–271); Townsend (2006: 86).
60. de Tapia in de Fuentes 1963: 39.
61. Aguilar in de Fuentes 1963: 147.
62. Interestingly, there are few descriptions of towers or beautiful cities in *Amadís*, leading Thomas (1995: 275) to question whether Díaz had actually read it.
63. Aguilar in de Fuentes 1963: 145–146.
64. Lockhart 1993: 108–112; see Terraciano (2010) on differences between the texts in Nahuatl and Spanish, and the images as a third type of text in Book XII.
65. Gardiner 1954, 1956: 35–44.
66. López Luján and Noguez 2011.
67. Díaz 2008: 160.

Chapter 7

1. Opening lines of Nahuatl poem from *Cantares Mexicanos* (circa 1523), translated by León Portilla (1966: 149).
2. Vázquez de Tapia 1972: 40–41; author's translation from original, "entramos en México y estuvimos en él ocho meses, poco más o menos, hasta la venida de Pámfilo de Narváez, en el cual tiempo pasaron grandes cosas que, para no alargar, las dejo." Narváez's first name is more commonly spelled Pánfilo.
3. Alcocer 1935; López Austin and López Luján 2017.

4. Evans 2004.
5. Marcus 2007: 63.
6. Cortés 1986: 86.
7. Aguilar in de Fuentes 1963: 148.
8. Díaz 2008: 165–183.
9. Lockhart 1993: 122; the Nahuatl description of the furnishing of Moctezuma's palace in Chapter 17 of Book XII fills 46 lines of text, whereas the Castilian version is 29 lines.
10. Velázquez Castro and Melgar Tísoc 2014.
11. Covey and Aland 2017: 565; Hassig 2006: 101; Mundy 2015: 1; see also Table 4.1 in Chapter 4.
12. de Tapia in de Fuentes 1963: 42.
13. López Luján 2017a.
14. Chávez Balderas 2018; Wade 2018.
15. Cortés 1986: 87–92; Díaz 2008: 184–192.
16. Alva Ixtlilxochitl in Brian et al. 2015: 22–29; Hassig 2006: 105; Oudijk and Castañeda de la Paz 2017: 164–165; Restall 2018: 217–218.
17. Díaz 2008: 202–204; López Luján 2017b.
18. Cortés 1986: 103; see also Díaz (2008: 206–207), who records three brigantines, and Gardiner (1954, 1956: 61–76) who provides overviews of the initial boat construction.
19. de Tapia in de Fuentes 1963: 44.
20. Thomas 1995: 337–357.
21. Duggan et al. 2016; Li et al. 2007.
22. Vågene et al 2018; Warinner et al. 2012.
23. Cortés 1986: 118–119; de Tapia in de Fuente 1963: 45; Vázquez de Tapia 1972: 41.
24. Thomas 1995: 391.
25. Restall 2018: 255–256.
26. Hassig 2006: 109; Thomas 1995: 379.
27. Gómara 1964: 206–208.
28. Boone 1989.
29. Lockhart 1993: 134.
30. Vázquez de Tapia 1972: 109–111.
31. Gómarra 1964: 208–211.
32. Hassig 2006: 109.
33. Brian et al. 2015: 24, who also note in a footnote that Native authors of the colonial period often portrayed the Tlaxcalteca in a negative light, not as "traitors," but because they had gained privileges from the Spanish Crown that other Native groups, including the Texcoca, wanted as well.
34. Díaz 2008: 215–220; Restall 2018: 286–287.
35. Vázquez de Tapia 1972: 43; see Hassig (2006: 112–113) and Restall (2018: 198) on the likelihood that Cortés had Moctezuma killed.
36. Lockhart 1993: 130.
37. Ixtlilxochitl provides a compressed chronology for Cuitlahuac's coronation, claiming that it occurred 20 days after the death of Moctezuma, which would have fallen in July 1520,

and that he only governed for a maximum of 40 days before dying of smallpox and being succeeded by Cuauhtemoc (Brian et al. 2015: 26). Note the neat intervals within the vigesimal system.

38. Martínez Baracs 2006: 101–122.
39. Díaz 1956: 313–314, 2008: 227; calculated distances along the escape route from footnote by Maudsley in Díaz (1956: 318).
40. Cortés 1986: 139.
41. Díaz 2008: 231–232. In using the term "Mexico" here, Díaz means the city of Mexico-Tenochtitlan, because later in the same chapter he mentions five Spanish women as part of the Narváez expedition (1844/2017: 279) who were killed in Tustepec while trying to join Cortés' group in Tlaxcala.
42. Lockhart 1993: 158–166.
43. Charlton et al. 2000, 2018; Evans 1998b; Fournier and Otis Charlton 2017.
44. Aguilar in de Fuentes 1963: 156; Díaz 1844/2007: 278–280, 2008: 232–234; Gómara 1964: 224–225.
45. Jarquín Pacheco and Martínez Vargas 2015, 2017; Martínez Vargas 2016; Martínez Vargas and Jarquín Pacheco 2010.
46. Hassig 2001.
47. Aguilar in de Fuentes 1963: 157; Cortés 1986: 144; see Grunberg (1994) for a review of all Spanish expeditions during these years.
48. Cortés 1986: 146–149; Díaz 1844/2017: 286–292, 1956: 330–338, 2008: 236–238.
49. Oudijk and Restall 2008.
50. Lockhart 1993: 180–182.
51. Cook 1998: 64–70; Melville 2000; Restall 2018: 314–317; Sandine 2015: 153–160; Vázquez de Tapia 1972: 46.
52. Cortés 1986: 157, 165.
53. Bierhorst 1992: 97–98; see also García Cook and Merino Carrión (1989) and Townsend (2014).
54. Brian et al. 2015: 28–31; Cortés 1986: 167–176; Díaz 2008: 239–245.
55. Restall 2018: 261–262.
56. Brian et al. 2015: 31–33.
57. Díaz (2008: 370) highlighted the connection between Sandoval's camp here during the conquest and where the miracles occurred and the chapel dedicated to the Virgin of Guadalupe stood when he wrote; see also Martínez Baracs (2000).
58. Gardiner 1956: 115–119; Hassig (2006: 147) estimates 12 of the brigantines were 42 feet (12.8 m) long, while the flagship was somewhat longer at 48 feet (14.6 m).
59. Cortés 1986: 183–186.
60. Brian et al. 2015: 36.
61. Mundy 2015: 62–67, 75–77, 193–205.
62. Cortés 1986: 232; Lockhart 1993: 218.
63. Aguilar in de Fuentes 1963: 159; see also Favila Vásquez (2014) on lacustrine battles.
64. Brian et al. 2015: 49–50; Cortés 1986: 239.
65. Lockhart 1993: 214–218.

66. Cortés 1986: 240–241.
67. Díaz 2008: 287.
68. Cortés 1986: 247, 262.
69. Lockhart 1993: 226–230.
70. Cortés 1986: 261.
71. Lockhart 1993: 246–250.

Chapter 8

1. Muñoz Camargo 1584/2000: 110–111. Translation by author from original passage: "Y aunque las gentes, desde el origen que hemos tratado, han investigado, desvelándose, para ensancharse más por el universo, jamás han podido pasar tan adelante con sus pensamientos vanos, que les quedase más por descubrir, pues vemos de HÉRCULES que, cuando llegó hasta donde puso y asentó sus columnas, entendiendo que no había más mundo, puso aquel tan bravoso blasón de NEQUE ULTRA, pensando que había llegado al fin y cabo de toda la tierra. Y en este engaño, cuántos reyes y monarcas habrán caído, ansí filósofos como cosmógrafos, y cuántos errores se habrán hallado [a]cerca desto que hablaron y escribieron."
2. Restall 2003: 64–76.
3. Scheidel 2016.
4. Silliman 2015: 286.
5. Boone and Cummins 1998; Burkhart 1989; Klor de Alva 1982; Mundy 2015; Gruzinski 1993; Ruiz Medrano and Kellogg 2010; Taladoire 2017; Townsend 2017, 2019. We will consider the terminology used for the culture mixture of the colonial period presented in the works of these authors and others throughout this chapter.
6. Cañizares-Esguerra 2004; Cummins 2010; see Rosenthal (1971) for debates concerning the origins of the slogan. It and the imagery of the Pillars of Hercules remain on the Spanish national crest today.
7. Restall and Asselbergs 2007: 4–8.
8. Herrera 2007.
9. Asselbergs 2007.
10. Restall and Asselbergs 2007: 29–30, 38.
11. Restall and Asselbergs 2007: 103–118, quote on 107.
12. Bueno Bravo 2019: 101–102; Carrasco 2008a: xx; Curiel Monteagudo 2007: 55–64.
13. Harris 2000: 118.
14. Restall et al. 2005: 56–61; Vargas Pacheco 2001.
15. Brian et al. 2015: 84–96, quote on 88.
16. Clendinnen 2003: 20–37.
17. Altman 2017.

18. Martínez Baracs 2008: 267–319; Oudijk and Restall 2008: 24; Taladoire 2017: 83–84.
19. O'Flanagan 2008: 30.
20. Burkholder 2018: 103–104; O'Flanagan 2008: 51–59.
21. Dietler 2009; Edmondson 2016; Scheidel 2016; Smith 2017c.
22. O'Flanagan 2008: 210; Parilla 1992: 108.
23. Wilkinson Zerner 2014.
24. Castañeda de la Paz 2017; Charlton et al. 2018: 148.
25. Mundy 2015.
26. Fowler and Card 2019.
27. Vinson 2018: 6.
28. Gibson 2019: 148–149.
29. McAndrews 1965: 93–120; Mundigo and Crouch 1977.
30. Mundy 2015; Rodríguez Alegría 2017.
31. Foster 1960: 39–46.
32. Low 1995; Pugh and Rice 2017; Wagner et al. 2013.
33. Alexander and Kepecs 2005.
34. Gibson 1964: 32–57, 368–402; Lockhart 1992: 14–58; the terms in Spanish are *ciudad, villa, pueblo, aldea, lugar*.
35. Slack 2012; Suárez Molina 2010.
36. Charlton et al. 2018; Dunmire 2004: 111–115; Evans 1998b: 341; Himmerich y Valencia 1991: 178; a succinct overview of all the encomiendas of the Basin of Mexico in the sixteenth century is provided by Gibson (1964: 415–434).
37. Gibson 1967: 62–65, 162; Martínez Baracs 2008: 71–107.
38. Gibson 1967: 89–123; Restall et al. 2005: 71–77; Sullivan 2001.
39. Crosby 2003; see also Mann (2011); Nunn and Quian (2010).
40. Gasco 2018.
41. Dunmire 2004: 55; Vargas and Casillas 1996: 159–160; see Curiel Monteagudo (2007) for a brief overview of colonial cuisine in New Spain, including hybrid cooking techniques and recipes.
42. Evans 1998b; Kepecs et al. 2018.
43. Curiel Monteagudo 2007: 79; Gibson 1967: 152, 155.
44. Compare Alexander et al. (2018), Borejsza (2013), and Melville (1997).
45. Population estimates and disease: for Mesoamerican generally, see Acuna-Soto et al. (2002), Gutierrez (2015), Nunn and Quian (2010); for the Basin of Mexico, see Sanders et al. (1979: 179); for Otumba subregion, see Charlton et al. (2018: 145); for Tlaxcala, see Borejsza (2013), Gibson (1967: 142); for the Soconusco, see Gasco (2018: 211); for northern Yucatan, see Alexander (2018: 266); for recent paleopathological studies, see Duggan et al. (2017), Li et al. (2012), Vågene et al. (2018), Warriner et al. (2012).
46. Newson 1993; Yalcindaga et al. 2012.
47. Alexander 2014.
48. Restall et al. 2005: 75–77.
49. Cummins and Feliciano 2017: 1039–1042.
50. Ricard 1966.

51. Moreno Villa 1942: 16–17; see also Aguilar-Moreno (2013), Cummins (1995).
52. McAndrew 1965: 21.
53. Cortés 2008; Morales 2014; Parilla 1992; Rubial García 2014.
54. McAndrew 1965: 30.
55. Parilla 1992: 152–153.
56. McClure 2018.
57. Motolinia 1536/2007: 69–70; see also McAndrew (1965: 253).
58. Don 2006; Ruiz Medrano 2014: 175.
59. Abbott 1996: 62.
60. Cortés 2008: 88–89; Gruzinski 1993: 47; López de la Torre 2016.
61. Ricard 1966: 235.
62. Townsend 2017: 137.
63. Barrientos García 2005; Fuertes Herreros 2015.
64. Medrano 2014.
65. Las Casas 1552/1992.
66. Restall 2018: 60–61.
67. Restall et al. 2005: 175.
68. Wright-Carr 2017.
69. Evans 2004: 47; McAndrew 1965: 202–254; Wagner et al. 2013: 51–54.
70. Clendinnen 2003: 114–115; McAndrew 1965: 242–243.
71. Gutiérrez Arriola 1997; McAndrew 1965: 419–423.
72. Charlton et al. 2018: 147.
73. Cummins and Feliciano 2017: 1027–1029.
74. McAndrew 1965: 251–254.
75. Saunders 2001: 226–228.
76. Restall et al. 2005: 186.
77. Harris 2000: 118–122; Matovina 2019: 69, 86; Peterson 2014: 207.
78. García 1991; Martínez 1990: 496–501; Remensnyder 2014: 209–223.
79. Illustrated in Curtis (1898).
80. López Medellín 2014; Martínez 1990: 501.
81. León-Portilla 2000: 13–14, 88–89.
82. Restall et al. 2005: 196–201.
83. López Luján and Noguez 2011; Martínez Baracs 2000.
84. Lockhart 1992: 428, 1998.
85. Curiel Monteagudo 2007: 72–76; Martínez 1990: 497; Restall 2018: 236, 275, 333–334.
86. Vázquez de Tapia 1972: 23, 53–55.
87. Gibson 1967: 98.
88. Gibson 1964: 257–299; Hicks 2009; Martínez Baracs 2008: 182–195; Restall et al. 2005: 94–100.
89. Robichaux 1997.
90. Lockhart 1992: 106–107; Restall et al. 2005: 129–133.

91. Gutierrez 2015; Vinson 2018, drawing for this paragraph particularly on pp. 11, 39, 61, 123; see Berdan et al. (2008) for pre-Hispanic notions of ethnic identity, and Whittaker (2016: 36–37) for racial identification of Alva Ixtlilxochitl.
92. Chance 2008.
93. Lockhart 1993: 288–297.
94. Mijares Ramírez 2010.
95. Rodríguez-Alegría 2010.
96. Vinson 2018: 86.
97. Slack 2012: 120–122.
98. Charlton et al. 2015: 463–465; Hernández Sánchez 2012: 112–140.
99. Evans 2005; Kirakofe 1995.
100. Juli 2002; Plunket and Uruñuela 2005.
101. Gibson 1967: 149–152; Restall et al. 2005: 130–132.
102. Charlton et al. 2018; Gibson 1964: 398; Pastrana et al. 2019.
103. Díaz 2008: 362–371; Harris 2000: 123–131.
104. Harris 2000: 132–147.
105. Dunmire 2004; Vargas and Casillas 1996.
106. Restall 2018: 231–233.
107. Taladoire 2017: 88; Thomas 2014: 76–86; Townsend 2017: 55–96.
108. Fernández de Velasco 1947.
109. Taladoire 2017: 231.
110. Cummins 2010; Harris 2000: 174–178; Taladoire 2017: 274–275.
111. Harris 2000: 213.
112. Taladoire 2017: 52, 55, 57, 64, 87, 113.
113. Cummins 2010; Parry 2014.
114. Kehoe 1979; Kilroy-Ewbank 2014.
115. Vargas and Casillas 1996: 165–166.
116. Nunn and Quian 2010.
117. Hamann 2010.
118. Altman 1989: 273; Taladoire 2017: 89.

Bibliography

Abbott, Don Paul. 1996. *Rhetoric in the New World: Rhetorical Theory and Practice in Colonial Spanish America*. University of South Carolina Press, Columbia.

Abulafia, David. 2011. *The Great Sea: A Human History of the Mediterranean*. Oxford University Press, Oxford.

Abulafia, David (ed.). 2003. *The Mediterranean in History*. Thames and Hudson, London.

Acemoglu, Daron, and James A. Robinson. 2013. *Why Nations Fail: The Origins of Power, Prosperity, and Poverty*. Crown Business, New York.

Acuna-Soto, Rodolfo, David W. Stahle, Malcolm K. Cleaveland, and Matthew D. Therrell. 2002. Megadrought and Megadeath in 16th Century Mexico. *Revista Biomédica* 13(4): 289–292.

Adorno, Rolena. 2008. Bernal Díaz del Castillo: Soldier, Eyewitness, Polemicist. In *The History of the Conquest of New Spain*, by Bernal Díaz del Castillo, edited by Davíd Carrasco, pp. 389–398. University of New Mexico Press, Albuquerque.

Aguilar-Moreno, Manuel. 2006. *Handbook to Life in the Aztec World*. Oxford University Press, New York.

Aguilar-Moreno, Manuel. 2013. Transculturation in Art: Sculpture in the Posa Chapels at the Monastery of Calpan, Mexico. *Colonial Latin American Review* 22(1): 39–66.

Aguilera, Carmen. 1984. *Códice de Huamantla*. First facsimile edition. Instituto Tlaxcalteca de la Cultura, Tlaxcala.

Aguirre-Samuido, Ana J., Blanca Z. González-Sobrino, Brenda A. Álvarez-Sandoval, Rafael Montiel, Carlos Serrano-Sánchez, and Abigail Meza-Peñaloza. 2017. Genetic History of Classic Period Teotihuacan Burials in Central Mexico. *Revista Argentina de Antroplogía Biológica* 19(1): 1–14.

Alberro, Solange. 2015. Hernán Cortés, heroico y piadoso. In *El Veracruz de Hernán Cortés*, edited by Juan Ortiz Escamilla, pp. 19–84. Secretaría de Educación/ Gobierno del Estado de Veracruz and Universidad Veracruzana, Xalapa.

Alcocer, Ignacio. 1935. *Apuntes sobre la antigua Mexico-Tenochtitlan*. Instituto Panamericano de Geografía e Historia, Mexico City.

Alexander, Rani T. 2014. Maya Collapse or Resilience? Lessons from the Spanish Conquest and the Caste War of Yucatan. In *The Ancient Maya of Mexico: Reinterpreting the Past of the Northern Maya Lowlands*, edited by Geoffrey E. Braswell, pp. 325–347. Routledge, New York.

Alexander, Rani T. 2018. Agrarian Ecology in Yucatán, 1450–2000. In *Colonial and Postcolonial Change in Mesoamerica: Archaeology as Historical Anthropology*, edited by Rani T. Alexander and Susan Kepecs, pp. 255–282. University of New Mexico, Albuquerque.

Alexander, Rani T., Janine Gasco, and Judith Francis Zeitlin. 2018. Agrarian Ecology and Historical Contingency in Landscape Change. In *Colonial and Postcolonial Change in Mesoamerica: Archaeology as Historical Anthropology*, edited by Rani T. Alexander and Susan Kepecs, pp. 53–72. University of New Mexico, Albuquerque.

Alexander, Rani T., and Susan Kepecs. 2005. The Postclassic to Spanish-Era Transition in Mesoamerica: An Introduction. In *The Postclassic to Spanish-Era Transition in Mesoamerica: Archaeological Perspectives*, edited by Susan Kepecs and Rani T. Alexander, pp. 1–12. University of New Mexico Press, Albuquerque.

Alexander, Rani T., and Susan Kepecs (eds.). 2018. *Colonial and Postcolonial Change in Mesoamerica: Archaeology as Historical Anthropology.* University of New Mexico, Albuquerque.

Alibhai, Ali Asgar. 2008. The Reverberations of Santiago's Bells in Reconquista Spain. *La corónica: A Journal of Medieval Hispanic Languages, Literatures, and Cultures* 36(2): 145–164.

Almagro Gorbea, Martín. 2014. La "tumba de Melqart" del Herákleion de Gadir. *Madrider Mitteilungen* 54: 159–202.

Altamira, Rafael. 1938. El texto de las Leyes de Burgos de 1512. *Revista de historia de América* 4: 5–79.

Altman, Ida. 1989. *Emigrants and Society: Extremadura and America in the Sixteenth Century*. University of California Press, Berkeley.

Altman, Ida. 2017. *Contesting Conquest: Indigenous Perspectives on the Spanish Occupation of Nueva Galicia, 1524–1545*. Pennsylvania State University Press, University Park.

Alva Ixtlilxochitl, Fernando de. 2015. Thirteenth Relation: On the Arrival of the Spaniards and the Beginning of the Law of the Gospel. In *The Native Conquistador: Alva Ixtlilxochitl's Account of the Conquest of New Spain*, edited and translated by Amber Brian, Bradley Benton, and Pablo García Loaeza, pp. 19–112. Latin American Originals 10. Pennsylvania State University, University Park.

Alvarado Tezozomoc, Hernando. 1878. *Crónica Mexicana*. Edited by Manuel Orozco y Berra. Biblioteca Mexicana, Mexico City.

Amaya Topete, Jesus. 1958. *Atlas mexicano de la conquista*. Fondo de Cultura Económica, Mexico City.

Anderson, Arthur J. O., Frances Berdan, and James Lockhart (eds. and trans.). 1976. *Beyond the Codices: The Nahua View of Colonial Mexico.* University of California Press, Berkeley.

Anderson, Arthur J. O., and Charles E. Dibble (eds. and trans.). 1959. *Florentine Codex: General History of the Things of New Spain* by Fray Bernardino de Sahagún, *Book 9: The Merchants*. School of American Research, Santa Fe.

Anderson, Arthur J. O., and Charles E. Dibble (eds. and trans.). 1975. *Florentine Codex: General History of the Things of New Spain* by Fray Bernardino de Sahagún, *Book 12: The Conquest of Mexico*. School of American Research, Santa Fe.

Andrews, Bradford, and Kenneth G. Hirth. 2006. Patterns of Stone Tool Consumption in Xochicalco's Civic-Ceremonial Core. In *Obsidian Production in Ancient Central Mexico*, by Kenneth G. Hirth, pp. 241–257. University of Utah Press, Salt Lake City.

Angulo Ramírez, Andrés. 2004. *Historia de Tlaxcala*. Compiled and edited by Roberto Suárez Ruiz. TRLS Ediciones, Tlaxcala.

Arruda, Ana Margarida. 2009. Phoenician Colonization on the Atlantic Coast of the Iberian Peninsula. In *Colonial Encounters in Ancient Iberia: Phoenician, Greek, and Indigenous Relations*, edited by Michael Dietler and Carolina López-Ruiz, pp. 113–130. University of Chicago Press, Chicago.

Asselbergs, Florine G. L. 2007. The Conquest in Images: Stories of Tlaxcalteca and Quauhquecholteca Conquistadors. In *Indian Conquistadors: Indigenous Allies in the Conquest of Mesoamerica*, edited by Laura E. Matthew and Michel R. Ouidijk, pp. 65–101. University of Oklahoma Press, Norman.

Aveni, Anthony F. 2001. *Skywatchers: A Revised and Updated Version of Skywatchers of Ancient Mexico*. University of Texas Press, Austin.

Bailey, Geoff. 2007. Time Perspectives, Palimpsests and the Archaeology of Time. *Journal of Anthropological Archaeology* 26(2): 198–223.

Barba Pingarrón, Luis A., and José Luís Córdova Frunz. 2010. *Materiales y energía en la arquitectura de Teotihuacan*. UNAM, Mexico City.

Barlow, Robert H. 1945. La Crónica X. *Revista Mexicana de Estudios Antropológicos* VII: 65–87.

Barrera Rodríguez, Raúl, and Gabino López Arenas. 2008. Hallazgos en el recinto ceremonial de Tenochtitlan. *Arqueología Mexicana* 16(93): 18–25.

Barrientos García, José. 2005. La Teología de la Universidad de Salamanca en los siglos XVI y XVII. In *Saberes y Disciplinas en las Universidades Hispánicas: Miscelánea Alfonso IX, 2004*, edited by Luis E. Rodríguez-San Pedro Bezares and Juan Luis Polo Rodrígues, pp. 51–96. Ediciones Universidad de Salamanca, Salamanca.

Barrientos García, José. 2006. La teología, siglos XVI–XVII. In *Historia de la Universidad de Salamanca*, Vol. III.1: *Saberes y confluencias*, edited by Luis E. Rodríguez-San Pedro Bezares, pp. 203–250. Ediciones Universidad de Salamanca, Salamanca.

Baucells Mesa, Sergio. 2013. *Aculturación y etnicidad: El proceso de interacción entre guanches y europeos (Siglos XIV–XVI)*. Instituto de Estudios Canarios, La Laguna, Spain.

Beard, Mary. 2015. *SPQR: A History of Ancient Rome*. W.W. Norton, New York.

Bellwood, Peter. 2005. *First Farmers: The Origins of Agricultural Societies*. Blackwell, Malden, MA.

Bellwood, Peter. 2014. *First Migrants: Ancient Migration in Global Perspective*. Wiley-Blackwell, Malden, MA.

Berdan, Frances F. 1992. Economic Dimensions of Precious Metals, Stones, and Feathers: The Aztec State Society. *Estudios de Cultura Náhuatl* 22: 291–323.

Berdan, Frances F., John K. Chance, Alan R. Sandstrom, Barbara Stark, James Taggart, and Emily Umberger. 2008. *Ethnic Identity in Nahua Mesoamerica: The View from Archaeology, Art History, Ethnohistory, and Contemporary Tthnography*. University of Utah Press, Salt Lake City.

Biar, Alexandra, and Mariana Favila Vázquez. 2016. Tradición de navegación indígena en Mesoamérica: Los casos lacustres mexica y tarasco. In *El mar: Una forma de vida en América*, edited by Alberto Hoces-García and Carlos Moral-García, pp. 97–124. Historia y Cultura del Mar, Madrid.

Bierhorst, John (ed. and trans.). 1992. *History and Mythology of the Aztecs: The Codex Chimalpopoca*. University of Arizona Press, Tucson.

Blanton, Richard E., and Lane F. Fargher. 2008. *Collective Action in the Formation of Pre-Modern States.* Springer, New York.

Blanton, Richard E., Lane F. Fargher, and Verenice Y. Heredia Espinoza. 2005. The Mesoamerican World of Goods and Its Transformations. In *Settlement, Subsistence, and Social Complexity: Essays Honoring the Legacy of Jeffrey R. Parsons*, edited by Richard E. Blanton, pp. 260–294. Cotsen Institute of Archaeology, University of California, Los Angeles.

Boatwright, Mary T. 2000. *Hadrian and the Cities of the Roman Empire*. Princeton University Press, Princeton, NJ.

Boatwright, Mary T. 2002. Trajan outside Rome: Buildings and Sculptural Commissions in Italian and Provincial Cities. In *Sage and Emperor: Plutarch, Greek Intellectuals, and Roman power in the Time of Trajan (98–117 A.D.)*, edited by Philip A. Stadter and Luc van der Stockt, pp. 259–277. Leuven University Press, Leuven.

Boix, Carles. 2015. *Political Order and Inequality: Their Foundations and Their Consequences for Human Welfare.* Cambridge University Press, New York.

Boone, Elizabeth Hill. 1989. Incarnations of the Aztec Supernatural: The Image of Huitzilopochtli in Mexico and Europe. *Transactions of the American Philosophical Society* 79(2): i–iv, 1–107.

Boone, Elizabeth Hill. 1998. Pictorial Documents and Visual Thinking in Postconquest Mexico. In *Native Traditions in the Postconquest World*, edited by Elizabeth Hill Boone and Tom Cummins, pp. 149–199. Dumbarton Oaks and Trustees for Harvard University, Washington, DC.

Boone, Elizabeth Hill. 2000. Venerable Place of Beginnings: The Aztec Understanding of Teotihuacan. In *Mesoamerica's Classic Heritage: From Teotihuacan to the Aztecs*, edited by Davíd Carrasco, Lindsay Jones, and Scott Sessions, pp. 371–396. University Press of Colorado, Boulder.

Boone, Elizabeth Hill. 2017. Aztec Pictography and Painted Histories. In *The Oxford Handbook of the Aztecs*, edited by Deborah L. Nichols and Enrique Rodríguez-Alegría, pp. 117–127. Oxford University Press, New York.

Boone, Elizabeth, and Tom Cummins (eds.). 1998. *Native Traditions in the Postconquest World*. Dumbarton Oaks, Trustees for Harvard University, Washington, DC.

Borejsza, Aleksander. 2013. Village and Field Abandonment in Post-Conquest Tlaxcala: A Geoarchaeological Perspective. *Anthropocene* 3: 9–23.

Bosch-Gimpera, Pedro. 1995. *El poblamiento antiguo y la formación de los pueblos de España*. Universidad Nacional Autónoma de México, Mexico City.

Braudel, Fernand. 1972. *The Mediterranean and the Mediterranean World in the Age of Philip II*. Vol. 1 & 2. University of California Press, Berkeley.

Brian, Amber, Bradley Benton, and Pablo García Loaeza (eds. and trans.). 2015. *The Native Conquistador: Alva Ixtlilxochitl's Account of the Conquest of New Spain*. Latin American Originals 10. Pennsylvania State University Press, University Park.

Brinton, Daniel G. 1896. The Battle and the Ruins of Cintla. *American Antiquarian* 18(5): 259–268.

Brittenham, Claudia. 2015. *The Murals of Cacaxtla: The Power of Painting in Ancient Central Mexico*. University of Texas Press, Austin.

Bruhn de Hoffmeyer, Ada. 1985. Las armas de los conquistadores. Las armas de los Aztecas. In *Hernán Cortés y su Tiempo, Actas del Congreso Hernán Cortés y su Tiempo V Centenario (1485–1985)*, pp. 244–260. Editora Regional de Extremadura, Mérida.

Budar, Lourdes. 2017. El puerto prehispánico de La Perla del Golfo. In *Arqueología de la Costa del Golfo: Dinámicas de la interacción política, económica e ideológica*, edited by Lourdes Budar, Marciel L. Venter, and Sara Ladrón de Guevara, pp. 291–314. Universidad Veracruzana, Xalapa, Mexico.

Bueno Bravo, M. Isabel. 2019. Doña Marina en la conquista de México. In *Mujeres en la guerra y en los ejércitos*, edited by Manuel Santirso Rodríguez and Alberto Guerrero Martín, pp. 93–105. Catarata, Madrid.

Burkhart, Louise M. 1989. *The Slippery Earth: Nahua-Christian Moral Dialogue in Sixteenth-Century Mexico*. University of Arizona Press, Tucson.

Burkholder, Mark A., Lyman L. Johnson, and Monica A. Rankin. 2018. *Exploitation, Inequality, and Resistance: A History of Latin America since Columbus*. Oxford University Press, New York.

Buxó, Ramon. 2009. Botanical and Archaeological Dimensions of the Colonial Encounter. In *Colonial Encounters in Ancient Iberia: Phoenician, Greek, and Indigenous Relations*, edited by Michael Dietler and Carolina López-Ruiz, pp. 155–168. University of Chicago Press, Chicago.

Calero, M., J. Gener, J. M. Pajuelo, M. A. Navarro, M. Torres, S. Palomo, C. Gomes, E. Arroyo, and C. González Wagner. 2015. Study of Mitochondrial DNA from Four Ancient Individuals (VIII century BC to IV AD) found in Gadir (Cadiz), Indicates the Possible and Subsequent Probable Interbreeding with Native European Population. *Journal of Paleopathology*, Supplement: XIII Spanish Paleopathology Association Meeting 25: 15, 36.

Calleja Puerta, Miguel. 2017. E l reino de los astures y el Imperio Carolingio: Historia y recreación histórica. In *Carlomagno: El sueño de una Europa unida. Una visión desde Asturias*, edited by Javier Ballina, pp. 43–62. Real Instituto de Estudios Asturianos, Oviedo.

Calnek, Edward. 1988. The Calmecac and Telpochcalli in Preconquest Tenochtitlan. In *The Work of Bernardino de Sahagun: Pioneer Ethnographer of Sixteenth-Century Aztec Mexico*, edited by J. José Klor de Alva, H. B. Nicholson, and Eloise Quiñones Keber, pp. 169–178. Institute for Mesoamerican Studies, State University of New York, Albany.

Calnek, Edward. 2003. Tenochtitlan-Tlatelolco: The Natural History of a City. In *Urbanism in Mesoamerica*, Vol. 1, edited by William T. Sanders, Alba Guadalupe Mastache, and Robert H. Cobean, pp. 149–202. Instituto Nacional de Antropología e Historia, and Pennsylvania State University, Mexico City and University Park, PA.

Calvín Velasco, María Eugenia. 2014. Estudio análisis y valoración social de la necrópolis Calcolítica de Los Millares (Santa Fe de Mondújar, Almería). *Arqueología y Territorio* 11: 1–13.

Camelo, Rosa. 2001. La matanza de Cholula. *Arqueología Mexicana* IX(49): 52–55.

Cañizares-Esguerra, Jorge. 2004. Iberian Science in the Renaissance: Ignored How Much Longer? *Perspectives on Science* 12(1): 86–124.

Carballo, David M. 2011. *Obsidian and the Teotihuacan State: Weaponry and Ritual Production at the Moon Pyramid*. University of Pittsburgh Memoirs in Latin American Archaeology No. 21. Center for Comparative Archaeology, Department of Anthropology, University of Pittsburgh, and Instituto de Investigaciones Antropológicas, Universidad Nacional Autónoma de México, Pittsburgh and Mexico City.

Carballo, David M. 2012. Trade Routes in the Americas before Columbus. In *The Great Trade Routes: A History of Cargos and Commerce over Land and Sea*, edited by Philip Parker, pp. 166–170. Conway, London.

Carballo, David M. 2013a. The Social Organization of Craft Production and Interregional Exchange at Teotihuacan. In *Merchants, Markets, and Exchange in the Pre-Columbian World*, edited by Kenneth G. Hirth and Joanne Pillsbury, pp. 113–140. Dumbarton Oaks and Trustees for Harvard University, Washington, DC.

Carballo, David M. 2013b. Labor Collectives and Group Cooperation in Pre-Hispanic Central Mexico. In *Cooperation and Collective Action: Archaeological Perspectives*, edited by David M. Carballo, pp. 243–274. University Press of Colorado, Boulder.

Carballo, David M. 2016. *Urbanization and Religion in Ancient Central Mexico.* Oxford University Press, New York.

Carballo, David M. 2017. American Pioneers and Traditions. In *Encyclopedia of Global Archaeology*, revised edition, edited by Claire Smith, https://doi.org/10.1007/978-3-319-51726-1_1532-2, pp. 1–6. Springer, New York.

Carballo, David M. 2018. Religion, Urbanism, and Inequality in Ancient Central Mexico. In *Beyond Integration: Religion and Politics in the Precolumbian Americas*, edited by Sarah B. Barber and Arthur A. Joyce, pp. 119–140. Routledge, New York.

Carballo, David M., Kenneth G. Hirth, Daniela Hernández Sariñana, Gina M. Buckley, Andrés G. Mejía Ramón, and Douglas J. Kennett. 2019. New Research at Teotihuacan's Tlajinga District, 2012–2015. *Ancient Mesoamerica* 30: 95–113.

Carballo, Jennifer, and Richard Lesure. 2014. Amomoloc. In *Formative Lifeways in Central Tlaxcala*, Vol. 1: *Excavations, Ceramics, and Chronology*, edited by Richard G. Lesure, pp. 13–50. Cotsen Institute of Archaeology Press, University of California, Los Angeles.

Carballo, David M., and Thomas Pluckhahn. 2007. Transportation Corridors and Political Evolution in Highland Mesoamerica: Settlement Analyses Incorporating GIS for Northern Tlaxcala, Mexico. *Journal of Anthropological Archaeology* 26(4): 607–629.

Carrasco, Davíd. 1999. *City of Sacrifice: The Aztec Empire and the Role of Violence in Civilization*. Beacon Press, Boston.

Carrasco, Davíd. 2000. *Quetzalcoatl and the Irony of Empire: Myths and Prophecies in the Aztec Tradition*. Revised edition. University Press of Colorado, Boulder.

Carrasco, Davíd. 2008a. Introduction: The Dream of the Conquistador and a Book of Desire and Destruction. In *The History of the Conquest of New Spain*, by Bernal Díaz del Castillo, edited by Davíd Carrasco, pp. xi–xxvii. University of New Mexico Press, Albuquerque.

Carrasco, Davíd. 2008b. The Exaggerations of Human Sacrifice. In *The History of the Conquest of New Spain*, by Bernal Díaz del Castillo, edited by Davíd Carrasco, pp. 439–447. University of New Mexico Press, Albuquerque.

Carrasco, Davíd. 2008c. Cortés and the Sacred Ceiba: A Maya Axis Mundi. In *The History of the Conquest of New Spain*, by Bernal Díaz del Castillo, edited by Davíd Carrasco, pp. 399–404. University of New Mexico Press, Albuquerque.

Carrasco, Davíd. 2014. *Religions of Mesoamerica*. 2nd edition. Waveland, Long Grove, IL.

Carrasco, Davíd. 2017. An Unfinished Biography of a Big Idea: "Nucleo Duro," Mircea Eliade, Fernand Braudel, Alfredo López Austin. In *Del saber ha hecho su razón de ser . . . : Homenaje a Alfredo López Austin*, edited by Eduarto Matos Moctezuma and Ángela Ochoa, pp. 39–55. Instituto Nacional de Antropología e Historia Universidad Nacional Autónoma de México, Mexico City.

Castañeda de la Paz, María. 2017. El acueducto del Padre Tembleque en Otumba y Zempoala: Patrimonio de la humanidad por la UNESCO. *Arqueología Mexicana* 24(143): 71–75.

Castro, José I. Castro. 2002. On the Origins of the Spanish Word "Tiburon," and the English Word "Shark." *Environmental Biology of Fishes* 65: 249–253.

Castro-Govea, Renato, and Claus Siebe. 2007. Late Pleistocene–Holocene Stratigraphy and Radiocarbon Dating of La Malinche Volcano, Central Mexico. *Journal of Volcanology and Geothermal Research* 162: 20–42.

Castro Morales, Efrain, and Roberto García Moll. 1972. Un entierro colectivo en la ciudad de Cholula, Puebla. In *Religion en Mesoamérica*, edited by Jaime Litvak King and Noemi Castillo Tejero, pp. 381–384. Sociedad Mexicana de Antropología, Mexico City.

Catlos, Brian A. 2018. *Kingdoms of Faith: A New History of Islamic Spain*. Basic Books, New York.

Celestino, Sebastián, and Carolina López-Ruiz. 2016. *Tartessos and the Phonecians in Iberia*. Oxford University Press, Oxford.

Celestino Pérez, Sebastián. 2008. Tartessos. In *De Iberia a Hispania*, edited by Francisco Gracia Alonso, pp. 93–345. Editorial Ariel, Barcelona.

Celestino Pérez, Sebastián. 2009. Precolonization and Colonization in the Interior of Tartessos. In *Colonial Encounters in Ancient Iberia: Phoenician, Greek, and Indigenous Relations*, edited by Michael Dietler and Carolina López-Ruiz, pp. 229–251. University of Chicago Press, Chicago.

Celestino Pérez, Sebastián, Francisco Gracia Alonso, and Esther Rodríguez González. 2017. Copas para un banquete: La distribución de cerámicas áticas en Extremadura. In *Homenaje a Glòria Trias Rubiés: Cerámicas griegas de la Península Ibérica: cincuenta años después (1967–2017)*, edited by Xavier Aquilué, Paloma Cabrera, and Margarita Orfila, pp. 140–149. Centro Iberia Graeca, Barcelona.

Celestino Pérez, Sebastián, and Esther Rodríguez González. 2017. Tarteso en Extremadura. *Revista de Estudios Extremeños* LXXIII(1): 13–56.

Cervantes de Salazar, Francisco. 2006. *Crónico de la Nueva España*. Biblioteca Virtual Universal, Buenos Aires.

Cervera Obregón, Marco Antonio. 2006. The Macuahuitl: An Innovative Weapon of the Late Post-Classic in Mesoamerica. *Arms and Armours: Journal of the Royal Armouires* 3: 127–148.

Cervera Obregón, Marco Antonio. 2011. *Guerreros aztecas: armas, técnicas de combate e historial militar del implacable ejército que conquistó Mesoamérica*. Ediciones Nowtilus, Madrid.

Cervera Obregón, Marco Antonio. 2019. La batalla de Tecóac, Tlaxcala y los enfrentamientos hispano-otomíes, una vision desde la perspectiva de la historia militar. *Revista Chicomoztoc* 1(1). Available online at http://revistas.uaz.edu.mx/index.php/chicomoztoc/article/view/502 (accessed January 1, 2019).

Chance, John K. 2008. Indigenous Ethnicity in Colonial Central Mexico. In *Ethnic Identity in Nahua Mesoamerica: The View from Archaeology, Art History, Ethnohistory, and Contemporary Ethnography*, edited by Frances F. Berdan, John K. Chance, Alan R. Sandstrom, Barbara L. Stark, James, M. Taggart, and Emily Umberger, pp. 133–149. University of Utah Press, Salt Lake City.

Chardon, Roland. 1980. The Elusive Spanish League: A Problem of Measurement in Sixteenth-Century New Spain. *The Hispanic American Historical Review* 60(2): 294–302.

Charlton, Thomas H., Patricia Fournier, and Cynthia L. Otis Charlton. 2015. Historical Archaeology in the Basin of Mexico and the Central Mexican Symbiotic Region: Development, Present Status, Future Prospects. *Ancient Mesoamerica* 26(2): 59–70.

Charlton, Thomas H., Deborah L. Nichols, and Cynthia L. Otis Charlton. 2000. Otumba and Its Neighbors: Ex oriente lux. *Ancient Mesoamerica* 11(2): 247–265.

Charlton, Thomas H., and Cynthia L. Otis Charlton. 2018. Historical Archaeology in the Basin of Mexico: The Otumba Case. In *Colonial and Postcolonial Change in*

Mesoamerica: Archaeology as Historical Anthropology, edited by Rani T. Alexander and Susan Kepecs, pp. 139–160. University of New Mexico, Albuquerque.

Chatters, James C., Douglas J. Kennett, Yemane Asmerom, Brian M. Kemp, Victor Polyak, Alberto Nava Blank, Patricia A. Beddows, Eduard Reinhardt, Joaquin Arroyo-Cabrales, Deborah A. Bolnick, Ripan S. Malhi, Brendan J. Culleton, Pilar Luna Erreguerena, Dominique Rissolo, Shanti Morell-Hart, and Thomas W. Stafford Jr. 2014. Late Pleistocene Human Skeleton and mtDNA Link Paleoamericans and Modern Native Americans. *Science* 344(6185): 750–754.

Chávez Balderas, Ximena. 2018. Effigies of Death: Representation, Use, and Reuse of Human Skulls at the Templo Mayor of Tenochtitlan. In *Social Skins of the Head: Body Beliefs and Ritual in Ancient Mesoamerica and the Andes*, edited by Vera Tiesler and María Cecilia Lozada, pp. 141–160. University of New Mexico Press, Albuquerque.

Chávez Jiménez, Ulises. 2007. Potonchán y Santa María de la Victoria: Una propuesta geomorfológico/arqueológica a un problema histórico. *Estudios de la Cultura Maya* XXIV: 103–139.

Christian, David. 2017. What Is Big History? *Journal of Big History* 1: 4–19.

Clendinnen, Inga. 1991a. *Aztecs: An Interpretation.* Cambridge University Press, New York.

Clendinnen, Inga. 1991b. "Fierce and Unnatural Cruelty": Cortés and the Conquest of Mexico. *Representations* 33: 65–100.

Clendinnen, Inga. 2003. *Ambivalent Conquests: Maya and Spaniard in Yucatan, 1517–1570.* 2nd edition. Cambridge University Press, Cambridge.

Codoñer Merino, Carmen. 2006. Las humanidades en latín. In *Historia de la Universidad de Salamanca*, Vol. III.2: *Saberes y confluencias*, edited by Luis E. Rodríguez-San Pedro Bezares, pp. 723–756. Ediciones Universidad de Salamanca, Salamanca.

Coleman, David. 2013. *Creating Christian Granada: Society and Religious Culture in an Old-World Frontier City, 1492–1600.* Cornell University Press, Ithica, NY.

Contreras Martínez, José Eduardo. 2014. La confrontación tlaxcalteca ante la Conquista. *Dimensión Antropológica* 21(61): 43–72.

Contreras Martínez, José Eduardo. 2015. La batalla de Tzompantepec: Continuación de los conflictos políticos entre los pueblos hegemónicos del postclásico tardío. In *Diversidad social, política y económica en distintos tiempos y espacios regionales*, edited by Marciano Netzahualcoyotzi Méndez. Universidad Autónoma de Tlaxcala, Tlaxcala.

Conway, Richard. 2012. Lakes, Canoes, and the Aquatic Communities of Xochimilco and Chalco, New Spain. *Ethnohistory* 59(3): 541–568.

Cook, Noble David. 1998. *Born to Die: Disease and New World Conquest, 1492–1650.* Cambridge University Press, Cambridge.

Cortés, Hernán. 1986. *Letters from Mexico.* Edited and translated by Anthony Pagden. Yale University Press, New Haven, CT.

Cortés, Rocío. 2008. The Colegio Imperial de Santa Cruz de Tlatelolco and Its Aftermath: Nahua Intellectuals and the Spiritual Conquest of Mexico. In *A Companion to Latin American Literature and Culture*, edited by Sara Castro-Klaren, pp. 86–105. Blackwell, Oxford.

Corzo Sánchez, Ramón. 2004. Sobre la imagen de Hercules Gaditanus. *Romula* 3: 37–62.

Covey, R. Alan, and Amanda S. Aland. 2017. Aztec Empire in Comparative Perspective. In *The Oxford Handbook of the Aztecs*, edited by Deborah L. Nichols and Enrique Rodríguez-Alegría, pp. 557–568. Oxford University Press, New York.

Cowgill, George L. 2012. Concepts of Collapse and Regeneration in Human History. In *The Oxford Handbook of Mesoamerican Archaeology*, edited by Deborah L. Nichols and Christopher A. Pool, pp. 301–308. Oxford University Press, New York.

Cowgill, George L. 2015. *Ancient Teotihuacan: Early Urbanism in Central Mexico*. Cambridge University Press, New York.

Crosby, Alfred W. 2003. *The Columbian Exchange: Biological and Cultural Consequences of 1492*. Vol. 2. Greenwood, Westport, CT.

Cucina, Andrea (ed.). 2014. *Archaeology and Bioarchaeology of Population Movement among the Prehispanic Maya*. Springer, New York.

Cucina, Andrea, Allan Ortega, and Vera Tiesler. 2008. When East Meets West: Biological Affinities between Coastal Populations in the Yucatan Peninsula during the Postclassic Period. *Mexicon* XXX: 39–43.

Cummins, Thomas B. F. 1995. The Madonna and the Horse: Becoming Colonial in New Spain and Peru. In *Native Arts and Patrons in Colonial Latin America*, edited by Emily Umberger and Tom Cummins, pp. 52–83. *Phoebus: A Journal of Art History*, Arizona State University, Tempe.

Cummins, Thomas B. F. 2010. Through the "Devil's Looking-Glass" Darkly: Brazilians, Peruvians, Aztecs, and Zemis in Europe; Serlio and Hercules in the Americas. In *The Arts of South America, 1492–1850: Papers from the 2008 Mayer Center Symposium at the Denver Art Museum*, edited by Donna Pierce, pp. 19–46. Denver Art Museum, Denver.

Cummins, Thomas B. F., and María Judith Feliciano. 2017. Mudejar Americano: Iberian Aesthetic Transmission in the New World. In *A Companion to Islamic Art and Architecture*, edited by Finbarr Barry Flood and Gülru Necipoğlu, pp. 1023–1050. John Wiley and Sons, London.

Cunliffe, Barry. 2001. *Facing the Ocean: The Atlantic and its Peoples 8000 BC–AD 1500*. Oxford University Press, Oxford.

Cunliffe, Barry. 2015. *By Steppe, Desert, and Ocean: The Birth of Eurasia*. Oxford University Press, Oxford.

Cunliffe, Barry. 2017. *On the Ocean: The Mediterranean and the Atlantic from Prehistory to AD 1500*. Oxford University Press, Oxford.

Curiel Monteagudo, José Luis. 2007. *La mesa de Hernán Cortés*. Editorial Porrúa, Mexico City.

Curtis, William Eleroy. 1898. *The Relics of Columbus: An Illustrated Description of the Historical Collection in the Monastery of La Rabida*. William H. Lowdermilk, Washington, DC.

Cyphers, Ann, and Anna Di Castro. 2009. Early Olmec Architecture and Imagery. In *The Art of Urbanism: How Mesoamerican Kingdoms Represented Themselves in Art and Architecture*, edited by William L. Fash and Leonardo López Luján, pp. 21–52. Dumbarton Oaks Trustees of Harvard University, Washington, DC.

Cyphers, Ann, and Kenneth G. Hirth. 2016. *Transporte y producción artesanal en los albores del mundo olmeca*. Universidad Nacional Autónoma de México, Instituto de Investigaciones Antropológicas, Mexico City.

Daniel, Douglas A. 1992. Tactical Factors in the Spanish Conquest of the Aztecs. *Anthropological Quarterly* 65(4): 187–194.

Davies, Arthur. 1956. The "English" Coasts on the Map of Juan de la Cosa. *Imago Mundi* 13(1): 26–29.

Davies, Malcolm. 1991. *Poetarum melicorum Graecorum fragmenta*. University of Oxford, Oxford.

Day, John. 2002. *Yahweh and the Gods and Goddesses of Canaan*. Sheffield Academic Press, London.

de Fuentes, Patricia (ed. and trans.). 1963. *The Conquistadores: First-Person Accounts of the Conquest of Mexico*. Orion Press, New York.

Deamos, María Belén. 2009. Phoenicians in Tartessos. In *Colonial Encounters in Ancient Iberia: Phoenician, Greek, and Indigenous Relations*, edited by Michael Dietler and Carolina López-Ruiz, pp. 193–228. University of Chicago Press, Chicago.

Delgado Hervás, Ana. 2008. Fenicios en Iberia. In *De Iberia a Hispania*, edited by Francisco Gracia Alonso, pp. 347–474. Editorial Ariel, Barcelona.

Di Sciacca, Claudia. 2008. *Finding the Right Words: Isidore's Synonyma in Anglo-Saxon England*. University of Toronto Press, Toronto.

Diamond, Jared. 1997. *Guns, Germs, and Steel: The Fates of Human Societies*. W. W. Norton, New York.

Díaz del Castillo, Bernal. 1844/2017. *The Conquest of New Spain*, Vol. 1. Translated by John Ingram Lockhart. Enhanced Media, New York.

Díaz del Castillo, Bernal. 1956. *The Discovery and Conquest of Mexico, 1517–1521*. Edited and Translated by Alfred P. Maudslay. Farrar, Straus and Cudahy, New York.

Díaz del Castillo, Bernal. 2008. *The History of the Conquest of New Spain*. Edited by Davíd Carrasco. University of New Mexico Press, Albuquerque.

Dietler, Michael. 2009. Colonial Encounters in Iberia and the Western Mediterranean: An Exploratory Framework. In *Colonial Encounters in Ancient Iberia: Phoenician, Greek, and Indigenous Relations*, edited by Michael Dietler and Carolina López-Ruiz, pp. 3–48. University of Chicago Press, Chicago.

Dietler, Michael, and Carolina López-Ruiz (eds.). 2009. *Colonial Encounters in Ancient Iberia: Phoenician, Greek, and Indigenous Relations*. University of Chicago Press, Chicago.

Don, Patricia Lopes. 2006. Franciscans, Indian Sorcerers, and the Inquisition in New Spain, 1536–1543. *Journal of World History* 17(1): 27–49.

Dugan Iverson, Shannon. 2017. The Enduring Toltecs: History and Truth during the Aztec-to-Colonial Transition at Tula, Hidalgo. *Journal of Archaeological Method and Theory* 24(1): 90–116.

Duggan, Ana T., Maria F. Perdomo, Dario Piombino-Mascali, Stephanie Marciniak, Debi Poinar, Matthew V. Emery, Jan P. Buchmann, Sebastian Duchêne, Rimantas Jankauskas, Margaret Humphreys, G. Brian Golding, John Southon, Alison Devault, Jean-Marie Rouillard, Jason W. Sahl, Olivier Dutour, Klaus Hedman, Antti Sajantila, Geoffrey L. Smith, Edward C. Holmes, and Hendrik N. Poinar. 2016. 17th Century Variola Virus Reveals the Recent History of Smallpox. *Current Biology* 26: 3407–3412.

Dunmire, William W. 2004. *Gardens of New Spain: How Mediterranean Plants and Foods Changed America.* University of Texas Press, Austin.

Edmondson, Jonathan. 2011. "A Tale of Two Colonies": Augusta Emerita (Mérida) and Metellinum (Medellín) in Roman Lusitania. In *Roman Colonies in the First Century of Their Foundation*, edited by Rebecca J. Sweetman, pp. 32–54. Oxbow Books, Oxford.

Edmondson, Jonathan. 2014. Hispania capta: Reflexiones sobre el proceso e impacto de la conquista romana en la Península Ibérica. In *Conquistadores y conquistados: relaciones de dominio en el mundo romano*, edited by Gonzalo Bravo and Raúl González Salinero, pp. 19–44. Signifer Libros, Madrid.

Edmondson, Jonathan. 2016a. Monuments of Empire in Roman Spain and Behond: Augusta Emerita (Mérida), the "Spanish Rome." In *Altera Roma: Art and Empire from Mérida to Mexico*, edited by John M. D. Pohl and Claire L. Lyons, pp. 69–107. Cotsen Institute of Archaeology Press, UCLA, Los Angeles.

Edmondson, Jonathan. 2016b. The Administration of Lusitania from the Reforms of Diocletian to c. 340. In *A Lusitânia entre Romanos e Bárbaros*, edited by José D'Encarnção, M. Conceição Lopes, and Pedro C. Carbalho, pp. 179–221. Universidade de Coimbra, Coimbra, Portugal.

Elliott, John H. 1967. The Mental World of Hernán Cortés. *Transactions of the Royal Historical Society* 17: 41–58.

Elliott, John H. 1986. Cortés, Velázquez and Charles V. In *Letters from Mexico* by Hernán Cortés, edited and translated by Anthony Pagden, pp. xi–xxxvii. Yale University Press, New Haven, CT.

Eshel, Tzilla, Yigal Erel, Naama Yahalom-Mack, Ofir Tirosh, and Ayelet Gilboa. 2019. Lead Isotopes in Silver Reveal Earliest Phoenician Quest for Metals in the West Mediterranean. *Proceedings of the National Academy of Sciences* 116(13): 6007–6012.

Evans, Susan Toby. 1998a. Sexual Politics in the Aztec Palace: Public, Private, and Profane. *RES* 33: 167–183.

Evans, Susan Toby. 1998b. Toltec Invaders and Spanish Conquistadors: Culture Contact in the Postclassic Teotihuacán Valley, Mexico. In *Studies in Culture Contact: Interaction, Culture Change, and Archaeology*, edited by James G. Cusick, pp.

335–357. Center for Archaeological Investigations, Occasional Paper No. 25. Board of Trustees, Southern Illinois University, Carbondale.

Evans, Susan Toby. 2004. Aztec Palaces and Other Elite Residential Architecture. In *Palaces of the Ancient New World*, edited by Susan Toby Evans and Joanne Pillsbury, pp. 7–58. Dumbarton Oaks Research Library and Collection, Washington, DC.

Evans, Susan Toby. 2005. The Aztec Palace under Spanish Rule: Disk Motifs in the Mapa de México de 1550 (Uppsala Map or Mapa de Santa Cruz). In *The Postclassic to Spanish-Era Transition in Mesoamerica: Archaeological Perspectives*, edited by Susan Kepecs and Rani T. Alexander, pp. 13–33. University of New Mexico Press, Albuquerque.

Evans, Susan Toby. 2013. *Ancient Mexico and Central America: Archaeology and Culture History*. 3rd edition. Thames and Hudson, New York.

Everitt, Anthony. 2009. *Hadrian and the Triumph of Rome*. Random House, New York.

Fagan, Brian. 2020. Big History and Archaeology. In *The Routledge Companion to Big History*, edited by Craig Benjamin, Esther Quaedackers, and David Baker, pp. 156–169. Routledge, London.

Fargher, Lane F., Richard E. Blanton, and Verenice Y. Heredia Espinoza. 2010. Egalitarian Ideology and Political Power in Prehispanic Central Mexico: The Case of Tlaxcallan. *Latin American Antiqutiy* 21(3): 227–251.

Fargher, Lane F., Richard E. Blanton, and Verenice Y. Heredia Espinoza. 2017a. Aztec State-Making, Politics, and Empires: The Triple Alliance. In *The Oxford Handbook of the Aztecs*, edited by Deborah L. Nichols and Enrique Rodríguez-Alegría, pp. 143–159. Oxford University Press, New York.

Fargher, Lane F., Richard E. Blanton, and Verenice Y. Heredia Espinoza. 2017b. The Independent Republic of Tlaxcallan. In *The Oxford Handbook of the Aztecs*, edited by Deborah L. Nichols and Enrique Rodríguez-Alegría, pp. 535–542. Oxford University Press, New York.

Fargher, Lane F., Richard E. Blanton, Verenice Y. Heredia Espinoza, John Millhauser, Nezahualcoyotl Xiuhtecutli, and Lisa Overholtzer. 2011a. Tlaxcallan: The Archaeology of an Ancient Republic in the New World. *Antiquity* 85: 172–186.

Fargher, Lane F., Verenice Y. Heredia Espinoza, and Richard E. Blanton. 2011b. Alternative Pathways to Power in Late Postclassic Highland Mesoamerica. *Journal of Anthropological Archaeology* 30: 306–326.

Faudree, Paja. 2013. How to Say Things with Wars: Performativity and Discursive Rupture in the *Requerimiento* of the Spanish Conquest. *Journal of Linguistic Anthropology* 23(2): 182–200.

Favila Vázquez, Mariana. 2014. Lacustrine Battles in Tenochtitlan: Use of War Canoes by Mexicas. In *Proceedings of the 2nd Asia-Pacific Regional Conference on Underwater Cultural Heritage*, Vol. 2, *Sessions 8–15*, edited by Hans Van Tilburg, Sila Tripati, Veronica Walker, Brian Fahy, and Jun Kimura, pp. 1037–1046. Museum of Underwater Archaeology, Honolulu.

Favila Vázquez, Mariana. 2016. *Veredas de mar y río: Navegación prehispánica y colonial en Los Tuxtlas, Veracruz*. Universidad Nacional Autónoma de México, Mexico City.

Fernández, Damián. 2017. *Aristocrats and Statehood in Western Iberia, 300–600 C.E.* University of Pennsylvania Press, Philadelphia.

Fernández de Velasco, Manuel. 1947. El descubrimiento de los restos de Hernán Cortés. *Revista de Indias* 8: 271–282.

Fernández Gallardo, Luis. 2005. Santiago Matamoros en la historiografía hispanomedieval: Origen y desarrollo de un mito nacional. *Medievalismo* 15: 139–174.

Ferrer, Eulalio. 2000. El color entre los pueblos nahuas. *Estudios de Cultura Náhuatl* 31: 203–219.

Fletcher, Richard. 1989. *The Quest for El Cid.* Oxford University Press, New York.

Folan, William J., Abel Morales L., Raymundo González H., José Antonio Hernández T., Linda Florey Folan, Donald Forsyth, Vera Tiesler B., María José Gómez C., Aracely Hurtado C., Ronald Bishop, David Bolles, Geoffrey Braswell, Jerald Ek, Joel D. Gunn, Christopher Götz, Gerardo Villanueva, Alicia Blanco, Tomás Arnabar G., María del Rosario Domínguez C., and Trenton Noble. 2012. Chakanputun, Campeche: 3,000 años de sustentabilidad. In *Arqueología de la costa de Campeche: La época prehispánica*, edited by Rafael Cobos, pp. 257–279. Ediciones de la Universidad Autónoma de Yucatán, Mérida.

Ford, Gordon B., Jr. (ed.). 1970. *The Letters of St. Isidore of Seville.* 2nd edition. Adolf M. Hakkert, Amsterdam.

Foster, George M. 1960. *Culture and Conquest: America's Spanish Heritage.* Quadrangle Books, Chicago.

Fournier, Patricia G., and Cynthia L. Otis Charlton. 2017. Post-Conquest Rural Aztec Archaeology. In *The Oxford Handbook of the Aztecs*, edited by Deborah L. Nichols and Enrique Rodríguez-Alegría, pp. 643–660. Oxford University Press, New York.

Fowler, William R., and Jeb J. Card. 2019. Material Encounters and Indigenous Transformations in Early Colonial El Salvador. In *Material Encounters and Indigenous Transformations in the Early Colonial Americas*, edited by Corinne L. Hofman and Floris W. M. Keehnen, pp. 197–220. Brill, Leiden.

Frankl, Victor. 1962. Hernán Cortés y la tradición de las Siete Partidas. *Revista de historia de América* 53–54: 9–74.

Freidel, David. 2010. Maya Divine Kinghsip. In *Religion and Power: Divine Kingship in the Ancient World and Beyond*, edited by Nicole Brish, pp. 191–206. The Oriental Institute of the University of Chicago, Chicago.

Fuentes, Carlos. 1992. *The Buried Mirror: Reflections on Spain and the New World.* Houghton Mifflin, Boston.

Fuertes Herreros, José Luis. 2015. Una filosofía para el Viejo y Nuevo mundo en la Universidad de Salamanca (siglos XV–XVI). In *La Escuela de Salamanca: Filosofía y Humanismo ante el mundo moderno*, pp. 23–82. Editorial Verbum, Madrid.

Futrell, Alison. 1997. *Blood in the Arena: The Spectacle of Roman Power.* University of Texas Press, Austin.

Galindo Leal, Carlos, José Sarukhán Kermez, and David Charles Wright Carr. 2017. Una historia natural del emblema nacional de México. In *Escudo nacional: Flora, fauna y biodiversidad*, edited by Cora Ma. A. Falero Ruiz, pp. 42–61. Gobierno de la República, Secretaría de Medio Ambiente y Recursos Naturales, Secretaría de Cultura, Instituto Nacional de Antropología e Historia, Mexico City.

Gamio, Manuel, Adolfo Best, and Frans Boas. 1921. *Álbum de colecciones arqueológicas*. Museo Nacional de Arqueología, Historia y Etnografía, Mexico City.

García, Sebastián. 1991. *Guadalupe de Extremadura en América*. Comunidad Franciscana de Guadalupe, Gráficas Don Bosco, Madrid.

García Cook, Ángel, and Beatriz Leonor Merino Carrión. 1977. Notas sobre caminos y rutas de intercambio al este de la Cuenca de México. *Comunicaciones* 14: 71–82 (FAIC, Puebla).

García Cook, Ángel, and Beatriz Leonor Merino Carrión. 1988. Integración y consolidación de los señoríos en Tlaxcala, siglos IX al XVI. *Arqueología* 2: 155–168.

García Cook, Ángel, and Beatriz Leonor Merino Carrión. 1989. La cultura Tlaxco o señorío de Tliliuhquitepec en el norte de Tlaxcala. In *Homenaje a Román Piña Chán*, edited by Roberto García Moll and Ángel García Cook, pp. 145–158. Instituto Nacional de Antropología e Historia, Mexico City.

García-Des Lauriers, Claudia. 2008. The "House of Darts": The Classic Period Origins of the *Tlacochcalco*. *Mesoamerican Voices* 3: 3–21.

García Martínez, Bernardo. 2001. Los caminos prehispánicos y la estrategia de la conquista. *Arqueología Mexicana* IX(49): 44–47.

Gardiner, C. Harvey. 1954. First Shipping Constructed in New Spain. *The Americas* 10(4): 409–419.

Gardiner, C. Harvey. 1956. *Naval Power in the Conquest of Mexico*. Greenwood Press, New York.

Gasco, Janine. 2018. Anthropogenic Landscapes of Soconusco, Past and Present. In *Colonial and Postcolonial Change in Mesoamerica: Archaeology as Historical Anthropology*, edited by Rani T. Alexander and Susan Kepecs, pp. 205–226. University of New Mexico, Albuquerque.

Gener Basallote, José María, María de los Ángeles Navarro García, Juan-Miguel Payuelo Sáez, Mariano Torres Ortíz, and Ester López Rosendo. 2014. Arquitectura y urbanismo de la Gadir fenicia: el yacimiento del "Teatro Cómico" de Cádiz. In *Los Fenicios en la bahía de Cádiz: Nuevas investigaciones*, edited by Massimo Botto, pp. 14–50. Fabrizio Serra Editore, Pisa and Rome.

Gibson, Carrie. 2019. *El Norte: The Epic and Forgotten Story of Hispanic North America*. Atlantic Monthly Press, New York.

Gibson, Charles. 1964. *The Aztecs under Spanish Rule: A History of the Indians of the Valley of Mexico, 1519–1810*. Stanford University, Stanford, CA.

Gibson, Charles. 1967. *Tlaxcala in the Sixteenth Century*. 2nd edition. Stanford University Press, Stanford, CA.

Gilman, Antonio. 1987. Unequal Development in Copper Age Iberia. In *Specialization, Exchange, and Complex Societies*, edited by Elizabeth Brumfiel and Timothy Earle, pp. 22–29. Cambridge University Press, New York.

Glick, Thomas F. 1996. *Irrigation and Hydraulic Technology: Medieval Spain and Its Legacy*. Variorum, Hampshire, UK.

Glick, Thomas F. 2005. *Islamic and Christian Spain in the Early Middle Ages*. 2nd edition. Brill, Boston.

Glick, Thomas F., Antonio Malpica, Félix Retamero, and Josep Torró (eds.). 2018. *From Al-Andalus to the Americas (13th–17th Centuries): Destruction and Construction of Societies*. Brill, Leiden.

Golitko, Mark, James Meierhoff, Gary M. Feinman, and Patrick Ryan Williams. 2012. Complexities of Collapse: The Evidence of Maya Obsidian as Revealed by Socialnetwork Graphical Analysis. *Antiquity* 86: 507–523.

Gómez Espelosín, Javier. 2009. Iberia in the Greek Geographical Imagination. In *Colonial Encounters in Ancient Iberia: Phoenician, Greek, and Indigenous Relations*, edited by Michael Dietler and Carolina López-Ruiz, pp. 281–297. University of Chicago Press, Chicago.

González Arévalo, Raúl. 2018. Cabalgadas y ganadería en la frontera castellano-granadina según la cronística cristiana. *Revista del CEHGR* 30: 71–89.

González-Rubial, Alfredo. 2004. Facing Two Seas: Mediterranean and Atlantic Contacts in the North-West of Iberia in the First Millennium BC. *Oxford Journal of Archaeology* 23(3): 287–317.

González-Rubial, Alfredo. 2006. House Societies vs. Kinship-Based Societies: An Archaeological case from Iron Age Europe. *Journal of Anthropological Archaeology* 25: 144–173.

González-Rubial, Alfredo. 2008. Los pueblos del noroeste. In *De Iberia a Hispania*, edited by Francisco Gracia Alonso, pp. 899–930. Editorial Ariel, Barcelona.

Gracia Alonso, Francisco. 2008. Colonización y comercio púnico en la península Ibérica. In *De Iberia a Hispania*, edited by Francisco Gracia Alonso, pp. 845–897. Editorial Ariel, Barcelona.

Gracia Alonso, Francisco (ed.). 2008. *De Iberia a Hispania*. Editorial Ariel, Barcelona.

Grove, David C., and Susan D. Gillespie. 2009. People of the *Cerro*: Landscape, Settlement, and Art at Middle Formative Period Chalcatzingo. In *The Art of Urbanism: How Mesoamerican Kingdoms Represented Themselves in Art and Architecture*, edited by William L. Fash and Leonardo López Luján, pp. 53–76. Dumbarton Oaks Trustees of Harvard University, Washington, DC.

Grunberg, Bernard. 1994. The Origins of the Conquistadores of Mexico City. *The Hispanic American Historical Review* 74(2): 259–283.

Gruzinski, Serge. 1993. *The Conquest of Mexico: Westernization of Indian Societies from the 16th to the 18th Century*. Polity Press, Malden, MA.

Gutiérrez, Gerardo. 2013. Negotiating Aztec Tributary Demands in the *Tribute Record of Tlapa*. In *Merchants, Markets, and Exchange in the Pre-Columbian World*, edited by Kenneth G. Hirth and Joanne Pillsbury, pp. 141–167. Dumbarton Oaks and Trustees for Harvard University, Washington, DC.

Gutiérrez, Gerardo. 2015. Identity Erasure and Demographic Impacts of the Spanish Caste System on the Indigenous Populations of Mexico. In *Beyond Germs: Native Depopulation in North America*, edited by Catherine M. Cameron, Paul Kelton, and Alan C. Swedlund, pp. 119–145. University of Arizona Press, Tucson.

Gutiérrez Arriola, Cecelia. 1997. El convento de Nuestra Señora de la Asunción de Tlaxcala en el siglo XVI: Notas sobre un dibujo de Diego Muñoz Camargo. *Anales del Instituto de Investigaciones Estéticas* 71: 5–36.

Hamann, Byron Ellsworth. 2010. The Mirrors of Las Meninas: Cochineal, Silver, and Clay. *The Art Bulletin* 92(1–2): 6–35.

Hanke, Lewis. 1965. *The Spanish Struggle for Justice in the Conquest of America*. Little, Brown, Boston.

Harris, Max. 2000. *Aztecs, Moors, and Christians: Festivals of Reconquest in Mexico and Spain*. University of Texas Press, Austin.

Harrison, Richard J. 1988. *Spain at the Dawn of History: Iberians, Phoenicians, and Greeks*. Thames and Hudson, London.

Hassig, Ross. 1992. *War and Society in Ancient Mesoamerica*. University of California Press, Berkeley.

Hassig, Ross. 2001. Xicotencatl: Rethinking an Indigenous Mexican Hero. *Estudios de la Cultura Nahuatl* 32: 29–49.

Hassig, Ross. 2006. *Mexico and the Spanish Conquest*. University of Oklahoma Press, Norman.

Hassig, Ross. 2016a. *Polygamy and the Rise and Demise of the Aztec Empire*. University of New Mexico Press, Albuquerque.

Hassig, Ross. 2016b. Combat and Capture in the Aztec Empire. *British Journal for Military History* 3(1): 2–25.

Healan, Dan M., and Robert H. Cobean. 2012. Tula and the Toltecs. In *The Oxford Handbook of Mesoamerican Archaeology*, edited by Deborah L. Nichols and Christopher A. Pool, pp. 372–384. Oxford University Press, New York.

Heath-Stout, Laura E. 2019. Pottery on the Periphery: Contact-Period Ceramics and Regional Integration at La Laguna, Tlaxcala, Mexico. *Journal of Anthropological Archaeology*, 56: 101088.

Helmke, Christophe. 2019. Tactics, Trophies, and Titles: A Comparative Perspective on Ancient Maya Raiding. *Ancient Mesoamerica*, online first version. doi:10.1017/S0956536118000287.

Hernández Sánchez, Gilda. 2012. *Ceramics and the Spanish Conquest: Response and Continuity of Indigenous Pottery Technology in Central Mexico*. Brill, Leiden.

Herrera, Robinson A. 2007. Concubines and Wives: Reinterpreting Native-Spanish Intimate Unions in Sixteenth-Century Guatemala. In *Indian Conquistadors: Indigenous Allies in the Conquest of Mesoamerica*, edited by Laura E. Matthew and Michel R. Ouidijk, pp. 127–144. University of Oklahoma Press, Norman.

Herodotus. 1987. *The History*. Translated by David Grene. University of Chicago Press, Chicago.

Heywood, Linda M., and John K. Thornton. 2007. *Central Africans, Atlantic Creoles, and the Foundation of the Americas, 1585–1660*. Cambridge University Press, New York.

Hicks, Frederic. 1999. The Middle Class in Ancient Central Mexico. *Journal of Anthropological Research* 55(3): 409–427.

Hicks, Frederic. 2009. Land and Succession in the Indigenous Noble Houses of Sixteenth-Century Tlaxcala. *Ethnohistory* 56(4): 569–588.

Hill, Jane H. 2017. The Languages of the Aztec Empire. In *The Oxford Handbook of the Aztecs*, edited by Deborah L. Nichols and Enrique Rodríguez-Alegría, pp. 129–141. Oxford University Press, New York.

Himmerich y Valencia, Robert. 1991. *The Encomenderos of New Spain, 1521–1555*. University of Texas Press, Austin.

Hirth, Kenneth G. 2016. *The Aztec Economic World: Merchants and Markets in Ancient Mesoamerica*. Cambridge University Press, New York.

Hirth, Kenneth G., David M. Carballo, and Barbara Arroyo (eds.). 2019. *Teotihuacan: The World beyond the City*. Dumbarton Oaks and Trustees for Harvard University, Washington, DC.

Hoffman, Philip T. 2015. *Why Did Europe Conquer the World?* Princeton University Press, Princeton, NJ.

Hosler, Dorothy. 1995. Sound, Color, and Meaning in the Metallurgy of Ancient West Mexico. *World Archaeology* 27(1): 100–115.

INAH. 2018. En aguas veracruzanas, expertos del INAH emprenden búsqueda de los navíos hundidos por Hernán Cortés. *Boletín* 246, July 31, 2018. Instituto Nacional de Antropología e Historia, Mexico City.

INAH. 2019. A 500 años del desembarco de Cortés, investigadores descubren dos anclas de hierro en la Villa Rica, Veracruz. *Boletín* 551, December 16, 2019. Instituto Nacional de Antropología e Historia, Mexico City.

Jaenicke-Després, Viviane R., and Bruce D. Smith. 2006. Ancient DNA and the Integration of Archaeological and Genetic Approaches to the Study of Maize Domestication. In *Histories of Maize in Mesoamerica: Multidisciplinary Approaches*, edited by John E. Staller, Robert H. Tykot, and Bruce F. Benz, pp. 83–95. Elsevier, Amsterdam.

Jarquín Pacheco, Ana María, and Enrique Martínez Vargas. 2015. Tecoaque: Encuentro entre dos mundos en una página de la conquista de México. In *Itinerario de Hernán Cortés: Catálogo de la exposición, Centro de Exposiciones Arte Canal, 3 diciembre 2014–3 mayo 2015*, edited by Martín Almagro Gorbea and Cristina Esteras Martín, pp. 133–143. Fundación Canal de Isabel II, Madrid.

Jarquín Pacheco, Ana María, and Enrique Martínez Vargas. 2017. El tzompantli en Zultépec-Tecoaque. *Arqueología Mexicana* 148: 75–77.

Jay, Felix (ed., trans.). 2002. *Three Dominican Pioneers in the New World: Antonio de Montesinos, Domingo de Betanzos, Gonzalo Lucero*. Spanish Studies Volume 16. Edwin Mellen Press, Lewiston, NY.

Jiménez, Alicia, and José R. Carrillo. 2011. *Corduba/Colonia Patricia*: The Colony That Was Founded Twice. In *Roman Colonies in the First Century of Their Foundation*, edited by Rebecca J. Sweetman, pp. 55–74. Oxbow Books, Oxford.

Jiménez Ávila, Javier. 2016. Ancha es Tartesos: El periodo orientalizante (siglos VIII–VI a.C.) en el tramo extremeño del Guadiana. In *El Rio Guadiana y Tartesos*, Siderum Ana III, edited by Javiér Jiménez Ávila, pp. 69–106. Consorcio de la Ciudad Monumental Histórico-Artística y Arqueológica de Mérida, Spain.

Joyce, Rosemary A. 2000. Girling the Girl and Boying the Boy: The Production of Adulthood in Ancient Mesoamerica. *World Archaeology* 31(3): 473–483.

Juli, Harold D. 2002. The Museum of the City of Cholula, Puebla, Mexico. *American Anthropologist* 104(3): 956–957.

Junco, Roberto, Christopher Horrell, Frederick Hanselmann, Melanie Damour, and Josué Guzmán. 2019. *Arqueología Subacuática en la Villa Rica, Tras los pasos del Del Paso y Troncoso y los barcos hundidos de Hernán Cortés.* Technical report on file at the Consejo de Arqueologia, Instituto Nacional de Antropología e Historia, Mexico City.

Karttunen, Frances. 1994. *Between Worlds: Interpreters, Guides, and Survivors.* Rutgers University Press, New Brunswick, NJ.

Kaufman, Terrance, and John Justeson. 2009. Historical Linguistics and Pre-Columbian Mesoamerica. *Ancient Mesoamerica* 20: 221–231.

Keegan, William F., and Corinne L. Hofman. 2017. *The Caribbean before Columbus.* Oxford University Press, New York.

Kehoe, Alice. 1979. The Sacred Heart: A Case for Stimulus Diffusion. *American Ethnologist* 6: 763–771.

Kennett, Douglas J., Heather B. Thakar, Amber M. VanDerwarker, David L. Webster, Brendan J. Culleton, Thomas K. Harper, Logan Kistler, Timothy E. Scheffler, and Kenneth Hirth. 2017. High-Precision Chronology for Central American Maize Diversification from El Gigante Rockshelter, Honduras. *Proceedings of the National Academy of Sciences* 114(34): 9026–9031.

Kepecs, Susan, Patricia Fournier García, Rani T. Alexander, and Cynthia L. Otis Charlton. 2018. Commodities Production and Technological Change. In *Colonial and Postcolonial Change in Mesoamerica: Archaeology as Historical Anthropology*, edited by Rani T. Alexander and Susan Kepecs, pp. 29–52. University of New Mexico, Albuquerque.

Kilroy-Ewbank, Lauren G. 2014. Holy Organ or Unholy Idol? Forming a History of the Sacred Heart in New Spain. *Colonial Latin American Review* 23(3): 320–359.

Kiracofe, James B. 1995. Architectural Fusion and Indigenous Ideology in Early Colonial Teposcolula the Casa de la Cacica: A Building at the Edge of Oblivion. *Anales del Instituto de Investigaciones Estéticas* 17(66): 45–84.

Kirchhoff, Paul. 1943. Mesoamérica: Sus límites geográficos, composición étnica y caracteres culturales. *Acta Americana* 1: 92–107.

Klemm, Friedrich. 1964. *A History of Western Technology.* MIT Press, Cambridge, MA.

Klor de Alva, J. Jorge. 1982. Spiritual Conflict and Accommodation in New Spain: Toward a Typology of Aztec Responses to Christianity. In *The Inca and Aztec States, 1400–1800: Anthropology and History*, edited by George A. Collier, Renato I. Rosaldo, and John D. Wirth, pp. 345–366. Academic Press, New York.

Knight, Vernon James, Jr. 2010. La Loma del Convento: Its Centrality to Current Issues in Cuban Archaeology. In *Beyond the Blockade: New Currents in Cuban Archaeology*, edited by Susan Kepecs, L. Antonio Curet, and Gabino La Rosa Corzo, pp. 26–46. University of Alabama Press, Tuscaloosa.

Kohler, Timothy A., and Michael E. Smith (eds.). 2018. *Ten Thousand Years of Inequality: The Archaeology of Wealth Differences.* University of Arizona Press, Tucson.

Kohler, Timothy A., Michael E. Smith, Amy Bogaard, Gary M. Feinman, Christian E. Peterson, Alleen Betzenhauser, Matthew Pailes, Elizabeth C. Stone, Anna Marie Prentiss, Timothy J. Dennehy, Laura J. Ellyson, Linda M. Nicholas, Ronald K. Faulseit, Amy Styring, Jade Whitlam, Mattia Fochesato, Thomas A. Foor, and Samuel Bowles. 2017. Greater Post-Neolithic Wealth Disparities in Eurasia than in North America and Mesoamerica. *Nature* 551(7682): 619. doi:10.1038/nature24646.

Kugel, James L. 2004. *The God of Old: Inside the Lost World of the Bible.* Free Press, New York.

Ladero Quesada, Miguel Ángel. 2008. *Las Indias de Castilla en sus primeros años: Cuentas de las Casa de la Contratación (1503–1521).* Editorial Dykinson, Madrid.

Ladero Quesada, Miguel Ángel. 2018. *La España de los Reyes Católicos.* 4th edition. Alianza Editorial, Madrid.

Las Casas, Bartolomé de. 1552/1992. *In Defense of the Indians.* Translated by Stafford Poole. Northern Illinois University Press, DeKalb.

Lee, Jongsoo, and Galen Brokaw (eds.). 2014. *Texcoco: Prehispanic and Colonial Perspectives.* University Press of Colorado, Boulder.

León Portilla, Miguel. 1966. *The Broken Spears: The Aztec Account of the Conquest of Mexico.* Beacon Press, Boston.

León Portilla, Miguel. 2000. *Tonantzin Guadalupe: Pensamiento náhuatl y mensaje cristiano en el "Nican mopohua."* Colegio Nacional and Fondo de Cultura Económica, Mexico City.

León Portilla, Miguel. 2003. *Aztec Thought and Culture: A Study of the Ancient Nahuatl Mind.* University of Oklahoma Press, Norman.

Lesure, Richard G. 2008. The Neolithic Demographic Transition in Mesoamerica? Larger Implications of the Strategy of Relative Chronology. In *The Neolithic Demographic Transition and its Consequences*, edited by Jean-Pierre Bocquet-Appel and Ofer Bar-Yosef, pp. 107–138. Springer, New York.

Lesure, Richard G. (ed.). 2011. *Early Mesoamerican Social Transformations: Archaic and Formative Lifeways in the Soconusco Region.* University of California Press, Berkeley.

Leveau, Philippe. 2007. The Western Provinces. In *The Cambridge Economic History of the Greco-Roman World*, edited by Walter Scheidel, Ian Morris, and Richard P. Saller, pp. 649–670. Cambridge University Press, Cambridge.

Levine, Marc N., and David M. Carballo (eds.). 2014. *Obsidian Reflections: Symbolic Dimensions of Obsidian in Mesoamerica*. University Press of Colorado, Boulder.

Li, Yu, Darin S. Carroll, Shea N. Gardner, Matthew C. Walsh, Elizabeth A. Vitalis, and Inger K. Damon. 2007. On the Origin of Smallpox: Correlating Variola Phylogenics with Historical Smallpox Records. *Proceedings of the National Academy of Sciences of the United States of America* 104(40): 15787–15792.

Lind, Michael. 2012. La estructura político-territorial del *altepetl* de Cholula. In *El poder compartido: ensayos sobre la arqueología de organizaciones políticas segmentarias y oligárquicas*, edited by Annick Daneels and Gerardo Gutiérrez Mendoza, pp. 99–113. Centro de Investigaciones y Estudios Superiores en Antropología Social, Colegio de Michoacán, Mexico City.

Linné, S. 1942. *Mexican Highland Cultures: Archaeological Researches at Teotihuacan, Calpulalpan and Chalchicomula in 1934/35*. The Ethnographical Museum of Sweden, Stockholm, Publication No. 7. Lund, Sweden.

Lockhart, James. 1992. *The Nahuas after the Conquest: A Social and Cultural History of the Indians of Central Mexico, Sixteenth through Eighteenth Centuries.* Stanford University, Stanford, CA.

Lockhart, James. 1993. *We People Here: Nahuatl Accounts of the Conquest of Mexico*. University of California Press, Berkeley.

Lockhart, James. 1998. Three Experiences of Culture Contact: Nahua, Maya, and Quechua. In *Native Traditions in the Postconquest World*, edited by Elizabeth Hill Boone and Tom Cummins, pp. 31–51. Dumbarton Oaks and Trustees for Harvard University, Washington, DC.

López Austin, Alfredo. 1993. *Myths of the Opossum*. University of New Mexico, Albuquerque.

López Austin, Alfredo. 1997. *Tamoanchan, Tlalocan: Places of Mist*. Translated by Bernard R. Ortiz de Montellano and Thelma Ortiz de Montellano. University Press of Colorado, Boulder.

López Austin, Alfredo. 2001. El núcleo duro, la cosmovisión y la tradición mesoamericana. In *Cosmovisión, ritual e identidad de los pueblos indígenas*, edited by Johana Broda and Félix Báez-Jorge, pp. 47–65. Conaculta/INAH, Mexico City.

López Austin, Alfredo, and Leonardo López Luján. 2009. *Monte sagrado—Templo mayor: el cerro y la pirámide en la tradición religiosa mesoamericana*. UNAM/IIA and INAH, Mexico City.

López Austin, Alfredo, and Leonardo López Luján. 2017. State Ritual and Religion in the Sacred Precinct of Tenochtitlan. In *The Oxford Handbook of the Aztecs*, edited by Deborah L. Nichols and Enrique Rodríguez-Alegría, pp. 605–621. Oxford University Press, New York.

López Corral, Aurelio, Lane F. Fargher, and Ramón Santacruz Cano. 2016. La república de Tlaxcallan. *Arqueología Mexicana* 139: 42–53.

López de Gómara, Francisco. 1552/1964. *Cortés: The Life of the Conqueror by His Secretary*. Translated and edited by Lesley Byrd Simpson. University of California Press, Berkeley.

López de Gómara, Francisco. 1552/1988. *Historia de la Conquista de México*. Editorial Porrúa, Mexico City.

López de la Torre, Carlos Fernando. 2016. El trabajo misional de fray Pedro de Gante en los inicios de la Nueva España. *Fronteras de la Historia* 21(1): 90–116.

López Luján, Leonardo. 2006. *La Casa de las Águilas: Un ejemplo de la arquitectura religiosa de Tenochtitlan*, Vol. 1. Fondo de Cultura Económica, Mexico City.

López Luján, Leonardo. 2015. *El capitán Guillermo Dupaix y su álbum arqueológico de 1794*. Ediciones del Museo Nacional de Antropología. Instituto Nacional de Antropología e Historia, Mexico.

López Luján, Leonardo. 2017a. El Proyecto Templo Mayor (1991–2017): Recuento de cinco lustros de actividades. In *Templo Mayor: Revolución y estabilidad*, edited by Eduardo Matos Moctezuma and Patricia Ledesma Bouchan, pp. 37–57. Instituto Nacional de Antropología e Historia, Mexico City.

López Luján, Leonardo. 2017b. El oro de las ofrendas y las sepulturas del recinto sagrado de Tenochtitlan. *Arqueología Mexicana* XXIV(144): 58–63.

López Luján, Leonardo. 2018. Cuando la gente "se uno-aconejó": la gran sequía de 1454 en la Cuenca de México. *Arqueología Mexicana* XXV(149): 36–45.

López Luján, Leonardo, and Alfredo López Austin. 2009. The Mexica in Tula and Tula in Mexico-Tenochtitlan. In *The Art of Urbanism: How Mesoamerican Kingdoms Represented Themselves in Art and Architecture*, edited by William L. Fash and Leonardo López Luján, pp. 384–422. Dumbarton Oaks Trustees of Harvard University, Washington, DC.

López Luján, Leonardo, and Xavier Noguez. 2011. The Codex Teotenantzin and the Pre-Hispanic Images of the Sierra de Guadalupe, México. *Res: Anthropology and Aesthetics* 59–60: 93–108.

López Medellín, Xavier. 2014. Hernán Cortés y la joya del alacrán. *¿Cómoves? Revista de divulgación de ciencias de la Universidad Nacional Autónoma de México* 188: 26–29.

López-Merino, Lourdes, Antonio Martínez Cortizas, Guillermo S. Reher, José A. López-Sáez, Tim M. Mighall, and Richard Bindler. 2014. Reconstructing the impact of human activities in a NW Iberian Roman mining landscape for the last 2500 years. *Journal of Archaeological Science* 50: 208–218.

Lothrop, S. K. 1924. *Tulum: An Archaeological Study of the East Coast of Yucatan*. Publication 335. Carnegie Institution, Washington, DC.

Low, Setha M. 1995. Indigenous Architecture and the Spanish American Plaza in Mesoamerica and the Caribbean. *American Anthropologist* 97(4): 748–762.

Lozano, José Antonio Lozano, Gerardo Ruiz-Puertas, Manuel Hódar-Correa, Fernando Pérez-Valera, and Great Menga Dolmen (Málaga, Spain): A Geometric and Geoarchaeological Analysis. *Journal of Archaeological Science* 41: 759–771.

Mahoney, James. 2000. Path Dependence in Historical Sociology. *Theory and Society* 29: 507–548.

Maldonado, Blanca E. 2012. Mesoamerican Metallurgical Technology and Production. In *The Oxford Handbook of Mesoamerican Archaeology*, edited by

Deborah L. Nichols and Christopher A. Pool, pp. 616–627. Oxford University Press, New York.

Mann, Charles C. 2005. *1491: New Revelations of the Americas before Columbus*. Alfred A. Knopf, New York.

Mann, Charles C. 2011. *1493: Uncovering the New World Columbus Created*. Vintage, New York.

Marciniak, Stephanie D., Ann Herring, Alessandra Sperduti, Hendrik N. Poinar, and Tracy L. Prowse. 2018. A Multi-faceted Anthropological and Genomic Approach to Framing *Plasmodium falciparum* Malaria in Imperial Period Central-Southern Italy (1st–4th c. CE). *Journal of Anthropological Archaeology* 49: 210–224.

Marcus, Joyce, and Kent V. Flannery. 1996. *Zapotec Civilization: How Urban Society Evolved in Mexico's Oaxaca Valley*. Thames and Hudson, New York.

Marquina, Ignacio. 1970. Pirámide de Cholula. In *Proyecto Cholula*, Vol. 19, edited by Ignacio Marquina, pp. 31–45. Instituto Nacional de Antropología e Historia, Mexico City.

Martínez, José Luis. 1990. *Hernán Cortés*. Universidad Nacional Autónoma de México and Fondo de Cultura Económica, Mexico City.

Martínez Baracs, Andrea. 2008. *Un gobierno de indios: Tlaxcala, 1519–1750*. Fondo de Cultura Económica, Fideicomiso Colegio de Historia de Tlaxcala, and Centro de Investigaciones y Estudios Superiores en Antropología Social, Mexico City.

Martínez Baracs, Rodrigo. 2000. Tepeyac en la conquista de México: Problemas historiográficos. In *Tepeyac: Estudios históricos*, edited by Carmen Aguilera and Ismael Arturo Montero García, pp. 55–118. Universidad del Tepeyac, Mexico City.

Martínez Baracs, Rodrigo. 2006. *La perdida Relación de la Nueva España y su conquista de Juan Cano*. Instituto Nacional de Antropología e Historia, Mexico City.

Martínez Ramírez, Ivonne. 2010. La mula en la vida cotidiana del siglo XVI. In *Caminos y mercados de México*, edited by Janet Long Towell and Amalia Attolini Lecón, pp. 291–310. Universidad Nacional Autónoma de México, Instituto Nacional de Antropología e Historia, Mexico City.

Martínez Vargas, Enrique. 2016. La historia no escrita de Zultépec-Tecoaque, Tlaxcala. *Arqueología Mexicana* 139: 54–59.

Martínez Vargas, Enrique, and Ana María Jarquín Pacheco. 2010. El tzompantli de Zúltepec-Tecoaque. *Letras Libres* 133: https://www.letraslibres.com/mexico/el-tzompantli-zultepec-tecoaque.

Matos Moctezuma, Eduardo. 1988. *The Great Temple of the Aztecs: Treasures of Tenochtitlan*. Thames and Hudson, London.

Maya Torcelly, R., G. Jurado Fresnadillo, J. M. Gener Basallote, E. López Rosendo, and M. Torres Ortiz. 2015. Nuevos datos sobre el Kronion de Gadir: resultados de la intervención arqueológica en el Castillo de San Sebastián (Cádiz). In *Actas del VII encuentro de arqueología del suroeste peninsular*, edited by Nieves Medina Rosales, pp. 429–451. Ayuntamento de Aroche, Huelva.

Mayoral, Victorino, Francisco Borja Barrera, César Borja Barrera, José Ángel Martínez del Pozo, and Maite de Tena. 2012. The Evolution of an Agrarian

Landscape: Methodological Proposals for the Archaeological Study of the Alluvial Plain of Medellin (Guadiana Basin, Spain). In *Landscape Archaeology between Art and Science: From a Multi- to an Interdisciplinary Approach*, edited by S. J. Kluiving and E. B. Guttmann-Bond, pp. 97–114. Amsterdam University Press, Amsterdam.

McCafferty, Geoffrey. 2000. The Cholula Massacre: Factional Histories and Archaeology of the Spanish Conquest. In *The Entangled Past: Integrating History and Archaeology*, edited by M. Boyd, J. C. Erwin, and M. Hendrickson, pp. 347–359. The Archaeological Association of the University of Calgary, Calgary.

McCafferty, Geoffrey. 2016. La matanza en Cholula. *Elementos* 102: 3–16.

McClure, Julia. 2018. The Charitable Bonds of the Spanish Empire: The Casa de Contratación as an Institution of Charity. *New Global Studies* 12(2): 157–174.

McGrail, Sean. 2004. *Boats of the World: From the Stone Age to Medieval Times*. Oxford University Press, Oxford.

McKillop, Heather. 2010. Ancient Maya Canoe Navigation and Its Implications for Classic to Postclassic Maya Economy and Sea Trade: A View from the South Coast of Belize. *Journal of Caribbean Archaeology* 3: 93–105.

Melville, Elinor G. K. 1997. *A Plague of Sheep: Environmental Consequences of the Conquest of Mexico*. Cambridge University Press, New York.

Melville, Elinor G. K. 2000. Disease, Ecology, and the Environment. In *The Oxford History of Mexico*, edited by M. C. Meyer and W. H. Beezley, pp. 213–243. Oxford University Press, New York.

Mendoza, Ruben G. 1977. World View and the Monolithic Temples of Malinalco, Mexico: Iconography and Analogy in Pre-Columbian Architecture. *Journal de la société des américanistes* 64: 63–80.

Merino Carrión, Beatriz Leonor. 1989. *La Cultura Tlaxco*. Serie Arqueológica, Colección Científica 174. Instituto Nacional de Antropología e Historia, Mexico City.

Michener, James A. 1968. *Iberia: Spanish Travels and Reflections*. Random House, New York.

Mijares Ramírez, Ivonne. 2010. La mula en la vida cotidiana del siglo XVI. In *Caminos y mercados de México*, edited by Janet Long Towell and Amalia Attolini Lecón, pp. 291–310. Universidad Nacional Autónoma de México, Instituto Nacional de Antropología e Historia, Mexico City.

Millhauser, John K., Lane F. Fargher, Verenice Y. Heredia Espinoza, and Richard E. Blanton. 2015. The Geopolitics of Obsidian Supply in Postclassic Tlaxcallan: A Portable X-Ray Fluorescence Study. *Journal of Archaeological Science* 58: 133–146.

Millon, René. 1973. *The Teotihuacan Map, Part One: Text*. University of Texas Press, Austin.

Millon, René. 1988. The Last Years of Teotihuacan Dominance. In *The Collapse of Ancient States and Civilizations*, edited by Norman Yoffee and George L. Cowgill, 102–164. University of Arizona Press, Tucson.

Miteva, Yuliya. 2015. *Árabes, Beréberes y autóctonos en el proceso de arabización lingüística del al-Ándalus (ss. VIII–X)*, I: *Los Árabes y los Beréberes*. Research Papers, Vol. 53, Book 1, Part A, Languages and Literature, University of Plovdiv, Bulgaria.

Mora Rodríguez, Luis Adrián. 2013. Política, imperio e imperialismo: Una aproximación crítica desde las cartas de relación de Hernán Cortés. *Tabula Rasa* 18: 147–163.

Moral García, Carlos. 2015. Santiago en la conquista de Nueva España. *Mirabilia Ars* (Ideas, ritos e imágenes de la muerte) 3(2): 13–35.

Morales, Francisco. 2014. Pedro de Gante, Martín de Valencia, Toribio Motolinía. *Arqueología Mexicana* XXI(127): 37–42.

Morales-Arce, Ana Y., Geoffrey McCafferty, Jessica Hand, Norma Schmill, Krista McGrath, and Camilla Speller. 2019. Ancient Mitochondrial DNA and Population Dynamics in Postclassic Central Mexico: Tlatelolco (AD 1325–1520) and Cholula (AD 900–1350). *Archaeological and Anthropological Sciences* 11(7): 3459–3475. doi: https://doi.org/10.1007/s12520-018-00771-7.

Moreno Villa, José. 1942. *La escultura colonial mexicana*. Fondo De Cultura Económica, Mexico City.

Morey, William C. 1903. *Outlines of Greek History*. American Book, Chicago.

Morris, Ian. 2010. *Why the West Rules—For Now: The Patterns of History, and What They Reveal about the Future*. Picador, New York.

Morris, Ian. 2015. *Foragers, Farmers, and Fossil Fuels: How Human Values Evolve*. Princeton University Press, Princeton, NJ.

Motolinia, Toribo Benavente de. 1903. *Memoriales*. Edited by Joaquin García Icazbalceta. Luis García Pimentel, Mexico City.

Motolinia, Toribo Benavente de. 2007. *Historia de los Indios de la Nueva España*. Linkgua ediciones, Barcelona.

Mundigo, Axel I., and Dora P. Crouch. 1977. The City Planning Ordinances of the Laws of the Indies Revisited. Part I: Their Philosophy and Implications. *The Town Planning Review* 48(3): 247–268.

Mundy, Barbara. 2015. *The Death of Aztec Tenochtitlan, the Life of Mexico City*. University of Texas, Austin.

Muñoz Camargo, Diego. 1584/2000. *Descripción de la ciudad y provincia de Tlaxcala*. 2nd edition. Colegio de San Luis and Gobierno del Estado de Tlaxcala, San Luis Potosí.

Murphy, Cullen. 2012. *God's Jury: The Inquisition and the Making of the Modern World*. Houghton Mifflin Harcourt, Boston.

Newman, Sarah E. 2016. Sharks in the Jungle: Real and Imagined Sea Monsters of the Maya. *Antiquity* 90(354): 1522–1536.

Newson, Linda A. 1993. Highland-Lowland Contrasts in the Impact of Old World Diseases in Early Colonial Ecuador. *Social Science and Medicine* 36(9): 1187–1195.

Nichols, Deborah L., Frances F. Berdan, and Michael E. Smith (eds.). 2017. *Rethinking the Aztec Economy*. University of Arizona Press, Tucson.

Nicholson, Henry B. 2001a. *Topiltzin Quetzalcoatl: The Once and Future Lord of the Toltecs*. University of Oklahoma Press, Norman.

Nicholson, Henry B. 2001b. *The "Return of Quetzalcoatl": Did It Play a Role in the Conquest of Mexico?* Labyrinthos, Lancaster, CA.

Nunn, Nathan, and Nancy Qian. 2010. The Columbian Exchange: A History of Disease, Food, and Ideas. *The Journal of Economic Perspectives* 24(2): 163–188.

O'Flanagan, Patrick. 2008. *Port Cities of Atlantic Iberia c. 1500–1900.* Ashgate, Hampshire, UK.

O'Scanlan, Timoteo. 1831/2003. *Diccionario marítimo español.* Museo Naval, Madrid.

Olivares Pedreño, Juan Carlos. 2006. Urbanismo e interacción religiosa en las ciudades de la Hispania céltica. *Iberia* 9: 79–106.

Ossa, Alanna, Michael E. Smith, and José Lobo. 2017. The Size of Plazas in Mesoamerican Cities and Towns: A Quantitative Analysis. *Latin American Antiquity* 28(4): 457–475.

Oudijk, Michel R. 2012. The Conquest of Mexico. In *The Oxford Handbook of Mesoamerican Archaeology*, edited by Deborah L. Nichols and Christopher A. Pool, pp. 459–467. Oxford University Press, New York.

Oudijk, Michel R., and María Castañeda de la Paz. 2017. Nahua Thought and the Conquest. In *The Oxford Handbook of the Aztecs*, edited by Deborah L. Nichols and Enrique Rodríguez-Alegría, pp. 161–171. Oxford University Press, New York.

Oudijk, Michel R., and Matthew Restall. 2007. Mesoamerican Conquistadors in the Sixteenth Century. In *Indian Conquistadors: Indigenous Allies in the Conquest of Mesoamerica*, edited by Laura E. Matthew and Michel R. Oudijk, pp. 28–64. University of Oklahoma Press, Norman.

Oudijk, Michel R., and Matthew Restall. 2008. *La conquista indígina de Mesoamérica: El caso de Don Gonzalo Mazatzin Moctezuma.* Universidad de las Américas Puebla, Cholula, Mexico.

Pagden, Anthony. 1986. Translator's Introduction. In *Letters from Mexico* by Hernán Cortés, edited and translated by Anthony Pagden, pp. xxxix–xl. Yale University Press, New Haven, CT.

Parilla, José Antonio. 1992. *La llamada del Nuevo Mundo: Galicia y América en el siglo XVI.* Gráfico Galaico, A Coruña.

Parsons, Jeffrey R. 2010. The Pastoral Niche in Pre-Hispanic Mesoamerica. In *Pre-Columbian Foodways: Interdisciplinary Approaches to Food, Culture, and Markets in Ancient Mesoamerica*, edited by John Staller and Michael Carrasco, pp. 109–136. Springer, New York.

Parsons, Jeffrey R., and Yoko Sugiura Y. 2012. Teotihuacan and the Epiclassic in Central Mexico. In *The Oxford Handbook of Mesoamerican Archaeology*, edited by Deborah L. Nichols and Christopher A. Pool, pp. 309–323. Oxford University Press, New York.

Pastrana, Alejandro, and David M. Carballo. 2017. Aztec Obsidian Industries. In *The Oxford Handbook of the Aztecs*, edited by Deborah L. Nichols and Enrique Rodríguez-Alegría, pp. 329–341. Oxford University Press, New York.

Pastrana, Alejandro, and Silvia Domínguez. 2009. Cambios en la estrategia de la explotación de la obsidiana de Pachuca: Teotihuacan, Tula y La Triple Alianza. *Ancient Mesoamerica* 20: 129–148.

Pastrana, Alejandro, and Patricia Fournier. 1997. Cuicuilco desde Cuicuilco. *Actualidades Arqueológicas: Revista de Estudiantes de Arqueología en México* 3(13): 7–9.

Pastrana, Alejandro, Patricia Fournier G., William J. Parry, and Cynthia L. Otis Charlton. 2019. Obsidian Production and Use in Central Mexico after the Spanish Invasion. In *Technology and Tradition in Mesoamerica after the Spanish Invasion: Archaeological Perspectives*, edited by Rani T. Alexander, pp. 15–34. University of New Mexico, Albuquerque.

Pérez García, L. C., and Francisco Javier Sánchez-Palencia Ramos. 1992. Los yacimientos de oro de Las Médulas de Carucedo (León). In *Recursos minerales de España*, edited by Javier García Guinea and Jesús Martínez Frías, pp. 861–893. Consejo Superior de Investigaciones Científicas, Madrid.

Pérez Macías, Juan Aurelio, Diego González Batanero, and Manuel Javier Rodríguez Martín. 2013. El fondeadero romano de Isla del Moral y el comercio marítimo en la desembocadura del Guadiana. *Espacio, Tiempo y Forma, Serie II, H.ª Antigua* 26: 339–370.

Peset, Mariano, and María Paz Alonso Romero. 2006. Las facultades de leyes. In *Historia de la Universidad de Salamanca*, Vol. III.1: *Saberes y confluencias*, edited by Luis E. Rodríguez-San Pedro Bezares, pp. 21–74. Ediciones Universidad de Salamanca, Salamanca.

Peterson, Jeanette Favrot. 2014. *Visualizing Guadalupe: From Black Madonna to Queen of the Americas.* University of Texas Press, Austin.

Piña Chan, Román. 1998. *Cacaxtla: Fuentes históricas y pinturas.* Fondo de Cultura Económica, Mexico City.

Piperno, Dolores R. 2011. The Origins of Plant Cultivation and Domestication in the New World Tropics: Patterns, Process, and New Developments. *Current Anthropology* 52(S4): S453–S470.

Piperno, Dolores R., and Bruce D. Smith. 2012. The Origins of Food Production in Mesoamerica. In *The Oxford Handbook of Mesoamerican Archaeology*, edited by Deborah L. Nichols and Christopher A. Pool, pp. 151–164. Oxford University Press, New York.

Plunket Nagoda, Patricia, and Gabriela Uruñuela Ladrón de Guevara. 1998. Preclassic Household Patterns Preserved under Volcanic Ash at Tetimpa, Puebla. *Latin American Antiquity* 9: 287–309.

Plunket Nagoda, Patricia, and Gabriela Uruñuela Ladrón de Guevara. 2005. Recent Research in Puebla Prehistory. *Journal of Archaeological Research* 13(2): 89–127.

Plunket Nagoda, Patricia, and Gabriela Uruñuela Ladrón de Guevara. 2008. Mountain of Sustenance, Mountain of Destruction: The Prehispanic Experience with Popocatépetl Volcano. *Journal of Volcanology and Geothermal Research* 170: 111–120.

Plunket Nagoda, Patricia, and Gabriela Uruñuela Ladrón de Guevara. 2012. Where East Meets West: The Formative in Mexico's Central Highlands. *Journal of Archaeological Research* 20(1): 1–51.

Plunket Nagoda, Patricia, and Gabriela Uruñuela Ladrón de Guevara. 2017. Cholula in Aztec Times. In *The Oxford Handbook of the Aztecs*, edited by Deborah L. Nichols and Enrique Rodríguez-Alegría, pp. 523–533. Oxford University Press, New York.

Plunket Nagoda, Patricia, and Gabriela Uruñuela Ladrón de Guevara. 2018. *Cholula.* Fondo de Cultura Económica, Mexico City.

Pohl, John M. D., and Claire L. Lyons (eds.). 2016. *Altera Roma: Art and Empire from Mérida to Mexico.* Cotsen Institute of Archaeology Press, UCLA, Los Angeles.

Postigo Castellanos, Elena. 1985. Los órdenes militares castellanas en tiempos de Hernán Cortés: una coyuntura de cambio (1488–1527). In *Hernán Cortés y su Tiempo, Actas del Congreso Hernán Cortés y su Tiempo V Centenario (1485–1985)*, pp. 178–182. Editora Regional de Extremadura, Mérida.

Powers, Karen Vieira. 2005. *Women in the Crucible of Conquest: The Gendered Genesis of Spanish American Society, 1500–1600.* University of New Mexico Press, Albuquerque.

Prescott, William H. 1843. *History of the Conquest of Mexico: With a Preliminary View of the Ancient Mexican Civilization, and the Life of the Conqueror, Hernando Cortés.* Vol. 2. Richard Bentley, London.

Pugh, Timothy W., and Prudence M. Rice. 2017. Early Urban Planning, Spatial Strategies, and the Maya Gridded City of Nixtun-Ch'ich', Petén, Guatemala. *Current Anthropology* 58(5): 576–603.

Quigley, Carroll. 1983. *Weapons Systems and Political Stability: A History.* University Press of America, Washington, DC.

Quiroga, Jorge L., and Mónica R. Lovelle. 1999. Ciudades atlánticas en transición: La "ciudad" tardo-antigua y alto-medieval en el noroeste de la Península Ibérica (s. V–XI). *Arqueología Medieval* XXVI: 257–268.

Rabasa, José. 2008. Writing Violence. In *A Companion to Latin American Literature and Culture*, edited by Sara Castro-Klaren, pp. 49–67. Blackwell, Oxford.

Ramírez, Felipe. 2012. La erupción del Xitle y el fin de Cuicuilco. *Revista de Arqueología Americana* 30: 61–89.

Ramírez de Alba, Horacio. 2013. Análisis de las construcciones en la Ruta de Cortés. *Revista Ideas en Ciencia* 39: 37–48. http://hdl.handle.net/20.500.11799/49952.

Remensnyder, Amy G. 2014. *La Conquistadora: The Virgin Mary at War and Peace in the Old and New Worlds.* Oxford University Press, New York.

Restall, Matthew. 2003. *Seven Myths of the Spanish Conquest.* Oxford University Press, New York.

Restall, Matthew. 2012. The New Conquest History. *History Compass* 10(2): 151–160.

Restall, Matthew. 2018. *When Montezuma Met Cortés: The True Story of the Meeting That Changed History.* Harper Collins, New York.

Restall, Matthew. 2019. "There Was a Time When We Were Friends": Las Casas and Cortés as Monstrous Doubles of the Conquest Era. In *Bartolomé de las Casas, O.P.: History, Philosophy, and Theology in the Age of European Expansion*, edited by David Thomas Orique O.P. and Rady Roldán-Figueroa, pp. 58–70. Brill, Leiden.

Restall, Matthew, and Florine Asselbergs. 2007. *Invading Guatemala: Spanish, Nahua, and Maya Accounts of the Conquest Wars.* Pennsylvania State University Press, University Park.

Restall, Matthew, and Felipe Fernández-Armesto. 2012. *The Conquistadors: A Very Short Introduction.* Oxford University Press, New York.

Restall, Matthew, Lisa Sousa, and Kevin Terraciano (eds. and trans.). 2005. *Mesoamerican Voices: Native-Language Writings from Colonial Mexico, Oaxaca, Yucatan, and Guatemala*. Cambridge University Press, New York.

Reynolds, Paul. 2015. Material Culture and the Economy in the Age of Saint Isidore of Seville (6th and 7th Centuries). *Antiquité Tardive* 23: 163–210.

Ricard, Robert. 1966. *The Spiritual Conquest of Mexico: An Essay on the Apostolate and the Evangelizing Methods of the Mendicant Orders in New Spain, 1523–1572*. Translated by Lesley Byrd Simpson. University of California Press, Berkeley.

Richerson, Peter J., Robert Boyd, and Robert L. Bettinger. 2001. Was Agriculture Impossible during the Pleistocene but Mandatory during the Holocene? A Climate Change Hypothesis. *American Antiquity* 66(3): 387–411.

Richter, Kim N. 2017. Bright Kingdoms: Trade Networks, Indigenous Aesthetics, and Royal Courts in Postclassic Mesoamerica. In *Golden Kingdoms: Luxury Arts in the Ancient Americas*, edited by Joanne Pillsbury, Timothy Potts, and Kim N. Richter, pp. 99–109. J. Paul Getty Museum and Getty Research Institute, Los Angeles.

Rius, J. Font. 1972. Asturias, León y Castilla en los primeros siglos medievales. In *Historia de España y América social y económica*. Volumen I: *Antigüedad. Alta Edad Media. América primitiva*, edited by J. Vicens Vives, pp. 297–409. 2nd edition. Editorial Vicens-Vives, Barcelona.

Robichaux, David Luke. 1997. Residence Rules and Ultimogeniture in Tlaxcala and Mesoamerica. *Ethnology* 36(2): 149–171.

Robin, Cynthia. 2006. Gender, Farming, and Long-Term Change: Maya Historical and Archaeological Perspectives. *Current Anthropology* 47(3): 409–433.

Rodríguez-Alegría, Enrique. 2010. Incumbents and Challengers: Indigenous Politics and the Adoption of Spanish Material Culture in Colonial Xaltocan, Mexico. *Historical Archaeology* 44(2): 51–71.

Rodríguez-Alegría, Enrique. 2017. A City Transformed: From Tenochtitlan to Mexico City in the 16th century. In *The Oxford Handbook of the Aztecs*, edited by Deborah Nichols and E. Rodríguez-Alegría, pp. 661–674. Oxford University Press, New York.

Rodríguez-Corral, Javier. 2012. Las imágenes como un modo de acción: Las estatuas de guerreros castreños. *Archivo Español de Arqueología* 85: 79–100.

Rodríguez González, Esther. 2018. The Tartessian Tumuli of the Guadiana. *Rivista di Studi Fenici* XLVI: 117–135.

Rodríguez González, Esther, and Sebastián Celestino Pérez. 2017. Las estancias de los dioses: la habitación 100 del yacimiento de Casas del Turuñuelo (Guareña, Badajoz). *CuPAUAM* 43: 179–194.

Rodríguez Gordillo, Eduardo. 2015. *Apuntes Históricos de la Villa de Medellín (Provincia de Badajoz): Reunidos por el que es hoy Cura Párroco de la Iglesia de San Martín, de dicha Villa*. Facsimile edited and annotated by José Angel Calero Carretero, José Mª Custodio Simón, and Tomás García Muñoz. Federación Extremadura Histórica, Cáceres.

Rodríguez-San Pedro, Luis E., ed. 1625/1990. *Estatvtos hechos por la Vniversidad de Salamanca 1625.* Ediciones de la Universidad de Salamanca, Salamanca.

Rojas, Gabriel de. 1985. *Relación de Cholula* (1581). In *Relaciones geográficas del siglo XVI*, Vol. II, edited by René Aguña, pp. 121–145. Instituto de Investigaciones Antropológicas, Universidad Nacional Autónoma de México, Mexico City.

Rojas, José Luis de. 2011. La historia de México contando con los indios. *Anales del Museo de América* 19: 195–210.

Rojas, José Luis de. 2012. *Tenochtitlan: Capital of the Aztec Empire.* University Press of Florida, Gainesville.

Rojas, José Luis de. 2016. *Imperio Azteca: Historia de una idea.* Rosa Ma Porrúa Ediciones, Madrid.

Rosenthal, Earl. 1971. Plus Ultra, Non plus Ultra, and the Columnar Device of Emperor Charles V. *Journal of the Warburg and Courtauld Institutes* 34: 204–228.

Rossi, Franco D. 2018. Pedagogy and State: An Archaeological Inquiry into Classic Maya Educational Practice. *Cambridge Archaeological Journal* 28(1): 85–102.

Rouillard, Pierre. 2009. Greeks and the Iberian Peninsula: Forms of Exchange and Settlements. In *Colonial Encounters in Ancient Iberia: Phoenician, Greek, and Indigenous Relations*, edited by Michael Dietler and Carolina López-Ruiz, pp. 131–151. University of Chicago Press, Chicago.

Rubial García, Antonio. 2014. Hernán Cortés y los religiosos. *Arqueología Mexicana* XXI(127): 26–36.

Ruiz, Teofilo F. 2001. *Spanish Society: 1400–1600.* Pearson Education, Essex.

Ruiz, Teofilo F. 2007. *Spain's Centuries of Crisis: 1300–1474.* Blackwell, Oxford.

Ruiz-Gálvez, Marisa. 2015. Before "the Gates of Tartessos": Indigenous Knowledge and Exchange Networks in the Late Bronze Age Far West. In *The Cambridge Prehistory of the Bronze and Iron Age Mediterranean*, edited by A. Bernard Knapp and Peter van Dommelen, pp. 196–214. Cambridge University Press, Cambridge.

Ruiz Medrano, Ethelia. 2014. Don Carlos de Tezcoco and the Universal Rights of Emperor Carlos V. In *Texcoco: Prehispanic and Colonial Perspectives*, edited by Jongsoo Lee and Galen Brokaw, pp. 165–181. University Press of Colorado, Boulder.

Ruiz Medrano, Ethelia, and Susan Kellogg (eds.). 2010. *Negotiation within Domination: New Spain's Indian Pueblos Confront the Spanish State.* University Press of Colorado, Boulder.

Runggaldier, Astrid. 2014. Mesoamerica: Strengths and Weaknesses of the Current Classification. In *Encyclopedia of Global Archaeology*, edited by Claire Smith, pp. 4806–4815. Springer, New York.

Runnels, Curtis, Chad DiGregorio, Karl W. Wegmann, Sean F. Gallen, Thomas F. Strasser, and Eleni Panagopoulou. 2014. Lower Palaeolithic Artifacts from Plakias, Crete: Implications for Hominin Dispersals. *Eurasian Prehistory* 11(1–2): 129–152.

Russo, Alessandra. 2011. Cortés's Objects and the Idea of New Spain: Inventories as Spatial Narratives. *Journal of the History of Collections* 23(2): 229–252.

Sabloff, Jeremy A., and William L. Rathje. 1975. The Rise of a Maya Merchant Class. *Scientific American* 233(4): 72–83.

Sabloff, Paula L. W. 2019. The Political Agency of Royal Women: A Comparative Analysis of Eight Premodern States According to Societal Rules and Roles. *Journal of Archaeological Research*. https://doi.org/10.1007/s10814-019-09131-y.

Sallares, Robert. 2002. *Malaria and Rome: A History of Malaria in Ancient Italy*. Oxford University Press, Oxford.

Sánchez Gamero, Juan Pedro (ed.). 2017. *Cisneros: Arquetipo de Virtudes, Espejo de Prelados*. Cabildo Primado Catedral de Toledo, Toledo.

Sánchez-Pardo, José Carlos. 2012. Los contextos de fundación de las Iglesias tardoantiguas en Galicia (ss. V–VIII): Substratos arqueológicos, distribución y significados. *Antiquité Tardive* 20: 255–273.

Sanders, William T. 1956. *The Cultural Ecology of the Teotihuacan Valley*. Department of Sociology and Anthropology, Pennsylvania State University, University Park.

Sanders, William T., Jeffrey R. Parsons, and Robert S. Santley. 1979. *The Basin of Mexico: Ecological Processes in the Evolution of a Civilization*. Academic Press, New York.

Sandine, Al. 2015. *Deadly Baggage: What Cortés Brought to Mexico and How It Destroyed the Aztec Civilization*. McFarland, Jefferson, NC.

Saturno, William, Franco D. Rossi, Heather Hurst, and David Stuart. 2017. A Maya *Curia Regis*: Evidence for a Hierarchical Specialist Order at Xultun, Guatemala. *Ancient Mesoamerica* 28(2): 423–440.

Saunders, Nicholas J. 2001. A Dark Light: Reflections on Obsidian in Mesoamerica. *World Archaeology* 33(2): 220–236.

Sayahi, Lotfi, and Juan Antonio Thomas. 2005. Morphophonological and Semantic Adaptation of Arabisms in Galician. *Languages, Literatures and Cultures Faculty Scholarship* 7: http://scholarsarchive.library.albany.edu/cas_llc_scholar/7.

Scheidel, Walter. 2007. Demography. In *The Cambridge Economic History of the Greco-Roman World*, edited by Walter Scheidel, Ian Morris, and Richard P. Saller, pp. 38–86. Cambridge University Press, Cambridge.

Scheidel, Walter. 2016. Rome, Tenochtitlan, and Beyond: Comparing Empires across Space and Time. In *Altera Roma: Art and Empire from Mérida to Mexico*, edited by John M. D. Pohl and Claire L. Lyons, pp. 21–32. Cotsen Institute of Archaeology Press, UCLA, Los Angeles.

Schwaller, John F. 2014. *The First Letter from New Spain: The Lost Petition of Cortés and His Company, June 20, 1519*. Authored with Helen Nader. University of Texas Press, Austin.

Schwartz, Stuart B. (ed.). 2000. *Victors and Vanquished: Spanish and Nahua Views of the Conquest of Mexico*. Palgrave Macmillan, New York.

Scott, James C. 1990. *Domination and the Arts of Resistance: Hidden Transcripts*. Yale University, New Haven, CT.

Scullard, H. H. 1982. *From the Gracchi to Nero: A History of Rome 133 B.C. to A.D. 68*. 5th edition. Routledge, London.

Serra Puche, Mari Carmen. 2005. Xochitécatl y sus volcanes: Pasado y presente. In *IV Coloquio Pedro Bosh Gimpera: El occidente y centro de México*, edited by E. Vargas Pacheco, pp. 331–347. UNAM, Mexico City.

Serra Puche, Mari Carmen, J. Carlos Lazcano Arce, and Liliana Torres Sanders. 2001. Actividades rituales en Xochitécatl-Cacaxtla, Tlaxcala. *Arqueología* 25: 71–88.

Shady Solis, Ruth. 2006. America's First City? The Case of Late Archaic Caral. *Andean Archaeology III*: 28–66.

Shryock, Andrew, and Daniel Lord Small. 2011. *Deep History: The Architecture of Past and Present*. University of California Press, Berkeley.

Silliman, Stephen W. 2015. A Requiem for Hybridity? The Problem with Frankensteins, Purées, and Mules. *Journal of Social Archaeology* 15(3): 277–298.

Simerka, Barbara A. 1998. "That the rulers should sleep without bad dreams": Anti-Epic Discourse in *La Numancia* and *Arauco domado*. *Cervantes: Bulletin of the Cervantes Society of America* 18(1): 46–70.

Simpson, Lesley Byrd. 1969. Introduction. In *Cortés: The Life of the Conqueror by His Secretary Francisco López de Gómara*, translated and edited by Lesley Byrd Simpson, pp. xv–xxvi. University of California Press, Berkeley.

Slack, Edward R., Jr. 2012. Orientalizing New Spain: Perspectives on Asian Influence in Colonial Mexico. *México y la Cuenca del Pacífico* (43): 97–127.

Smith, Colin. 1983. *The Making of the Poema de mio Cid*. Cambridge University Press, Cambridge.

Smith, James L. 2014. Europe's Confused Transmutation: The Realignment of Moral Cartography in Juan de la Cosa's *Mappa Mundi* (1500). *European Review of History: Revue européenne d'histoire* 21(6): 799–816.

Smith, Michael E. 1984. The Aztlan Migrations of the Nahuatl Chronicles: Myth or History? *Ethnohistory* 31(3): 153–186.

Smith, Michael E. 1994. Hernan Cortés on the Size of Aztec Cities: Comment on Dobys. *Latin American Population History Bulletin* 25: 25–27.

Smith, Michael E. 2005. City Size in Late Postclassic Mesoamerica. *Journal of Urban History* 31(4): 403–434.

Smith, Michael E. 2008. *Aztec City-State Capitals*. University Press of Florida, Gainesville.

Smith, Michael E. 2017a. Cities in the Aztec Empire: Commerce, Imperialism, and Urbanization. In *Rethinking the Aztec Economy*, edited by Deborah L. Nichols, Frances Berdan, and Michael E. Smith, pp. 44–67. University of Arizona Press, Tucson.

Smith, Michael E. 2017b. Aztec Urbanism: Cities and Towns. In *The Oxford Handbook of the Aztecs*, edited by Deborah L. Nichols and Enrique Rodríguez-Alegría, pp. 201–217. Oxford University Press, New York.

Smith, Michael E. 2017c. Bounding Empires and Political/Military Networks Using Archaeological Data. *Journal of Globalization Studies* 8(1): 30–47.

Smith, Michael E. 2020. Mesoamerica's First World City: Teotihuacan in Comparative Perspective. In *Teotihuacan: The World Beyond the City*, edited by Kenneth G. Hirth, David M. Carballo, and Barbara Arroyo, in press. Dumbarton Oaks and Trustees for Harvard University, Washington, DC.

Smith, Michael E., Aleksander Borejsza, Angela Huster, Charles D Frederick, Isabel Rodríguez López, and Cynthia Heath-Smith. 2013. Aztec Period Houses and Terraces at Calixtlahuaca: The Changing Morphology of a Mesoamerican Hilltop Urban Center. *Journal of Field Archaeology* 38: 227–243.

Smith, Michael E., Abhishek Chatterjee, Angela C. Huster, Sierra Stewart, and Marion Forest. 2019. Apartment Compounds, Households, and Population in the Ancient City of Teotihuacan, Mexico. *Ancient Mesoamerica* 30(3): 399–418.

Smith, Michael E., and Frederic Hicks. 2017. Inequality and Social Class in Aztec Society. In *The Oxford Handbook of the Aztecs*, edited by Deborah L. Nichols and Enrique Rodríguez-Alegría, pp. 423–436. Oxford University Press, New York.

Smith, Michael E., and Lisa Montiel. 2001. The Archaeological Study of Empires and Imperialism in Pre-Hispanic Central Mexico. *Journal of Anthropological Archaeology* 20: 245–284.

Smith, Michael E., and Peter Peregrine. 2012. Approaches to Comparative Analysis in Archaeology. In *The Comparative Archaeology of Complex Societies*, edited by Michael E. Smith, pp. 4–20. Cambridge University Press, New York.

Smith, Virginia. 2000. The Iconography of Power at Xochicalco: The Pyramid of the Plumed Serpents. In *The Xochicalco Mapping Project*, Vol. 2, edited by Kenneth Hirth, pp. 57–82. University of Utah Press, Salt Lake City.

Solís, Felipe, Gabriela Uruñuela, Patricia Plunket, Martín Cruz, and Dionisio Rodríguez. 2006. *Cholula: The Great Pyramid*. CONACULTA, INAH, and Grupo Azabache, Mexico City.

Spence, Michael W., Christine D. White, Evelyn Childs Rattray, and Fred J. Longstaffe. 2005. Past Lives in Different Places: The Origins and Relationships of Teotihuacan's Foreign Residents. In *Settlement, Subsistence, and Social Complexity: Essays Honoring the Legacy of Jeffrey R. Parsons*, edited by Richard E. Blanton, pp. 155–197. Cotsen Institue of Archaeology, University of California, Los Angeles.

Stevens, Wesley M. 1980. The Figure of the Earth in Isidore's "De natura rerum." *Isis* 71(2): 268–277.

Suárez Molina, María Teresa. 2010. Los mercados de la ciudad de México y sus pinturas. In *Caminos y mercados de México*, edited by Janet Long Towell and Amalia Attolini Lecón, pp. 435–457. Universidad Nacional Autónoma de México, Instituto Nacional de Antropología e Historia, Mexico City.

Suárez Otero, José. 2014. The Cult of St. James at Compostela: From Antiquity to the Middle Ages. *Boletín Avriense* 44: 165–182.

Sugiyama, Nawa, Andrew D. Somerville, and Margaret J. Schoeninger. 2015. Stable Isotopes and Zooarchaeology at Teotihuacan, Mexico Reveal Earliest Evidence of Wild Carnivore Management in Mesoamerica. *PloS One* 10(9): e0135635.

Sugiyama, Saburo. 2005. *Human Sacrifice, Militarism, and Rulership: Materialization of State Ideology at the Feathered Serpent Pyramid, Teotihuacan*. Cambridge University Press, New York.

Sugiyama, Saburo, and Rubén Cabrera Castro. 2007. The Moon Pyramid Project and the Teotihuacan State Polity: A Brief Summary of the Excavations in 1998–2004. *Ancient Mesoamerica* 18(1): 109–125.

Sullivan, John. 2001. Construcción de dos enunciados colectivos en el Cabildo de Tlaxcala. *Estudios de Cultura Náhuatl* 32: 297–322.

Taggart, James M. 2017. Nahua Ethnicity. In *The Oxford Handbook of the Aztecs*, edited by Deborah L. Nichols and Enrique Rodríguez-Alegría, pp. 411–421. Oxford University Press, New York.

Taladoire, Éric. 2017. *De América a Europa: Cuando los indígenas descubrieron el Viejo Mundo (1493–1892)*. Fondo de Cultura Económica, Mexico City.

Tarradell, Miguel. 1972. España Antigua. In *Historia de España y América social y económica*. Volumen I: *Antigüedad. Alta Edad Media. América primitiva*, edited by J. Vicens Vives, pp. 47–198. 2nd edition. Editorial Vicens-Vives, Barcelona.

Tarkanian, Michael J., and Dorothy Hosler. 2011. America's First Polymer Scientists: Rubber Processing, Use and Transport in Mesoamerica. *Latin American Antiquity* 22(4): 469–486.

Tedlock, Dennis (ed. and trans.). 1985. *Popol Vuh: The Mayan Book of the Dawn of Life*. Simon & Shuster, New York.

Terraciano, Kevin. 2010. Three Texts in One: Book XII of the Florentine Codex. *Ethnohistory* 57(1): 51–72.

Thibodeau, Alyson M., David J. Killick, Saul L. Hedquist, John T. Chesley, and Joaquin Ruiz. 2015. Isotopic Evidence for the Provenance of Turquoise in the Southwestern United States. *GSA Bulletin* 127(11–12): 1617–1631.

Thomas, Hugh. 1993. *Conquest: Cortes, Montezuma, and the Fall of Old Mexico*. Simon & Schuster, New York.

Thomas, Hugh. 2014. *World Without End: Spain, Philip II, and the First Global Empire*. Random House, New York.

Torquemada, Fray Juan de. 1995. *Monarquía Indiana*. 3rd edition, edited by Miguel León Portilla. Universidad Nacional Autónoma de México, Mexico City.

Torró, Josep. 2018. Partners-in-Arms. Medieval Military Associations: From the Iberian *cabalgada* to the American *entrada*. In *From Al-Andalus to the Americas (13th–17th Centuries): Destruction and Construction of Societies*, edited by Thomas F. Glick, Antonio Malpica, Félix Retamero, and Josep Torró, pp. 19–77. Brill, Leiden.

Townsend, Camilla. 2003. Burying the White Gods: New Perspectives on the Conquest of Mexico. *The American Historical Review* 108(3): 659–687.

Townsend, Camilla. 2006. *Malintzin's Choices: An Indian Woman in the Conquest of Mexico*. University of New Mexico, Albuquerque.

Townsend, Camilla. 2014. Polygyny and the Divided Altepetl: The Tetzcocan Key to Pre-conquest Nahua Politics. In *Texcoco: Prehispanic and Colonial Perspectives*, edited by Jongsoo Lee and Galen Brokaw, pp. 93–116. University Press of Colorado, Boulder.

Townsend, Camilla. 2017. *Annals of Native America: How the Nahuas of Colonial Mexico Kept Their History Alive*. Oxford University Press, New York.

Townsend, Camilla. 2019. *Fifth Sun: A New History of the Aztecs*. Oxford University Press, New York.

Turnquist, Gary M. 1974. The Pillars of Hercules Revisited. *Bulletin of the American Schools of Oriental Research* 216: 13–15.

Trautmann, Wolfgang. 1981. *Las transformaciones en el paisaje cultural de Tlaxcala durante la época colonial*. Franz Steiner Verlag, Wiesbaden, Germany.

Trend, J. B. 1967. *The Civilization of Spain*. Oxford University Press, Oxford.

Tylor, Edward B. 1861. *Anahuac: or, Mexico and the Mexicans, Ancient and Modern*. London: Longman, Green, Longman and Roberts.

Tylor, Edward B. 1867. Phenomena of the Higher Civilisation: Traceable to a Rudimental Origin among Savage Tribes. *Anthropological Review* 5(18–19): 303–314.

Umburger, Emily. 2015. Tetzcatlipoca and Huitzilopochtli: Political Dimensions of Aztec Deities. In *Tezcatlipoca: Trickster and Supreme Deity*, edited by Elizabeth Baquedano, pp. 83–112. University Press of Colorado, Boulder.

Uruñuela y Ladrón de Guevara, Gabriela, Patricia Plunket Nagoda, and Amparo Robles Salmerón. 2009. Cholula: Art and Architecture of an Archetypal City. In *The Art of Urbanism: How Mesoamerican Kingdoms Represented Themselves in Architecture and Imagery*, edited by William L. Fash and Leonardo López Luján, pp. 135–171. Dumbarton Oaks Trustees for Harvard University, Washington, DC.

Vågene, Åshild J., Alexander Herbig, Michael G. Campana, Nelly M. Robles García, Christina Warinner, Susanna Sabin, Maria A. Spyrou, Aida Andrades Valtueña, Daniel Huson, Noreen Tuross, Kirsten I. Bos, and Johannes Krause. 2018. Salmonella Enterica Genomes from Victims of a Major Sixteenth-Century Epidemic in Mexico. *Nature Ecology & Evolution* 2(3): 520–528.

Valdeón Baruque, Julio. 2008. *Historia de Castilla y León*. Ámbito Ediciones, Valladolid.

Vargas, Luis Alberto, and Leticia E. Casillas. 1996. El encuentro de dos cocinas: México en el siglo XVI. In *Conquista y comida: Consequencias del encuentro de dos* mundos, edited by Janet Long, pp. 155–168. Universidad Nacional Autónoma de México, Mexico City.

Vargas Pacheco, Ernesto. 2001. El viaje de Cortés a Las Hibueras. *Arqueología Mexicana* IX(49): 58–61.

Vázquez de Tapia, Bernardino. ca. 1544/1972. *Relación de méritos y servicios del conquistador Bernardino Vázquez de Tapia, vecino y regidor de esta gran ciudad de Tenustitlan, México*, edited by Jorge Gurría Lacroix. Universidad Nacional Autónoma de México, Mexico City.

Vázquez Galicia, Sergio Ángel. 2008. Interpretación histórica e identidad en dos cronistas novohispanos: Análisis historiográfico de las obras de Diego Muñoz Camargo y Chimalpain Cuauhtlehuantzin. MA thesis, Department of History, Universidad Nacional Autónoma de México.

Velázquez Castro, Adrián, and Emiliano Ricardo Melgar Tísoc. 2014. Producciones palaciegas tenochcas en objetos de concha y lapidaria. *Ancient Mesoamerica* 25: 295–308.

Vicens Vives, J. (ed.). 1972. *Historia de España y América social y económica. Volumen I: Antigüedad. Alta Edad Media. América primitiva.* 2nd edition. Editorial Vicens-Vives, Barcelona.

Villalibre, Javier. 2005. *Las Médulas y su entorno.* Ediciones Lanica, Léon.

Villella, Peter B. 2016. *Indigenous Elites and Creole Identity in Colonial Mexico, 1500–1800.* Cambridge University Press, New York.

Vinson, Ben, III. 2018. *Before Mestizaje: The Frontiers of Race and Caste in Colonial Mexico.* Cambridge University Press, New York.

Vizuete Mendoza, José Carlos. 2017. Cisneros y las Indias. Evangelización y Reforma. In *Cisneros: Arquetipo de Virtudes, Espejo de Prelados*, edited by Juan Pedro Sánchez Gamero, pp. 125–133. Cabildo Primado Catedral de Toledo, Toledo.

Wade, Lizzie. 2018. Feeding the Gods: Hundreds of Skulls Reveal Massive Scale of Human Sacrifice in Aztec Capital. *Science*, June 21, pp. 1288–1292. https://www.sciencemag.org/news/2018/06/feeding-gods-hundreds-skulls-reveal-massive-scale-human-sacrifice-aztec-capital.

Wagner, Logan, Hal Box, and Susan Kline Morehead. 2013. *Ancient Origins of the Mexican Plaza: From Primordial Sea to Public Space.* University of Texas, Austin.

Warinner, Christina, Nelly Robles García, Ronald Spores, and Noreen Tuross. 2012. Disease, Demography, and Diet in Early Colonial New Spain: Investigation of a Sixteenth-Century Mixtec Cemetery at Teposcolula Yucundaa. *Latin American Antiquity* 23(4): 467–489.

Webster, David. 2018. *The Population of Tikal: Implications for Maya Demography.* Archaeopress, Oxford.

Wendt, Carl J. 2009. The Scale and Structure of Bitumen Processing in Early Formative Olmec Households. *Archeological Papers of the American Anthropological Association* 19(1): 33–44.

Westner, K. J., T. Birch, H. Höfer, H.-M. Seitz, F. Kemmers, and S. Klein. 2017. Rome's Rise to Power as Deduced by Analysis of Silver Coinage. Paper presented at Goldschmidt Conference, August 14, Paris.

Whittaker, Gordon. 2016. The Identities of Fernando de Alva Ixtlilxochitl. In *Fernando de Alva Ixtlilxochitl and His Legacy*, edited by Galen Brokaw and Jongsoo Lee, pp. 29–76. University of Arizona, Tucson.

Wickham, Chris. 2009. *The Inheritance of Rome: Illuminating the Dark Ages, 400–1000.* Penguin Books, New York.

Wilkinson Zerner, Catherine. 2014. The Spanish Habsburgs and the Arts of Islamic Iberia. In *The Habsburgs and Their Courts in Europe, 1400–1700*, edited by Herbert Karner, Ingrid Ciulisová, and Bernardo J. García García, pp. 336–348. Österreichische Akademie der Wissenschaften, KU Leuven, Slovakia.

Williams, John. 1997. Isidore, Orosius and the Beatus Map. *Imago Mundi* 49: 7–32.

Wilson, Andrew. 2012. Raw Materials and Energy. In *The Cambridge Companion to the Roman Economy*, edited by Walter Scheidel, pp. 135–155. Cambridge University Press, Cambridge.

Winchester, Simon. 2010. *Atlantic: Great Sea Battles, Heroic Discoveries, Titanic Storms, and a Vast Ocean of a Million Stories.* Harper Perennial, New York.

Wright, Elizabeth. 2008. New World News, Ancient Echoes: A Cortés Letter and a Vernacular Livy for a New King and His Wary Subjects (1520–23). *Renaissance Quarterly* 61: 711–749.

Wright-Carr, David Charles. 2015. One Culture, Two Languages: What Calques Tell Us about Central Mexican Society at the Time of the Spanish Conquest. In *Perspectivas sobre la Investigación Cualitativa/Perspectives on Qualitative Research*, edited by M. Martha Lengeling and Irasema Mora Pabolo, pp. 457–468. Universidad de Guanajuato, León.

Wright-Carr, David Charles. 2017. Signs of Resistance: Iconography and Semaisography in Otomi Architectural Decoration and Manuscripts of the Early Colonial Period. *Visible Language* 51(1): 58–87.

Wolf, Eric. 1959. *Sons of the Shaking Earth: The People of Mexico and Guatemala—Their Land, History, and Culture.* University of Chicago Press, Chicago.

Yalcindaga, Erhan, Eric Elgueroa, Céline Arnathaua, Patrick Duranda, et al. 2012. Multiple Independent Introductions of Plasmodium Falciparum in South America. *Proceedings of the National Academy of Sciences* 109(2): 511–516.

Zeder, Melinda A. 2008. Domestication and Early Agriculture in the Mediterranean Basin: Origins, Diffusion, and Impact. *Proceedings of the National Academy of Sciences* 105(33): 11597–11604.

Zeder, Melinda A. 2011. The Origins of Agriculture in the Near East. *Current Anthropology* 52: S221–S235.

Zilhão, João. 2001. Radiocarbon Evidence for Maritime Pioneer Colonization at the Origins of Farming in West Mediterranean Europe. *Proceedings of the National Academy of* Sciences 98(24): 14180–14185.

Index

Tables and figures are indicated by *t* and *f* following the page number.

For the benefit of digital users, indexed terms that span two pages (e.g., 52–53) may, on occasion, appear on only one of those pages.